HITLER'S
SHADOW
EMPIRE

HITLER'S SHADOW EMPIRE

Nazi Economics and the Spanish Civil War

PIERPAOLO BARBIERI

Harvard University Press

Cambridge, Massachusetts
London, England
2015

Library of Congress Cataloging-in-Publication Data

Barbieri, Pierpaolo.
  Hitler's shadow empire : Nazi economics and the Spanish Civil War / Pierpaolo Barbieri.
      pages cm
  Includes bibliographical references and index.
  ISBN 978-0-674-72885-1 (alkaline paper)
1. Spain—History—Civil War, 1936–1939—Economic aspects.   2. Spain—History—Civil
War, 1936–1939—Finance.   3. Spain—History—Civil War, 1936–1939—Participation,
German.   4. Spain—Foreign economic relations—Germany.   5. Germany—Foreign
economic relations—Spain.   6. Military assistance, German—Spain—History—20th
century.   7. Intervention (International law)—Economic aspects—Germany—
History—20th century.   8. Intervention (International law)—Economic aspects—
Spain—History—20th century.   9. Schacht, Hjalmar Horace Greeley, 1877–1970.
10. Germany—Economic policy—1933–1945.   I. Title.
  DP269.8.E2B37 2015
  946.081'343—dc23

                                                                        2014036049

A mis padres, Adriana and Franco,
por enseñarme el significado del sacrificio

CONTENTS

HITLER'S SHADOW EMPIRE

The Two Spains, July 25, 1936

Republican Spain

Nationalist Spain

Planned Airlift of Nationalist
Troops to the Mainland

introduction

BONES BENEATH

España de los inquisidores	Spain of the inquisitors
que padecieron el destino	who suffered the fate,
de ser verdugos,	of being henchmen,
y hubieran podido ser	[when] they could have
mártires.	been martyrs.

—JORGE LUIS BORGES, "España," 1965

"Spain is different," proclaimed advertisements around the world in the 1960s.[1] Their aim was to encourage tourism to an introverted, authoritarian country—and it worked wonders with affluent travelers eager for Mediterranean sun. At the time, Spain was ostracized by its continental neighbors, but sustained by a U.S. State Department more concerned with preventing a "red plague" descending over Western Europe than with the anachronistic, autocratic rule of Generalísimo Francisco Franco.[2]

Spain is different indeed. By any quantifiable standard, it is a rare late twentieth-century success story, one that not even a gargantuan real estate boom and bust (compounded by a Eurozone debt crisis) could overshadow. When Franco finally died in 1975, Spain went through a relatively clean democratic transition, rapid economic growth, decreasing poverty, declining irredentist claims, and seamless European integration, not to mention the revival of its cultural primacy in the Ibero-American world. Today it is home to some of the world's best-run corporations as well as a prolific publishing industry in the world's second most common native language.[3] In spite of a long recession and distressingly high unemployment and in contrast to some of its neighbors, Spain has developed no successful anti-European political parties. Even those who dream about regional self-determination or independence in Catalonia or the Basque Country embrace an integrated Europe.

Yet there is more to Spain than a successful transition into globalized modernity. Distant battles, contested memories, and unspoken crimes routinely return to disturb its newfound normalcy. Quite literally, half-forgotten bones lurk beneath the arid Iberian soil. Successful as the society built on them has become, these bones creep up in the most unexpected places. In a fit of Nietzschean recurrence, they return: in courts, in politics, and in culture. Silenced though they have been, silent they are not.

The Spanish Civil War was fought seventy-five years ago. The battle over its memory, however, rages on; it is legally contested, culturally relevant, and politically explosive. Its echoes are loud in Spain and beyond.[4] But essential parts of the story of how Franco came to impose his will on a divided country remain buried like the bones in his mass graves. Among the deepest buried is the intervention that brought German Nazi and Italian Fascist troops, know-how, and supplies into Spain and to Franco's aid. This book seeks to unearth the project of Nazi informal empire on Iberian soil, to explain how it came to be, and to elucidate the economic framework within which it operated. What I call Adolf Hitler's "shadow empire" during the Spanish Civil War was fundamentally different from his later attempts at formal empire; it involved a relationship with Franco's Nationalists that was distinctive from that which bound Nationalists with their other key sponsor, Benito Mussolini's Fascist Italy. Yet Franco long outlived his fascist backers. After their demise he was keen to forget all debts and to erase what they implied for Spain's role in any future German-dominated European economic system.

Strictly speaking, this is not a book about Spain. Rather it is a story of political economy and war in the tumultuous 1930s, one that by definition transcends national borders. Although my focus is Spain, Germany, and the relationship between them, I take crucial detours to Italy, France, and Britain, moving from battlefields to boardrooms and banks. The way Nazi Germany sought to profit from the Spanish Civil War could have taken place only in the context of the dysfunctional, Depression-era international system. Nazi imperialism in Spain contrasts starkly with the established views of Berlin's domestic and international priorities in those years, as well as central tenets of the Hitlerian regime's evolving ideology. Hence this study lays bare profound differences among key figures in Nazi-era Berlin, many of whom have been lost in the historiography of an "inexorable" road to world war.

German intervention in the Spanish Civil War is unique when compared not only with the behavior of other great powers like Britain and France but also with "fascist" policy as implemented by Rome. The Nazis' first international military adventure encapsulates a strategy different from the one they tried to impose on Europe in World War II. Although the shadow empire in Spain was not the one Hitler ultimately chose to build, it provides a useful counterfactual for German projection of power in Europe. In many ways informal integration under German informal power—as exercised in Spain more thoroughly than even in the well-studied Balkans—had the potential to yield more lasting results than the formal, genocidal, and ultimately ephemeral Nazi empire ever did.

Other histories are written. The history of the Spanish Civil War is exhumed. A particular set of bones leads to the first indictment relating to Francoist crimes during the war. They belonged to Federico García Lorca, one of the most prominent intellectuals to fall victim to the conflict. His remains had long been rumored to lie in an unmarked mass grave along a winding road in Granada. Early in the conflict a Nationalist death squad found the poet in hiding and, after a few days of improvised imprisonment, took him "for coffee, lots of coffee"—a peculiar Iberian euphemism for facing the firing squad. There has been a decades-long, heated debate about precisely why Lorca was shot. In spite of his closeness to prominent reactionaries, his being an outspoken Socialist with a trail of male lovers surely did not help.[5] Seven decades later, the legal case for exhuming Lorca's bones was anything but straightforward. At the center of the case lay Spain's post-Francoist amnesty law. Yet in 2008 a judge ordered that bones belonging to nineteen victims of the "Francoist repression," including Lorca's, be exhumed, even when the alleged perpetrators had themselves been six feet under for decades.[6]

To Spanish liberals, unearthing the bones was one of many battles in the long war to reclaim their country's memory after decades of dictatorship; it amounted to painful but necessary reckoning. Historians sought details about Lorca's last hours. The granddaughter of a schoolteacher who had the dubious honor of being executed alongside the author was exultant, having "spent a decade waiting for the moment."[7] She would be disappointed: there was little to be found at the designated location.

Yet elusive bones led to an even greater setback for proponents of exhumation: the only person to be indicted in the case was the judge who ordered the digging.[8] This was not just any judge. Baltasar Garzón has had a long, controversial history with cases featuring crimes against humanity. In 1998 he became internationally recognized when he prosecuted former Chilean dictator Augusto Pinochet for the murder of Spanish citizens during his junta rule. Garzón banked on the "universal principle" ascribed by Iberian jurisprudence, which limited Pinochet's jurisdictional arbitrage in the European Union while the former dictator was in the United Kingdom. Pinochet subsequently spent eighteen months under house arrest in London. Many scholars judged the case to be a defining moment for international law. After all, having personally managed Chile's transition to democracy, Pinochet had dodged indictment; it was only through the probing of a Spanish judge in the name of a few obscure victims that he came close to actually facing trial. Garzón's judicial activism had consequences beyond the prosecution of a decrepit octogenarian: it contributed to challenges against postdictatorship amnesty laws in countries as diverse as Argentina, Bosnia, and Kyrgyzstan—all of which experienced "managed" democratic transitions.

Around the world, but in particular within Spain, Garzón became a Manichaean figure. To his supporters he was a restless crusader for justice; to his opponents he was a careless, overstepping judge, fighting a past buried for good reason. British courts eventually found Pinochet unfit for trial, but the dictator's life back in Chile would never be the same; the autumn of the patriarch had finally arrived.[9]

After a series of causes célèbres targeting Latin American juntas and Islamic terrorists, Garzón focused on his own backyard. In response to a filing by twenty-two civil organizations, he produced a sixty-eight-page judicial opinion arguing that Civil War–era murders qualified as "crimes against humanity," meaning neither statutes of limitations nor the deaths of alleged perpetrators allowed them to lapse.[10] He then requested Franco's death certificate, a sine qua non for indictment, as well as those of other central figures of his regime. In so doing he implicitly challenged Spain's amnesty law. Even though it had been originally designed to protect Franco's victims rather than his perpetrators, the law originally passed in 1977 became crucial to the transition that allowed for the return of democracy to Spain.[11] It allowed old Francoists and the Spanish military to engage in the constitutional monarchy that King Juan Carlos I established.[12] It was a gamble and, by (almost) all measures, a successful one. Some of Franco's old ministers were soon elected to office. Some bumps in the road notwithstanding, a stable democratic transition ensued. And integration into Europe flourished.

When Garzón settled on Lorca's undignified resting place to launch his crusade into Civil War crimes, two right-wing organizations with Francoist roots fought back. Manos Limpias (Clean Hands) and Falange Española—Franco's old political party turned civil organization—filed a suit arguing that the judge was overstepping his responsibilities and violating the amnesty law. Conservative magistrate Luciano Varela agreed, suspending Garzón from the bench. Public opinion was fiercely divided. Thousands took to the streets to protest the ruling; among other symbols, Garzón's supporters waved flags of the Second Spanish Republic, the very one the Civil War had ended.

In early 2012 the Spanish Supreme Court cleared Garzón of abuses of power in a six-to-one decision.[13] Yet the Court also suspended Garzón for illegal wiretaps in another, technically unrelated case involving corruption in Spain's leading conservative party, the Partido Popular; the Court judged that Garzón conducted investigations with "methods only found in totalitarian societies." Few believed the cases against Garzón to be independent of each other, and the result was unequivocal: suspended from the bench, the judge could not upset the legal status quo any longer. Garzón's lawyer complained that the verdict amounted to a "career death sentence." NGOs and the world press suggested the judge was being persecuted.[14] Garzón has since gone before the Constitutional Tribunal, questioning the impartiality of the Supreme Court in light of new evidence linking one of the Court's judges to the very political party he was investigating.[15] The Supreme Court's ruling implicitly gave its imprimatur to Garzón's investigation into Francoist crimes—but no other judge has thus far dared step into such a minefield. There are powerful reasons why Spain's bones have remained buried, both literally and figuratively.

The battle over Spain's bones transcends its courts. On March 2, 2009, for instance, the country's troubled past made the cover of the *Wall Street Journal*, which reported on a legislative initiative that stirred social divisions akin to Garzón's legal probes.[16] Although the ominously titled Law of Historical Memory did not directly revisit the 1977 amnesty law, it sought to redress public memory of the conflict and Franco's rule.[17] It allowed the Socialist administration of José Luis Rodríguez Zapatero to issue apologies for thousands of illegal executions and offer citizenship to living members of the international brigades—the volunteers from all over the world who poured into Spain to fight Franco's Nationalists. It also launched a crusade against Franco's iconography: yokes and arrows, eagles, street names, statues.

A few years earlier the Socialist-controlled Parliament had decreed that the last remaining statue of Franco be removed from the heart of Madrid.[18] Copied from a sixteenth-century equestrian piece by Donatello, it portrayed a victorious Franco marching on the capital after its defenders had finally capitulated. Through three decades of constitutional monarchy, the statue had stood erect in the center of Madrid, epitomizing the unapologetic view of the Francoist past that so enraged the Iberian left. The Socialist government's decision was unambiguous: Francoism had no place in modern Spain's public sphere. But as with Garzón's case, not everyone agreed. Before dawn and armed with lit candles, old Francoists gathered to protest the statue's removal. The effigy was confined to a government warehouse, away from the public eye but not gone forever.

In light of such tensions it is unsurprising that Spain's bones were first unearthed by neither courts nor congress, but rather by Iberian culture. Generations of artists broke the silence surrounding Civil War crimes well before Franco had passed away; by adding music to poetry, artists like Joan Manuel Serrat revived artistic statements in ways that echoed Picasso's paintings and Neruda's verses in defense of the Second Republic. Arguably Spain's finest twentieth-century troubadour, Serrat came to prominence in his native Catalonia when he withdrew from the 1968 Eurovision contest—a fixture of European pop culture—in protest of Franco's repression of the Catalan language. He would later declare he found forbidden languages the best conduits for expression.[19]

A year later the songwriter took up a cause that made him renowned everywhere. It began with a twelve-track LP, "To Antonio Machado, Poeta."[20] Featuring a red cover with a photograph of the left-leaning Civil War–era poet, the record should have raised Francoist eyebrows, but it somehow got past the censors. Serrat revived Machado's poems by crafting them into song. The album was more political statement than artistic homage; not unlike Lorca's, Machado's was a telling Civil War tragedy.[21] The album's first track, "Cantares," revived the poet's best-known couplet, penned shortly before his death in 1939. By then the Civil War was lost. Machado, who, like many vanquished Republicans, literally walked into exile in France, wrote, "Walker, your footsteps are road / and nothing else. / Walker, there are no roads / you make roads walking."[22] Spaniards knew of the poet's ignominious death in exile. Serrat's own lines, intertwined with the original verse, laid bare the political message:

> The poet died, far from home
> he's covered by dust from a foreign land,
> walking away he was heard to cry:
> "Walker, there are no roads,
> you make roads by walking."

Serrat too soon found himself in exile. In 1972 he turned the work of Miguel Hernández into song. This time he added not a single word of commentary. Perhaps the most powerful statement in this set is to be found in Hernández's "onion lullaby," a tragic, almost final communication between the poet and his family before tuberculosis overcame him in one of Franco's many prisons. Receiving desperate letters from his wife, Hernández had nothing but couplets on borrowed paper to send back:

> Laugh, my boy,
> Your laughter frees me,
> it gives me wings;
> it vanquishes my loneliness,
> it rips my prisons.[23]

The stanzas became a sensation. It is still moving to watch the recording of a young Serrat, eyes looking into the distance, singing Hernández's words on Spain's public television, Televisión Española, in the early 1980s. By then Franco was long dead and Spanish democracy very much alive. Serrat's sung poetry inspired new generations and the *trova*—the troubadour movement—became a cultural conduit through which to explore the buried past.

More recently younger generations have taken up this distinctively Spanish blend of remembrance and guitars. Among others, Javier Bergia and Ismael Serrano—two young artists outspoken in their support of Garzón's inquiries and public memory initiatives—stand out. They epitomize a cohort that did not stop at denouncing Francoism for its authoritarianism; their challenge ran deeper. In between allusions to Che Guevara and miniskirts, Serrano's breakout 1997 single, "Dad, Tell Me Once Again," asked:

> Dad, tell me once again how after so many a barricade,
> so many clenched fists, so much spilled blood,
> by the end of the game, there was nothing you could do,
> and below the cobblestones there lay no beach sand.[24]

Such lyrics—cleverly playing with student revolutionaries' slogan "Under the cobblestones, the beach"—questioned the whole edifice of Iberian society as it emerged from the managed democratic transition.[25] Franco's downfall left more than beach beneath the cobblestones.

This book begins with an earlier downfall: Spain's. Chapter 1, "Two Spains," traces the ideologies that clashed in the Civil War. When the Bourbons fell in 1931, the country seemed to settle on universal democracy, yet the democratic system led to further polarization. Between seemingly endless political tumult and economic crisis, two radically dissimilar versions of Spain emerged: a liberal, Republican, and secular Spain and a conservative, monarchical, and Catholic Spain. Yet the country was too poor to fund its fratricidal conflict. Neither Republicans nor Nationalists could prevail without foreign aid; they needed weapons, supplies, and hard currency, and, although the Great Depression was not quite over, they found them. Spain became the only place where Communists and fascists waged open war against each other before World War II; between 1936 and 1939 it became Europe's open wound.

Even before the first shot was fired, the Spanish Civil War was an international affair. It was state-of-the-art Junkers and Heinkel bombers from Nazi Germany's Condor Legion, with Italian aerial support, that wrought the destruction of Guernica later immortalized by Picasso; Madrid's Communist defenders charged against Franco's Foreign Legion with American weapons purchased from, of all places, Stalinist Russia. In a world of crumbling globalization, Spain saw the internationalization of localized violence. Intervention favored the side that started the war at a marked disadvantage: the Nationalists. The diplomatic decisions across great power capitals reversed the Republic's advantage and undermined its government.[26] Chapter 2 approaches these decisions by analyzing simultaneously the domestic politics and evolving international perceptions in Paris, London, Moscow, Washington, Rome, and Berlin. With sources in six languages from archives in three continents, it is now possible to reconstruct not only strategic outcomes but also the news reports, rumors, diplomatic cables, coalition battles, and personal biases that influenced decision making. As the chapter concludes, it will become clear how the great power decisions that determined the Civil War's outcome were made within twenty-four hours on one crucial day—July 25, 1936.

But what exactly were German Nazis and Italian Fascists looking for in Spain? Answering that question gets to the central purpose of this book. The historiography of foreign intervention in the Spanish Civil War has, by and large and in particular outside of Spain, remained unchanged in spite of a considerable reassessment of Nazi economic and foreign policy.[27] Shortly after inception Nazi Germany's project in Spain changed radically, becoming more pragmatic and far more ambitious than anything its ally on Spanish soil, Fascist Italy, ever attempted. The Third Reich's first foreign military foray three years after its seizure of power and three years before the beginning of World War II became an exercise in informal empire. This is definitely not the type of imperialism we traditionally associate with Nazi Germany.[28] Indeed the Nazi project in Spain fit into a primarily economic conception of German power that was sidelined in Berlin as

Hitler drifted toward a wider war and the Polish frontier that finally triggered it.[29]

One man above others may be said to have inspired this economics-focused foreign expansion: Hjalmar Schacht. His personal ascent mirrored Germany's, and Chapter 3 tracks his development while sketching the debates that drove German political economy in the decade before Nazism. Two overarching, interrelated concerns had dictated continental policy since the fall of Bismarck. One was the fear of encirclement, an issue that addressed both geostrategic and economic concerns. The other was what a young Henry Kissinger summarized as "unassimilated greatness"—essentially how to cope with Bismarck's delicate European balance of power once the grand master was gone.[30] By the time Schacht became the Weimar Republic's currency commissioner, the great successes of the nineteenth century—Prussian industrialization and German unification—had been overshadowed by the spectacular failures of the early twentieth century: defeat in World War I and the Weimar Republic's hyperinflation. As president of the Reichsbank, Germany's central bank, Schacht wandered away from economic liberalism and toward reactionary nationalism. His historicist economics, rooted in the "historical" German tradition of the burgeoning discipline, encouraged this fundamental shift. When globalization crumbled, Schacht threw himself into the arms of Hitler. Germany soon followed.

Schacht's personal and professional ascent crystallizes the policy debate among economists during the Great Depression. Dismissing most of them as "Party thugs," the banker believed he could "rule through the Nazis." His goal was recasting Germany's role in the European economic system, and the price was enabling Hitler's rearmament, which lay at the core of the ensuing—and still contested—"economic miracle." This is the topic of Chapter 4. With power over monetary affairs through the Reichsbank and economic organization from his years-long acting control over the Economics Ministry (Reichswirtschaftministerium), Schacht wielded unprecedented power in Nazi Germany. He was not the only economic nationalist in 1930s Europe, but he was by far the most powerful and successful one, and I show how Hitler's "economic dictator" crafted an economic program that would later allow for the informal projection of German power in Spain, one ironically run by men he distrusted.

Schacht managed Germany's vast foreign debt, remade its industrial organizations, and revolutionized its trade relationships in a neomercantilist tradition. The implosion of the liberal international financial system that Britain was unable and the United States unwilling to sustain allowed him unprecedented room for maneuver. He labored to redirect trade to less developed countries where power could tilt the terms of trade. Borrowing from the British imperial experience, Nazi Germany's economic dictator sought to develop an "economic empire" to address Germany's structural weaknesses, which he—like many other nationalists—linked to the Treaty of Versailles. Thus Schacht became the mastermind of a nationalist economic strategy that made Nazi intervention in Spain not only possible but also profitable.

The Nazis swiftly transcended the strategic rationale of Hitler's Wagnerian decision to aid Franco in his civil war, reconstructed in detail in Chapter 5.[31] The regime soon began seeking economic profit from the dislocations created by the conflict and Franco's utter dependence on their favor. Fascist support from Rome and Berlin had made Franco primus inter pares among Nationalist generals. To prevail he needed the products of the Schacht-fueled German armaments boom, but these did not come for free for long. Nazi intervention in Spain eventually became more about resources than ideology. As early as September 1936 and for the remainder of the Civil War, a central motivation for German intervention became economic in nature. It was not that strategic motivations did not matter to Hitler or, for that matter, Mussolini, but because of its natural wealth and relative stage of development, Spain fit perfectly into Schachtian economic designs.[32] To an extent other historians have overlooked, Chapter 7 traces how Schachtian economics came to dominate German policy in Spain.[33] In far better studied cases, a similar phenomenon later took place in Eastern Europe and the Balkans. Yet the Spanish project was far more ambitious than anything ever attempted in those geographies. Informal empire relied on political power to direct trade: without sacrificing scant foreign exchange, Germany could unload in Spain those products being produced by the Nazi Sparta and, in exchange, extract what its constrained industry needed to keep growing. All this was executed through monopolistic companies with the full backing of the Nazi apparatus. That is how, within two years and in the midst of civil war dislocations, German trade with Spain had eclipsed centuries of Anglo-French dominance.

Until mid-1937 Nazi economics was—to a large extent—Schachtian economics. Even afterward most of Schacht's key policy patterns and economic structures endured. Yet the "Party thugs" he so derided outmaneuvered the banker in Berlin power circles. Intervention in Spain may have been Schachtian in design, but it came to be run by Schacht's nemesis, Hermann Göring. For his part Hitler moved toward transformative economic choices that sent Germany closer to world war. These choices are detailed in Chapter 6. Schacht's departure from the higher echelons of Nazi decision making was part of a key transformation in the regime, one that sacrificed the possibility of informal empire, an idea inspired by the tradition of *Weltpolitik,* on the altar of *Lebensraum.*[34]

Those who replaced Schacht ensured that "essential living space" would be sought to the east, through force, and underpinned by racialist pseudo-science.[35] Hitler unleashed armaments spending far beyond Schacht's targets, leading to crisis in a system that was already too reliant on armaments to deliver growth and full employment. I contrast the banker's downfall in Berlin with the effectiveness of his preferred imperial strategies on Iberian soil.

In order to establish the exceptional character of Germany's Iberian project, Chapters 8 and 9 contrast it with another intervention and another empire, respectively. In terms of lives and lire, Mussolini invested far more in Spain than Hitler did.[36] Intervention fit il Duce's longstanding foreign policy.[37] New archival findings detail a Fascist "connivance" with Iberian conspirators.[38] The Civil War and the specter of Communism arguably brought the Axis together while the dictators collaborated on Spanish battlefields.[39] The gargantuan investment in Spain, however, depleted Italy's resources at a rate that the Fascist regime could not realistically hope to sustain. Together with Mussolini's empire building in Africa, the sheer scale of Iberian commitments crippled Rome's economic standing ahead of world war. Fascists had little to show for intervention, in particular when contrasted with an "Axis partner" that effectively undermined them.[40] The stark differences between both fascist interventions underscore the uniqueness of the Nazi project and is symptomatic of an Axis that worked, to paraphrase Italian foreign minister Count Galleazzo Ciano, for only one of its parts.[41]

Understanding an empire that could have been requires a comparison with the empire that was, albeit fleetingly. Chapter 9 therefore contrasts the informal empire in Spain with the formal empire Hitler ultimately chose to build. German behavior in occupied territories between 1937 and 1945 was anything but a coordinated affair. It was haphazard, often contradictory, and ever dependent on Hitler's personal diktats. Austria and the former Czechoslovakia were swiftly integrated into the Reich; meanwhile territories farther east fell victim to the most radical *Lebensraum* designs. With particular intensity in Poland and the Soviet Union, the Nazi empire involved a racially driven plan of uneconomic mass deportations, forced labor, and unspeakable genocide. By contrast, occupation in Western Europe involved relatively less outright plundering and violence, at least at first. The degree of direct exploitation increased when Blitzkrieg failed to deliver a decisive world war victory. Yet the degree of geographic variability in Nazi imperial experience underscores a relative lack of experience and ex ante planning, as well as managerial problems exacerbated by centralized Nazi rule and the inherent difficulties of long-term extractive exploitation. Neither the western nor the eastern Nazi empires were as potentially sustainable as the informal projection of German power attempted, as we shall see, on Iberian soil.

Chapter 9 also concurrently traces the decline of German hegemony on Iberian soil, concluding with a hitherto unappreciated paradox; an analysis of bilateral documents in the context of the wider war shows the extent to which the advent of world war crippled the Nazis' standing with Franco. Only after September 1939 were Franco and his government able to successfully resist German economic penetration and debt repayment. World war yielded unexpected benefits to Franco. Debts are rarely paid when creditors are obliterated. That is what came of Nazi Germany's large claims on Nationalist Spain, as well as its network of resource-focused long-term investments.

The shadow empire in Spain previewed the economic exploitation of the European periphery at the service of the industrial German core. Although this strategy was ultimately abandoned in favor of a far more ruthless and less effective policy, an informal empire did function on Iberian soil to Germany's benefit. Some might counter that such an empire never appeared on European maps. They would be right. And yet, as John Gallagher and Ronald Robinson wrote in a classic study of the British Empire, "for purposes of economic analysis it would clearly be unreal to define imperial history exclusively as the history of those colonies coloured red on the map."[42] Hitler did possess a shadow empire, one that in hindsight would have provided a more effective blueprint for continental dominance than his preferred alternative.

We live in different times. Today a peaceful, democratic, and increasingly federal Europe faces challenges inherent to the birth defects of its monetary union.[43] Frequently populist politicians in the so-called periphery complain of German dominance; they even explicitly evoke the memory of the Nazi past. But institutions are rarely, if ever, ex ante constructions. More often than not they evolve in the context of political cultures, economic realities, social aspirations, and demographic constraints—a point made long ago by adherents to the historical school of economics. As Europe's federal institutions evolve, the experience of the Spanish Civil War and Germany's designs for economic hegemony should remind us of far less palatable alternatives to the current process of "ever closer union." I have heard it said that, after the Civil War, one Spain abandoned freedom for the motherland and the other Spain abandoned the motherland for freedom. Today that is no longer the case; integrated Europe is at the core of modern, democratic Spain's successes. It has underpinned its democratic transition, its accelerated development, and even the difficult—but ultimately bloodless—debates about its buried past. Similarly "Europe" as idea and reality has been crucial to the political and economic successes of both reunified Germany and postwar Italy.

My interpretation of Nazi Germany's project in Spain departs from the work of scholars like Michael Burleigh, who see Nazism as a political religion largely devoid of economic rationale.[44] The argument herein also diverges from the theory of an overdetermined racial empire as proposed by Mark Mazower and Timothy Snyder, among others.[45] German exploitation of Spain predated the (initially) profitable Western European conquests highlighted by Alan Milward and others, while providing a case study in economic hegemony that has been largely ignored in the best economic histories of the period, among which Adam Tooze's stands out.[46] This book thus sets Nazi Germany's

Iberian project in a novel, comparative economic framework within the shipwreck of globalization in the 1930s.

Above all, however, this study challenges the view that Germany's informal empire in Spain was a mere "failure," as advocated by learned Civil War scholars in Germany (Hans-Henning Abendroth), Britain (Christian Leitz), and Spain (Angel Viñas and Rafael García Pérez).[47] That surely goes too far, in particular in the context of the amazing successes of economic penetration before the advent of world war. Hence counterfactual questions can be raised about the sustainability of the Iberian shadow empire if Hitler had chosen a different foreign policy. Without fascist intervention, Franco could never have written, as he did on April 1, 1939, "Today, with the Red army imprisoned and disarmed, national troops have achieved their final military objectives. The war is over."[48] And without Iberian resources Germany would have been less ready for war five months later. Not so Fascist Italy, a point that can only be made through the comparison of both interventions. The Spanish Civil War left many bones to bury beneath the arid Iberian soil. Among them was an alternative version of German empire—and indeed of European integration—that deserves to be unearthed.

chapter one

TWO SPAINS

Aquí yace media España;   Here lies half Spain;
murió de la otra mitad.   it died of the other half.

—MARIANO JOSÉ DE LARRA, "All Saints' Day," *Figaro,* 1836

More so than London's British Museum or New York's Metropolitan, and perhaps comparable only to the relationship that binds the Louvre to Paris, El Prado defines Madrid. No visitor can hope to comprehend the city's layout without understanding the centrality of its leading museum. Both its neoclassical façade and sleek, modern expansion stand tall, unavoidable, on a street that bears its name *(Calle del Prado)* and connects one of the city's central arteries *(Calle de Alcalá),* where one can find the imposing Bank of Spain and the beautiful curves of Cibeles, with Atocha station, the country's busiest and its rail connection to the rest of Europe.[1] El Prado is at the heart of Madrid. Close to it is the Retiro, the *madrileña* answer to Hyde Park or Central Park, as well as the Royal Botanical Gardens, whose serene leafy vistas retain that distinctively Gallic aesthetic of Bourbon kings. El Prado's forty-five thousand square meters cannot rival the Napoleonic grandiosity of the Louvre or the vastness of New York's Met, yet in the words of Iberian modernist Antonio Saura, it "may not be the most extensive [museum], but it's the most intense."[2]

If El Prado defines Madrid, then Goya defines El Prado. The Diego Velázquez and El Greco collections may be favorites among tourists on busy morning tours, but Francisco de Goya is el Prado's most carefully curated artist. Its halls exhibit no fewer than 100 of Goya's works, which may explain why the curatorial staff includes a position dedicated to the master. It is Goya's oversize, stern-looking effigy that oversees the museum's main entrance, unsurprisingly named "Goya Gate."

The master's most evocative paintings are also his last, collectively called the "black paintings."[3] As touching as they are troubling, these fourteen murals epitomize the transformation of a romantic forced to taste invasion, war, illness, and even ostracism. Excluded from the royal court, deaf, and aged, Goya retreated to a solitary enclave in the outskirts of Madrid; at this so-called Deaf Man's Villa, he produced paintings so private that they were—as far as we know—not even titled. As if to hide them from his statue's sight, they now reside in a gallery at the farthest corner from Goya Gate.

Upon entering the room, most visitors are immediately taken by Saturn's gaze as he devours one of his sons lest his progeny overthrow him. Others may be drawn to the disfigured faithful in *A Pilgrimage to San Isidro* (1820–1823). Yet Goya's most astute political message is hidden in the deceptive simplicity of *Duel by Clubs* (1820–1823), which masterfully captures the promise of violence of a duel frozen in time.[4] Against an arid landscape that could be almost anywhere in Spain, one of the duelists is about to die a painful death by clubbing, a curiously Iberian form of dueling devoid of the stiff formality—and relative civility—of Anglo-French rules. The raw physicality of such duels ended with the victor bloody and entangled with his victim, making it difficult to ascertain who ultimately prevailed.

Duel by Clubs is a fitting metaphor for the centuries-long dichotomy that culminated in the Spanish Civil War, a theme also touched upon by contemporaries of the war like Antonio Machado and Miguel de Unamuno.[5] The "two Spains" underscore antagonistic answers to an elusive question: Who—and what—was Spain? Was it the absolutist, Catholic, conservative kingdom of the Bourbon kings or the free-thinking, secular, Republic of liberals?

When King Philip II commissioned a traditional bronze suit of armor to depict all the territories he ruled, the product looked like the shield of Achilles—a legendary shield, as described by Homer, which Hephaestus crafted to depict the whole world. In the last decade of the sixteenth century, Philip ruled over the greatest seafaring powers (Spain,

Portugal, and the Low Countries), Sicily and Naples, an uninterrupted tract of the Americas from the viceroyalty of New Spain bordering present-day Canada all the way down to Patagonia, trading ports throughout India and South Asia, the Spanish East Indies, and select holdings in Guinea and North Africa. He even had a claim on England by marriage. To say the sun never set on Philip's empire was, strictly speaking, an understatement.[6]

The empire fit the motto of Philip's father, Charles, which endures on the Spanish coat of arms: *Plus ultra*. Their Spain was running out of "further beyonds." And yet, lacking the communication and bureaucratic apparatus of Queen Victoria's empire two centuries later, Spain's was an empire too vast to rule. A system of regional viceroyalties tied to Madrid's absolutist control failed to deliver effective management. Under Philip's underwhelming successors, the viceroyalty system became expensive and chaotic. The monarchy went largely unchecked by the Cortes (Parliament) and was backed by a Church keen on empire building.[7] The Spanish Empire threw away the metallic wealth of its South American colonies in failed ventures fought with imported weapons and, increasingly, imported men. Not least of those ventures was Philip's Grand Armada fiasco, an ill-fated, hubristic attempt to conquer Elizabethan England. The Spanish treasury's chronic bankruptcy weakened Spain's foreign influence, an early modern version of imperial overstretch.[8] Not unlike the decline and fall of other great empires, Spain's involved a self-reinforcing process linking the overcommitting of military resources with the loss of economic preeminence.

As Spain's foreign influence declined, foreign involvement in Spanish affairs increased. It was not until Napoleon upset the European balance of power that Spain began in earnest its duel with itself. Bonaparte was the first to challenge Iberian territorial integrity since the so-called Reconquista, the process of Spanish unification under one crown (Ferdinand and Isabella's) and one faith (Catholicism) in the 1490s. By the time Napoleon's imperial army crossed the Pyrenees, two centuries of financial mismanagement had taken their toll: the country was another piece in the European puzzle, far from the world's undisputed hegemon. It was the terror Napoleon's men brought that Goya immortalized in *The Third of May of 1808* (1814), a momentous development in political art.[9] In it, a pure Spain rises against the invader's firing squad, an iconic scene of Catholic martyrdom.

Europe's internal wars meanwhile emboldened self-government movements throughout the Spanish colonies. Starting in Buenos Aires in 1810, creoles evicted Bourbon viceroys in favor of self-government.[10] Along with foreign troops, Enlightenment ideals also crept into the Iberian peninsula—as they did in the colonies. Many of those who died to deliver Bourbon Spain from Bonaparte did not merely want independence from foreign rule; they also sought deep domestic reforms. Indeed, the liberal revolutions are best understood as a single historical process linking the metropolis with the colonies, where independence broadly conceived was the central goal.[11]

In 1812 the provisional government passed the liberal Constitution of Cádiz promising limits on both Crown and Church. It was an inspired document that challenged the traditionalist Bourbon king, Ferdinand VII. The exiled monarch did little to oppose it lest it inspire his subjects to seek more radical reform than the (mere) establishment of a constitutional monarchy. But when the Battle of Waterloo did away with the Napoleonic threat once and for all, Ferdinand swiftly abolished the Constitution. He lived up to the most famous dictum about his kin: the Bourbons "forgot nothing and learned nothing."[12]

Yet Ferdinand failed to restore an ancien régime that was bankrupt both literally and figuratively.[13] Not unlike the Latin American independence hero José de San Martín, Iberian officers devoted themselves to the constitutional cause. In the port of Cádiz, Gen. Rafael del Riego staged a liberal mutiny. Meeting no resistance, he marched on Madrid, where a cornered Ferdinand signed on the dotted line. Not for the last time change proved short-lived. While a new government planned long-delayed reforms, Ferdinand appealed to the Holy Alliance, the guarantor of absolutist monarchies in post–Napoleonic Europe. Conservative Russia and Prussia hesitated. Austria's Prince Metternich, mastermind of the Alliance, pressed France's Louis XVIII to aid his cousin. To stop the spread of liberalism, French troops crossed the Pyrenees once again, this time armed with an ideology diametrically opposed to Napoleon's. François-René Chateaubriand, the author–cum–ultraroyalist foreign minister, fondly recalled a historically charged campaign: "Striding across the Spains, succeeding where Bonaparte had failed, triumphing on the same soil where a great man's arms had suffered setbacks, doing in six months what he was unable to do in seven years, was a true miracle!"[14] Financed by two Rothschild loans, the "Hundred Thousand Sons of St. Louis" reestablished absolutist power.[15]

Ferdinand's retaliation was vicious. Yet his notoriously unchaste daughter, Isabella, also struggled to maintain Bourbon autocracy. Some argued the queen was not the rightful heir, favoring instead Ferdinand's brother, Carlos; these royalists became known as "Carlists" and, a century later, would play a key part in the Spanish Civil War. It was during the first of the "Carlist wars" that the salient romantic journalist Mariano José de Larra wrote of a Spain "dying of the other half." Less than a year later, spurned by his love and depressed about his fatherland, he committed suicide.[16] In spite of the Carlist threat and unstable constitutional arrangements, Isabella's nightmare was the *pronunciamiento*—the Iberian version of a coup d'état—from an army eager to put limits on the Crown.[17] There were other enemies too: the clergy reacted against some of Isabella's measures, particularly *desamortización,* the process of selling off Church-owned "dead lands" to finance Spain's fiscal excesses.[18] Reactionary forces did not move fast enough. A naval mutiny began—again—in Cádiz, leading to the "glorious revolution" of 1868. But while the Industrial Revolution gathered momentum in northern Europe, Spain stagnated. When the queen went into exile, Iberian liberals looked for a more reliable dynasty. Prussia's Iron Chancellor, Otto von Bismarck, saw a strategic opportunity; he proposed a German prince for the throne. It would not be long before the Hohenzollern prince abandoned the bid, yet the row served Bismarck's purpose of souring relations between Prussia and France's Napoleon III.[19] This "Spanish diversion" therefore helped pave the way for German unification under Prussian—and Bismarckian—leadership. Meanwhile Catalonian general Juan Prim scouted Europe for a monarch willing to swear on a liberal constitution. In the 1870s this was no simple task: "looking for a democratic monarch in Europe," Prim was quoted saying, "is like trying to find an atheist in heaven."[20]

Eventually he settled for Amadeo of Savoy, younger son of Italy's unifier, Victor Emmanuel II. The arrival of the new king in Madrid coincided with Prim's assassination. It was a bad omen. Upon Prim's corpse, outside the Cortes, Amadeo swore to uphold the Constitution. At last Spain had a constitutional monarchy. But in a country in desperate need of reform, Amadeo could rely neither on the reactionary Church, for which he was too liberal, nor on radicalizing liberals, who now looked to the Paris Commune for inspiration. Carlists also opposed him. Before Amadeo had time to get used to Madrid, Madrid had had enough of him; the same Parliament that made him king in 1870 proclaimed a Republic in 1873. That evening deposed king Amadeo declared Spain to be "ungovernable."[21]

In a time of irredentism all over the Continent, the Spanish Republic promised increased autonomy for regions like the Basques and Catalonia. Yet such initiatives deepened the gulf between Republicans and the army. Increasingly conservative generals argued that moves toward federalism would destroy Spain's integrity and render the country impossible to rule. It would also weaken what remained of Spain's empire. A solution was once again sought from abroad: Isabella's son, Alfonso XII, went from cadet at Sandhurst to king of Spain in a fortnight.[22] His passion for "all things military" pleased the generals. During Alfonso's rule the army was driven into the monarchical camp, seduced by the promise of renewed imperial glory.[23]

The restoration's ideological architect, Antonio Cánovas del Castillo, sacrificed modernization for stability. Although he admired the British prime ministers Gladstone and Disraeli enough to have memorized their speeches at Westminster, Cánovas was deeply pessimistic about his parliamentary system. A historian by training, he had achieved fame by penning a book about Iberian decline and was widely believed to have said, "[The] Spanish are those who cannot be anything else."[24] Cánovas's Conservatives took turns with the Liberals in power.[25] The latter's name, however, was misleading; the only issues that differentiated the parties were the Liberals' relative anticlericalism and support for public education.[26]

Cánovas's restoration was so effective that newspapers published results ahead of elections.[27] In time popular discontent with such blatant rigging grew. An 1891 volume comparing Spain's system with the rest of the continent epitomized disenchantment: "In Spain . . . one cannot speak about a system like the French . . . of numerical despotism, or like in Italy and Belgium, of the omnipotence of parliamentary majorities, but about ministerial omnipotence and the utter lack of an electoral base, substituted by the most scandalous corruption of electoral processes."[28] Eventually the parties resorted to slightly more elaborate vote rigging; in a trick still occasionally used in some former Spanish colonies, for instance, all seven hundred dead in a Castilian cemetery cast votes for the Conservatives; the deceased, it seemed, were not Liberals.[29]

Without lasting development, however, stability turned stale. The ruling elites cheered King Alfonso XIII in his attempt to seek renewed imperial grandeur in Cuba and Morocco. Not so the lower classes. Having lost faith in the corrupt Parliament and the royalist Church, masses of landless agricultural workers turned to yet another foreign solution: ideology. Socialism, Communism, and anarchism took root in Spain.[30] Like Prim decades before, Cánovas was assassinated when leaving the Cortes.[31] Following an uprising in Barcelona in 1909 that met ferocious military repression, Catalonia's governor, Ángel Ossorio y Gallardo, famously confided to his diary, "In Barcelona, a revolution does not have to be prepared, since it is always prepared."[32]

During World War I Spain did enjoy an export boom, not uncharacteristic for nonbelligerent nations. Yet this growth spurt did little to increase the real income of the lower classes, at this point among the poorest in Europe. The economic burst after the end of the war, however, managed to boost support for fringe politics, on both the right and the left. Economic crisis deepened polarization. Not for the last time, King Alfonso XIII feared the end was nigh; and like his predecessors, he opted for reaction over revolution. On September 13, 1923, the king acquiesced in Gen. Miguel Primo de Rivera's *pronunciamiento.* "We have reason on our side and, therefore, force, though we have used force with moderation. . . . We shall not shrink from bloodshed."[33] During Primo's ensuing six years of dictatorship, however, there were no political executions. The general flirted with fascism but ruled like a despot from a bygone century.[34]

During the early years of his rule, cheap foreign credit put Spain's deeply rooted economic problems on hold. Although foreign trade grew considerably, loans to furnish the military, develop education, modernize infrastructure, and build extravagant cinemas—a passion of Primo's that left its mark in the landscape of Madrid—eventually dried up. Iberian capital markets closely followed the flow of foreign funds. Their withdrawal was particularly painful.[35] With the first signs that the 1929 Wall Street crash heralded a global crisis, Primo fell. Spain's intellectuals called for a new Republic. As yet another Bourbon went into exile, a new generation proclaimed, "This young and eager Spain has at last arrived at its majority."[36]

★   ★   ★

Virtually all analyses of the Spanish economy in the "long nineteenth century" agree on one thing: industrialization failed.[37] At the core lies Spain's backward agricultural sector, which employed over two thirds of its labor force until well into the twentieth century.[38] Admittedly the country's physical endowment is poor for agriculture. Narrow coasts surround the *meseta central*—the high, dry central Iberian plateau—and over 90 percent of the country receives less than 750 millimeters per year in precipitation; this complicated the introduction of intensive agricultural techniques. Most of the innovations that led to higher productivity before industrial takeoff—the so-called agrarian revolution, including new husbandry, crop rotation, and heavy plows—did not easily fit the Iberian landscape; technologically, therefore, Spain remained trapped in Roman times.[39] Most Spaniards' diets were kept barely above subsistence levels, with agricultural yields far below not only industrial "first-movers" like England and France but also Mediterranean neighbors like Italy.[40]

When reforms were attempted, a politically weak state exacerbated suboptimal distribution, creating the twin problems of *latifundios* in the South and *minifundios* in the North.[41] Agricultural backwardness became intertwined with the failure of education. Notwithstanding a liberal pet project, the Instituto de la Libre Enseñanza, Spanish education lagged far behind most of western Europe. Tellingly the number of students enrolled in primary schools peaked in the 1880s and plummeted for the next three decades.[42] Spanish human capital was behind even its Latin neighbors.[43]

Economists also agree on the centrality of Iberian fiscal irresponsibility.[44] Having famously defaulted no fewer than fourteen times between 1557 and 1696, Spain was by no means new to fiscal crisis, yet public finance in the long nineteenth century was, to use a technical term, chaotic. To borrow from a leading historian of the period, "old debts were consolidated, deferred, reformed, and reactivated, but rarely paid."[45] As usual, financial mismanagement created a negative feedback loop. Not unlike many emerging markets in the late twentieth century, Spain's track record of bad debt and chronic deficits increased long-term interest rates, negatively affecting investment. This vicious circle was both a cause and a consequence of Spain's duel with itself.

Some Iberian economists argue that the relative openness of trade in the mid-nineteenth century and the loss of empire hurt modernization efforts.[46] Others disagree, estimating from admittedly imperfect statistics that Spain's small and poorly managed late nineteenth-century empire was too small to have a definitive impact on development.[47] Data strongly suggest that the only problem with open trade policies in the 1860s and 1870s was that they were rolled back as soon as the Bourbons were restored.[48] Ultimately Spanish development fell victim to a familiar misalignment of incentives: protectionist policies appealed to the inefficient but politically powerful agricultural sector. Meanwhile successive Bourbon governments imposed import taxes on cheap food, the so-called *arancel,* aiming toward food self-sufficiency in a country unfit for the task.[49]

In short, a combination of agricultural backwardness, poor human capital management, dismal state finances, and protectionism explain the failure of Spanish modernization. The sole exceptions were Catalonia's textiles and Viscaya's metallurgy, largely in the hands of foreign-controlled firms like Rio Tinto. By and large, however, Spain lacked the impulse for a "takeoff" or a "great sprout"; protected industries were not competitive for international markets, poor agricultural incomes limited the growth of the domestic market, and capital accumulation was simply insufficient for industrial development. A government perennially in deficit crowded out industry rather than encourage the move from consumer to capital goods.[50] In another great line ahead of his time, de Larra had joked ironically that "Spanish credit" was buried at the Madrid stock exchange, wondering, "Like with the pyramids, why such a big building for a body so small?"[51] And that was in 1836.

By the advent of the Second Republic, Spain was in a position of backwardness; educational attainment, industrial production, urbanization, and public health were all decades behind Italy and Germany, not to mention Britain and France. Indeed, some have suggested that by then Spain was "a colony of Europe."[52] Taking advantage of the further economic dislocations produced by Spain's ongoing duel with itself, one of the intervening powers in the looming Civil War would seek to make this "colony" primarily theirs.

In late 1930 an opinion piece by philosopher José Ortega y Gasset in *El Sol* captured the mood of the time. He argued that the Bourbons lacked legitimacy: "The normality of civil union between Spaniards is broken, the continuity of legal history is splintered." He closed with a flourish worthy of Cato:[53] "It is us, and not the regime, the people from the streets . . . who must tell other citizens: Spaniards, your state is no more. *Delenda est monarchia.*"[54]

The Second Republic was meant to rebuild the state and put an end to polarization. It was to provide Spaniards with an outlet for dissent. It was to bring the social peace and political legitimacy intellectuals so desired. It was to end Spain's "duel by clubs." Briefly it seemed that it might succeed. Neither Communists nor anarchists—nor monarchists for that matter—were included in the first Republican Cabinet. But leaving aside extremes, it was a plural project. A former Bourbon supporter, Niceto Alcalá-Zamora, led a Cabinet that included men from a surprising variety of backgrounds. A majority of them were secularists, yet both Alcalá-Zamora and Miguel Maura, the interior minister, were practicing Catholics. The Ministry of the Navy went to future prime minister Santiago Casares Quiroga and the Foreign Ministry to Alejandro Lerroux, a corrupt politician who had long given up on the principles his Radicals were supposed to espouse.[55]

It was said disparagingly of "National Economy Minister" Nicolau d'Olwer that, as an economist, he was "a great Hellenist."[56] It was in keeping with Iberian tradition not to have financial experts in senior government positions; d'Olwer was a choice meant to appease Catalan nationalists. Yet the Banque de France expressed confidence in the new regime by extending a loan to the Republican Bank of Spain.[57]

The Socialists in the Cabinet accurately represented the ideology's diverging strands. Justice Minister Fernando de los Ríos was a bourgeois humanist. Labor Minister Francisco Largo Caballero, leader of the mighty Unión General de Trabajadores, was a proletarian through and through; he had worked in construction before joining the ranks of the Spanish Socialist Party in the aftermath of the particularly bloody 1890 strike.[58] He was often called "the Spanish Lenin," an epithet he sought to live up to. And then there was Finance Minister Indalecio Prieto. Young and charismatic but less proletarian and popular in the movement than Largo Caballero, Prieto had come into conflict with the labor minister twice before. After the Great War Prieto had chosen exile rather than the imprisonment that Largo Caballero endured. During Primo's dictatorship, however, when Largo Caballero chose collaboration, Prieto remained aloof. Responsibility over finances would have been unenviable in any Iberian government, but it was particularly toxic during the Depression.

Perhaps the most interesting man in the Cabinet, however, was the minister of war. Born in the same town as Cervantes, Manuel Azaña was celebrated for his polemics and translations of Voltaire. "Enlightened" is probably an anachronistic way to describe him, but then again, Azaña himself was anachronistic. Self-consciously ugly, he had a natural tendency toward seclusion. The unparalleled Miguel de Unamuno once said of Azaña that he would be willing to start a revolution if only so that his books would be read. During the Civil War he would return to letters, publishing a sarcastic dialogue while his country tore itself apart.[59] But in 1931 Azaña's star rose unchallenged; he represented the liberal model of post-Bourbon Spain: progressive, secular, and wary of the army. The barracks were not pleased.

If there was one demography that placed its hopes in the government, that was long-suffering peasants.[60] According to the great Iberian historian Salvador de Madariaga, powerful landlords and their offspring, deridingly called *señoritos,* tried to impose conservative electoral choices among their poor workers when the Republic first went to the polls. In one of the plantations of meager Andalusia, a peon had refused to cast his vote for his *señorito*'s choice: "In my hunger, it is my choice."[61]

The new government introduced changes ranging from the foundational to the figurative. A key priority was making religious education optional; this was a long-held secular goal. Although the Vatican was willing to compromise, the Iberian clergy was not. Primate Pedro Segura violently attacked it in a pastoral letter, while also expressing nostalgia for the monarchy.[62] "When the enemies of Christ's kingdom advance resolutely," he wrote, "no Catholic can remain inactive." In a sermon he added, "May the Republic be cursed!"[63] The otherwise centrist justice minister described the letter as "a frank assertion indicating the hostility of the Church to the Republican regime."[64] Henceforth government intransigence toward the Church and its perceived nonchalance toward church burnings escalated hostilities. The burning of Spanish churches was not strictly a Republican phenomenon: it symbolized the proletarian, anarchist rejection of a Church all too prone to side with Spain's Crown, aristocracy, and military. Otherwise peaceful liberals came close to justifying it; for instance, renowned teacher José Castillejo once famously remarked, "The anarchists have destroyed many churches, but the clergy had first destroyed the Church."[65]

Republicans were well aware that if any rebellion were to challenge their new order, it would not spring from the convents but from the barracks. Bloated and anachronistic, the army hierarchy remained in denial about decline. The fact that the army had approximately one general for every hundred soldiers in 1898 did not prevent its humiliating defeat in the Spanish-American War; it likely precipitated it. More recent military disasters in Africa, such as the battle of Annual in 1921, compounded difficulties. Those who had been hardened in the deserts of Morocco—commonly referred to as Africanistas to differentiate them from the cozier Peninsulares—saw the Republic with particular disdain, fearing for their hard-fought African empire. But could Spain afford that never-ending war? In the hands of Azaña, military modernization meant cuts and civilian subordination. He made few friends in the army ranks. Some measures admittedly went too far: while it was sensible to cut back on automatic advancements by seniority, it was nothing short of bizarre for an army to do away with bravery promotions altogether.

The government also restored the liberal "Himno de Riego" as the national anthem. Its strident lyrics oozed confidence in the Republic's daunting task: "The world never saw braver courage / . . . soldiers, the fatherland calls / to prevail or die." Yet the mirage of workable government quickly began to fade. On an otherwise tranquil Sunday morning in downtown Madrid, the simple exchange of shouts between two groups—liberals crying "Viva la República!" and conservatives replying "Viva la Monarquía!"—somehow culminated in the burning of the offices of Spain's leading monarchist daily, *ABC*. The government was soon in the uncomfortable position of protecting the property of its staunchest political opponents. The threat of street violence loomed large. While the extreme left dreamed of revolution in mines and slums, the right plotted in palaces, churches, and barracks.

Episodes like the *ABC* burning help explain why neither the left-leaning Republican coalitions under Alcalá-Zamora and Azaña between 1931 and 1933 nor the conservative government between 1934 and 1936 sustained by a right-wing alliance, the Confederación Española de Derechas Autónomas (Confederation of the Autonomous Right, CEDA),

could successfully hold on to power. Facing a triad of thorny situations—
Azaña's military reforms, an edict allowing for more Catalonian autonomy, and a bizarre incident in the sleepy town of Castilblanco where
four civil guard officers had been brutally massacred, seemingly by the
whole town[66]—monarchists conjured a coup. In the summer of 1932,
aged, eccentric Gen. José Sanjurjo launched a *pronunciamiento;* it was
successful only in Seville, and only for a few hours. Azaña later boasted
that he knew about it well in advance, allowing it to happen just to
watch it fail.[67]

The so-called Sanjurjada was disastrous for reactionaries. Amid the
uncertainty, however, the economic situation deteriorated. Investment
collapsed. Although rising Republican wages improved the incomes
of the lower classes, theoretically increasing domestic demand, they impaired competitiveness. Declining exports put pressure on the balance
of trade. Both coalition governments tried to enact deep reforms, only
in opposite directions. Land reform was at the core of Republican
politics—wholly unsurprising in light of Spain's deep inequalities. The
Instituto de la Reforma Agraria (Agrarian Reform Institute, IRA) was
an essential project of the Azaña coalition. Even though Cortes approved its creation in 1932, conservative deputies packed the final bill
with amendments that undermined its implementation. So numerous
were the changes, in fact, that respected historians such as Preston have
argued it was a mistake for the government to send it through Parliament in the first place.[68] Other goals included enforcing the forty-hour
work week and improving the legal standing of landless peasants.

Unsurprisingly Spain's landed aristocracy resisted, often resorting to
the same violent tactics of the workers' movement. Following the Republic's 1934 elections, conservatives sought to end land redistribution
by creating a complex bureaucracy at the IRA.[69] The aptly named Law
of Agricultural Counter-Reformation all but stopped redistribution.[70]
Similarly conservatives halted the exclusion of Jesuits from education
as well as the development of a lay school curriculum. They even released political prisoners, allowing figures like Sanjurjo to go abroad
to resume their plotting.[71] In spite of warnings from even their own
parliamentary representatives, landlords also took the chance to slash
wages and fire activist workers. The strategy was shortsighted both economically, because it furthered deflation, and politically, because it invited retaliation in the ballot box and beyond.

Paradoxically the introduction of universal suffrage helped the right in the 1934 polls. Conservative politicians targeted first-time female voters effectively. While the right stood squarely against radical changes to the status quo, the workers' movement chastised the Republican government for not going far enough. Different groups saw in the 1934 results whatever they wanted: the right saw an opportunity to turn back the clock; Socialists saw a justification for radical measures. To the dismay of democrats, Socialist newspapers ran articles denouncing the Republic as no better than the monarchy it had deposed.[72] At a meeting in early October, Largo Caballero burned bridges: "Our party is ideologically [and] tactically, a revolutionary party . . . that believes this regime must disappear." The "regime" was the Republic.

While Largo Caballero dreamed of living up to his nickname, the moderate left worried about José María Gil Robles. Founder and mastermind of the victorious right-wing CEDA alliance, Gil Robles expressed sympathies for Nazism and liked to be addressed as "Jefe" (literally, "boss"), in the tradition of Mussolini's Duce and Hitler's Führer. Iberian leaders enjoyed their foreign allegories. Echoing Italian slogans, one of Gil Robles's electoral mottos was "All power to the Jefe."[73]

Gil Robles was not among the CEDA members to join the Cabinet in 1934 because the president was reluctant to hand him power the way President Hindenburg had yielded to Hitler a year earlier. But he was not far away. In this context the far left had its shot at revolution. On October 4 miners in Asturias called a strike to protest against CEDA joining the government. In a region with a history of rebellion, the strike soon graduated into revolution.[74] Armed with rifles, dynamite, and plenty of fervor, miners set up committees and took over industries. Facing little resistance, they took over the regional capital, Oviedo. They proclaimed an "Asturian Socialist Republic." The agenda involved the usual revolutionary fare: eradicating property, capitalism, landlords. From a traditional hotbed of Iberian anarchism, the most hopeful dreamed of marching on Madrid.[75]

Was this to be Spain's Red October? Seeing this as an opportunity, the president of Catalonia, Lluis Companys, addressed Barcelona: "Catalans, the monarchical and fascist forces that for a while have sought to betray the Republic have achieved their objective and launched a [violent] bid for power." That was factually inaccurate, but his direction was obvious enough: "In this solemn hour . . . the government [over

which] I preside assumes all faculties of power in Catalonia, [and] pro-
claims the Catalan state of the Spanish Federal Republic." There was
no such thing as an Iberian "federal republic" in 1934; indeed, it does
not exist today. Yet Companys at least paid lip service to Spanish unity
by expressing the "hope to build a free and magnificent" Republic.
Companys invited secession.

Madrid would have neither Asturian revolution nor Catalan independence. Diego Hidalgo, a far more conservative war minister than
Azaña, was not keen on having conscripts repress in Asturias. To have
Spanish youth firing against the Spanish proletariat would not sit well
with Republican supporters, not to mention the press. So Hidalgo called
on a precocious general who had made his name in North Africa. In
order to take back Asturias, the government shipped troops from the
war-seasoned Army of Africa, the so-called Africanistas. The solution
devised by Gen. Francisco Franco did not shy from bloodshed.[76]

Among those shipped from Morocco were members of Spain's finest
fighting force: the Foreign Legion. Modeled after its French equivalent, it had developed an Iberian identity under the leadership of
Lt. Col. José Millán Astray. Historical gravitas permeated the Legion:
its formations were deemed *tercios* after the Reconquista unit that had
fought off Moors in the sixteenth century. Millán Astray—who had
lost an arm and several fingers in action—encouraged a cult of death
that would acquire dark fame in the Civil War.[77] His legionnaires called
themselves "bridegrooms of death," and their motto was no less disqui-
eting: "Long live Death!"[78] Their presence in mainland Spain came as
a shock.[79] Although Catalonia did not put up military resistance, Asturian miners received treatment previously reserved for Spain's "civilizing mission" in Morocco. Aerial bombing, torture, and thousands
of casualties were the result of the campaign that ended the revolution. Just as Sanjurjo's *pronunciamiento* had failed in 1932, so did the
Asturian miners in 1934.

And the two Spains fought on. The repression in Asturias gave the
Republican left a powerful rallying cry against "October murderers."
By February 1936 the center-right coalition called for elections under
the pretext of seeking a more comfortable majority. It was a gross mis-
calculation. Though lacking in ideological unity, the left came together
to form a Popular Front with Azaña at its head. The Front massed cen-

trists, Socialists, and Communists—a rare occurrence in 1930s electoral politics. Even usually apathetic anarchists went to the polls, eager to see their Asturian comrades released from prison.

There were omens that this would be the Republic's last election. Four weeks earlier Largo Caballero again toyed with revolution. "I want to tell the Right that if we win, we will collaborate with our allies [Azaña's Front]," he wrote, "but, if the Right wins, our work will be double, collaborate with our allies within legality, but [also] we will have to go to declared Civil War."[80] His rhetoric suggested the time for subtlety was gone: "Let them not say we say things to say things—for we will accomplish them."[81] Would the Spanish Lenin deliver?

On February 6 the Popular Front narrowly defeated a CEDA-led National Front. Azaña triumphantly returned to power. Largo Caballero stayed out of government, but Communists did join Azaña. This was a crucial difference between Spain's and France's Popular Fronts. Wary of losing his hold of the proletariat, Largo Caballero's rhetoric out of government veered closer to revolution. The government soon granted amnesty to political prisoners, just as the right had done two years earlier.[82] This time it benefited anarchists, but it did not buy their support for long.

On the streets, violence escalated. At a May Day parade a rumor spread that nuns were giving poisoned candy to the workers' children.[83] Before the day was through, an angry mob burned down a convent. Throughout Spain dozens of churches burned; a strike followed. Gil Robles taunted the Azaña administration: "The workers' groups know perfectly well where they are headed: to change the existing social order, and whenever they can, to violently assault power, to exercise from above the dictatorship of the proletariat; but meanwhile, they go for the destruction, constant and efficient, of the system of individual and capitalistic production in Spain. . . . [This] precipitates the collapse of our economy . . . not for legitimate labor complaints, but rather with the purpose of killing capitalistic production."[84] Yet the right had already moved to another type of killing. Faced with Gil Robles's reluctance to rise up against the Republic, the ranks of an even more extreme group multiplied.

The Falange Española, a rapidly growing proto-fascist group led by José Antonio Primo de Rivera, first born of the former dictator, emulated Mussolini's blackshirts threatening to "march on Madrid." If Gil Robles was the "boss," then José Antonio was the fascistic *philosophe* of Iberian reaction. He was a forceful orator obsessed with restoring the memory of his father—to whom, he maintained, Spain had been deeply ungrateful. In a momentous speech he disguised his authoritarianism in Hegelian cloth: "The [Spanish] Fatherland is a transcendent synthesis, an indivisible synthesis, with its own goals to achieve."[85] Like any self-respecting reactionary, he directed many a diatribe against Rousseau. Though certainly no Burke, José Antonio blamed the French philosopher for the Revolution, and the Revolution for the "most notorious system of wasted energies"—his chosen epithet for democracy.[86] Taking his cues from the "liberation" of fascism, he asked rhetorically, "Why do we need the intermediate and pernicious element of political parties?" Perhaps the future would favor the Spain of this aristocratic proto-fascist over that of Largo Caballero's workers. Yet for all his literary references, the Reconquista, and the "unmatched glory" of Iberian culture, José Antonio's followers were keener to terrorize than to attend literary gatherings. They were another group eager to tear the Republic apart to impose their Spain on the rest.

In the same North where Asturian revolutionaries had been freed, a general plotted. Negotiating with illiberal forces from Carlists—who still favored their different branch of Bourbon pretenders—to José Antonio's Falanges, Emilio Mola was deserving of his nickname, "the Director." He amassed an antidemocratic coalition in the shadows, ready to rise up against the Popular Front. Mola imagined an army-led *pronunciamiento* to succeed where the Sanjurjada and the Asturian revolution had failed. With Azaña now installed as president in the midst of a polarized country, his time had come.

In Madrid, meanwhile, the situation was so tense that Prieto asked the government to distribute weapons among workers. The Popular Front government may have relied on Socialist and Communist votes to obtain electoral success, but the Cabinet had the liberal, Republican middle classes to answer to. Premier Casares Quiroga judged that arming the workers was a step too far; President Azaña agreed. The Second Republic was not ready to invite revolution for fear of rebellion. Prieto visited the premier's bureau so many times that Casares Quiroga sardonically reminded him it was not his office. Nor was it his ultimate decision.

In those tense hours a group of shady characters furnished with a false arrest warrant picked up a famous monarchist, José Calvo Sotelo, from his home. His captors appear not to have had a plan; under the influence of hatred likely mixed with alcohol, they sought revenge for the death of a Socialist guard, José Castillo, murdered in cold blood.[87] While the police car in which they drove Sotelo roamed the streets of a sleepy Madrid, a young Socialist in the backseat put a gun to the back of the prisoner's head and pulled the trigger. Bearing a sly smile, the murderer allegedly soon boasted, "One of Castillo's [murderers] has fallen."[88]

The shot that killed Sotelo was just another in the seemingly endless duel between the two Spains, yet it mattered more than most. One of the most brilliant and respected leaders of the Spanish right now lay dead; violence only escalated further in a July with over 200 political killings. At the height of the ensuing confusion, Largo Caballero warned his followers to refrain from collaborating with the Republican government. He believed the end of the regime was nigh. Meanwhile José Antonio waited in a Madrid prison for a reactionary coup to free him or, alternatively, for revolutionaries to finish him.[89] In Burgos, General Mola hastened plans for a coup he had painstakingly planned, even though he was increasingly doubtful of its chances. After all, the late Sotelo was one of the potential leaders of the postcoup government. And many members of the military, including Franco of Asturian fame, now sent by the wary government to the Balearics, dithered about whether or not to join the conspiracy.[90] When his brother Ramón visited Mola, he expressed doubts about their chances in Barcelona, a traditional hotbed of the left. "I do not doubt you know how to die like a gentleman," Mola replied frostily.[91] The Director knew his time had come: before the government would move against them, before Largo Caballero's men would rise, before José Antonio could steal their thunder. "Men must endure," *King Lear*'s Edgar would have it. "Ripeness is all."

For the third time in its brief half-decade of existence, the Republic faced an existential threat. The regime had failed to stop Spanish polarization: divisions in 1936, exacerbated by economic crisis, ran deeper than ever. The country, however, was too poor and evenly matched for a fratricidal war to have a quick resolution. In an unstable Europe the murderous climax of the two Spains triggered a new political crisis. Yet the ultimate outcome of the looming Spanish Civil War would be determined by decisions across the great power capitals of Europe, taken with remarkable synchronicity on a momentous day in the hot summer of 1936.

chapter two

"TODAY IS SO FAR FROM YESTERDAY"

Este amor que quiere ser,	This love that wants to be,
acaso pronto será;	perhaps soon will be;
pero ¿cuándo ha de volver	but when will return
lo que acaba de pasar?	what has just been?
Hoy dista mucho de	Today is so far from
ayer	yesterday
¡Ayer es Nunca jamás!	Yesterday is Never again

—Antonio Machado, "Consejos" (Advice)

In the years leading up to the Spanish Civil War, Dolores Ibárruri was known as La Pasionaria, or "Passion Flower," a rather curious name for a revolutionary.[1] A sly, zealous Communist with ties all the way up to Stalin, she had been thrown in jail more times than she had visited Moscow—three versus two—but that was precisely the type of achievement that gave early twentieth-century revolutionaries their credentials. Though moving, her words consistently seemed to incite violence. Her parliamentary orations became symbols of the polarized atmosphere of Republican Spain.[2] Among the many speeches she delivered during her tenure at a democratic legislature she increasingly distrusted, her June 16, 1936, address encapsulates the abyss Spain stood before. That day La Pasionaria was in no mood to abide by procedure. The right, her usual target, was still shaken by the electoral defeat back in the February elections. Yet, as I have shown, violence had only increased since then: "To avoid disturbances, not only should we make responsible of what may happen [in Spain] a man like Mr. Calvo Sotelo, but also we must begin by incarcerating all those landlords who refuse to abide by the [Republican] government." She was referring to government initiatives from the new ruling left-wing administration of President Manuel Azaña, fiercely rejected by elites and conservatives, whom Sotelo represented. Ibárruri's problem with the government was that they did not dare go far enough: "And when this work of justice has begun, there will be no government with stronger support . . . than this, for the popular masses of Spain will rise against those forces that, for decorum, we should not even tolerate having sat here [in Parliament]." Uproar ensued.

La Pasionaria was not merely challenging the right; she was also pushing Azaña farther left. Her Communists remained out of government, believing power would be theirs when the democratic charade came to an end. In the meantime they pressed for the type of radicalization that cemented the reactionary opposition. In the following days the right would blame Ibárruri's words, among others, for the blood spilled on the streets in a recurring cycle of violence and vendettas. One such cycle ended with Sotelo's murder.

When she campaigned for the Popular Front, La Pasionaria was merely abiding by the Soviet decision to join forces with Socialists in elections. The strategic goal was avoiding the electoral atomization of the left that had contributed to Hitler's salient electoral performance before the Nazi seizure of power.[3] Moscow's tactics notwithstanding, La Pasionaria never abandoned her innermost conviction: the Spain of tomorrow had little to do with constitutions and everything to do with revolution. A few weeks later, when Nationalist forces first threatened to overtake Madrid as revolution and civil war spread across the country, it was her radio address that rallied resistance. In what soon became the key cry of the left, La Pasionaria said over the airwaves, "They shall not pass!"[4]

But who were "they"? The army officers that led the coup d'état launched on July 17, 1936, had the support of key members of the Spanish Armed Forces—though most definitely not all—and a plethora of reactionary groups subscribing to ideologies as dissimilar as Catholic traditionalism and José Antonio's fascistic Falangismo. On their side was a peculiarly Iberian agglomeration of monarchists, consistently nostalgic for Philip II's old imperial glory but in deep disagreement about which royal house was best fit to deliver the country from democracy. There were those who favored the exiled Bourbon king, Alfonso XIII—aware of coup preparations—and those who supported the Carlist contender, Alfonso Carlos. A considerable section of the Spanish middle classes eventually sided with this eclectic group because they feared the very revolution Largo Caballero and La Pasionaria dreamed of leading. And indeed it was the revolution that materialized in Republican territory in the aftermath of the failed coup.

At first it seemed "they" would indeed not pass. An extended confrontation seemed tilted in favor of the Republic and not its reactionary opponents.[5] In spite of General Mola's planning, the uprising was badly synchronized. Owing to disorganization and bad communication, the coup began in Morocco on July 17, but it took until July 21 to reach certain parts of northern Spain. A delay of over fifty hours all but destroyed the element of surprise in the cities where military officers chose to "declare" for the rebellion a tad too late. There were those who dithered until the last minute. Prominent officers in the armed forces had upheld their oath of allegiance to the Republican government, so the military was immediately divided. It was not without reason that Azaña and the government had been promoting and reshuffling military leaders for months, based on conspiracy reports.[6]

Local authorities across Spain had managed to stay in control with the support of revolutionary urban militia that government officials had armed, not always reluctantly. Arming workers had been Largo Caballero's price for supporting the Republic on the eve of the revolt, which in hindsight undermined the power of the Republican state. Militias, as would soon become clear, were often volatile and sometimes unpredictable; hatred of the Nationalists notwithstanding, their allegiance to Madrid was questionable at best.[7] Yet this Faustian pact was necessary for the government: it was in no small measure thanks to mobilized trade unions—Largo Caballero's Socialist Unión General del Trabajo, the anarchist Confederación Nacional del Trabajo, and the Federación Anarquista Ibérica—that the coup failed swiftly in Spain's most populous cities. It was only briefly successful in Barcelona and never gathered momentum in Madrid. Large cities were, for the most part, in "antifascist" hands. (Not so some smaller cities and rural areas.) The net effect of this was plainly visible in the numbers: by July 21, 240,000 square miles remained loyal to Madrid, as opposed to 110,000 to the scattered Nationalists. Significantly the Republican government or workers' militias maintained tight control over strategic industries in urban surroundings, including steel, chemicals, and explosives.[8] Azaña's Republic had a clear strategic advantage.

Faced with the prospect of vengeance and reprisals, many owed their allegiance to the location in which the coup had found them. The air garrison in Barcelona, for instance, included many monarchists who remained dutifully loyal to the government only because they found themselves in a sea of Catalonian anarchism. If one thing was clear in the chaos of a divided country, it was that the uprising was far from the clear-cut success that Mola had hoped for.[9] (His brother Ramón committed suicide when the uprising collapsed in Barcelona.)[10]

Access to friendly neighbors like France as well as the resources to pay for war supplies also, in theory, contributed to the Republican advantage. It may seem odd that the Republic's financial standing was sound, particularly given the revolutionary outbursts that soon threatened Madrid's grip on its own territory. Yet the Bank of Spain had the fourth largest bullion reserve in the world, sitting undisturbed in an underground Madrid vault, largely accumulated during World War I.[11] Meanwhile the control of the state apparatus allowed—in theory—for the continued influx of taxes and levies. Outside the gold standard, bullion reserves had survived the constant strains of Republican finances since 1931. Madrid controlled most (if not all) local governments in its jurisdiction, along with the civil service. By contrast, leaving aside the wealth of prominent aristocratic backers, the Nationalists had almost no hard currency in the country, to say nothing of precious metals.[12] And most of the industries and export production capacity were in Republican hands. Unlike in the U.S. Civil War, Nationalists had no central bank to speak of, so they remained reliant on Republican money circulating in the areas under their control.[13] The revolt was therefore in an inauspicious financial position from which to start a protracted civil war, notwithstanding some key moneyed backers.

The Nationalists were also at a geographical disadvantage, with their territories cut in two by a strongly Republican core. Given that the government decisively suffocated even the hint of rebellion in the navy, Director Mola and the rebellion's commander in Morocco, Francisco Franco—a decidedly late addition to the cause—could not transport the best forces in Spain from North Africa to the mainland.[14] Nationalists thus lacked even access to the troops that could lead a military offensive akin to the retaliation against Asturian miners in 1934. From loyal Catalonia, the Republic also controlled the two railway links into France, where Prime Minister Léon Blum's own Popular Front government had been in office since June 6.[15] France's ideological allegiance clearly lay with Spain's legitimate, constitutional government. Strategically as well as financially the Republican situation was thus auspicious.

And yet, on July 29, ten Junkers Ju52s—the glittering new transport airplane of the German air force, the Luftwaffe—landed in Morocco to airlift General Franco's Foreign Legion, Spain's most experienced ground forces. Also that day twelve Savoia-Marchetti 81s from the Italian air force, the Regia Aeronautica, were sent from Sardinia to join in the task. (Although Mussolini often boasted about his state-of-the-art air force, three of the first batch of planes sent to Spain did not make it due to technical complications.)[16] These German and Italian planes may not have had an immediately decisive impact on the war in the mainland; the dawning war, after all, would last three long years. But they reversed a key initial Nationalist disadvantage: according to certain sources, on July 20 the Nationalists had only forty planes, as opposed to 173 available to the Republic.[17] More important, despite Republican pleas, no similar planes came from Paris, London, Washington, or Moscow until a full two weeks later.[18]

The importance of planes in mid-twentieth-century warfare had already been established not only within military hierarchies but also in the public sphere. The Great War had suggested a central role for aircraft in any future conflagration. But when the Spanish Civil War began, there were only around four hundred aircraft in the whole country, including about fifty fighters, a hundred reconnaissance aircraft, and thirty light bombers. They were mostly French and over a decade old.[19] A contemporary observer kindly referred to the Republican air force as "old coffins."[20] In this context the pristine German and Italian aircraft symbolized the crucial tilting factor in the Spanish Civil War: fascist intervention.

The poor and polarized character of Spain by mid-1936 made aid from abroad not only useful but essential for Civil War victory. Barely ten days into a war that would span years, the strategic choices of great power diplomacy—interlocked and largely taken within twenty-four hours—had already planted the seeds of Republican defeat. Having detailed the key issues in Iberian political economy and society, this network of European decision making established the foreign context in which Hitler's "shadow empire" came to be. For Azaña's Republic, Machado's lines were tragically fitting: one day above all others—July 25, 1936—marked a fateful break with the past.

Spaniards of all political leanings expected a challenge to the constitutional order in mid-1936. Two of those who worried most were Constancia de la Mora, niece of a former conservative minister, and her husband, Ignacio Hidalgo de Cisneros, deputy head of the (humble) Republican air force. From his position Cisneros knew as well as anyone the state of the air force; it was not reassuring. De la Mora later wrote in her diary, "Madrid was on tenterhooks. . . . [Ignacio and I] sat up many a night beside the telephone, waiting for the terrible news that a Madrid garrison, or some other garrison, had risen against the Republic. . . . Ignacio would go off to the War Ministry and beg his immediate superior, the War Minister and Prime Minister . . . Casares Quiroga, to act. But Casares would laugh. 'You are an alarmist, Cisneros.'"[21]

Cisneros was a realist. The latest accounts suggest the government had known a coup attempt was forthcoming since the Cabinet meeting of July 10 at the latest. Yet it decided to emulate the successful strategy of 1932: let the military try, and fail. But 1936 proved to be very different from 1932. When the coup materialized, Prime Minister Casares Quiroga submitted his resignation. President Azaña asked Diego Martínez Barrios to form a new government, in the hope that he could form a national unity one with union backing. It was to no avail; garrisons all over Spain continued to rise, unsynchronized, against the Republic while workers once again set off strikes with revolutionary pretensions. Though Largo Caballero had long prophesized it would happen thus, he remained intransigent about entering the government in July; this could not but undermine Republican institutions. All over Spain the seeds of an extended confrontation were being sown. Paradoxically the military rebellion actually triggered the revolution it purported to prevent.

Azaña then offered the premiership to José Giral, a democrat, former minister, and friend. His task was Herculean: to persuade Mola and the other generals to give up the coup, while simultaneously preparing to fight them.[22] Contacts with the military began immediately, and, in order to prepare for the worst, Giral knew exactly where to turn. In his first foreign communiqué as prime minister, he wrote a personal note to his French peer, Léon Blum. The telegram, not even encrypted, was as succinct as it was grave: "We are surprised by a dangerous military coup. [I] beg you arrange assistance with arms and planes. Fraternally, Giral."[23] It was fitting for the new premier to sign the message so informally; surely he expected nothing short of full cooperation from Blum's Popular Front across the border.

Upon receiving the telegram on the morning of July 20, Blum was saddened but not surprised; Giral's was old news. Two days earlier, on the afternoon of July 18, Blum was meeting with a delegation of trade union teachers at Hôtel Matignon. The regal setting probably seemed like an incongruous location for a Socialist prime minister, but it had been the setting of key achievements for Blum's government in his tumultuous first weeks of office.[24] As Blum struggled to pull off another victory with the trade unionists, an urgent telegram from the French ambassador in Spain, Jean Herbette, interrupted the meeting. "[Last] night, it became apparent to Madrid that a military revolt had taken place in Melilla [Morocco]," wrote the conservative ambassador. "The government could neither contact commander Romenales, the [military] chief of East Morocco, nor the civilian commander of Morocco."[25] Blum became visibly upset as he read. Rumors of instability in Spain were ubiquitous. Yet that very morning he had met with a Spanish jurist who had assured him the situation was "excellent." Little did his guest know that before dawn garrisons in Spanish Morocco had risen against the Republic. Even on the afternoon of July 18 Blum was late to find out the news. His trade union guests at Hôtel Matignon were, for their part, surprised the prime minister was unaware of the Spanish crisis; *Paris-Midi* had already printed a report of what was then described as a "military" uprising. Blum's first words after digesting the telegram suggest he sensed how central the issue would become for the continent, for his government, and for himself: "If we succeed, no one will be able to say that we were helped by the circumstances!"[26]

Blum could be forgiven for his acidity; his had not been an easy path. As a young militant during the (in)famous Dreyfus case, he had come into contact with Jean Jaurès, a legendary Socialist and antiwar leader many Frenchmen considered the best orator since Mirabeau.[27] At

L'Humanité they became close, and when a young nationalist shot Jaurès on the eve of the Great War, Blum became his political heir. At the trial of Jaurès's murderer, Blum eulogized his mentor: "For him, socialism was the republic of things extending the republic of persons."[28] No doubt their Socialism was idealistic. Patient and prolific, Blum aimed to achieve the one thing Jaurès had not: power. For a decade he edited *Le Populaire,* the party broadsheet. Slowly but steadily he became a fixture of the French left and, eventually, its leader.

Not only a pacifist but also a Jew, Blum was the bane of the Gallic right. Only weeks before the crucial 1936 election, he had been beaten almost to death by a gang of Camelots du Roi, a fringe royalist group close to Charles Maurras's Action Française.[29] They were the types who avidly read the vitriolic editorials in *L'Echo de Paris* penned by Henri de Kérillis. As it happened across the Pyrenees, the spike in violence could be interpreted as a sign of reactionary desperation ahead of the parliamentary polls. At least in France the integrity of the Republic was never openly challenged. But that did not always seem to be the case. French conservatives were scattered and unable to create a viable alliance to counter the Front Populaire, amassing together Blum's Socialists, the Radicals, and, for the first time, the Communist Party. A month before the French elections, de Kérillis worried about the Iberian elections: "The parallel between the situations and the political structures of the two countries is striking," he wrote as he saw Azaña march on to victory. "Spain today is our guinea pig, and everything that unfolds there constitutes a supreme warning for us."[30] For once, Paris looked to Madrid.

In contrast to the splintered right, Blum's Popular Front had produced a clear reform agenda. Politically it promised the nationalization of war industries, the dissolution of fascist leagues—then so active that they had almost killed the Socialist leader—and the extension of obligatory schooling. But it was its economic program that attracted most voters. Blum promised a reduction of the workweek, a program of proto-Keynesian public works (not unlike Hitler's, even though French Socialists invited comparisons with Roosevelt's New Deal instead), and the establishment of a national unemployment fund. Though not explicitly stated, a central policy goal was to reverse deflation, precipitated in France by restrictive monetary and fiscal policy in the Depression.[31] Many of these reforms would eventually become staples of

the French welfare state. Playing with the long-established French distrust of financiers, Blum also pledged reform at the central bank, the
Banque de France, in order to increase its dependence on the central
government and reduce the influence of the "200 families"—France's
richest, stockholders at the Banque—on monetary policy. It was, to say
the least, an unorthodox electoral platform.

On the night of the election, May 3, *Le Populaire* prepared a historic
headline: "After the Electoral Triumph, Power!"[32] On the streets Socialists chanted the "Internationale." And at a café in downtown Paris,
author-cum-aviator André Malraux sat with his wife and other prominent left-wingers. Malraux was increasingly attracted to Communism,
so much so that he had penned a proto-existential novel on Shanghai's
failed revolution, *La Condition Humaine* (1933), which won him the Prix
Goncourt. In it he describes Socialism in words that echoed Blum:
"men struggling to become more than men." As results were announced,
mass celebrations erupted and a stranger approached the author's party:
"Are you happy now, Malraux?"[33]

The left was elated, but Blum trod carefully; like Azaña, he feared
reaction as well as revolution. His refusal to take power before it was
constitutionally due angered part of his electoral base. One of his most
zealous supporters challenged him: "In our place, do you think the Fascists would have hesitated for a minute?" Yet Blum did not give in, lest
haste bring about chaos. As the first Jew and first Socialist to become
prime minister of the Third Republic, he knew there were outcomes
to be avoided at all costs: political uncertainty, the very fears of revolution that could create the self-fulfilling prophecy of reaction, and crip-
pling capital flight. "No," Blum acknowledged. "But the point is that
we are not Fascists."[34]

His first weeks in office before the Spanish crisis were successful,
but only in retrospect. Bitter electoral defeat had revitalized the right,
which was at its most effective in frightening elites and inducing
reflexive fears of economic crisis. Conservatives criticized Blum's economics and his origins, betraying a veritable sense of French social instability. During the presentation of the Cabinet, Paul Reynaud
wondered out loud if the increased social spending would not hurt
French exports without a devaluation. Extreme right deputy Xavier
Vallat was incendiary: "I have a special duty to say aloud what everyone
is thinking. . . . To govern this peasant nation of France it is better to

have someone whose origins, no matter how modest, spring from our soil than to have a subtle Talmudist."[35] The Banque de France's reserves had suffered, while traders tested its ability to maintain the gold standard. Workers opted not to wait for Blum to pass legislation but to take what they wanted: they occupied factories. France was paralyzed.

In early June, though, Blum consolidated power. On June 7 he brokered the Matignon Agreements—named after his office—that put an end to the strikes. The wage hikes the agreements implied contributed to reversing deflation. Even the head of the Communist Party, himself outside the government, wrote in *L'Humanité,* "One must know how to finish a strike at the moment that the main points have been obtained."[36] It was a victory for labor, but a bigger one for the prime minister. Thereafter reforms flew through the National Assembly. On June 20 it passed paid vacations; a day later, the forty-hour workweek; on June 24, the legalization of collective bargaining. In a matter of days the French left achieved milestones it had sought since before the Great War. Some even dared to dream Blum's government would last a full parliamentary term—a considerable achievement in the Third Republic.[37]

A few weeks later, back at Hôtel Matignon, Blum pondered the consequences of the Spanish coup. Ambassador Herbette's telegram had given him a few days to meditate on his first true foreign policy test, but now he faced Giral's. Blum was convinced that the fates of the Popular Fronts in Madrid and Paris were intertwined; after all, hadn't they come to power democratically, within weeks of each other, and through the vote of analogous constituencies? Now that his rule in Paris seemed at last to stabilize, Blum saw his own worst fears materialize across the Pyrenees. If reaction prevailed in Spain, France would be surrounded in the continent by hostile, militaristic regimes. The Spanish rebels could also inspire the likes of Maurras to give up on democracy once and for all. Given Blum's (legitimate) worries about Germany's newly assertive foreign policy, the international dimension to the crisis cannot be understated.

Faced with the choice, the French prime minister decided that the danger of not doing enough to support the Spanish Republic was greater than that of acting. Madrid needed planes and weapons; Paris could afford to supply them. So Blum would sell them to the legitimate government of Spain, to be paid from its sizable gold reserves. The plan was discussed at a meeting held on July 20 and attended by all relevant Cabinet members: Foreign Minister Yvon Delbos, Defense Minister Édouard Daladier, Air Minister Pierre Cot, and Minister of Finance Vincent Auriol. Legally Blum's plan was workable: a 1935 accord between the conservative government that preceded Blum's and the similarly minded CEDA coalition in Spain allowed for the legal sale of a sizable amount of weapons. There seemed to be little resistance at the meeting. With some creative accounting, French aid could be escalated further. Almost immediately Cot began working on it with his direct subordinate, Jean Moulin.[38] Deputy Minister Moulin, a staunch antifascist and future eminence of the Résistance, could soon be found smuggling weapons for the Republic. He also involved a trusted friend: Malraux, who once expressed his conviction that "when man faces destiny, destiny ends and man comes into his own," was not one to pass up such an adventure.[39]

But when Blum met the Spanish ambassador, Juan de Cárdenas, early on July 21 to discuss Giral's telegram, he encountered the first of many obstacles that would doom his best intentions. Cárdenas was an aristocratic diplomat whose posting dated from the Bourbon era. It therefore comes as no surprise that his allegiances lay closer to the Nationalists than to Azaña's Republicans. He was the type of public servant who undermined the Spanish Republic from within.[40] Madrid was well aware that a monarchist held the strategic embassy in Paris and had decided to replace him with a reliably left-wing author. Unfortunately for the Republic, however, the ambassadorial switch had been scheduled for August 15. Meeting Blum, Cárdenas bid for time. At a time when delays could only erode Republican legitimacy, he suggested waiting for a more detailed list of required materials before proceeding with any sale.

The morning after their meeting, two loyal air force officers delivered such a list from Madrid. Giral's shopping list was modest: twenty modern Potez 540 bombers, a thousand Lebel rifles, and a quarter million machine-gun bullets, among other items.[41] Cárdenas was now in an awkward position: if he delayed further, he risked being found out as a Nationalist sympathizer. The duplicitous ambassador relayed the list to Blum, but he knew the sale could not yet be finalized; there were more bureaucratic hurdles to surmount. Blum nevertheless pledged to deliver on his promise. That same day Minister Cot confirmed to the premier and a new Spanish chargé d'affaires loyal to Madrid, former minister Fernando de los Ríos, that most supplies would be ready to ship as soon as the Cabinet signed off. Despite the conservative leanings of most private weapons factory owners in France, Cot's threats of nationalization had worked wonders on their desire to sell to the Spanish Republic.[42] French aid therefore hinged on explicit approval from the Cabinet, but that would have to wait. There was a trip the prime minister was unwilling to skip.

Despite the stabilizing domestic situation, Blum could not arm the Spanish Republic in a diplomatic vacuum. Early on July 23 he accompanied Foreign Minister Delbos across the English Channel for a conference on the future of Anglo-French relations with the Third Reich, unambiguously the Entente's chief foreign policy concern since the so-called March crisis.[43] Back on March 7 Hitler had marched unopposed on the Rhineland, and in so doing wrecked yet another pillar of the Versailles Treaty. Though technically German territory, by international law the area was supposed to remain demilitarized.[44] The aggressive move revived in Paris and London fears of a new continental war, yet neither French nor British armed forces had mobilized. Both governments had shown themselves just as unwilling to enforce the demilitarization of the Rhineland as they had the prohibition of conscription in Germany (reintroduced by Hitler) and strict limits on rearmament (plainly ignored by the Nazi government). The democracies' armies were unready, they argued; their electorates and governments, unwilling. Hitler's Rhineland bet, daring as it was, has since been revealed as a most successful bluff. "The forty-eight hours after the march into the Rhineland were the most nerve-racking in my life," Hitler would later declare. "If the French had then marched into the Rhineland we would have had to withdraw with our tails between our legs, for the military resources at our disposal would have been wholly inadequate for even a moderate resistance."[45]

At the time, however, French intelligence had not relayed such information to Paris. Perhaps more important, the government had not felt confident in British support.[46] The administration that preceded Blum's struggled to elicit even a vague statement from the British foreign secretary, Anthony Eden, linking French and British security interests. It was not much, but it was all that was forthcoming from London.[47] Constrained by his own National Coalition politics, ever since Blum's election British Prime Minister Stanley Baldwin had further hedged his bets, refusing to meet with his Socialist French peer ahead of the scheduled July conference.[48] Hence Blum decided to head to London with Delbos while his government finalized plans for sending war supplies across the Pyrenees.

Although the Spanish coup d'état was not formally on the agenda—and apparently was not explicitly discussed—the final London communiqué stated that the first priority of "the nations of Europe [was] the consolidation of peace."[49] Considering the havoc in Spain, the statement was not without irony. Against the art deco backdrop of Claridge's Hotel, Eden approached Blum privately to inquire about the weapons sale to Spain; news had traveled swiftly across the Channel. It has been suggested that Cárdenas or one of the pro-rebellion Spaniards in Paris had told the British ambassador, hoping 10 Downing Street would act as a conservative bulwark to halt Blum's activism.

Another diplomat who worked against the French premier was Charles Corbin, the French ambassador in London. Not quite the traitor Cárdenas was, Corbin was so staunchly Anglophile that in the higher echelons of French diplomacy, officials jokingly addressed him as the "English ambassador to the Court of St. James."[50] Moreover public servants at Quai d'Orsay, home to a Foreign Ministry far more conservative than Blum, also worked to limit the premier's freedom of action. The following morning they published a sour reminder to eager Minister Cot: "No sale of arms to a foreign country can be made without the formal agreement of this [Foreign Ministry]."[51]

According to Blum's later deposition, when he told Eden of his intention to honor Giral's request, the Briton's reply was almost stereotypically cold: "It is your affair. But I ask you one thing: be prudent."[52] An experienced diplomat like Eden probably sensed such a carefully worded warning would plant seeds of doubt, whereas an outright threat might move the Frenchman into action. Eden would eventually come to regret such admonitions.[53] Before flying home Blum met a French journalist who also inquired about "planes for Spain." His intentions had leaked to the press. The reporter remarked that Baldwin's National Coalition government would disapprove, further straining relations with France's closest ally against Hitler's ascendancy.[54] Yet Blum continued to prioritize his initial instinct over Entente diplomacy: "Possibly, but I know nothing about it and in any case we are going to do it."[55]

But would he? Back in France, Blum saw the first sign of trouble even before deplaning: the deputy prime minister waited on the runway. In the few hours of Blum's absence the mood in Paris had changed dramatically. A member of the French Cabinet had told the German ambassador, Count Johannes von Welczeck—an aristocratic, old school German diplomat with enviable contacts in Paris—about Blum's desire to arm the Spanish Republic.[56] Although it is impossible to pinpoint who was to blame, more than one of Blum's ministers shared Eden's reservations.[57] This was most likely due to an association of the Republican cause with revolutionary Socialism, a confusion that the Baldwin government would later knowingly and willingly exacerbate.[58]

Left-leaning French dailies made Spain look like a country with the dubious honor of suffering both revolution and fascist reaction; considering the armed workers and the feeble institutional arrangement in Madrid, it was not a wholly inaccurate representation. Regardless of what was accurate, this media spin only exacerbated domestic opposition to Blum's efforts, adding to the international pressures. In fact on July 24 a headline on the cover of the *L'Intransigeant* read, "By Special Airplane [*l'Intran*] Reports Tonight the First Photos of the Revolution in Madrid."[59] The newspaper worried more about La Pasionaria's revolutionaries than Mola's rebels. Welczeck also reported Blum's plans to his superior in Berlin, Hans Heinrich Dieckhoff, as fait accompli: "I have learnt in strict confidence that the French Government declared itself prepared to supply the Spanish Government with considerable amounts of war materiel during the next few days. . . . Franco's situation is likely to deteriorate decisively especially as a result of the supplying of bombers to the Government."[60] Welczeck had topped his diplomatic move with a more informal one: he divulged details to the French reactionary press. The French High Command can also be suspected of leaking government plans.[61] Hungry for ammunition after Blum's successes, the right-wing press jumped on the news. On the pages of *L'Echo,* de Kérillis was harsh, but *L'Action Française* topped him. Denouncing the two Spanish Air Force officers who had brought Giral's list to Blum, its editorial page asked, "What do they want? Money? Guns? Planes? Whatever it is, the French people forbid the Jew Blum to give it!"[62]

Deputies in the National Assembly complained and did so loudly.[63] Furthermore, André François-Poncet, who had the unenviable duty of being French ambassador to the Third Reich in the late 1930s, sent an urgent telegram to Paris that afternoon, which arrived an hour before the Cabinet meeting was due to begin. His message could not be clearer: "It is considered here that [France], which has always upheld the notion of non-intervention in the internal affairs of other peoples, will create a terrible precedent . . . [with the sale]."[64] At this point President Albert Lebrun had had enough; calling on Blum ahead of the Cabinet meeting, he reprimanded him, arguing that his actions were pushing France to war.[65] Some accounts suggest the president even shed tears. Lebrun made another point: if the French government had not mobilized when Hitler marched on the Rhineland, how could it risk continental war over a coup in another country and against a different government? He may as well have called it "a quarrel in a far-away country between people of whom we know nothing." The president was far from alone; two other important domestic stakeholders agreed with this interpretation: the French Armed Forces under Maurice Gamelin sided with the conservative Foreign Ministry of Delbos, wary of both aiding "revolution" in Europe and alienating London.[66] The French High Command held the view that the rebels had better odds than they actually did at that juncture;[67] at least later Gamelin would admit his personal sympathies always lay with the "dedicated and clear-headed professional" Francisco Franco, an emergent "Francophile" leader in the Nationalist camp.[68]

Thus began the July 25 Cabinet meeting that would set the framework for French involvement in the Spanish Civil War. Predictably Cot urged the government to honor Giral's request.[69] Yet Delbos and Daladier sided with Lebrun and the reactionary press.[70] It was just too dangerous, they argued, and their Cabinet support was wider than Blum had foreseen. The debate dragged on, and eventually the premier yielded. He seemed willing to put the question to the National Assembly itself, but his advisors agreed it would likely mean the end of his government. Not even the Republican envoys in Paris wanted to run such a risk.[71] The government released a communiqué announcing it would decline Giral's request as well as guarantee that all private sales to Spain included no arms. It must have come as a terrible surprise to de los Ríos and other Republicans in Paris. No sooner had the announcement been released than conservative French diplomats began to lobby other foreign diplomats for a concerted nonintervention agreement for Spain, which would eventually turn into the infamous Committee of Non-Intervention. Meanwhile Foreign Minister Delbos rushed to hold a press conference. Though Giral's was a legal request from a legitimate government, Delbos claimed the French Cabinet "did not wish to give *any pretext* to those who might be tempted to furnish war materials to the insurgents."[72] A truer statement would have explained that Blum had ultimately chosen to prioritize his administration's hard-won stability, domestically and internationally. Yet Blum's passionate conviction to help had been kept anything but private; German diplomats needed only to pick up a copy of *L'Action Française* or *L'Echo* to find all the "pretexts" for action they could have wanted.[73]

In the next thirty-two months of war, France would never fully reverse its July 25 decision to forbid military material from being shipped across the border. The most glaring exceptions to this policy were Cot's smuggling and Malraux's missions to Spain, as well as some selective help to future Republican administrations. The air minister actively participated in the clandestine sale of weapons, though it was very problematic for Malraux, Moulin, and Cot to go around official supply channels. Most of the businessmen who went to the inexperienced de los Ríos to offer supplies for the Republic did so for selfish reasons that, in aggregate, cost the Republic too much money and effort.[74] These were often old and defective supplies, much inferior to what the French government itself could have provided—particularly after Cot's nationalization of these industries.[75] At the governmental level France would never truly intervene in the Spanish Civil War, a choice that only furthered the strategic weight of fascist intervention.[76]

Protective of his government and on the defensive about Spain, Blum would remain loyal to this nonintervention framework even when Italy's and Germany's breaches of the agreement became blatantly obvious.[77] Lacking a change of tack from London, Blum's successors would also embrace this policy.[78] Aside from short and marked exceptions, French railway borders would remain closed for military aid, which a few months later would start pouring into Spain from other sources.[79]

Had Blum reacted more conservatively at first or followed through on the intentions first publicly laid out in London, the end result for the Republican war effort would have likely been better. As it stood, however, it was "fraternal" Giral and his moderate Republicans who suffered the most from the intricate decision making in London and Paris that reached their climax on July 25. Devoid of French aid, the Republic would have to turn elsewhere for help.

The traditional British strategy of balancing against any continental hegemonic power did not require a military presence in Spain in 1936 as it had in 1808, when Wellington first faced Napoleon's armies. The 1930s called for a more tactful approach. Seen from London, where appeasement was on the rise, the Spanish Civil War was a nuisance in the path to hedging continental polarization between Soviet Moscow and Nazi Berlin. At the time, anti-Communist worries were running high.[80] In this context the Spanish crisis was a hindrance, preferably to be ignored or brushed aside, lest it move the French to precipitate a continental war that was—from a British perspective—neither wanted nor winnable.[81] Hence the British warnings to Blum, both officially and unofficially, during his crucial trip to London.[82]

Diplomatic documents suggest Foreign Secretary Eden heard about the rebellion in Spain at least as early as the French premier did. British Ambassador Henry Chilton, another conservative career diplomat who leaned toward the rebellion, had written a succinct telegram about it: "Report has reached me which is confirmed by local military authorities that the Foreign Legion in Morocco has revolted against the régime."[83] It arrived in London at 19:25 on July 18 from San Sebastián, the traditional elite summer resort on the Basque coast. As the days unfolded, however, no policy emerged from Eden's Foreign Office, save caution. Priorities clearly lay elsewhere. The Entente meeting on July 23, which brought Blum to London, amounted to Prime Minister Baldwin's best hope for Germany and Italy to agree on a general European settlement; it would not be the last such attempt. One of the possible goals of the conference was "another Locarno," a reference to the series of treaties that had stabilized continental tensions a decade earlier, in 1925.[84] In mid-1936 "the chief concern of British policy-makers" was peace with the fascistic dictators, so as to focus on Communist worries.[85] As most other European capitals prepared to make crucial decisions in the wake of the Iberian crisis, Eden sent long telegrams to his envoys in Berlin and Rome late in the evening of July 24 that reflected how important Spain was in the national government's foreign policy calculations: the Iberian coup was mentioned not once. Eden focused entirely on how to find reassurances for a great power arrangement that would satisfy Hitler and Mussolini.[86]

The foreign secretary did not go unsupervised. Premier Baldwin may not have cared much about foreign affairs, but the prospect of alienating the fascist dictators concerned him. Ever since the 1935 general election, the focus on British rearmament had been diminished, a policy that answered to the electorate's choices and opposition from both Liberals and Labour. This implied military parity with the dictators' rearmament had given way to deterrence.[87] A few weeks after the remilitarization of the Rhineland, Baldwin had said privately, "With two lunatics like Mussolini and Hitler you can never be sure of anything. But I am determined to keep the country out of war."[88] This was tried and tested British electoral strategy.

The portrayal of the spreading Spanish war in the European press as a battle between revolution and reaction was a contributing factor to the pressure Baldwin exerted on Eden. The foreign secretary seemed to share the prime minister's reluctance to become heavily involved, a view invariably influenced by the British desire to avoid complications with its Gibraltar base and strategic access to the Mediterranean.[89] This fits the well-established view that before mid-1937 Eden worried far more about Communism than he did about fascism.[90] On July 22 the government of Portuguese dictator António de Oliveira Salazar— not only a rebellion supporter but also an avid anti-Republican propagandist[91]—asked a rather biased question to Eden's Foreign Office: What would Britain do to "stop the spread of communism in Spain"?[92] The "oldest ally" replied in a way that surely pleased the Portuguese dictator.[93] Assistant Undersecretary Victor Wellesley responded that "whatever the situation" Britain would not intervene militarily; the justification was political: "The Government . . . would not have the support of public opinion."[94] The Fascist government made a similar— but, interestingly, less overtly biased—inquiry a few days later, to which the Conservative chief whip replied that British interests favored a rebellion victory, yet the government could not afford anything but strict neutrality: "This is the only possible way to counter labor agitation."[95] A freer and more aggressive Rome noted the political constraint on any further British action.[96]

The Labour opposition—far stronger within the trade union movement than in Parliament—still found a way to attack the national government, the chief worry of the Tory whip. Despite their traditionally antiwar stance, Labour leader Clement Attlee pledged "all practicable support" for the Spanish Republic as early as July 20. Rhetoric aside, there was little he could do. It remains unclear how much Labour would have actually done differently in office, particularly when one considers 1935 campaign statements by Attlee himself. Winston Churchill, a Tory out of the government, was later said to have urged "an absolutely rigid neutrality" from the start.[97] In private correspondence to Eden, however, Churchill had been far more explicit than that. On August 9, 1936, he demonstrated an acute understanding of the situation on the ground. "The Spanish business cuts across my thoughts," he wrote in between references to books exchanged with the secretary. "It seems to me most important to make Blum stay with us strictly neutral, even if Germany and Italy continue to back the rebels and Russia sends money to the government. If the French government take sides against the rebels it will be a god-send to the Germans and pro-Germans."[98] An astute point, to be sure, but one that underscored the Republic's international isolation.

Downing Street's orders to the Foreign Office were nothing short of adamant. Baldwin later confided to his friend Thomas Jones, "I told Eden yesterday [on July 25] that on no account, French or other, must he bring us into the fight on the side of the Russians." Perhaps the prime minister's fear of Moscow was more pressing than his fear of Rome or Berlin. "I reminded him of the prophecy," Baldwin continued, "made to me two months ago that Moscow looked forward for a Communist government in Spain in three months."[99] At least some quarters of the Foreign Office agreed.

Another character vying for Eden's attention in the aftermath of the prime minister's warning was the Spanish ambassador, Julio López Oliván. From the Regency-style mansion on 24 Belgrave Square—purchased during the easy money days of the Primo dictatorship—López Oliván worked to undermine the Azaña government; not unlike his peer in Paris, he sympathized with the rebellion.[100] Two days after the July 25 warning, the ambassador penned a private note to the foreign secretary, suggesting he and his wife join him for "lunch or dinner, alone, at the Embassy, on any day that is convenient to you."[101] It was a pressing request for time alone. Vaguely López Oliván professed a desire to discuss "urgent matters connected with recent events in Spain."

He also tried to leverage their past relationship: "I am aware this is not perhaps the most correct form an Ambassador seeks . . . a quiet conversation with a Foreign Secretary, . . . but I am hoping that as a friend you may find it possible to forgive this procedure." Less than a month later Eden's professed "friend" officially resigned his embassy in open support of the Nationalists.[102]

Like Blum, Baldwin and Eden shaped their Iberian policies within the delicate balance of their own domestic coalition politics, an intricacy of democracy the dictators did not have to contend with. But the British Cabinet never changed their professed view as starkly as Blum did. The original, cautious British stance was neither abandoned nor substantially altered; if anything, the anarchist-led, bloody reprisals against "reactionary" prisoners in Republican prisons exacerbated the British distrust of the Republic, along with that of other diplomatic emissaries.[103]

Baldwin's opposition to rearmament had arguably granted him victory in the 1935 general elections, even if it implicitly jeopardized Britain's chances against a rapidly rearming Third Reich.[104] Churchill, ever the warmonger from the perspective of appeasers, never forgave Baldwin for "putting party before country." Years later, in characteristic Churchillian fashion, he would say of his predecessor, "I wish Stanley Baldwin no ill, but it would have been much better had he never lived." The policy with regard to Spain could be considered complementary to Baldwin's antiwar view, along with his preference for hedging his bets with left-leaning France. His successor, Neville Chamberlain, would not be much different; seen from Paris, London was an ever unreliable ally.

By fiercely upholding a policy of nonintervention while Italy and Germany blatantly disregarded it, Britain avoided having to side with fascism or Communism on the continent. Applied to the Spanish question, this dichotomy had existed in Eden's mind at least since Baldwin's July 25 warning. The foreign secretary, however, would eventually come to realize the balancing act did not appease Hitler but actually encouraged him. This would be the cause for his resignation in February 1938, by which time Chamberlain was prime minister and the Munich Agreement loomed. "It is with the great democracies in Europe and America that our national affinities must lie," he would then write in a moving but much delayed resignation. "We must stand by our conception of international order, without which there can be no lasting peace." If only Azaña's Spanish Republic had qualified back on July 25, 1936.[105]

Another key British actor deserves mention. Shortly after the rebellion, First Sea Lord Ernle Chatfield apparently declared to a guest, "Franco's was a much nobler cause than that of the Reds."[106] A similar perspective was relayed to French admiral François Darlan when he visited Chatfield, inquiring on Blum's behalf for support for the Republic; this view made it back to the French premier around the time he changed his original position on aiding the Republic. With Chatfield's opinion dominating its ranks, it is rather unsurprising how unneutrally the British Navy behaved thereafter. Without any authorization from London on record, Spanish rebels had been allowed to use phone lines at the Gibraltar base to contact their allies in northern Spain and Morocco, as well as their agents in Rome and Berlin.[107] This British position was not merely the result of Chatfield's conservatism, even though he held considerable sway within the navy.[108] British strategists worried—and would continue to worry throughout the Civil War—about the fate of its Gibraltar base, a crucial strategic asset in the Mediterranean.[109] Everyone knew that Mussolini's Italy fervently desired a larger role in the Mediterranean, which the British resisted. The flagship of the Royal Navy, HMS *Hood*, was eventually deployed off Spain's northern coast—a useful reminder of British naval preeminence.[110] A domestic Iberian issue also seems to have factored into early naval strategic calculations. As early as July 19, amid the badly synchronized coup that had already taken over in Morocco, Giral encouraged Republican sailors to execute their officers at sea before they could change sides and provide Franco with the transport he so needed. The purge further alienated the powerful navy establishment—and it had very tangible consequences.[111] Less than a week later the British Navy refused Republican refueling requests in Gibraltar.[112]

Last but not least, commercial relations should not be overlooked. Before the Civil War Britain had been the main foreign direct investor in Spain.[113] After two centuries of commercial preeminence in Spain, Britain controlled no less than 40 percent of all foreign investment on Iberian soil.[114] Yet, as we shall see, economic dislocations created by the Spanish Civil War and, at least in part, Britain's "neutrality" allowed for another great power to move in. London would honor its historic

Iberian ties by opening trade negotiations with Franco's Nationalists almost as soon as their considerable Spanish investments—mostly in the strategically crucial mining sector—became Hitler's spoils of war.[115]

Considered holistically Britain's formal neutrality and informal favors to the Nationalists evidently worked against Republican interests. It would later be profitable to orchestrate a rapprochement with Franco, who eagerly welcomed it.[116] From a strategic perspective, it seems clear British policymakers always considered the Spanish Civil War a secondary concern to the much larger issue of continental stability. Hence the bitter irony of the July 24 communiqué about a prospective great power conference that had so worried Baldwin, which explicitly argued for "the consolidation of peace in Europe" even as Spain descended into a fratricidal war.

Soviet military aid to the Republic, as well as the organization of the international brigades throughout the Civil War, has been hailed for decades as the key reason why the Republic—isolated by Britain and France—held on as long as it did.[117] Russia was the only great power that armed the Republic with the weapons, planes, and men it needed to sustain a true war effort, even if Stalin was known to complain about the overly "defensive" attitude of a republic that often seemed too feeble from within to prevail on the battleground. In recent years, however, some sources have cast serious doubts on the prices charged for Soviet aid. The specifics of this ongoing debate are beyond the scope of this study. What matters most is that Stalin did provide aid to the Spanish Republic—and it was certainly not free.

Available evidence may be limited, but it is possible to discern that on July 25, 1936, Gaston Monmousseau, the chief of the European office of the Communist Trade Union Organization (Profitern), directed a joint meeting with the Soviet equivalent of the Nazi Auslandorganisation (Comintern) to decide how to aid the besieged Spanish Republic. The unions then decided to send 1 million francs to Madrid; it was a popular collection for the Spanish comrades. In Spain a Communist committee, including La Pasionaria and Largo Caballero, would be in charge of managing the funds. For President Azaña, Soviet aid was a mixed blessing from the start. It was well-known that some of those administering Russian aid expected nothing short of revolution to follow the defeat of the Nationalist rebellion. In a way, the Western democracies' nightmare of a "Red Spain" came close to materializing, if anything exacerbated by their lack of strong action; infighting within Republican ranks throughout the war—involving Republicans, nonrevolutionary Socialists, Moscow-inspired Bolsheviks, Catalonian anarchists, and the odd opportunist—only intensified while garrisons around Spain declared for the Nationalists. Respected historians from Preston to Viñas describe in painstaking detail the revolutionary outbursts, dangerous from the perspective of international opinion.[118] The entry of Communists into the Republican government in September—a desperate move by a besieged Azaña—only exacerbated these tendencies.

A few days before July 25 the official Soviet propaganda machine, mainly through *Pravda,* began celebrating the Iberian struggle against fascism, which contributed to the European media's characterization of the war along Marxist lines. In government circles weary of "Reds," this approach only weakened the Republic's international standing. French Radicals such as Daladier and Delbos were particularly concerned about helping "the Reds" win a war that would bring about a Soviet regime in the Iberian peninsula.[119] This dynamic unsurprisingly played to the dictators' hands, at a time when both Hitler and Mussolini engaged in extensive, public diatribes against Bolshevism. The British prime minister, as we have seen, was similarly inclined. Yet— as some Iberian historians have argued—this remained a self-fulfilling prophecy: the democracies' lack of support for Madrid pushed the government closer to Moscow and weakened the more moderate elements in its leadership. This tragic dynamic did not go unnoticed among struggling moderates in Madrid.

Despite the financial soundness that extensive gold reserves furnished, the Republic quickly faced tremendous difficulties making use of its wealth. Resources that are impossible to mobilize, after all, can hardly count as such.[120] The Republican government was soon forced to organize the largest weapons-smuggling operation in modern history, one very hard to disguise in countries with a free press and without the help of state apparatuses. Men like de los Ríos in Paris were constrained by limited knowledge, cunning weapons dealers, closed borders, fascist intervention aiding the rebellion, and, if that were not enough, the Non-Intervention Pact.[121] This pushed their activities to the shadows, the very opposite of the contemporaneous fascist strategy.

On October 25, when Franco's Foreign Legion first threatened Madrid, a new Republican minister of finance, Juan Negrín, and Giral's successor to the premiership, Largo Caballero, decided to ship their gold to Stalin's Russia.[122] The Soviet government insisted on keeping on Russian soil the Spanish officers who accompanied the huge shipments by sea, but reaching a final count of the gold seems to have been challenging for the Kremlin, since the Spaniards were not freed until two years later.[123] According one of his closest confidants, Aleksandr Orlov, Stalin organized a banquet to celebrate the gold's arrival in late 1936, where he was inspired to make a sarcastic toast over vodka: "The Spaniards shall never see their gold again, just as one cannot see one's own ears."[124] And yet the official receipt claimed that the Spaniards would be able to re-export the gold at any time they wished.[125]

The quote may be apocryphal, but the point stands nonetheless. The gold—as well as what it paid for—remains an issue of heated debate. Ronald Radosh, along with others, claim Stalin's men *ex post* tweaked both currency conversion tables and, eventually, history books to overstate their aid to the Republic. In this analysis the Soviets overcharged items by more than 100 percent and Soviet books overstated sent aid by at least 25 percent, thus magically matching fascist support to Franco. For generations thereafter it was possible for Soviet historians to argue their government had done all they could to prevent a Republican defeat. Howson's analysis of planes yields a similar conclusion about overcharging, at least for air supplies. These seem indicative of overcharging elsewhere.[126] But Viñas has recently challenged Radosh's calculations, claiming the nonconvertibility of the Russian ruble (and its multiple exchange rates) had something to do with the price discrepancies, and that Stalin—unlike Hitler and Mussolini—went out of his way to seek Republican approval of what was being charged to Spain. In most sold items Viñas failed to find evidence for a "betrayal" of the Republic, to borrow Radosh's terminology.[127]

Beyond this academic debate, the abandonment of the European democracies implied that the Spanish Republic had basically no choice but to turn to Moscow for help, as Largo Caballero himself acknowledged in a missive to an agent of Moscow's in December 1936. Without shipping the gold, it is unclear that Russia would have helped the way it did.[128] The "Spanish Lenin" soon realized this did not strictly benefit his personal agenda. Yet the resulting rise of Communist influence in Madrid was most problematic for President Azaña, who had no alternative but to allow Communists in the Cabinet as of September—

beginning with Largo Caballero, who became prime minister. This dynamic only worsened certain foreign perceptions of the Republican government. Such was the self-fulfilling prophecy 10 Downing Street had feared all along—and its domestic policies as well as pressures on France only helped to materialize it.

With the doors slammed shut in London and Paris and Stalin's self-serving strategy being implemented in Moscow, there was one more potentially saving source of help for the Spanish Republic: the United States. Yet the relationship between Madrid and Washington had long been a problematic one. Although there were considerable and rising commercial exchanges in the interwar period, relations had not decisively moved beyond 1898; the brief but bitter Spanish-American War weighed on both national consciousnesses.[129] In Spain that war represented the most obvious symbol of its imperial downfall. The once great empire was great no longer; it could not even hold on to Cuba, then its most profitable possession.[130] Yet the crisis had also sparked renewal, empowering an enlightened generation of writers, the Generación del '98, of which Ortega y Gasset, Unamuno, and Machado were prominent members. Eager for cultural renewal, their writings denounced the stale Iberian monarchy. The war's effect on the United States was the diametric opposite. The formation of an "anti-imperialist" league notwithstanding, the decisive American victory illustrated its anti-imperial rhetoric in the service of a decidedly imperial foreign policy. Eight decades after its formulation, the Monroe Doctrine proclaiming "America for the Americans" had finally become a tangible reality ninety miles off the coast of Florida.[131] And that was leaving aside the American success in the Pacific theater, extending American control all the way to former Spanish outposts in the Philippines and Guam. The Spanish-American War had slain one empire and given birth to another.

In the decades that followed, the countries remained far apart, save perhaps for cultural exchanges and rising American investments in the Iberian economy, with the International Telephone & Telegraph Company as the most prominent among them. Such ventures were symbolic of American commercial ascendency in what had been traditional British-dominated markets.[132] Beyond that, however, Spain mattered little to the United States. As the two Spains drifted to war in 1936,

President Franklin D. Roosevelt campaigned for his (first) reelection. With polls scheduled for November 3, 1936, the focus remained squarely on domestic recovery, having only briefly emerged from the Great Depression. On the campaign trail, Roosevelt's key promise was peace at all costs, consistent with the growing consensus on Capitol Hill, made into law through the Neutrality Acts. Passed in July 1935, the first of these prohibited the export of "arms, ammunition, and implements of war" to any belligerent nation. There was a caveat: they applied only once the president had declared a "state of war." It also required arms manufacturers in the private sector to apply for specific export licenses for weapons. On February 29, 1936, Congress renewed the act for 1937 and added a loan prohibition, so that the government could not financially sustain other nations at war through loans. Though Roosevelt was never too keen on congressional constraints, he largely agreed with an electorally promising antiwar strategy. Barely a week after the Spanish coup he would famously declare in a landmark speech in Chautauqua, New York, "I have seen war. . . . I hate war."[133] As it had for Britain's Baldwin, the strategy—together with FDR's popularity and the moderate economic recovery—paid off: FDR won 523 electoral votes against a mere 8 for Republican Alf Landon. It was the most lopsided election in U.S. history.

As early as July 14 the U.S. ambassador in Spain, Claude Bowers, had written a long memorandum on the fragile political situation in Madrid from San Sebastián, where he summered alongside other diplomats. An intellectual and a liberal, Bowers was perhaps the most avid supporter of the Republic among great power envoys in Spain. His memo to Washington was straightforward: "Unless the [Republican] Government acts energetically, to enforce the respect for law and order, its position may become untenable."[134] After Calvo Sotelo's murder, Bowers argued to Washington that Azaña's Republic ought to act forcefully against both left and right, particularly considering the danger of escalating reprisals. "The political situation is made particularly serious, aside from the [Sotelo] death," he summarized, "by the fear on an attempt on the part of Fascists and other reactionary elements to overthrow the Government itself." And yet, accurately predicting how much the State Department would care about the issue, he dispatched the memo by mail rather than telegram. It did not reach Washington until July 27, at which time war was a reality.[135]

On July 18, however, as the Spanish government contacted U.S.-owned IT&T to stop all outgoing calls from Madrid in the hopes of blocking rebel communications, Bowers cabled an urgent note to Washington: "[Embassy official] Wendelin in Madrid telephones by special permission *coup d'état* planned for noon today."[136]

Despite the affinity for the Republic of American intellectuals like Ernest Hemingway and Cabinet members ranging from Treasury Secretary Henry Morgenthau to Interior Secretary Harold Ickes, the president was in no mood for international activism. He sided with the more cautious Secretary of State Cordell Hull. Their careful impartiality and focus on trade freedom was not only respectful of Congress's Neutrality Acts, but it also spoke to the "Bolshevik key," with which American diplomats saw European events. It was an approach that resembled Britain's at the time.[137] Though Bowers became increasingly critical of Franco's fascistic tendencies, this did not seem to upset the State Department. At this stage, like Eden, Hull still considered fascism, dangerous as it was, to be a viable bulwark against Russia-sponsored Communism.

According to the U.S. diplomatic dispatches in those crucial July hours, the only issue that interested Washington aside from the safety of its citizens was the protection of its commercial fleet and assets on Moroccan coasts, where Franco was desperately trying to mobilize his forces.[138] On July 21 the U.S. consul in Tangier asked for advice from Washington, for "[the] question of fueling Spanish war vessels in the Tangier bay [is] causing a menacing situation. General Franco threatens bombardment of ships in the harbor if supplies are furnished."[139] Although Franco's planes bombed ships, including the U.S. steamer *Exmouth,* Hull explicitly ordered Blake on July 22 to remain uninvolved: "In the interest of international cooperation for the avoidance of complications, [Washington] would not be disposed to support American nationals in Tangier in any effort to furnish supplies for either side to the present conflict."[140] Neutrality had to be preserved.

A debate regarding the Spanish Civil War soon flooded the U.S. press, with the left being far more active in pushing for aid to the Republic. So much so that on August 11 the German ambassador in Washington, former Reichsbank president Hans Luther—ostracized from Berlin in curious circumstances—sent a memorandum to Berlin detailing the popular outrage in America regarding "Germany's alleged intentions to intervene" in Spain. He dutifully enclosed a selection of "protesting telegrams that the Embassy has receiv[ed] . . . from pacifist and Communist organizations."[141] While America's intellectual establishment called for Republican support, Soviet involvement and the Republic's anticlericalism became objects of scrutiny in government circles and among Catholic groups.[142]

The North American democracy that most involved itself in the Spanish Civil War was Mexico, a left-leaning republic since its own revolution in the 1910s. Despite its limited financial resources, the Mexican government did all it could to deliver weapons to the Republic and would eventually become the home (and resting place) of the Republican government-in-exile.[143] In a stark contrast, in a thinly veiled reference to Spain, the U.S. Congress expanded the Neutrality Acts to cover sales to countries undergoing civil wars. When FDR proposed a "cash-and-carry" provision to make room for trade, he suffered a humbling defeat on the Hill.

In the private sector allegiances were unsurprisingly tilted in favor of the rebellion: Texas Oil had a contract to supply oil to the Republic, which it canceled unilaterally as soon as the war broke out. According to an unconfirmed yet telling story, Henry Ford once told Texas Oil president Torkild Rieber, "With my trucks and your oil, we are preventing Communism in Spain." What we do know is that years later, on April 1, 1954, Rieber received the Isabel la Católica award for "services to Spain" from Franco's regime. It is estimated that during the war this company provided the Nationalists with 1,886,000 tons of fuel, almost all on credit and without any collateral.[144] Bowers's protests meanwhile fell on deaf ears. Staunch neutrality remained the official U.S. government policy, though in the context of other great power decisions, as well as the actions of private U.S. interests, it only further impaired the Republic.[145]

Thirty blood-soaked months after July 1936, Roosevelt asked Bowers to the White House. It was a strange invitation, particularly since Bowers had long retired from public service to return to teaching at Columbia University. Before the ambassador had taken a seat in the Oval Office, an unusually somber Roosevelt looked at him in the eye and addressed his administration's policy on Spain: "We have made a mistake. You have been right all along."[146] It was too late. Most U.S. investments had been protected, yet there was no Republic left to protect. A week earlier Franco had marched on Madrid. On horse, as the later Donatello-style statue would have him, he is rumored to have mocked La Pasion-aria: "We have passed!"

The strategic decisions in Paris, London, Moscow, and Washington stand in radical opposition to those taken by the fascist powers in sup-port of "the other Spain." If ephemeral Republican Premier Giral sent his first telegram to Paris, it was only fitting for Nationalists to contact Rome first. It was a decision rooted not only in ideological coherence but also in Italy's past foreign policy.[147] As the latest Iberian research on the issue clarifies, it also answered to existing contractual arrange-ments between a particular set of anti-Republican conspirators and Rome.[148] Loyal to the monarchy, tolerant of the Church, militaristic, and as of late decidedly imperial, Italian Fascism had opposed the Second Spanish Republic arguably since before its inception. It was therefore natural for the Nationalists to count on Fascist support; paradoxically it was Mussolini's previous foreign policy commitments that somewhat delayed the Italian intervention in July 1936.

Always desirous to expand his influence in European affairs, Mus-solini had close relations with Spain during the Primo de Rivera dic-tatorship. The two dictators simply got along. King Alfonso XIII had famously introduced Primo de Rivera to his Italian peer as "my Mus-solini." Yet King Vittorio Emanuele III had something that Alfonso XIII did not: Mussolini, an enthralling speaker and tireless egomaniac who saw in his relationship with his people shades of both Napoleon and Jesus Christ. He blended a rejection of democracy with romantic nationalism little updated from Verdi's operas and D'Annunzio's po-etry, a convenient anti-Communist support for heavy industry, and a futurist spin on Roman imperial legacy.[149] Although he looked up to his authoritarian neighbor in Rome, Primo de Rivera had no similar syncretic ideology; he was closer to an old-fashioned *caudillo* than the *uomo nuovo* of Fascistic dreams.[150]

Predictably the advent of a Second Republic brought cooler rela-tions between Rome and Madrid.[151] Yet Spain still figured prominently in Mussolini's Mediterranean plans. Rome kept close tabs on the Re-public basically since the regime change; during the Decennale—the bombastic tenth anniversary of Fascist rule—close contacts with Ibe-rian monarchists were established. But in March 1934 plans moved further. Iberian monarchists traveled to Rome looking for il Duce's support, moral and otherwise, for a coup against the Republic. Their plan was to release General Sanjurjo and establish him as head of state. At il Duce's bequest, the Italian government delivered financial aid in the form of hard currency, gold, and weapons ranging from machine guns to grenades. Conditions were simple enough: Sanjurjo's regime need only be "monarchist and of a corporative and representative nature."[152] But neither Antonio Goicoechea nor General Emilio Barrera, the two leading monarchists who traveled to Rome, managed to garner enough support back home. With the conservative CEDA prevailing in the 1934 elections, many of the Republic's opponents hoped reaction could be attained without another *pronunciamiento*.[153] After all, Primo de Rivera's collapse had brought disgrace to the Spanish Army, and a return to the monarchical order seemed farfetched in light of the ebullient social mood in favor of the new regime. The plans were postponed, but not canceled. And Mussolini never got a refund.

Two years and a Popular Front victory later, the situation had changed significantly. We now know that early on July 1 four contracts were signed in Rome detailing war material to be supplied to Iberian rebels. A first contract, to be fulfilled in July, stipulated the sale of twelve Savoia-Marchetti 81 transport aircraft, precisely what the conspirators would need in Morocco to move troops to the mainland. Banker Juan March, long rumored to have supported the uprising financially, allegedly provided the funds, contracting directly with Italy's state-sponsored companies. Other contracts stipulated the sale of Fiat fighter planes, more transport aircraft, weapons, and explosives.[154] This has led respected Iberian historian Viñas to speculate that Rome must have known about the date of the uprising.[155]

Whether Franco knew about these contracts between conspirators and Rome remains unclear; as we have seen, he declared late for the rebellion and was in Morocco, geographically and logistically far from the key monarchist conspirators. What we do know, however, is that as soon as the unsynchronized coup materialized, Franco sent an agent to Rome directly. Though the rebellion was barely a day old, Luis Bolín had already proven his worth. As the London correspondent of a prominent monarchist newspaper, it had fallen to him to rent a plane in the United Kingdom to fetch Franco from the Balearic Islands, where President Azaña had sent him so that he would be kept "farther away from temptations," an unsubtle way to refer to a possible coup.[156] Bolín had disguised the operation by bringing two women along for the ride on-board the *Dragon Rapide* bimotor, with whom he delivered Franco from the Balearics, where he was commander to Morocco; there the general had taken control of the Foreign Legion and the Army of Africa.[157] Many of those war-seasoned men were the same ones Franco had led against Asturian miners in 1934; by late July 1936 they prepared to march on mainland Spain yet again. According to the grandson of the plane's British pilot, none other than March—also known as the "pirate of the Mediterranean"—funded the operation.[158] This makes sense given March's role in the August contracts. With a mission akin to Premier Giral's, Franco ordered Bolín to "England, Germany, or Italy" on his behalf in a desperate search for supplies.[159]

In order to establish his credentials, Bolín made a stop in Portugal first, so that Sanjurjo could add his signature to Franco's, requesting aid for a coup against the Republic. The almost illegible order may well have been the old general's last, for he died shortly after in a bizarre plane accident apparently precipitated, of all things, by the heavy suitcases he had packed for his triumphant return.[160] Arriving in Rome, Bolín liked to say he headed straight to Piazza Venezia, setting of Mussolini's long orations and home to his private office. According to his pompous (and disputed) autobiography, Bolín was direct with the palace ushers: "I want to see *il Duce*."[161]

Rather than Mussolini, it was Count Galeazzo Ciano who received him. Not merely Europe's most precocious foreign minister but also Mussolini's son-in-law, Ciano had spent his childhood in Argentina before moving back to Italy to join the Fascist Party that his father had cofounded with Mussolini.[162] Thereafter Ciano had married his way into il Duce's closest circle. In conversation with Franco's agent, Ciano proceeded to celebrate the rebellion's cause with a heavy *porteño* accent. "We must end the communist threat in the Mediterranean," he allegedly said, clearly associating the Popular Front with Moscow.[163] Anti-Bolshevism, both rhetorically and effectively, was on the rise in fascist capitals. Yet in a regime as pharaonic as Mussolini's, intervention would require the approval of il Duce. Franco's envoy would have to wait.[164] And regardless of the July contracts, such support did not come for several days.

Bolín sensed the hours were crucial; what he had seen in Franco's Morocco was anything but encouraging. Nor were press reports alluding to French plans. Yet Mussolini was noncommittal—at least until July 25. Did Mussolini question whether to honor the July contracts? On July 24 the seasoned conspirator Goicoechea arrived in Rome, where he explained to Ciano the connection between the plotters of 1934 and 1936.[165] The names may have changed, but the goal remained unaltered: *Delenda est Republica.* Yet it would take more than the interconnectedness of the reactionary plots to mobilize Mussolini. On July 25 he got further confirmation of financial and monarchical backing for the rebellion, which seemed to confirm it would not be as swiftly asphyxiated as Sanjurjo's. According to some (disputed) sources, Juan March also arrived in Rome in order to offer hard currency for the transport aircraft Franco so desperately needed in Morocco. This seemed to complement his role in the July contracts. Without the transport aircraft, there seemed to be no way for Franco to move his seasoned troops to the mainland; even if by dubious means, the Republican government had succeeded at crushing revolt within naval ranks. Some sources even claim March went as far as to purchase a considerable stake in Italian aircraft maker Savoia-Marchetti.[166] In any event, it is now clear that Mussolini approved the fulfillment of the crucial July 1 contract to supply Iberian rebels; support went to a Franco desperate to move his troops. Italian aircraft were soon to become a fixture of the clear Iberian skies.[167]

As if that were not enough, il Duce also received a call from an old acquaintance. King Alfonso XIII telephoned him from exile in the Metternich Palace in Austria urging support for the uprising. For someone as obsessed with status as Mussolini, it was perhaps piquant that the call was placed from the home of the mastermind of the Congress of Vienna and for half a century Europe's foremost strategist.[168] As is the case with France, international considerations must not be overlooked: in the days since Bolín's landing in Rome, the Fascist press had begun emulating French right-wing newspapers in printing reports about Blum's convictions and "looming" French intervention. As with any Fascist policy, the perception element cannot be overlooked: How would the world see Italy if it did not at least match French force? Mussolini—unlike Blum—was unconstrained by parliamentary queries or, for that matter, the reaction across the Channel.[169] In the complex game of 1936 European diplomacy, London worried about not alienating Rome far more than Rome worried about alienating London.[170]

With the order to send twelve Savoia-Marchetti 81s from Sardinia to Morocco to aid Franco, Fascist intervention in the Spanish Civil War began in earnest. In the coming months, despite the policy of nonintervention, Italian military support for the Nationalists became so extensive that some scholars called it an "undeclared Italian invasion of Spain."[171] In light of the fact that Italy provided around seventy-five thousand troops, six hundred planes, and a thousand artillery pieces to the Nationalist war effort, the characterization is not farfetched.[172]

Yet Italian intervention in Spain must also be contextualized with regard to a newfound ally. Though feeble, the boycott sponsored by the League of Nations that resulted from Mussolini's imperial venture in Ethiopia in 1935 opened an unexpected door to an old adversary: it led to Berlin. It was collaboration in the Spanish Civil War that brought the old adversaries closer together and eventually played a central role in the formation of the so-called Rome-Berlin Axis. As we shall see, there were powerful reasons beyond ideology for both Germany and Italy to intervene on behalf of Franco. Yet only one of the fascist partners was able to truly profit from the arrangement.

By the time the Civil War broke out in Spain, Hitler had tasted only success in foreign policy.[173] By mid-1936 the Third Reich was getting away with rearmament on a scale that made a mockery of the Treaty of Versailles, not to mention mandatory conscription, abandonment of the League of Nations, and the effective end of the reparations payments that had so burdened the Weimar Republic. More recently, on March 7, Hitler had successfully bluffed his way into remilitarizing the Rhineland.

The attainment of such goals was nothing short of unthinkable before the Nazi seizure of power in early 1933. Yet Hitler had achieved them, along with a strong rebound of the German economy. Granted, the Nazi regime had its weaknesses, including the conflict with churches and the feebleness of its financial standing, but by 1936 few could challenge Hitler's grip on power.[174] The remilitarization of the Rhineland seemed like the peak of the German "rebirth" Nazi propagandists were so keen to proclaim; the European balance of power was now obviously altered. Yet the surprise military crossing of the Rhine was also the closest Europe had come to another continental conflagration since 1918.[175] The chancellor, it turns out, was well aware of both triumph and doubt.[176] Would moderation follow success? As the Spanish war ran its course from July 1936 to May 1939, the Führer's foreign policy would become only more centralized, more assertive, and more aggressive. Yet that was not yet established on July 24, 1936.

The first Nationalist request for German support was not directed to Hitler. On July 22, a day after Bolín arrived in Rome, Franco's deputy in Morocco, Juan Beigbeder, sent a "very urgent request" to the German military attaché in Paris asking for "ten transport aircraft with maximum seating capacity." The goal was clear enough: airlifting the experienced troops into the mainland.[177] But Beigbeder never received a firm reply. In the North, Director Mola, now in the National Defense Junta, also attempted contact with German private companies through the German legation in Lisbon.[178]

That same day the aged Nazi Party leader in the minuscule Tetuán legation, Adolf Langenheim, and a failed, overweight Prussian businessman who had lost his small fortune in the 1929 stock market crash, Johannes Bernhardt, met Franco. Unlike Mola, Franco was not part of the rebellion's National Defense Junta.[179] With its troops trapped in Morocco, little ammunition, and next to no hard currency, the rebellion's status was dire, particularly when facing the prospect of an extensive war. Likely sensing an opportunity, a younger Bernhardt was passionate enough to talk his way onto the trip: Franco and the generals needed all the help they could get.[180] They would need far more, and Franco must have known it. Bernhardt was then handed a personal letter for the Führer's eyes only; years later he would claim not only to have read it but also that Franco's missive was "infantile in style."[181] Like much Bernhardt later claimed, there was a sizable element of self-aggrandizement. What is beyond dispute is that the Germans and a young Spanish official requisitioned a Luft Hansa mail plane to deliver the letter as fast as possible, having seized the only aircraft in the vicinity capable of reaching Berlin.[182] Avoiding bad weather and Republican forces, it would take them no less than three days to reach Germany.[183]

If it had been up to the Reich's diplomatic service, Franco's emissaries would have received the same response Beigbeder and Mola got—or lack thereof. Writing on July 25, Hans Heinrich Dieckhoff, acting head of the Reich Ministry of Foreign Affairs,[184] wrote a cautious memorandum: "There arrived in Berlin yesterday [July 24] by *Luft Hansa* plane at Tempelhof [Berlin airport] two officers of the Spanish rebels bearing instructions of General Franco to negotiate with our authorities for the purchase of planes and war materials. . . . It is necessary that at this stage German governmental and [Nazi] Party authorities continue to refrain from any contact with the two officers. Arms deliveries to the rebels would become known very soon. All government authorities should remain completely aloof."[185] On the original document, "Yes" and "Correct" appear in the handwriting of Dieckhoff's superior, Foreign Minister Konstantin von Neurath, the aristocratic diplomat in charge of the Wilhelmstraße and who had, up until then, resisted pressures to join the Nazi Party.[186] But both of them had been kept in the dark. The career diplomats—far from the inner circle of Hitlerian decision making—were unaware that on July 25 the Führer himself had chosen a different German strategy with regard to the nascent conflict. And it was anything but "aloof."

The head of the foreign section of the Nazi Party, the Auslandorganisation, Gauleiter Ernst Wilhelm Bohle, had become aware of Franco's emissaries traveling to Germany. Rebuffed by the Foreign Office, Bohle had contacted the deputy head of the Nazi Party, Rudolf Heß, through his brother Alfred.[187] Heß then arranged for his personal plane to pick up the visitors in Berlin and bring them to Thuringia, where he vacationed at his parents' summer retreat, for a meeting.[188] Bohle seemed reticent at first, yet after a lengthy discussion featuring an old school mate of the Heß brothers in the diplomatic service, Rudolf thought it pertinent to place a phone call directly to the Führer.[189] At the time an "old fighter" like Heß had Hitler's ear as did few others. It was through the Auslandorganisation that a meeting with Hitler was arranged for the evening of July 25.

The Führer was then at the Bayreuth Festival, the yearly Richard Wagner extravaganza he never missed. Arriving in Bavaria, Langenheim and Bernhardt did not know what to expect. The evening featured a stirring performance of *Siegfried* conducted by Wilhelm Furtwängler.[190] Late that night, usually his most productive hours, the Führer was in a fiery mood and eager to discuss international politics. We cannot but assume he had already been briefed on the inauspicious situation of the Iberian rebels. A report from the German embassy in Madrid early that morning presciently predicted that the failed coup d'état would trigger a full-scale civil war. It also argued that a Franco-Soviet alliance—formally a reality since 1935—would be strengthened by a Republican victory, since the ensuing regime would certainly be left-leaning and perhaps even revolutionary. According to Adm. Erich Raeder's memories, Hitler had expressed a desire for caution a few days before, eager to avoid a German naval presence in Spain for fear of triggering an international conflict.[191] This suggests that Hitler's initial thoughts on Spain—rarely a feature of his European strategic calculations— were close to Britain's and France's official policy after July 25. But that was before the post-Siegfried meeting.

War Minister Werner von Blomberg, Adm. Wilhelm Canaris, then commander of the German intelligence office (Abwehr), and Hermann Göring, the ubiquitous Luftwaffe head were also at the meeting.[192] Even though he was at Bayreuth, Propaganda Minister Joseph Goebbels apparently did not attend; perhaps he had already retired for the evening. Canaris knew Spain better than anyone else in the room; he had visited repeatedly in the 1920s as an envoy from the Weimar Republic.[193] In fact a key prototype of the German Navy (Kriegsmarine)—then illegal under Versailles terms—had been built in Cádiz under Canaris's direct supervision, eagerly welcomed by the Spanish king. Given our lack of precision on who exactly was there, it is unsurprising there is disagreement about the discussion that evening. Yet the end result is unequivocal. Hitler ordered to send Franco more supplies than he had originally requested: twenty Junkers Ju52 transporters, six Heinkel He51S fighters, artillery, and more. The supplies would be sent with airmen, mechanics, and even a medical unit.[194]

The importance of this decision cannot be overstated: Hitler's Wagnerian choice not only began his first foreign military adventure but also directly challenged the Anglo-French desire to build "a new European peace" that occupied the Wilhelmstraße and the London conference hosted by Eden in those very hours. In a move that drove Director Mola to contemplate the same fate of his brother Ramón, Hitler also decided to supply Franco—and *only* Franco. In so doing the Führer immediately and irrevocably altered the dynamics of the rebellion's leadership, completely disregarding the Spanish junta structure in place since a few days before. It is indeed very hard to argue that Franco would have so easily monopolized power within the uprising so early in the Civil War had it not been for Hitler's steadfast vote of confidence. Langenheim and Bernhardt proved their worth.

As early as July 26 the Luftwaffe was given a new special unit, Sonderstab W, to recruit "volunteers" and dispatch weapons to Spain. The codename for the operation—allegedly Hitler's idea—paid homage to the decision's Wagnerian roots: Unternehmen Feuerzauber (Operation Fire Magic) referred to the ring of fire Siegfried courageously faces in order to free the fallen Valkyrie, Brünnhilde, and fulfill his destiny. Beyond the historiographical debates about the evening, the personal role of Hitler's decision stands out.

Although four of the first batch of Junkers Ju52s lost their way and ended up in Seville, German aircraft were airlifting Nationalist troops from Morocco as early as July 29, aiding Franco in the key task of overcoming the Republican naval blockade. Mussolini would soon be speaking publicly of a "Rome-Berlin Axis," but the closer relationship with Italy was not at the core of Hitler's overruling of his diplomatic officers.[195] The Führer's strategy was subtler than il Duce's; there were elements of anti-Communism, a desire to test new German weapons (as Göring would later boast), and at least some limited sense of "fascist solidarity" in the face of a Communist threat in Spain.[196] But there was also something else.

Under Bernhardt's direction, a Spanish monopoly company (Compañía Hispano-Marroquí de Transportes, HISMA) would be established a few days later to buy equipment from a German peer (Rohstoffe-und-Waren-Einkaufsgesellschaft, ROWAK), which bought from German weapons producers. As we shall see, Bernhardt's business was an instant success—and would become a vehicle for German influence on Iberian soil. Although no minutes of the Bayreuth meeting survive, the synchronicity of military and commercial moves suggests Bernhardt did not set up HISMA unsupervised. From the very beginning, if only as an afterthought, the commercial side of the venture was a product of Hitler's Wagnerian bravado on July 25.

With European public opinion still convinced that Blum's government would aid the Republic, Hitler's interventionism would become more nuanced and far more profitable. Unlike Blum or Baldwin, Hitler did not have to worry about parliamentary opposition or public opinion; his decisive volte-face on July 25 was a matter of *Gleichschaltung*.[197] His early, daring bet on Franco is a perfect illustration of his growing and very personal role in German foreign policy decision making, taken explicitly against the directions of the Reich's career diplomats.[198] Von Blomberg did not even bother to communicate Hitler's Iberian policy to von Neurath when they met at the Munich horse races on July 26.[199] Von Neurath and Dieckhoff were simply briefed on the new government policy days later, a harbinger of centralization around the figure of the Führer that would contribute to the Anschluß and the Sudeten crises in the next two years. The Nazi project in Spain was to become not only the Third Reich's first foray into foreign war but also a unique project of informal empire.

By mid-1936 Spain was economically backward, socially volatile, and politically explosive. After a rebellion's coup failed and with a dawning civil war on their hands, it was unsurprising that the two Spains sought supplies from the great powers to make up for their deficits in armaments and technology. Foreign supplies were, as of the coup, a necessary—if not sufficient—element of victory in the dawning civil war. But only one side received the decisive support that allowed it to overcome its initial material, territorial, and financial inferiority, and it was not the side that had the initial economic, geographic, and strategic advantage. Eventually fascist intervention allowed Franco to undertake another Reconquista, cleansing Spain not of Moors but of Reds. In the thirty-two months of protracted war, all powers would somehow change their original strategic stance toward the "Spanish question," but not enough to alter the strategic decisions at the dawn of the conflict. The course of great power diplomacy was dictated, through a web of interlocked and synchronized decision making, on a momentous day: July 25, 1936.

Intentions notwithstanding, Premier Blum ultimately gave in to domestic and foreign political pressures by declining Giral's "fraternal" aid request and choosing to preserve his own Front Populaire at the expense of the Spanish one. This sequence of events proved harmful both in terms of fact and appearance. The French did not supply the Republic but provided plenty of excuses for others to arm the Nationalists. Britain's formal neutrality fit its policy objective of localizing the war in Spain while containing political and naval strategic considerations. The "continental arrangement" sought by Eden's Foreign Office would not come, yet appeasement of the dictators with an eye to Moscow had already fundamentally altered Britain's centuries-old strategy of balancing continental hegemons. Through official inaction and selective favors to the Nationalists, the British too undermined the Republic. A similar conclusion can be reached about the behavior of the United States: FDR's government prioritized the protection of its investments in Spain, choosing a middle path that only further isolated moderate Republicans. The Soviet Union did sell war material to Madrid, but Soviet involvement often contributed to important rifts within the Republican government. All in all, Moscow ultimately contributed less to the Republican cause than originally believed. Foreign investors understood the implications of these diplomatic decisions very early in the war, and, fearing both Republican defeat and Communist victory, lacked trust in the Republican peseta for the remainder of the conflict.

After the fateful July 25 the two decisive intervening powers in the Spanish Civil War were therefore Fascist Italy and Nazi Germany. Hitler and Mussolini decided on intervention in favor of Franco's Nationalists independently, yet within hours of each other. Their analogous answer to the Spanish question would bring them closer together; but whereas Mussolini merely continued his foreign policy objective of ending the left-leaning Spanish Republic, Hitler challenged his traditional Reich diplomatic service by betting on Francisco Franco.

It would prove to be a lucrative gamble. The following chapters approach these interventions individually, focusing on the rise and fall of Hitler's shadow empire on Iberian soil. The contrast between the two interventions will serve to highlight the uniqueness of Nazi designs. As will become clear, fascist intervention was not driven by ideology. While Italian leadership worried primarily about international appearances, the Germans—often ruthlessly—played their hand differently, obtaining concessions fully compatible with their domestic economic needs. In a matter of months Spain would move decisively toward becoming an informal German colony. Unlike the Führer's daring foreign policy, Germany's grand economic strategy did not originate with Hitler—who was uninterested and largely incompetent in financial affairs—but with a man who was, at the time of the Civil War's outbreak, his most independent and powerful minister: Hjalmar Schacht.

chapter three

THE RISE AND RISE OF HJALMAR SCHACHT

If the German people are going to starve, there are going to be many more Hitlers.

—HJALMAR SCHACHT, October 30, 1930

Hitler's decision on July 25, 1936, to back Franco was not the only one he took while at the Bayreuth Festival that shaped German involvement in the Spanish Civil War.[1] Two years before, on July 26, 1934, he had summoned Dr. Hjalmar Schacht, president of Germany's central bank, the Reichsbank, to Bayreuth for a private audience. The chancellor could ill afford to immerse himself in Wagner; the strains of a foreign exchange crisis had almost claimed the life of Minister of Economics Kurt Schmitt, who had suffered a stroke while delivering a speech.[2] Schmitt's subsequent leave of absence extended beyond the necessary recovery time; it appears that he was eager to find a way out of a seemingly impossible job. If this was so, one cannot blame him. Few within the Nazi regime liked the former head of insurance giant Allianz. They derided him as a symbol of outdated conservatism, a bulwark against the populist revolution so many Nazi "old fighters" hoped for. The paramilitary SAs (Sturmabteilung), for instance, sang sarcastically, "The stockbrokers are party members / and capital's protector is Herr Schmitt."[3] Meanwhile Hitler and his Cabinet pressured Schmitt to deliver on their economic priorities. By mid-1934 only a few economies had begun pulling out of the Depression. German growth and employment were improving from the economic trough, but exports languished. During a publicized national tour, Schmitt called this a problem of "export fatigue"; he promoted "exports as national duty"—even if that involved "dumping" or selling abroad below cost.[4]

The macroeconomic quandary was anything but straightforward. Although employment had seen a marked improvement since early 1933, with such depressed exports in the context of low international trade it seemed impossible to reduce the large (and growing) trade deficit.[5] The problem was compounded by two interwoven, politically driven obsessions: maintaining the international value of the Reichsmark and resisting inflation, lest it remind the German public of bleaker Weimar days. At the time Germany's closest trading partners were competing to see how swiftly they could abandon the "fetters" of the international gold standard of pegged exchange rates, gaining world export market share through cheaper currencies. If there was ever a currency war, this was it.[6]

Yet international markets did not buy Nazi promises; they expected a Reichsmark devaluation against the U.S. dollar and British sterling. It was neither the first nor the last time they would be disappointed.[7] There was no way around it: in the summer of 1934 Nazi Germany faced a financial dilemma.[8] Summoning the successful president of the Reichsbank to Bayreuth was part of Hitler's plan to solve the crisis so that he could focus on other pressing political issues. A few weeks earlier, he had unleashed the Gestapo on his own SAs and other political rivals, including a former chancellor.[9] The bloodbath, in what became known as the "Night of the Long Knives," gave Hitler more power, while pleasing the conservative armed forces, the Wehrmacht.[10] Yet managing the domestic and international backlash required the chancellor's full attention.[11] With Schmitt out and the financial crisis unresolved, it was time for a new face: at Bayreuth Hitler offered Schacht the Economics Ministry.

In his unashamedly unapologetic autobiography, Schacht claimed he already foresaw the dangers inherent in Hitler's unchecked power, yet the evidence suggests that, if he did, Schacht did not let it interfere with his accumulation of power.[12] He wanted the new portfolio to complement his second coming at the Reichsbank, and it is plausible that he had been working behind the scenes to oust Schmitt, a man he never considered his intellectual equal.[13] But then again, who was? The

Reichsbank president was not known for his humility. It was Schacht who was credited internationally for pulling Weimar back from hyperinflationary chaos in 1924; it was Schacht who had given legitimacy to many a German delegation in 1920s and 1930s international economic conferences; it was Schacht who was a member sine qua non of the transatlantic financial establishment. The press lauded him as the "the wizard of international finance," an epithet that he embraced wholeheartedly.[14]

The result of the Bayreuth meeting was the financial equivalent of the papal union of temporal and spiritual power: henceforth Schacht wielded unprecedented power over both monetary and fiscal affairs. Within months foreign media began addressing him as "Germany's economic dictator," while expressing confidence in his able management. Markets agreed, reacting positively to his appointment.[15] The domestic media was no less exultant. But given the many constraints on Depression-era German economics, which path was right? The answer had escaped Schmitt and his predecessor, Alfred Hugenberg.[16] To Schacht, however, it seemed clear: the Reich's salvation required the emphatic—or, rather, ruthless—application of nationalist economic principles he had developed throughout his meteoric career. Schacht was not the only successful economic nationalist in the Depression. Yet it was his economic framework that changed the face of the German economy, its foreign economic relations, and eventually drove the type of foreign intervention the Nazis brought to warring Spain.[17]

Hjalmar Horace Greeley Schacht had never been just another German; by some accounts, in fact, he was not even one. Born to a traditional family from Schleswig-Holstein in 1877, Schacht grew up in a region Prussian Chancellor Bismarck acquired for the Hohenzollern dynasty through the 1864 Danish War after decades of the type of argument that allegedly led Lord Palmerston to say, "Only three people have ever really understood the Schleswig-Holstein business—the Prince Consort, who is dead—a German professor, who has gone mad—and I, who have forgotten all about it."[18] The acquisition of the duchies was one of Bismarck's many brilliant moves in the long process leading to German unification.[19] Schacht's parents had recently returned from several years in New York, where his father had emigrated for a job.[20] Though they had not managed to *fare l'America*—as Italian immigrants called finding success in the New World—the seemingly endless possibilities of the American republic fascinated the Schachts, so much so that they wanted to name their son Horace Greeley.[21] The reference to the *New York Tribune* editor was symbolic of the reformist, liberal American ideal the Schachts so admired.[22] Yet the maternal grandmother resisted such an affront to the family roots, insisting her grandson should have a proper Danish name, even though she was now a subject of the Kaiserreich.[23] To be sure, the boy with a partly American name, Danish blood, and German citizenship had mixed roots, but his years at the reputable Gelehrtenschule des Johanneums school in Hamburg bred a proud German nationalist. Surrounded by shipping scions, he was keenly aware of his modest origins.[24] Yet it was not for nothing that the Kaiserreich's educational system in the late nineteenth century allowed for a degree of meritocracy unknown elsewhere: intellect and dedication trumped connections and family name.[25]

While his father moved from failed business to failed business, Schacht moved through Germany's finest universities, reading medicine in Kiel, literature in Berlin, and finally economics in Munich.[26] By the turn of the century, back at Kiel, he was pursuing a doctorate under the supervision of Professor Wilhelm Hasbach. Although none of Schacht's biographers seem to have looked into the issue in detail, Hasbach had been particularly active in the confluence of philosophy, politics, and economics that had shaped the growing field of economics in the previous three decades.[27] In the tradition of German proto-economists such as Friedrich List and Friedrich Hegel, Hasbach had been most interested in issues of moral philosophy, the predecessor to what we today call "economics."[28] During his tenure Schacht's supervisor wrote extensively on the German influences on two of the intellectual pillars of the growing field: François Quesnay and Adam Smith.[29] He had also published on contemporary political economy issues, drawing from history and theory to inform policy. Schacht's supervisor was a "historical" economist through and through.[30]

The so-called Historical School of economics, more influential in Germany than perhaps anywhere else, was a branch of economics that prioritized the study of empirical evidence (History) as distinct from the mostly theoretical and increasingly mathematical frameworks preferred by the proponents of the discipline in Britain. This preference pitted the historicists against the best-known successors of Adam Smith,

men like Stanley Jevons and Alfred Marshall, credited with the founding
of neoclassical economics.[31] The historical approach deplored the theoretical and mathematical turn in nineteenth-century British economics,
epitomized by the birth of *Homo economicus* and its strictly rational
preferences. They questioned its ability to provide effective answers
to policy questions. Rather than mathematical modeling, they argued,
economics was best served by studying policy in the context of history,
pursuing the sociological study of peoples—the nation-state was the
preferred unit of analysis—while taking into consideration customs
and cultures.[32]

Historicists expected policy recommendations, almost by definition,
to vary greatly based on experience, a cultural variable far too complex to account for mathematically. Abstractions and models, so popular with Marshall and his followers, were for them only of secondary,
limited value.[33] Unsurprisingly, therefore, the moral philosophy of the
German historicists did not chiefly concern itself with theoretical constructs: it sought to address the social tensions created by Germany's
rapid industrialization, evolving from the micro *Ökonomie* into the
macro, internationally focused *Wirtschaft*.[34] This skeptical tendency in
German economic thought toward neoclassicism would famously be
highlighted in John Maynard Keynes's introduction to his *General Theory*'s first German translation in 1936. In it Keynes went so far as to
hypothesize that because of this intellectual divergence, Germans would
be far more receptive to his ideas than were his own British contemporaries.[35] Like his peers, Schacht's advisor remained drawn to qualitative comparisons with the British system, but they were firmly
grounded in German arguments and German policy concerns.

The interests of the teacher evidently influenced the student. In 1900,
ten years after the publication of Marshall's *Principles of Economics* and
under Hasbach's supervision, Schacht submitted a doctoral dissertation
addressing "the theoretical content of English mercantilism" ("Der theoretische Gehalt des englischen Mercantilismus"). The few biographical accounts that even mention the study focus on its thoroughness
and "typically German" dispassion.[36] Given the evolution of "Schachtian
economics" in the 1920s and 1930s, the thesis deserves a closer look.
Intellectually subtle, it ponders whether the mercantilist framework constitutes "a complex of systematically developed opinions, which, aimed
at a common goal, can and should be addressed as an 'economic

system.'"[37] Schacht then sets out to analyze the foundational texts of British mercantilism to judge the construct as a whole. The thesis finds that the staple positions of mercantilist thought—namely the emphasis on the accumulation of bullion, the planned promotion of exports, and state control of imports—emerged not from a coherent logical system but rather through a series of pamphlets aimed at addressing the constraints of British imperial trade policy. Unlike the adherents of Marshall's *Principles,* Schacht does not conclude that this mercantilism, lacking a theoretical framework, is to be declared intellectually bankrupt. On the contrary, he argues that the mercantilist ideas represent a rational, effective response to the conditions of international trade and finance faced by the British state during the eighteenth century. For Schacht, therefore, mercantilism is a response to the needs of British imperial policy.

Although the origins of mercantilism are traced back to Elizabethan England—"We must always take heed that we buy no more from strangers than we sell to them, for so we should impoverish ourselves and enrich them," reads a tome from 1549—the school had avid followers in Germany. It was popular among historicists, including Adam Müller and List, even Hegel.[38] List, a key German thinker heavily inspired by Alexander Hamilton's arguments during a sojourn in the young United States, subscribed to selectively protectionist ideas in the domestic arena and aggressively expansionist concepts abroad.[39] In List's eyes, Germany had an inherent "territorial defect," which in truth was more of a territorial deficit. In order to properly compete with other empires—namely Britain's dominions and the vast internal U.S. empire—List advocated a "metropolitan-colonial protective system."[40] That was the ultimate goal of his "national economics": a vehicle for German imperial strength to be projected abroad. More mainstream mercantilist theory essentially considered foreign trade to be of central importance for national (and imperial) strength, a point also made by pre-Smithian economists in France and Austria.[41] Beyond bullion, mercantilism sought a positive trade balance and consequently a positive net international investment position.[42] From a philosophical standpoint, this considered trade closer to a zero-sum game than the mutually beneficial activity that mathematically inclined neoclassicists favored.

Schacht's choice of dissertation topic is interesting in and of itself. He focused on the economics of empire at the very beginning of his career by analyzing the intellectual background of British mercantilism. His dissertation therefore suggests a strong association with German historicists against Britain's economists, at a time when in government circles Bismarck's successors advocated for a German empire to rival Britain's. From the Wilhelmine perspective of the early years of the twentieth century, the preeminent goal was to access within an exclusively German sphere of influence the natural resources that routinely pushed the empire's trade balance to negative territory; in short, it was a time of aspirational colonialism for strategic reasons, underpinned by economic theories.[43] The debate was not about whether imperialism was a worthy goal, but rather was about what *kind* of imperialism Germany should pursue.

Schacht's argument about the inherent pragmatism of mercantilist thought prefigured one that would be made more forcefully during the 1930s by Marshall's most brilliant student, Keynes. He would argue that the mercantilist preoccupation with gold bullion came not from worship of gold as the ultimate commodity but from a rational appraisal of its ability to provide the national economy with liquidity and a common medium of exchange.[44] From an economic point of view, it is a valid contention: in the absence of reliable international financial markets that can alleviate liquidity constraints, the provision of liquidity falls back on central bank reserves. As the British Empire expanded, the maintenance of gold reserves became more and more central to the unhindered operation of colonial trade. Gold—later replaced by a gold-convertible pound sterling—acted as the ultimate lubricant of international trade. Perhaps more interesting, as Schacht was careful to note, it was not out of conviction but in response to their circumstances that British mercantilist policymakers sought to accumulate the contemporary equivalent of foreign exchange "reserves." More than three decades later and during an epoch of crumbling internationalism, Schacht would not hesitate to seek a comparable solution to Germany's dilemmas.

Schacht's thesis synthesized the main tenets of a mercantilist tradition that had evolved and adapted over time. First, there is the acknowledgment of a bias in what kind of trade is conducted: "The gain in export goods is greater, when they are processed goods, rather than raw materials." This is a point that "dependency theorists" would revive, with varying degrees of effectiveness, in the 1970s.[45] More important, however, was the role of political influence in furthering economic preeminence. "Of the greatest advantage," Schacht wrote, "is the trade with such countries over which one maintains political influence, or which one holds as colonies in complete dependency." And then there was the role of the state apparatus in turning political advantage into trade preeminence: "Only planned state intervention can give trade the form in which it will benefit the country." Finally, he underlined the importance of an inherently virtuous cycle of power in mercantilist theory: "The political influence is also increased as a consequence of a higher economic influence."[46]

It was this blend of economic and political choices that would come to influence Schacht's policymaking in both domestic and foreign arenas. His "statism" in the 1930s would completely transform the German economy, and yet his choices also can be synthesized as a partial return to the mercantilist principles inherent in his doctoral work. Ultimately the mercantilist system does not pass Schacht's test as a "cohesive theoretical construct," but there is nothing to suggest that he was not supportive of its policy implications. In fact much of the language is supportive and adaptability was a central pillar of the historicist construct.

With the new century Schacht entered the workforce. First he worked at the Office for the Preparation of Trade Agreements. Later, in the private sector, he became a Dresdner Bank "economist," though his role involved mostly public and press relations. Flawless English and respectable French allowed him to get involved in international issues. At one of Germany's universal banks in the (first) age of globalization, he became acquainted with the main features of global finance.[47] Confidence and hard work paid off: by 1908 he had been promoted to deputy director.[48] As Schacht rose through the ranks in the elite world of Wilhelmine banking, European politics came to a sudden halt. The guns of August, however, did not halt Schacht's meteoric ascent; in fact they furthered it.

Though exempt from military service, Schacht took a detour from the private sector following the "Rape of Belgium," Germany's bloody invasion of its neighbor that brought Great Britain into the Great War.[49] He left the Dresdner to advise the German Army on the economics of occupation. Working under a former Reichsbank executive, he was given power to turn the economic ideas he had been developing in a

variety of publications into policy.[50] The finances of occupied Belgium
were complicated. Faced with an uncooperative central bank with no
foreign reserves, what Schacht encountered in Brussels was not unlike
what he would have to deal with at the Reichsbank a decade later. The
Belgian government had transferred all reserves to London shortly before following their bullion into exile. So Schacht came up with a pragmatic solution: outstanding loans and payments in kind between Bel-
gians and the occupying Germans would henceforth guarantee currency
issuance. It was a solution that went back to the future of monetary
theory; Schacht saw barter as a viable way to compensate for the lack
of hard currency.[51] What could be described only as heterodox policy
worked on the ground, at least initially; it allowed payments to pro-
ceed with a new exchange rate to benefit German forces. Schacht would
later justify these wartime measures by claiming they were the only
viable answer to the exigencies of war.[52] German occupation eventually deteriorated into disastrously high inflation, but by then Schacht
had returned to Germany due to disagreements with his superior.

Back in the private sector, Schacht joined the Danatbank. Granted,
it was a humbler home than the Dresdner, but the Danat gave Schacht
a board position that allowed for a flexible schedule. This gave him time
to write and develop contacts.[53] From a now secure financial position,
Schacht watched the Second Reich unravel. The literature on the effects of defeat and revolution on Germany is extensive; for our purposes, suffice to say the pain of the Kaiserreich's downfall, a period of
political dithering between revolution and reaction not unlike Spain's
in the 1930s, and ultimately the experience of hyperinflation all had a
profound impact on the banker, both personally and in his economic
thinking. In short, they worked to strengthen his nationalist leanings.[54]

As was true for many of his contemporaries, for Schacht postwar humiliation had a proper name: Versailles. A Carthaginian peace to say
the least, the negotiations in Paris in 1919 had profound internal consequences for the young Weimar Republic. The domestic effects of the
peace are perhaps best illustrated by the stab-in-the-back legend *(Dolch-
stoßlegende)*, a populist theory that claimed the military had been "stabbed
in the back" by the politicians who signed the armistice and subsequent
peace. Versailles had negative consequences far beyond Germany. As
British prime minister David Lloyd George once said, it was hard to
be "between Jesus Christ and Napoleon Bonaparte" at the negotiations,

referring to the idealistic U.S. president Woodrow Wilson and the intransigent French premier Georges Clemenceau. Yet even Lloyd George obliged the public mood with his "Hang the Kaiser" campaign.[55] This view played with a public used to propaganda like Rupert Julian's hit film *The Kaiser, Beast of Berlin* (1918). Punishment of the vanquished deepened existing rifts between the victorious powers, which only hastened America's withdrawal into postwar isolationism.[56]

For a nationalist like Schacht, the result was a debacle. He would later open a book on reparations for Anglo-Saxon audiences with a pithy line: "What is called the peace treaty of Versailles is no treaty, and it has not brought peace." Reasoning along the most reactionary of lines, he continued, "[It] was presented to the Germans, and they were compelled, under threat of force, to sign it. . . . It was an act of dictatorship . . . [and] it was erected upon a gross breach of an international compromise."[57] One of the key unstated goals of Versailles—at least from a French perspective—was to arrest German growth, so strong in the late nineteenth century; Clemenceau pressed for restrictions that would mostly lapse in 1925.[58] This was meant to remove the impetus for German continental hegemony and empire that had led the German High Command to gamble for "preventive war" while they "could still more or less pass the test" in 1914.[59] So Versailles rid Germany of its merchant marine, three quarters of its iron ore and a third of its coal supplies, its (relatively minor) African empire, and over 16 billion Marks of foreign assets. And that does not include the 132 billion Marks reparations bill set in 1921, totaling around 83 percent of pre-1914 German gross national product (GNP)—a considerable part of which had disappeared. Some leading historians have suggested Versailles ought to be measured against the "draconian" peace the Second Reich had imposed on warring Russia in the short-lived Treaty of Brest-Litovsk that sealed German victory in the Eastern Front.[60] Regardless of the frame for comparison, however, it cannot be disputed that Versailles reparations foresaw payments of up to 2.5 percent of GNP per year scheduled for no less than seven decades. Importantly the payment was denominated in gold-linked hard currency, which made it impossible for the Weimar Republic to inflate it away.[61]

This tally was far beyond what Keynes had estimated Germany could possibly pay in his *Economic Consequences of the Peace*, the tome that made a famous commentator into an international celebrity. In the following years Keynes's "maximum amount" oscillated between 20 and 22 billion, but a fraction of the Versailles total.[62] The peace had also severely constrained German access to key industrial imports, since the feeble republic had to maintain a trade balance positive enough to make reparations payments. The star Cambridge economist remained skeptical; seeing no hope for an international loan or payment in kind, Keynes focused on the "transfer problem": basically Germany after Versailles was required to run a current account surplus into the distant future with newly constrained resources, opening itself up to the possibility of destabilization if its trade relations worsened. Keynes's insightful commentary posed an unavoidable question: Could Weimar possibly stabilize?

One possibility, of course, was that it simply could not. Burdened with reparations Keynes (and Schacht) thought unpayable, deprived of colonies, geographically partitioned, internationally ostracized, and under the yoke of both reparations and postwar social expenditure, the Weimar Republic in the early 1920s descended into rampant hyperinflation. Of the myriad analogies devised to describe it, perhaps one of the first remains the finest: if one were to chart the German Mark to U.S. dollar exchange rate using a scale in which 10 Marks equal an inch, the prewar curve would have corresponded to four-tenths of an inch—representing a quote of largely 4 Marks to the dollar at prewar gold standard prices. By November 1923 the position of the curve would have been 160 million miles from the base, equaling almost a round trip to the sun.[63]

It has been convincingly argued that Weimar politicians and businessmen conceived of inflation as part of a political strategy to prove the burdens of Versailles were both unsustainable and unpayable, even when they could have put an end to it by stabilizing government finances. There is, however, a question about how politically viable that was.[64] Ultimately the "always and everywhere monetary phenomenon" materialized: the German elite took the road that led to political and economic ruin.[65] Regardless of who was ultimately responsible, there is no doubt hyperinflation left behind profound social fissures.[66]

As Schacht would later write, "even financially sophisticated people often assume that Germany gained a certain advantage from the fact that her internal loans were wiped out [by inflation]." What Keynes popularized as the "euthanasia of the rentier" did not really apply to Schacht's Germany, at least in the banker's view: "The same process wipes out the capital of the citizens [savings] and the citizens . . . are just so much the poorer."[67] Hyperinflation amounted to a radical experiment in wealth redistribution. Furthermore Schacht acknowledged a deeper consequence that Keynes had only indirectly touched upon: political humiliation.[68] In his words, "[Inflation] hurt still more, because it made our helplessness so evident, to watch the foreigners from the Army of Occupation [in the Ruhr] onwards, buying us out with their better money throughout this inflation period. They bought our goods cheap and robbed us of the value of our labor; they bought our houses, and stock in our businesses, for the cost of a sandwich."[69] (That does not sound so different from what the German occupation authority had imposed on Belgium during the war.) Not even the ruin of some speculators caught on the wrong side of the trade helped: "It was only slight consolation that so many of them, speculating on our currency, themselves suffered losses."[70] Yet it was this collapse of the German currency and ensuing hyperinflation that gave Schacht his finest career opportunity.

As billions of Marks turned into trillions, Weimar Food and Agriculture Minister Hans Luther approached Schacht to offer him a job: currency commissioner. He was not Luther's first choice; two others had already turned down what was perhaps the least appealing job in the government.[71] As at Bayreuth a decade later, Schacht did not hesitate. Run from an office that had previously been a wardrobe, the new task welcomed him on November 13, 1923, with a challenging agenda:[72] stabilizing the Mark, putting an end to secondary currency issuance—which, through nongovernment currencies, exacerbated the hyperinflationary spiral—and speeding up budgetary balancing across central and regional *(Länder)* governments.[73]

Schacht was as intransigent in crisis-ridden Berlin as he had been in wartime Brussels. He oversaw the introduction of a new currency, the Rentenmark, promising it would not behave like the devalued Mark. After all, over 99 percent of the Marks in Germany by the end of 1923 had been put into circulation in the previous thirty days.[74] Effectively this meant that Schacht and the Reichsbank apparatus would not allow the government to finance deficits by running the printing presses.[75] This contributed to a monetary "regime change" ultimately rooted in the fact that public consciousness caught up to the printing presses; expectations needed to change for hyperinflation to be arrested. The new currency's name had a raison d'être: real estate collateral technically guaranteed issuance. It was a somewhat fictitious construct, given how hard it would have been to ensure delivery, but the asset-backed quality of the paper appears to have added to its credibility. It was as good a regime change as could be attempted given the circumstances.[76]

At such a dire stage in the hyperinflationary spiral, however, controlling the quantity of money was necessary but not sufficient to arrest hyperinflation; Schacht had to induce people to slow the velocity of money as well. After all, during such an episode, it is entirely rational to spend as fast as possible so as to maximize one's swiftly decreasing spending power, which builds an expectation of further depreciation into daily behavior. In short, the government needed to replace the vicious cycle of distrust with one allowing for stability.[77]

The new Rentenmark was "nominally" linked to gold, yet it was not convertible. Not that there was an alternative: lacking foreign reserves in the context of Versailles, any type of convertibility as had been fashionable before the Great War was out of the question.[78] It was not entirely down to Schacht; with almost all the country's printers at the service of a Reichsbank running empty of credibility, the government had no alternative but to contemplate a fiscal tightening. Tired of a losing game against inflation, Germans wanted stability. The end of 1923 therefore brought a change in fiscal laxity: civil servants, railway workers, and postmen were laid off and expenditures cut.[79] Perhaps this rationalization a few years before would have avoided the hyperinflationary collapse altogether, but that was the path not taken.[80]

Schacht's routine involved endless hours in his tiny office. "Did he read letters? No, he read no letters. Did he write letters? No, he wrote no letters," his secretary later said. "He telephoned a great deal—he telephoned in every direction and to every German or foreign place that had anything to do with money. . . . And he smoked."[81] The Rentenmark, along with the government's change and Schacht's obstinate refusal to allow any exceptions, gained acceptance. At the core of this process lay no miracle: the Reichsbank was no longer allowed to discount government bills, which meant it could no longer monetize the deficit. The fact that Schacht refused to accept informal, nongovernment money—what the so-called *Notgeld* corporations had issued—led to considerable losses for international speculators and select domestic conglomerates. Monetarily it was another sign of stabilization. Where others had failed, Schacht managed to create a positive feedback loop closely associated with his stewardship; a new face allowed for new credibility. This was a collective effort of the administration aided by inflationary exhaustion, yet the press gave the new commissioner all the credit.[82] Some accompanied the accolades with musical tunes that surely massaged Schacht's ego: "The *Rentenmark* has saved the day, our hero Schacht has shown the way!"[83]

Before Christmas, Chancellor Gustav Stresemann put Schacht's name forward to succeed the late Reichsbank president Rudolf Havenstein. Although hyperinflation forever tarnished his reputation, Havenstein had run Germany's central bank diligently since 1908, through the Great War, the Weimar Republic's difficult birth, and into the chaotic 1920s.[84] When his advice went unheeded, Havenstein had behaved like a loyal subject, innovating in war finance and occupation management.[85] In old age he had yielded to inflation as the only politically palatable path for the Weimar Republic. A week before his passing, the threat of Weimar social instability was painfully illustrated by a putsch in Bavaria.[86] The coup failed, but the plotters—in particular a former private of Austrian origin with a talent for public speaking—gained notoriety. "Either the German revolution begins tonight and the morrow will find us in Germany a true nationalist government," a young Adolf Hitler threatened, "or it will find us dead by dawn!" As it turned out, neither was the case, but his putsch represented the gravest threat against the Weimar Republic since the failed Communist revolution of 1919.[87] Inflation had taken its social toll.

Schacht was inaugurated as president of the Reichsbank against the backdrop of the failed coup and Havenstein's death. If hyperinflation had subsided, perhaps there was a future of democracy in Germany, allowing the country to return to economic growth and international respectability.[88] The only meaningful opposition to Schacht's appointment came from within the Reichsbank, where directors used to Havenstein distrusted a man surrounded by media accolades but lacking in most other credentials. Successful as he had been, Schacht had been commissioner for barely a month and his private banking career had been mostly devoted to public affairs.[89]

With astonishing speed, however, Schacht turned into an international interlocutor for the Weimar Republic. Amid the bitter negotiations surrounding the Dawes and Young Plans that amended Versailles, he became an irreplaceable member of German delegations.[90] In a time

of turmoil he cultivated critical personal relationships with men like
Montagu Norman, the autocratic governor of the Bank of England.[91]
According to a British journalist writing in 1924, "Today he [Schacht]
is Germany's most prominent man, not only at home, but also, though
he has never held a diplomatic post, in international relations. He is
the only German who holds the ear of British and American finance."[92]
With notoriety grew his thirst for power. According to banker and U.S.
vice president Charles Dawes, Schacht's "pride is equaled only by his
ability and his desire for domination." What is more, "[Schacht] frankly
insinuated that as long as he was President of the *Reichsbank,* he was
the *Reichsbank.*"[93] The authoritarian tendencies Dawes identified would
only grow in the years ahead.

From the Reichsbank Schacht sought to restore access to foreign markets closed off to the Weimar Republic. If German exports did not
thrive, Keynes's "transfer problem" would only be exacerbated, making
it all the more difficult to honor reparations.[94] After the Dawes Plan,
total German debts were eased and Schacht's currency stabilization was
given international backing. Thereafter Germany became a preferred
destination for U.S. capital. This suggested a second possible answer to
Keynes's question about how to pay for reparations. But could more
liabilities be piled on Germany's already gargantuan debt pile?

The ultimate source of capital, for one, was eager. The United States
had remained politically isolationist throughout the presidency of Calvin
Coolidge, a pragmatist who interpreted Republican electoral fortunes
as rejection of Wilson's involvement in world affairs. The Senate had
never ratified Wilson's brainchild, the League of Nations, which left
the United States out of the international system it had helped set up
in Paris.[95] Successive Republican administrations remained introspec-
tive, yet the country had a considerable capital surplus and American
bankers enjoyed the newfound benefits of preeminence over their competitors across the Atlantic. Britain—home to Walter Bagehot's Lombard Street, once the "greatest combination of economical power and
economical delicacy that the world has ever seen"[96]—faced a difficult
decade of slow recovery and tense relations with its empire, not to mention its disgruntled Entente ally. Indeed Britain managed a return to
the gold standard only in 1925 and only after intense lobbying by Bank
of England governor Norman. Against the orthodoxy Keynes argued
for loose money to fuel the recovery, famously deeming gold a "bar-

barous relic."[97] Yet Norman seduced an ambitious (but financially inexperienced) Chancellor of the Exchequer, Winston Churchill, arguing that gold convertibility would return Britain to the stability of the prewar years and its role at the core of the international financial system. He promised to make Churchill "the golden Chancellor."[98]

Reality was far less glamorous than that. What amounted to an overvalued exchange rate pushed Britain back into recession, adding deflationary pressures on prices and wages. Britain had its own onerous war debts, which Americans refused to write off as war expense.[99] Deflation only made them harder to service by shrinking GDP and therefore increasing the relative weight of the debt. Norman was mistaken: the second-order consequences of a return to the gold standard further eroded Britain's role as the "world's banker." In this context American bankers—led by J. P. Morgan and Kuhn, Loeb—generously extended credit abroad while their British and French competitors struggled. During a 1924 discussion about German stabilization, for instance, banker Paul Warburg, then a Federal Reserve advisor, worried that "[the United States] may miss this quite unique opportunity for putting America's discount market [money market] on the map and complete our position as world bankers."[100] Schacht's newly respectable Weimar Republic became a preferred destination for U.S. surplus capital. The Dawes loans had given the German government breathing room; the country remained dependent on foreign funding but was comparatively developed and impressively productive. In short, it was cheap enough to be attractive and in need of huge amounts of capital to rebuild.[101]

The inflow of U.S. capital inherently tied the German economy to U.S. prosperity through short-term loans that linked, via reparations and Anglo-French debts, back to Wall Street.[102] Schacht would later write, "The danger in these short-term credits is thus not a danger for foreign countries [i.e., the United States], but for Germany." It was a line of reasoning he would hold on to during the Nazi regime. "For imagine what it would mean for an industrial country," he continued, "dependent upon the sale of the products of its working men, if suddenly its supplies of raw materials had to be utilized to pay off its short-term debts. . . . [The resulting reduction in available foreign exchange for trade] would have catastrophic consequences upon German economic life."[103] An interesting Brookings Institution study at the time detailed the sizable profits made by U.S. banks from selling German loans. Writing in the aftermath of a 1932 Senate hearing, German statistician Robert Kuczynski concluded that the U.S. banks had made net profits of around $50 million from the sale of no less than $1.289 billion in gross German loans in a few years. The eventual losses for buyers of such loans, however, would turn out to be more substantial than Kuczynski had envisioned.[104]

Schacht's personal relationship with the governor of the Bank of England was nothing short of essential for the establishment of the Gold Discount Bank (Golddiskontbank) that allowed for a new Reichsmark to succeed the Rentenmark. The Bank of England provided the liquidity reserve for the new currency to be viable.[105] But even if Britain's central bank provided the bullion for Schacht's new currency, it was America's private capital that oiled the German economic machine.[106] Yet Schacht believed that the combination of a vast foreign debt and social instability made Germany's standing inherently precarious. This bleak outlook distanced him from a fellow nationalist who came to symbolize an "Atlanticist strategy" in German politics: Chancellor Gustav Stresemann.[107] In 1923 Stresemann had had a central role in Schacht's appointment to the Reichsbank. But Schacht doubted Stresemann's careful diplomacy could prevent a crisis. What he saw at international gatherings was anything but promising. Although the Allies had written off some of the original reparations and relaxed rules through the Dawes Plan, Germany had no consistent access to foreign exchange and no meaningful reserves of its own.[108] Schacht worried there was no way to ensure the necessary imports for Germany's economy to thrive. The currency was now viable but utterly dependent on the state of its foreign payments and budget balancing, always a hard act in light of Weimar's deep social fissures. Meanwhile new short-term debts piled up on top of old ones.

German industry needed foreign raw materials to function, and other developed economies, to which Germany was increasingly indebted, could at any time raise trade barriers against her exports. As long as trade flowed freely, this would not be an issue. In Schacht's thinking the core of the problem, once again, lay in Versailles: the expropriation of colonies meant that Germany's highly developed industry could have accessed crucial inputs—among them iron ore, foodstuffs, rubber, and other industrial raw materials—without employing now sparse foreign exchange. After 1919 this "closed system" route was no longer available, which deepened Germany's need for short-term foreign capital without providing long-term solutions to its imbalance.[109] Foreign commentators rightly pointed out that Wilhelmine Germany had not developed its colonies extensively, to which Schacht retorted that what was accessible in international markets during the golden age of trade before the Great War was no longer so in the 1920s. Indebted as it was, Germany depended on open access to world markets to sell its exports and purchase raw materials. Then again an economically constrained Germany had been a purposeful consequence of Versailles. One crucial known unknown emerged: What if trade were to collapse, making it much harder to service foreign debts? A dichotomy emerged in Schacht's mind: either Germany was given unhampered access to markets for raw materials or else reparations would have to be revisited far more comprehensively than the Dawes Plan had allowed. Liberals, however, would have called it a false dichotomy.

Given both his academic roots and the Reichsbank actions, Schacht's pseudo-mercantilist belief in the economic weight of empire was perhaps best synthesized in a 1926 speech he delivered to the German Colonial Association. It is a surprisingly obscure document, ignored by Schacht's biographies, even if it was the Reichsbank presses that published it.[110] The Colonial Association had been one of the most influential institutions in late Wilhelmine Germany. Closely associated with private industrial conglomerates and the German East Africa Company, it advocated for a central construct of German imperialism: *Weltpolitik*.[111] Interestingly enough, in the late 1920s the Association would become closer to a populist fringe political party, at first sight distant from the organization's elite roots: the Nazis.[112]

There were essentially two intellectual strands in German imperialism. The first, *Weltpolitik,* favored a preeminently economic perspective on empire, arguing for the use of political influence to access new markets and provide a positive feedback loop on strategic influence at the world stage. It was a position advocated by both leading historicists and students of mercantilism, drawing heavily from late nineteenth-century British experiences with "informal empire."[113] During World War I these perspectives garnered much attention in the public sphere. A symbolic proponent of this idea was Friedrich Neumann, a pastor and influential politician who penned the instant best-seller *Mitteleuropa*

(1915), arguing for a discrete economic community in central Europe under German control.[114]

The outcome of the Great War shattered the dreams of all Wilhelmine imperialists. But in its aftermath proponents of economic-focused *Weltpolitik* had to contend with a new rival and rising trend in German imperialism: *Lebensraum*. Literally meaning "living space," the construct traced its roots back to the work of the Ober Ost, the military management agency that administered the occupied territories in the East and, following the Treaty of Brest-Litovsk, the ephemeral Russian territorial concessions to Wilhelmine Germany.[115] If briefly, the Kaiser's conquests during the Great War included the Baltic states—Estonia, Lithuania, and Latvia—as well as large swaths of Ukraine, effective control of Poland, and the promise of no Russian interference in Finland. During the interwar years, however, defeat turned what had been occupation lands *(Land)* into space *(Raum)*. This semantic change underscored an important change of meaning: *Raum* was, to quote a leading source on the issue, "triumphantly ahistorical, biological, and 'scientific.'"[116] Supporters of these views did not see geography as impartial; "geography" would be the study of space at the service of the state, creating the necessary consciousness for a formal Germanic empire in central Europe.[117] In the Weimar Republic many such centers of "geographic" study opened their doors. A rising political movement would soon appropriate these *Völkisch* themes, intertwining them with other themes in the tradition of *Blut und Boden*, namely the open celebration of a pseudo-scientific racial connection between a people and their land.[118]

By contrast *Weltpolitickers* traced its roots back to thinkers preoccupied with the international projection of the "national economy." Organizations like the Colonial Association supported "spheres of influence" for the ascendant Second Reich, namely Mitteleuropa in Central Europe and a Mittelafrika in Africa, concepts that had become popular in prewar Germany.[119] One such theorist was Karl Goering, who exerted great influence on Germany's relatively liberal 1892 tariff.[120]

Weltpolitik resonated with Schachtian thought on two main accounts. First, his educational roots and historicist training, culminating with his doctoral work on mercantilism. Second, supporting the projection of informal influence abroad implied a way out of Germany's inherent—and in his view unsustainable—economic imbalances. This was precisely what his 1926 speech to the Colonial Association argued.

Facing a friendly audience, Schacht began diplomatically: "It may seem at first a bit strange that the [Reichsbank president] should express his views on the colonial problem." Yet there was a purpose. "I say nothing of the political reasons which may have induced the victorious Powers [Britain, France, United States] to rob Germany of her colonies," he said diplomatically, "but I propose to show that their action in taking away these Colonies was an economic mistake which, if not corrected, must inevitably have political consequences." Thereafter Schacht trod on controversial ground for a central banker of such international repute: he argued that the Great War ought to be blamed, ultimately, on European overpopulation, for "the economic necessities of the European peoples were hampered by the traditional political framework" that existed before the war.[121] In Malthusian terms, nationalists argued that the only possible solution to Germany's demographic "problem" was more space. Yet Schacht's conception of "space" differed from that of the *Lebensraum* supporters; race and sovereignty mattered less than influence and market access.[122]

Protectionism in the form of trade barriers remained a particularly problematic enemy for an economy so reliant on foreign capital: "The principal difficulty in connection with the reparations payments is not in the collection of the required sum, but in their transfer to Allied recipients. . . . Germany is putting her surplus production in the world market . . . but the Allies can never desire such deliveries to anything like the amounts which are in question, whether on their own home markets or on the outside markets to which they have to look for their own exports."[123] Here Schacht was borrowing a page from Keynes's "transfer problem." Such rhetoric essentially made explicit Schacht's dichotomy: without colonies, Germany would find it economically unfeasible to attain the balance of payments surplus required to honor reparations payments.[124]

As for how colonies should be managed, Schacht believed in "big, privileged, Colonial companies, operated by private enterprise." His audience approved; the Association had had close contacts with state-sponsored conglomerates in Africa. Yet in this speech and elsewhere Schacht publicly expressed his belief in state-sponsored private enterprise as a fitting "third way" between capitalism and communism.[125] To Schacht "the victory of the conceptions [of free enterprise] underlying the Dawes Plan represents the victory of an enlightened individualist . . .

and capitalist view over nationalist imperialism on the one hand, the path which leads to the battlefield, and Bolshevist socialism on the other hand, the path of which leads to the wilderness." The sly banker illustrated this point by evoking the experience of the North American *Mayflower,* a rhetorical move that catered not only to a potential international audience—the speech, after all, was translated by the Reichsbank—but also to those in the audience who leaned toward a "late British" imperial conception of empire.[126] Schacht tracked *Weltpolitik* thinking closely.

The banker seemed to care very little, if at all, about racialist ideas. Even his examples featuring Germanic settlers were devoid of the elements characteristic of the *Lebensraum* world view and its *Blut und Boden* conceptions. Foreign exchange weighted more than ownership and the myth of German soil: "In Cameroon, Togo, in German South-West Africa and in all the German settlements in the South Seas, the German Mark was the prevailing currency down to the war. . . . That meant that all Germany's colonial enterprises—in spite of the complete economic independence of the Colonies as regards trade policy—could be carried on in Germany's own currency without any question of exchange risks or the necessity of procuring foreign currency." The implication was obvious: "It was on the rock of the German currency that the economic and financial demands of the forced Peace of Versailles eventually made shipwreck." "We must get back as soon as possible to the Colonial field," Schacht concluded; the "result will be to facilitate German payments to foreign countries, and to open for Germany herself economic prospects in the future which will ensure the possibility of lasting amicable understanding with her neighbors."[127] This was not the first time the president of the Reichsbank had referred to an "amicable understanding" with the Allies, if only to make the alternative clear. Nor would it be the last.[128]

Schacht was not the only member of the Weimar government to address the colonial issue. Despite his Atlanticist strategy, Chancellor Stresemann also sought a return to colonialism.[129] Stresemann's vision was theoretically attainable: Article 22 of the League of Nations covenant stipulated that any "advanced" country was to be allowed the same access to mandates in the developing world.[130] "When we shall again possess our own colonies I cannot say," Stresemann said while trying to appease the Reichstag in 1925, "but there is no doubt that the reacquisition of the colonies is an aim, and an acute aim, of German policy." Playing with the covenant's language, he added, "If there are 'advanced nations' then we belong to the advanced nations."[131] Some sources argue that Stresemann was at the time under a "Schachtian spell" on the colonial issue: the nationalist rationale made political sense, but the economic rationale was a matter of "survival."[132] Yet the British and French shunned all German foreign economic overtures, from Asia to its former colonies in Africa.[133] The destiny of Tanganyika, once the heartland of German East Africa, was symbolic of Anglo-French intransigence: to the dismay of Stresemann's administration and the Reichsbank, Tanganyika joined a customs union with British Kenya in 1927. Henceforth, from the perspective of Berlin, "League mandates" seemed little more than additions to the British Empire by another name, essentially "to be colored red on the map."[134]

Despite a roaring growth rate in the late 1920s, the domestic situation in Weimar Germany remained fragile. Trade deficits were large; consequently its net international investment position deteriorated further. Politically dependence on the United States made logical sense to Chancellor Stresemann: if all loans led back to Wall Street, it was better to depend on Washington than on bitter Paris or diminished London. But the United States remained adamant on not writing off British and French war debts. So the debt cycle continued, turning short-term loans into higher yields for Wall Street. How long could it hold? Though history books often refer to Stresemann's period as a "honeymoon," his Atlanticist strategy did not achieve its ultimate goal of giving the Weimar Republic long-lasting stability. The onerous debts were still there.[135] From his Reichsbank office, Schacht became ever more apprehensive, privately and increasingly publicly. He ran a campaign against "unproductive borrowing," publicly berating cities for spending on "stadiums, swimming pools, public squares, dining halls, convention halls, hotels, offices, planetariums, airports, theatres, museums, etc., and the purchase of land."[136] He also got into a very public newspaper row when he publicly criticized the 14 million Reichsmark redecoration of the Berlin State Opera.[137] According to his later autobiography, in those years he "did not hesitate to point out [he] had publicly and consistently opposed Germany's excessive foreign indebtedness."[138] Around this time he also began to openly criticize Versailles.[139]

Easy money also found its way to the Berlin stock market, pushing up valuations and encouraging risk taking. In 1927 Schacht became concerned about the buoyant market, so he pushed for a limit to credit extension in sectors he saw linked to stock market exuberance, including lending for leveraged investments. This endeared him to neither the press nor most Weimar politicians.[140] On May 13 this stance contributed to what newspapers baptized "Black Friday" at the Berlin stock exchange; it can be argued that he attempted what the U.S. Federal Reserve failed to do a year later: to burst the bubble.[141] The reputable *Frankfurter Zeitung,* however, called Schachtian policy "an unexampled attempt at regimentation, a planned economy action of the first rank."[142] Wittily playing with language, the self-assured banker responded by arguing that "profits so easily made on the stock market" did not go into business, as learned journalists were wont to point out, "but rather into hotels and fancy cars."[143] Nevertheless the *Zeitung's* point about Schacht's desire for control was not misplaced.

As Reichsbank president, Schacht was ultimately responsible for credit creation. Ever since changes to the institutional architecture of the Reichsbank in 1922 "strongly suggested" by the Allies, the bank had enjoyed unprecedented independence from political influence. This autonomy was, at the time, extremely rare and comparable only to Norman's tenure at the Bank of England.[144] Schacht used this power freely, to direct credit to the areas of the economy he thought most productive. His beneficiaries included large cartels and export-oriented industrial sectors. The inspiration for this top-down credit dirigisme has been traced back to the work of a Romantic proto-economist that preceded even Friedrich List: Adam Müller, a pioneer in the German preoccupation with its "national economy."[145] More influentially Joseph Schumpeter's 1911 masterpiece, *Theory of Economic Development (Theorie der wirtschaftlichen Entwicklung),* another product of the historicist tradition, argued for a direct linkage between credit and growth. By Schacht's time the idea had permeated into the German intellectual milieu, and had even influenced calls for state management of credit during the Great War.[146]

In strict monetary terms, Schacht ascribed to the "real bills" theory of money rather than the quantity theory advocated by Yale's Irving Fisher.[147] His monetary goals were therefore achieved through a combination of quantitative and qualitative measures; though the Reichs-

bank had its discount rate, effectively much depended on "credit recommendations" from the bank. This often entailed Schacht calling
bankers to his office for interrogation and admonishment. One could
call it "personal supervision."[148] The degree of bank oversight was also
unusually high; in this context it is unsurprising that commentators likened his Reichsbank to a "second government."[149] Yet the behavior of
government at regional and central levels as well as foreign capital remained beyond the bank's purview. In Schacht's view the unprecedented
power of the 1920s Reichsbank was actually not quite enough. Not
only did he need more power, but he also needed to oversee an economy
without the structural deficiencies that had plagued Germany since 1919.

In April 1929 Schacht led the German delegation to a preparatory
international conference in The Hague. The goal of what would become the Young Plan was to revisit reparations once and for all, even
if yet another Republican administration, one led by President Herbert Hoover, had not changed the long-standing U.S. position on war
debts.[150] During these discussions Schacht's emergent nationalism culminated in an infamous telegram. In it, and echoing some of his Colonial Association reasoning, he argued that Germany could not afford
any further reparations payments unless its colonies, along with the
Polish Corridor that cut the republic in two, were restored.[151] The
argument was nothing new: Germany's businesses needed guaranteed
access to raw materials to manufacture the industrial goods at the core
of its economic architecture. Yet the Corridor betrayed motives that
transcended the strictly economic; it was nakedly driven by an appeal
for German "territorial integrity."[152] Wasn't Schacht too ingenious to
overplay his hand so blatantly in a room filled with Anglo-American
diplomats? Perhaps it was time for an exit. Unsurprisingly his autobiography glances over this shocking telegram and subsequent resignation,
focusing instead on his role in the creation of the Bank of International
Settlements (BIS).

Perhaps Schacht's finest international brainchild, the BIS was established in the context of the Young Plan as the ultimate guarantor of
loans to Germany.[153] For the pragmatist at the Reichsbank, the BIS
would go beyond its goal of expediting remittances through internationally guaranteed financing; it would also serve as a promoter of cooperation. Schacht would later write, "My BIS remained the finest propaganda item for the Young Plan."[154] The organization also delivered

a nationalist goal by effectively replacing the reparations agent, whom so many Germans considered a "viceroy" in Berlin.[155] Yet his telegram on the colonial issue achieved the seemingly impossible in interwar diplomacy: it enraged London even more than it enraged Paris. Committed to Atlanticism, Chancellor Stresemann publicly disowned his central banker. What Schacht wrote might have resonated with the chancellor in private, but how could he have backed a banker seriously advocating such radical changes in such a vitriolic tone? This leads one to wonder whether Schacht had played a careful hand, furthering his appeal in other political quarters. Unsurprisingly the internationally repudiated telegram endeared him to more extreme German nationalists.

The next Young Plan meeting was no less problematic. This time around, however, it was the Chancellor of the Exchequer, Philip Snowden, who shocked the world. "The Yorkshireman," as *Time* was fond of addressing him, took advantage of the need to pass the agreement unanimously to demand a larger share of reparations for Britain. Versailles remained divisive not only with respect to Germany but also among the victorious powers. Snowden complained that German payments "in kind"—one of Schacht's ways to get around any deterioration of currency reserves—constituted trade dumping, which in turn hurt British trade.[156] Keynes had long pushed payment in kind, arguing a decade before that it was a logical reason the British government would not insist on German reparations for too long. No change of policy was imminent, however. Snowden, eager to defend a sagging British economy, wanted cash with which to pay its own debts. The British recovery continued to lag even though Benjamin Strong's Federal Reserve did what it could—and perhaps too much—to support Norman.[157] Snowden enjoyed cross-party support for his international position; the staunchly Tory *Morning Post* praised the Labour chancellor: "We are delighted that there is no nonsense about internationalism in the line that he [Snowden] has taken, and that he stands firmly upon the British interest." Even Churchill supported him from the opposite Westminster bench: "I think Snowden is opposing the Young Plan not on personal or party grounds but solely as an Englishman who wants fair play!"[158] Internationalism was showing cracks.

During the impasse Schacht discovered that he had been kept from negotiations between his government and Poland, which culminated in a clause by which Germany waived her claim to compensation for all property and land ceded at Versailles. This effectively meant the Corridor would remain forever Polish. Around the time the news of Wall Street's 1929 crash stole the headlines, Schacht wrote a vicious memorandum directed toward his own government. He sent it to the Cabinet and leaked it to the press. Surely with some delight he would later acknowledge it "came as a bombshell."[159] With his Reichsbank days numbered, Schacht intervened to stop one last U.S. loan, which Finance Minister Rudolf Hilferding—of *Das Finanzkapital* (1910) fame[160]—had laboriously arranged to keep the German economy afloat. Hilferding immediately resigned, complaining about the "interference of the *Reichsbank's* president in . . . national policy."[161] Schacht followed him out of office.

His timing—by chance or choice—could not have been better.[162] The coming years of Depression would be an ideal time to be freed from a truly unenviable menu of policy options. There remains vigorous debate about the ultimate causal relationships surrounding the economic downturn after the 1929 crash, which a young Ben Bernanke once described as the "holy grail of macroeconomics."[163] It is by now established that a wave of bank failures and misguided monetary strategies aimed at avoiding gold outflows severely contracted monetary supply in the United States and around the world.[164] A period of deleveraging led to deflationary pressures that created a vicious cycle linking a deepening slump with higher unemployment. Sticky wages made it hard to lower labor compensation equilibrium, deepening domestic imbalances, even if, as Keynes argued, it remained hard for specific groups of workers to successfully bargain with employers at a time of deep slump.[165]

The end of globalization was compounded by the international gold standard of pegged exchange rates that Britain's Norman was so wedded to.[166] Although U.S. protectionism long predated the (in)famous Smoot-Hawley tariff, it was this bill's debate in the U.S. Senate—with its hundreds of amendments—and eventual enactment in 1930 that spread panic around the world and escalated an all-out trade war.[167] Like seven decades later, the 1929 market crash in New York was the spark that lit a global fire.

The initial, sharp spike in risk aversion started the domino effect beyond U.S. markets.[168] With unemployment soaring and government popularity ratings in free-fall, electorates moved squarely to the political fringes, where both reactionary and revolutionary politicians argued against free trade and for protection. Schacht was increasingly attracted to such arguments. Given that countries tied to gold could not resort to the "best" beggar-thy-neighbor policy of competitive devaluation—due to the fixed exchange rates that characterized the gold standard—they had to enhance trade protection as a "second best" alternative.[169] The goal was nonetheless the same: to remain competitive at the expense of one's trading partners, a practice that could only further undermine the international system. It was soon painfully clear that protectionism— like a bank run—constituted a self-reinforcing phenomenon. It is important to remember that such policies were not emanating from authoritarian dictators; rather they emerged from democratic polities: far from resisting the end of globalization, Britain, France, and the United Sates sought to advance their individual positions to the detriment of their partners. It was a global *sauve qui peut,* implemented by politicians but driven by democratic forces and misguided economics. The worse the economic situation became, the harder it was to vote for the hard choices, even if they were "economically preferable" in the theoretical sense.[170] In dictatorships and democracies alike, nationalistic populism was the strongest currency around.

As Schacht had forewarned, the implosion of the world economy hit debt-shackled, export-reliant Germany particularly hard. Amid plummeting global trade and a current account deficit that was "structural" in nature—exacerbated by Weimar's payments abroad for short- and long-term debts—the German economy faced a painful squeeze.[171] As is usual in these types of crises, the financial sector was hit first, exacerbating the precarious capital position of banks large and small. The great Berlin banks were soon on the brink.[172] For decades historians have debated the relative importance of the gargantuan debts and the currency pressures on the 1931 German banking crisis, but for our purposes the trigger is beside the point. After the failure of Schacht's first private employer, the Danatbank, the crisis led to government capital injections into the banks. The result was an unusual degree of government control over the German banking sector.[173] Years later this would become a vehicle for a dictatorial reordering of the German economy, with Schacht once again at the helm.

Since late March 1930 a new chancellor, Heinrich Brüning, had implemented what economic orthodoxy prescribed. His *Deflationspolitik* has since become the most controversial decision in German economic history, if only for its connection with Hitler's ensuing electoral success.[174] Brüning's government implemented a brutal program of economic deflation, slashing prices and salaries. The 1930s austerity in Germany required government by decree; with the backing of aged Weimar president von Hindenburg and selective acquiescence from Social Democrats, Brüning's objective was to counter the loss of competitiveness that resulted from policy responses to the Depression.[175] Abroad many respected the ascetic technocrat implementing hard adjustments in Germany.[176] Within the country, however, the social cost spiraled. As Schacht moved toward the political fringes, so did the Weimar electorate.

Why did Brüning not choose a path of devaluation of the Reichsmark and new spending, amounting to what we could anachronistically call countercyclical fiscal policy? Some scholars have accused the administration of choosing deflation in order to achieve a Pyrrhic victory, showing the world that German debts could not possibly be paid back.[177] The latest evidence suggests that this counterfactual is deceiving. Brüning's Cabinet knew all too well that Reichsmark devaluation would only make it harder for Germany to service gargantuan debts denominated in foreign currency. Even in 1932 considerable debt forgiveness remained out of the question for Germany's creditors, not least the United States.[178] Yet this was not Brüning's only reason. "It would be unthinkable to inflict another inflation on the German people," the chancellor argued during a Cabinet meeting on October 2, 1931. Even then, fears of inflation outweighed even a harrowing banking crisis. "It would also be impossible to maintain the currency on a level 20% below the current one," he added, warning about a possible spiral of devaluation. Brüning did not trust the regime's credibility was enough for a small devaluation.[179] Both the domestic and the international intelligentsia worried that devaluation—and in particular a *German* devaluation, less than a decade after the hyperinflation—would prove unstoppable. If Brüning had any plausible alternative to deflation, it was visible neither to him nor to his closest advisors.

Economic historiography has since made Brüning's deflationary strategy into anathema, though governments today still resort to variations of the deflationary theme to maintain currency pegs.[180] The Reichskanzler's drastic reduction in government expenditure furthered the vicious cycle linking plummeting demand and lower output; not only were Germans and foreigners spending less, but the government was retrenching simultaneously, trimming the welfare extended by earlier Weimar administrations.[181] Four rounds of deflation between 1930 and 1932 depressed the domestic economy, pushing up unemployment and spare capacity to record levels. Thus Germany followed the dictums of the gold standard toward the social abyss.[182]

Brüning was not politically deaf; accurately reading the social reactions of the crisis, he greatly escalated nationalist rhetoric. In foreign economic policy, he pushed for a customs union with Austria. His government was never deeply popular, yet his policy of ever-closer union with Austria marked a clear break with Stresemann's more careful international balancing.[183] Unsurprisingly such a proposal was particularly unpalatable in Paris. In light of their gold hoarding, French opposition to Brüning had profound financial consequences during the banking crisis in 1931.[184] This rising nationalism exacerbated capital flight at a time when investors were already withdrawing rapidly for strictly fundamental reasons.[185] Brüning's became the "hunger dictatorship" for good reason.[186]

Out of office but not out of sight, the "bellwether" Schacht worked on his international reputation. In mid-1930, like his parents before him, he left Germany for a sojourn in the United States. Barely a couple of months after the passing of the Smoot-Hawley Tariff, he argued that trade restrictions—and not the rise of reactionaries—were the true enemies of stabilization. "Germany's economic system and her credit are not menaced," he held, "by the success of National Socialists, but only by the way we are oppressed by other countries."[187] The Nazis were, in his view, the democratic product of a general lack of prospects. This pointed to dangerous relativism, but for a pragmatist like Schacht, this was no anathema. Brüning's policies gave someone of his repute and out of office plenty of room to be populist. On a speaking tour Schacht took this reasoning further. When asked if Germany was headed toward a "Hitler revolution," Schacht's response made it to *Time* under a fitting headline, "Schacht Shocks." "If the German people are going to starve," he said cheekily at Yale, "there are going to be many more Hitlers." Reaction had been a decade in waiting. "You must not think that if you treat a people for ten years as the German people have been treated they will continue to smile," he said. "How would you like to be kept in jail for ten years? Tell your people that."[188]

Released from his central banking duties, Schacht also became more politically active domestically. As recession gave way to Depression, he flirted with right-wing groups sympathetic to his positions on reparations and imperialism. In open opposition to the government, he resumed his love affair with the media. With the whole German banking system on the brink of collapse, he publicly criticized the Reichsbank's leniency on capital requirements.[189] But when the Reichsbank did restrict domestic credit—as it attempted to do in July 1931—the ensuing panic created a full-blown banking crisis with global ramifications.[190] The government ended up with majority positions in two of the five universal German banks, including the Dresdner, and that was after the spectacular failure of the Danat.[191]

As part of this media blitz Schacht also published a controversial book entitled *The End of Reparations,* in which he viciously denounced Versailles.[192] The argument was familiar reactionary fare, but it came from a highly respected source.[193] Schacht's position on colonies, meanwhile, remained intact. Imperialism mattered less as an issue of "geopolitical equality" and more as a way to address Germany's resource constraints. Imperialism, in one way or another, had the power to yield sources of raw materials within Germany's economic system.[194]

A "Hitler revolution" drew closer. Schacht had been introduced to the political sensation at a dinner thrown by Mrs. Hermann Göring in February 1931. Joseph Goebbels, future minister of propaganda, and Fritz Thyssen, of the eponymous industrial empire, also attended.[195] The banker had flirted with several reactionary groups, but his approach to the Nazis was not based merely on a strategic assessment of their strength. Schacht's "stout, placid," and reactionary wife, Louise, was particularly taken by National Socialist politics after her husband's involvement in the short-lived Harzburg Front.[196] Among reactionaries and populists, by 1931 Hitler had developed a powerful electoral apparatus of his own, putting him in a unique position to deliver.

Soon enough Schacht would find himself introducing Hitler to individuals who would become staples of Nazi policymaking. Among them was Walther Funk, a former financial reporter bound for Goebbels's ministry. Although Schacht initially failed to be independent of

Wilhelm Keppler's "circle"—an early point of contact between German business and the Nazis—the banker enjoyed relative freedom to maneuver.[197] At a meeting on June 20, 1932, Hitler declared himself to be "no doctrinaire" on economic issues.[198] Although he later denied ever being part of it, one of the circle's members remembered vividly Schacht's "eulogy" *(Lobrede)* following Hitler's speech.[199] The banker seems to have been taken by such pragmatic politics, so much so that in 1932 a "special office" bearing his name, Arbeitsstelle Schacht, was set up to centralize heavy industry support for the Nazi electoral effort and pave the way for Hitler's entry into government.[200]

A few months earlier, in the spring of 1931, a progressive American journalist interviewed Schacht. Dorothy Thomson asked him directly if he would ever join a Nazi administration, in so doing providing it with the international economic legitimacy that Hitler utterly lacked. "The Nazis cannot rule," Schacht responded decisively, "but I can rule through them."[201] The Nazis could therefore serve as the ultimate vehicle for Schacht's personal ascendency, one so far, so fast that it seems almost devoid of setbacks—unlike the many that plagued his Fatherland. And it began with a second coming.

chapter four

"GIVE ME FOUR YEARS"

The Nazis cannot rule, but I can rule through them.

—HJALMAR SCHACHT, 1931

In the immediate aftermath of his seizure of power, Hitler did not see much of Hjalmar Schacht. Yet he was not far; when it mattered, Schacht was there. He "happened to be in the room with a mere handful of his entourage when Hitler made his first radio speech, beginning 'Give me four years [and you will not recognize Germany].'" The new chancellor would deliver on this promise: four years hence Germany would be radically different. The Nazi propaganda machine would soon admit as much, and there can be no doubt that Schacht was at the heart of this transformation. Politicians often talk about seeing into their peers' inner selves; so did Schacht: "Seeing [Hitler's] soul served to strengthen my hope that it would be possible to guide [him] in the path of righteousness." At the Nuremberg trials he would assert he had joined the Nazis not as a vehicle for personal advancement or allegiance to a party he cared little about but merely as a service to the Fatherland. "I would have preferred if [Chancellor] Brüning had asked me in July 1931 [to return to the Reichsbank]," he later wrote. Yet that had not happened, rather unsurprisingly considering Schacht's vociferous criticism. With Hitler, however, something was different: "Since I was now given the opportunity of ending unemployment for six and a half million persons, all other considerations must give way."[1] Was this confidence? Delusion? Or was it hubris?

From Hitler's perspective, Schacht's appointment made sense. The foreign press noted that Hitler had been seeking "fiscal advice" from Schacht for over a year.[2] Although the Party was critical of the Weimar elite to which the banker belonged, fighting the record levels of unemployment in 1933 Germany was sound electoral strategy—at least for as long as elections were needed. In parliamentary elections the Nazis promised "Arbeit und Brot" (work and bread). Yet they also had a third slogan: "Freiheit."[3] The Nazi conception of freedom meant liberation from the Versailles system; it implied rearmament. A choice would eventually have to be made between guns and butter—but not in early 1933. Hitler needed someone in charge of monetary affairs who was not only cooperative but also creative, so as to deliver on his promise of transforming Germany. He also needed an interlocutor respected abroad. The fiscal situation the chancellor inherited was inauspicious at best. Burdened with a large fiscal deficit and crisis across regional and local governments, Hitler had little room for maneuver.[4] The Reichsbank was different, if only its leadership shared Nazi goals.

At first Hitler tried for continuity and approached the sitting Reichsbank president Hans Luther.[5] His message was not strictly about jobs; it was also about guns. Yet Luther did not quite get it. After listening to a long, typically Hitlerian tirade about the strategic rationale for large-scale German rearmament, Luther pledged 100 million Reichsmarks to help the task. This would have equaled around £7 million or $23.8 million at the time, less than 0.25 percent of GDP. To say it was far from what Hitler envisioned was to put it mildly. "For a moment," Hitler later recounted, "I thought I must have misunderstood him, for I did not think it possible that a financier should have so little knowledge of the finances involved in the policy of rearmament." The conversation was over: "Further comment was obviously superfluous, so I simply asked the President of the *Reich* [von Hindenburg] to remove the man from his office."[6]

It was not so simple; in 1933 Hitler was far from the omnipotent dictator he would one day become. With the Weimar constitution in place, the chancellor could not just sack the central bank president.[7] Yet Hitler found a way to be persuasive: he offered Luther the Washington embassy and—though this contention remains unsupported by Reichsbank files—allegedly heeded Luther's request for 50,000 Reichsmarks added to his pension.[8] "I can see him still, his eyes modestly downcast," Hitler would say, "assuring me that it was pure patriotism which caused him to fall in with my suggestions!" Money talked. "So I had to pay good money to open the way for the appointment of a man of international reputation to the Presidency of the *Reichsbank*—Dr. Schacht."[9] In his memoirs Schacht naturally chose to focus on Hitler's desire to "furnish whatever will be necessary to take the last unemployed off the streets."[10] Yet there was a clear price for Schacht's second coming: it involved abandoning the central bank independence he had so zealously defended years before.

As of March 17, 1933, just over a month into Hitler's government, Schacht was back at the office where he had made his reputation. Yet 1933 was a world away from 1924. In between lay half a decade of exuberance and cheap credit, followed by the painful hangover of market collapse, bank failures, unemployment, and the implosion of the international financial system. It was this shipwreck of globalization that allowed Schacht a degree of freedom for unilateral action that would have been unthinkable before 1929. In the context of crumbling globalization, this "freedom" would first be applied to Germany's international liabilities and then to its economic architecture. And it would ultimately lead to a strategy of foreign power on Iberian soil.

The first two years of the Depression had seen a veritable explosion in trade protectionism. Symbolic of this trend was the passage of the Smoot-Hawley Tariff, best remembered by its nine hundred different tariffs and twenty pages of congressional debate on tomato duties. Contemporaries could see its inherent danger; as Thomas Lamont, managing director at J. P. Morgan, put it at the time, "I almost went down on my knees to beg Herbert Hoover to veto the asinine [bill]." In fact 120 economists urged Hoover not to sign it.[11] But political calculation trumped economic sense. As we have seen, from bad duties to worse quotas, countries engaged in a shortsighted attempt to shield their internal markets in ways that damaged the international system. In game theory terms, the unilateral action made everyone in the system worse off, yet the individual incentive for seeking relative advantage prevailed. Like the mythical Ouroboros, protectionism fed on itself, pushing global trade into a vicious cycle of ever more closure and ever less exchange. And then the banking crisis hit.

By most measures Creditansalt was a prestigious Austrian financial institution: founded by the Rothschilds in the 1850s, it had become Austria-Hungary's leading bank, lending generously to Austrian

eminences like Prince Metternich and the central European aristocracy.[12] In the spring of 1931, however, it was brought to its knees in
part due to the purchase of a smaller bankrupt competitor, underwritten
by none other than the central bank.[13] On May 11 the bank's failure
spread panic across the Austrian financial system. Bank runs multiplied.
International contagion followed, soon engulfing Germany, where the
Brüning administration was forced to provide unprecedented support
to the financial system.[14] The Weimar Republic suffered from "twin
crises," one challenging its banking sector leading to bank runs and
the other, a political crisis, challenging the Weimar commitment to the
gold standard.[15] Amid the capital flight the Reichsbank imposed controls, effectively limiting convertibility.[16] The 1931 banking crisis
turned a domestic recession into the Great Depression.

It is usually forgotten that it was none other than the Republican administration across the Atlantic that sought to arrest the panic.[17] This was
the objective when Hoover introduced a proposal for a debt moratorium
on June 20, 1931, following a "strong suggestion" by J. P. Morgan's
Lamont. It aimed at halting debt repayments from Britain and France
to the United States in exchange for a temporary freeze on German
reparations payments.[18] Eventually a moratorium materialized—but
not without its difficulties. The State Department neglected to notify
Paris; neither Prime Minister Pierre Laval nor Emile Moreau's Banque
de France had been informed in advance of Hoover's proposal. A later
standstill agreement dealt with shorter-term debts, giving Germany
breathing room for trade but still demanding considerable short-term
payments.[19] The German private sector that had so worried Schacht
at the Reichsbank—in particular agricultural banks, iron and steel
firms, and department stores—now faced default.[20] Domestic crisis
deepened.

This *sauve qui peut* attitude in London and Washington and inflex-
ibility in Paris fueled competition where there once had been cooperation.[21] The French hoarded reserves, modifying their gold coverage
ratio; this led to a "shortage" of reserves that prima facie benefited Paris
but in truth weakened the whole system.[22] Less than a week before,
the French ambassador in Washington had made a prescient toast at an
embassy party in the presence of high-ranking U.S. officials: "In the
brief moment that has left us between the crisis and the catastrophe,
we might as well grab a glass of champagne!"[23]

By September 1931 the debt and banking crisis had morphed into a currency crisis. Philip Snowden, the Chancellor of the Exchequer who had shocked his interlocutors at Young Plan negotiations, unilaterally took Britain off the gold standard. "It is safe to predict Monday September 21st will become a historic date," led the *Economist*. "The suspension of the gold standard in Great Britain marks the definite end of an epoch in the world's financial and economic development."[24] It was a move that would have seemed inconceivable only months earlier. By "amending" Churchill's Gold Standard Act of 1925, a new national government ended the historic peg to gold in the hopes of furthering domestic recovery.[25] Although there was no panic in Britain, the pound plummeted; soon Scandinavia and the Dominions followed suit.[26]

Such a blatant, unilateral abandonment of the international monetary system by its historical architect had second- and third-order consequences. It effectively meant the resumption of "economic hostility" on both sides of the Atlantic.[27] Indeed an internal memo at the British Treasury acknowledged the impact devaluation would have in the international economic arena, even if it made domestic political sense: "No country ever administered a more severe shock to international trade than we did when we both (1) depreciated the £ [and] (2) almost simultaneously turned from free trade to protection."[28] A few months later the *Economist* acknowledged, "The abandonment by Britain of the post-war gold standard, despite all the manifest shortcomings in both that standard and its working, has set in motion forces which have had lethal effects on the world's monetary and commercial activities."[29] From the viewpoint of trading partners outside the British Empire, "old authorities and rules on economic policy were shattered."[30]

As the pound devalued, Britain gained a price advantage over France, the United States, and Germany. Regardless of its positive domestic effects, this was the very definition of beggar-thy-neighbor policy. Snowden's successor, Neville Chamberlain, sought to further divert trade toward the British Empire by embarking on trade measures that built on devaluation. At the 1932 Ottawa Imperial Conference he proposed an "imperial preference system." For Chamberlain it was a personal struggle, for none other than his father had started the campaign for tariff reform two decades earlier.[31] Although he acknowledged some of Keynes's monetary insights—chiefly the need for lower effective rates in severe recessions—what Chamberlain sold as "imperial free trade" amounted to an abandonment of Britain's traditionally open policies.[32] If free trade was exclusive to the empire, then it was not all that free. These policies compounded the problem for the empire's trading partners, which saw themselves limited in terms of not only price (British goods were now cheaper) but also access (Chamberlain promised "imperial quotas"). British policy prioritized domestic needs over the longue durée of the international financial architecture.[33]

In early 1933, following a domestic bank panic, new U.S. president Franklin D. Roosevelt emulated Britain: he unpegged the dollar from gold.[34] Roosevelt's devaluation was a bid for domestic recovery at all costs, influenced by a Democratic Party eager for better export prices and concerned with rural stability.[35] British inability and American unwillingness to organize the international system were therefore rooted in domestic electoral choices.[36] At the preparatory discussions for the World Economic Conference in London, dollar devaluation took over as the key discussion topic. And where central bankers wanted to collaborate, it was politicians who refused—and they did so looking at their electoral calendars.[37] To paraphrase a modern take, they knew what to do but not how to get reelected after doing it. To borrow Kindleberger's famous terminology, no willing and able financial hegemon was to be found on either side of the Atlantic.

Hope was not immediately lost; after much negotiation the U.S. delegation in London agreed to a temporary deal with Britain and France to halt competitive devaluations. It implied that the great powers could eventually find a way to return to gold convertibility at a lower rate, preserving the globalized financial architecture. In the United States influential financiers like Bernard Baruch and rising foreign policy experts such as Dean Acheson backed it.[38] Yet Roosevelt sent a telegram that shunned even his own delegation: "The fetishes of so-called international bankers are being replaced by efforts to plan national currencies with the objective of giving those national currencies a continuing purchasing power." No wonder it became known as the "bombshell telegram."[39] It confirmed the administration's unwillingness to stabilize the dollar, snubbing even the semblance of international cooperation. Roosevelt's path may have been economically preferable for the United States, but what remained of the international system was all the weaker for it. Schacht, for his part, complained the strategy "provided benefits solely for Anglo-Saxon countries."[40] Such was the shipwreck of globalization.

By this time Hitler and Schacht were in power. In the context of Roosevelt's bombshell, an uncouth announcement by Alfred Hugenberg, Hitler's first economics minister, that Germany must return to colonialism to help end the Depression did not garner much attention.[41] Had Britain, France, and the United States achieved stabilization, then Hugenberg's move would have hurt Berlin's standing further. But they had not; in fact the *Economist* opined that the conference conveyed "the uncomfortable impression which is created [at] an operatic performance when there is a hitch in the raising of the curtain [and] the conductor has to repeat, in a grimly persistent da capo, the concluding passage of the overture."[42] Yet Hugenberg's memorandum still gave Hitler an excuse to replace him with Kurt Schmitt.[43] The appointment of the former Allianz head was a conciliatory move toward a rival group in the Nazi Cabinet led by aristocratic Foreign Minister von Neurath.[44] This internal battle between non-Nazi nationalists only augmented Hitler's power over them.[45]

Meanwhile Schacht's policymaking influence grew. With the great powers disunited, his main task was to provide a monetary framework for Hitler's goals. Although he had questioned Luther's "overly accommodative" monetary policy months before, Schacht pledged Reichsbank support for both the fight against unemployment and for rearmament.[46] With the economy depressed, the goals were temporarily one and the same.[47] As Hitler's later utterances underscore, however, work creation was not his overarching priority: "[Schacht] understood at once that it would be ridiculous to think of launching any rearmament program unless we were prepared to vote many billions [of Reichsmarks] for its implementation."[48] Though Schacht's autobiography mysteriously omits it, minutes note that he was part of the Cabinet meeting on June 8, 1933, when a rearmament program amounting to 35 billion Reichsmarks to be spent over the next eight years was approved. This was approximately 6 percent of German GNP.[49] This document singlehandedly undermines the view that the first years of Nazi rearmament were "mild." Indeed the best available data confirm that only 1933 can be described as such in terms of military spending. Even so, four months into the Nazi government, plans had been laid for a gargantuan expansion over the next half-decade. Even allowing for generous domestic and international growth—a prospect that hardly seemed in the cards then—this plan foresaw a military sector in excess of 10 percent of the economy, necessarily changing Germany's economic structure. Comparisons with the Weimar era were pointless; as Tooze pithily summarized, "the annual military spending by the Weimar Republic was counted in millions, not billions."[50] These figures were also high when compared to European budgets during the cold war.[51] The program was so large that when a delighted War Minister Werner von Blomberg told Finance Minister Lutz Graf Schwerin von Krosigk about it, the latter allegedly fainted.[52]

Although he was not yet formally part of the Cabinet, Schacht was there for a reason: Reichsbank support was nothing short of crucial for many of these initiatives.[53] The "motorization" of the economy and the building of the *Autobahnen* was—just like incipient rearmament—monumental; it was a scheme close to Hitler's heart, involving the creation of an interconnected network of highways as well as the popularization of the car as a civilian mode of transport.[54] Implementation of such goals was not left to old Party fighters but rather to traditionally trained men. It was like having Schacht rather than a Party parvenu at the Reichsbank. When Hitler allegedly asked the banker for his choice between engineer Fritz Todt and Gottfried Feder, a Party "theorician," to lead the Autobahn project, Schacht favored the former. "Do you know Herr Todt?" Hitler inquired. "No, Chancellor," he replied with characteristic sarcasm, "but I know Herr Feder."[55] Schacht had little respect for the anticapitalist Feder and his radical, anti-Semitic ideas. In contrast, Todt was an engineer with more moderate views. Schacht's choice was representative of the more economically conservative—yet no less nationalistic—tone of the new government. Todt got the job. Often by choice, and otherwise by force, big business was a partner in the young regime's efforts. From the central bank Schacht advanced a cause that was capitalistic in nature, if driven and directed by the state.[56]

In the midst of Goebbels's bombastic propaganda, Todt began his work; the formerly unemployed marched with shovels as placeholders for rifles. Hitler hailed the "tremendous task" ahead: no less than 6,500 kilometers of roads, to be fully appreciated only "in the course of future decades."[57] "Cooperation" had been required for "will to turn into reality"; he omitted to mention the private sector, but clearly signaled out Schacht's activist Reichsbank.[58] Indeed the banker was present and was acknowledged explicitly in the introduction. After required mentions of *Volksgemeinschaft,* Hitler filled a wheelbarrow with shovelfuls of dirt for the viewing pleasure of Goebbels's cameras.

The highway project employed many at relatively low cost, in particular blue-collar construction workers—victims of the Depression and prime Nazi electoral targets.[59] And it worked wonders for the 1934 referendum on Hitler's leadership.[60] At first Todt's administration minimized use of machinery to provide the greatest number of jobs in geographic areas worst hit by the crisis.[61] But the project also served a strategic rearmament purpose: the Wehrmacht conceived of the *Autobahnen* system as an efficient tool to mobilize divisions speedily should Germany again have to fight a two-front war. And then there was always tourism.

This Autobahnen project has taken up much academic ink as an example of a Keynesian aggregate demand boost before Keynes had published his *General Theory* in 1936.[62] In the same German introduction where Keynes argued his ideas might potentially be better received there than in neoclassical Britain, he also made a controversial claim that his theory of aggregate production "can be much more easily adapted" to the conditions of a totalitarian state ("eines totalen Staates").[63] Contemporary sources believed these Nazi projects made a major difference to the German economy. Yet the latest estimates suggest Nazi fiscal deficits were too small to provide the multiplicative effects of Keynesian demand stimulus.[64] Rather, a cyclical recovery after the 1932 bottom began to deliver jobs and improve the fiscal situation.[65] This benefited whoever was in power, suggesting an interesting counterfactual if Hitler had not accessed power in early 1933. Furthermore Ritschl's data suggest the weight of the rearmament, approved by Schacht and the Cabinet in early 1933, was crucial to growth as of 1934, earlier than previously assumed.

The necessary complement to Autobahnen was motorcars, a sector where Germany lagged.[66] In this respect Hitler's regime pushed ahead against established businesses in the pursuit of mass production.[67] It was another grand project, best exemplified by the support for Ferdinand Porsche's Volkswagen, the aggressively priced "car of the people" that moved many to save without hopes of actual delivery until after World

War II. These were examples of the state leading the way of structural investment through direct funding, subsidies, and guarantees. Schacht's Reichsbank underwrote the Autobahnen. Back in power and amid collapsing internationalism, his economic nationalism required a level of heterodoxy that quickly exceeded Roosevelt's New Deal.

Given Hitler's fiscal constraints, only having someone like Schacht at the Reichsbank made financing for work-creation projects and rearmament possible. The latter had to be kept from international eyes for as long as possible. Yet both involved credit creation and, ultimately, the kind of activist monetary policy that would eventually lead to inflation. By definition, funds spawned from a supposedly independent Reichsbank to, as it were, kick-start the economy risked price stability—if not immediately, at least in the medium term. The relative merits of a kick-start against a cyclical rebound are beside the point here: in 1934 Schacht came up with an off–balance sheet system to funnel credit into work projects and rearmament well beyond official targets. Both inflation hawks and international eyes made stealth a necessity.[68]

Thus Germany's largest industrial conglomerates jointly set up a new "private" company, the Society for Metallurgical Research *(Metallurgische Forschungsgesellschaft)*. The fact that the backers—Siemens, Krupp, Rheinstahl, and Gutehoffnungshüte—were champions of heavy industry closely involved with military contracts should have been suspicious to outside observers.[69] Indeed this was no run-of-the-mill joint venture and involved no research whatsoever; rather it was a vehicle for monetary stimulus.[70] The company issued IOUs, so-called Mefo bills, well beyond its capital base. These were then discounted by Schacht's Reichsbank, effectively creating credit for rearmament.[71] Through Mefo bills—a Schachtian concoction—monetary expansion could be concealed to appease traditionalists at home and go unnoticed abroad. Between 1933 and 1936 Mefo bills financed a considerable portion of public deficit spending.[72]

In theory the government would eventually compensate the Reichsbank for Mefo advances. Yet "temporary" central bank advances have a way of becoming permanent, particularly when fiscal and monetary responsibilities are blurred. Nowhere was this more blatant than in Schacht's Germany.[73] The multiplicative effects of credit creation with the backing of the lender of last resort were considerable. This off–balance sheet invention was an important illustration of Schacht exceeding his strict monetary priorities to attain the government's goals.[74] In 1934 heavy industry and the Wehrmacht were pleased with the inflow of orders, and the Nazis did not shrink from pressuring businesses to accept the Reichsbank-discounted bills whenever necessary.

Although there is plenty of historical debate about Germany's economic performance in the early years of the regime, from the means (Mefo bills) to the ends (rearmament and work creation), Schacht was at the heart of policy.[75] GDP revived vigorously from the Depression lows, with unemployment declining by a third during Hitler's first year in power.[76] It was a phenomenon at the very least aided by a cyclical rebound, but the ultimate source of growth mattered less to the Nazis than to future historians: Hitler took all the political credit. Within the government Schacht was increasingly regarded as the architect of recovery—and he would be rewarded handsomely.

On the very same day that the gargantuan rearmament program was approved, the Cabinet gave Schacht carte blanche to announce a further moratorium of Germany's foreign debts. The synchronicity betrays the priorities of both chancellor and central banker: Nazi Germany found money for its rearmament but not for its foreign liabilities. As we have seen, foreign indebtedness had been a key concern of Schacht's in the late 1920s.[77] The debt policy he implemented during his "second coming" amounted to an official repudiation of the Dawes and Young Plans he himself had helped negotiate and was the final nail in the coffin of Stresemann's Atlanticist strategy. So after the failure of the World Economic Conference, Schacht announced that only 50 percent of debt service would be paid in foreign currency, the rest coming in scrip, which through the intervention of his Reichsbank would reduce effective payments by 25 percent.[78] The new vigor in domestic state planning—from work creation to rearmament and labor relations—was therefore matched with newly aggressive foreign economic policy.[79] But how would the world react?

Back in 1923 French and Belgian troops had occupied the Ruhr when the Weimar Republic ceased reparations payments amid hyperinflation.[80] If anything, Germany's debts in 1933 dwarfed those of 1923, since the net decrease in reparations payments in the public sector was more than matched by a rise in private and regional *(Länder)* debts.[81] The French could ill afford a repeat of their response: they had suffered diplomatically and financially a decade earlier. And they lacked British backing.[82] This time around there was no Ruhr occupation. Through Schacht's tactics, Germany's trade partners were divided, lessening their ability to curtail the newfound economic assertiveness.

Despite the British and U.S. devaluations, Hitler was as unwilling as his predecessors to devalue; he associated his reputation with the value of the currency even amid global devaluations. So Schacht found a way to turn his unilateral 1933 "debt moratorium" into a tool to help German foreign trade and have someone else foot the bill.[83] First he sped up short-term debt repayment to present the bleakest possible picture to creditors, a fact that did not go entirely unnoticed abroad.[84] Then, at a conference with international creditors in June 1933, he presented them with a "new system" that, though no one dared call it such, amounted to selective debt default. Indebted German firms would continue to deposit Reichsmarks at the Reichsbank in order to honor their foreign debts, but those accounts would not be freely convertible.[85] Schacht's Reichsbank argued that Germany—low in foreign reserves after having canceled a loan with his brainchild, the BIS, earlier that year—could not afford such capital mobility. Of course the government promised that debts would be converted back to freely movable foreign currency when the balance of payments had recovered, but 1920s current accounts clearly suggested that was not forthcoming. Schacht called it a mere "transfer problem," pretending it did not involve an actual loss for creditors.[86] Beleaguered creditors disagreed. Yet without any credible enforcement mechanisms and a disunited foreign community, Schacht could effectively avoid retaliation.

To be sure, trade protectionism and economic nationalism were on the rise everywhere. But Germany was different: it was increasingly directed from an assertive central bank that centralized economic decision making like never before; indeed it can be argued that Schacht personally engineered many policies to be emulated elsewhere.[87] Following the default and capital controls, newspaper articles began referring to Schacht as the "debt dictator of the Third Reich."[88] It was a well-earned epithet: in order to protect the (nominal) convertibility of the currency and his central bank's paltry reserves, Schacht introduced draconian capital controls. By January 1937 there would be no fewer than seventeen different kinds of Reichsmark accounts, each with its own particular set of allowances and permissions.[89] The new system had bureaucratic consequences: through the new trading schemes, Schacht had constructed the institutional framework that enabled him to adjust the level of German foreign trade down to a product- and producer-specific levels. Expanding far beyond his (already extensive) 1920s powers, this system for import oversight gave the Reichsbank an unprecedented level of control over Germany's trade. Henceforth Schacht could pick winners and make losers. Conveniently for his re-emerging mercantilism, however, Germany's creditors were "free" to use their hostage wealth to purchase industrial goods domestically. This furthered investment into the domestic economy. Nazi Germany's central banker, it was now clear, did not shy away from economic authoritarianism, far less resisted in the 1930s than in the 1920s.

In macroeconomic terms Germany's problem lay at the intersection of foreign trade and foreign exchange. The recovery would only increase the need for foreign raw materials, meaning more imports. Key trading partners like Britain, France, and the Netherlands threatened trade war against Germany in retaliation for the Reichsbank's debt policy. Schacht had been blaming protectionist walls erected across the world for German falling exports since the advent of the Depression.[90] What he omitted was that Germany's exports suffered the consequences of its main partners going off the gold standard and therefore regaining competitiveness, a policy road at least in theory also open to Germany. Fewer exports meant more than sluggish growth and higher spare capacity, particularly in a trade-geared economy like Germany's. Fewer exports also jeopardized the main source of the Reichsbank's foreign reserves: without an improvement of the current account, Germany's foreign reserves situation could not grow.[91]

Yet the regime had to contend with Hitler's convictions on the currency, as well as the cultural legacy of inflation—against which the Nazis had in part built their power.[92] As Brüning has experienced years before, there were marginal benefits to remaining on gold: foreign currency commercial debts were effectively reduced by devaluations elsewhere. Yet that did not affect gold-denominated debts. The much-cited gold coverage ratio that had been at 45 percent in 1930 was at 8.5 percent by December 1933. By June 1934 the situation had reached a critical level: after a large late 1933 redemption, the Reichsbank foreign exchange reserves had plunged to only 100 million Reichsmarks—barely enough to cover a week's worth of imports.

Schacht also expanded a debt buyback operation into the largest buy-back in history to that date; Nazi Germany geared the system to ben-efit its goals.[93] Under Reichsbank direction, German exporters were encouraged to buy distressed German debt in foreign markets and get paid closer to face value within Germany, thus offsetting their uncom-petitive, overvalued exchange rate.[94] Reichsbank-controlled export pro-motion allowed German exporters to effectively mark down their over-priced goods abroad by allowing payment in German debt. This helped reverse the Reichsmark's overvaluation, at least for those sectors with Reichsbank backing. It was also an unprecedented level of economic micromanagement. In this system foreign buyers could purchase German debt trading at approximately a 50 percent discount on face value and use it to pay the face-value cost of (overvalued) German goods. This way the foreign importer partly offset the cost of Germany's overvalued currency, the exporter was able to sell abroad, and the Reichsbank re-tired debt.

German debt traded at a heavy discount in New York when com-pared to Berlin, underscoring a tangible difference of opinion on whether the debt would eventually be paid back.[95] Foreign observers initially dis-trusted Nazi economic management enough to expect an implosion.[96] In this context a German policymaker who knew no full default was forthcoming could therefore repurchase debt and reduce total indebt-edness. Germans were so keen on debt buybacks that some continued until 1944, shortly before Nazi Germany's final downfall. On April 23, 1933, Hitler made clear to his Economic Policy Committee that he did not intend to fully renege on German debts but did intend, through the Reichsbank, to take advantage of the situation. This implied no sudden, full exit from the world economic system as well as support for Schachtian management.[97] The goal was simultaneously debt reduc-tion and export promotion.

Since Schacht's return to the Reichsbank at least some buybacks were carried out in secret. As of 1934 they increasingly focused on sover-eign debt. This furthered the potential advantage from information asymmetry in the market. And it worked best through proxies. A re-tired British official, Lt. Col. Francis Norris, bought so much debt in the autumn of 1933 that the press began calling him "Colonel Law-rence of finance." The Reichsbank denied any connection, but a year later Scotland Yard and the French Sûreté revealed that Norris had acted as a front to fill Nazi Party coffers. None other than Schacht's nephew informed the Bank of England that as much as 300,000 Reichsmarks had been used in this operation, repurchasing 550,000 Reichsmarks of debt. These tricks added to the existing buyback policy. Modern neo-classical economic research suggests that debt buybacks do not represent a transfer from debtor to creditor, but an econometric analysis of Germany's historical experience suggests net gains at the expense of its foreign creditors.[98] Expectations eventually made it into the risk premium of German debt trading abroad, but not before annoying British Prime Minister Ramsay MacDonald. In a "bitter mood about Germany," Mac-Donald complained to the German ambassador that Berlin was talking up default to talk down debt price—only to buy it back on the cheap.[99] The Reichsbank objected. Yet Hitler would eventually vindicate Mac-Donald: years later he gloated in private about the success of the scheme and, in spite of their falling out, credited Schacht for it.[100] To borrow from Keynes's biographer, this use of buybacks was an act of "Schachtian devilry."[101]

Senior economic policymakers, including Economics Secretary Hans Posse and Finance Minister von Krosigk, resisted many of these heterodox, authoritarian turns. Yet Schacht prevailed, supported by the War Ministry and the Wehrmacht. Courtesy of the Nazis' debt dictator, it was the country's creditors that footed the bill for some of its authoritarian monetary innovations.[102] This would help increase exports that, according to foreign observers, had suffered greatly at the expense of inward-looking agricultural policies escalated by the Nazis.[103]

Within Germany another battle dawned. Though far from an advocate for free trade, Schacht was by no means interested in taking the German economy out of what remained of the international trading system. Aggressive and cynical as they were, operations like the Reichsbank's foreign exchange monitoring were designed to help sustain trade, not close off the country entirely. Nonetheless Schacht's vision of global trade had little to do with the laissez-faire tradition of Anglo-Saxon neoclassical economics. It was up to the state and not the market to direct the country's goals when engaging with the outside world. In Schacht's view Germany's fundamental economic strength lay in what he baptized as "reprocessing": turning raw materials, primarily of foreign provenance, into capital goods that could be exported to its global trading partners.[104] This double reliance on foreign trade rendered Germany especially vulnerable to the trade wars, as the Depression had laid bare. The state therefore ought to mediate.

According to Schacht, then, Germany need not be fully cut off from world markets to be powerful; indeed absolute independence would make it impossible to capitalize on the spoils of influence beyond its constrained borders. Yet within the regime there were advocates of full *Autarkie,* the concept of economic self-sufficiency that the *Economist* derided as "the modern nationalistic policy of *a poor thinge but my owne.*"[105] The Depression had also furthered this ideal among right-wing politicians. How exactly this "full autarky" was to be implemented remains opaque, not least because of the dubious economic expertise of those who advocated it. These "theoreticians" maintained close ties to the most racist strands of Nazi ideology, which simplistically argued that a "superior" Germany could not rely on others for sustenance.[106]

In a June 1933 article titled "Principles of German Foreign Trade Policy," Werner Daitz, director of the external trade division in the Party's Foreign Policy Office, defined *autarky* "as the vital right of every people and every nation to set up their economy in such a manner, so that she may be a fort [*Burg*] to them, so that they may not starve and thirst because of trade or monetary politics, or even in the case of war. The extent of [what we mean by] autarky should emerge out of this image."[107] It should come as no surprise that agrarian classes—represented in Party hierarchy by an idologue in charge of the Agriculture Ministry, Walther Darré, and his deputy, Herbert Backe—spearheaded the push toward self-sufficiency.[108] Darré was a leading exponent of *Blut und Boden* racialist ideas, so much so that he had penned a book advocating eugenics to improve the race, combining pseudo-science with romantic nationalism.[109] This telling *Burg* analogy contradicted not only the whole edifice of liberal trade theory but also the British imperial experience with mercantilism that Schacht followed. Darré and Backe were even more extreme than Daitz, as expressed by myriad pamphlets, pseudo-scientific books, and of course the policy of their ministry. Backe had even put his name on a book entitled *The End of Liberalism.*[110] Yet their conception of liberalism's "end" was radically different from Schacht's.

Schacht kept close tabs on the proponents of *Autarkie,* a fact evidenced by the Reichsbank's meticulous account of all press mentions of the word.[111] By 1934 the popularity of the cause had risen to an all-time high; the preceding years of misery were at least partly to blame. When the international system crumbled in the Depression, Germany suffered greatly; for instance, between 1929 and 1932 annual imports of iron ore plummeted from 17,000 tons to under 3,500.[112] The fact that the decline coincided with Brüning's successive deflationary drives—which would have made imported iron ore much more attractive than the lower-quality domestic variant—is a further indication of the German industry's strong dependence on world markets.

Examined from this perspective, it should not come as a surprise that Germany's leaders were looking for every way to reduce foreign dependence. This was fertile ground for the advocates of radical *Autarkie.* At first the Nazi regime promoted a strikingly uneconomic effort to produce substitute raw materials domestically, in effect stretching Germany's lower-quality resources to produce expensive end products. It was not ideal; domestically produced iron ore, for example, contained less than half the iron of the imported material and was far costlier to process. Similarly the extensive research on and development of synthetic fiber and fuel were examples of the power of the autarkic ideals among Nazi leaders.[113] Factions of the Wehrmacht and Göring, a man always eager to expand his responsibilities, also selectively favored it, particularly when thinking of scenarios that involved war. Autarky might have been an economic concept, yet it lay at the heart of a political framework driven by ideology. Its proponents did not advocate immediate closure since the deficiencies in Germany's resource architecture were obvious enough. Going back to Party scripture, Hitler's *Mein Kampf,* these men wanted Germany closed off so that it could concentrate on integrating an appropriate *Lebensraum* ("living space").

Talk of such economic introversion was anathema to Schacht, who, as we have seen, favored a rival conception of foreign influence and empire. Speaking before representatives of the American Chamber of Commerce in Berlin, Schacht warned that Germany's dire financial straits would only embolden autarkists: "Everyone keeps claiming that Germany is turning toward autarky; what we are seeing today vindicates my explanation: it is not Germany who is turning toward autarky, but rather the meaningless debt policy against Germany that forces us into autarky."[114] This was one way of looking at the issue, and a convenient perspective at that; indeed Schacht would routinely repeat these arguments at the U.S. embassy.[115] Yet the logic could be turned around:

"How could it be reasonable for an indebted but export-driven country to attain complete agricultural autarky, preventing the cheaper agricultural commodities traded on the world markets from drastically raising the German living standards?"[116] Despite his extensive powers, Schacht's control of the German economy was limited by intense competition within what has often been described as a polycratic administration.[117]

In the context of these battles within the regime, the "debt dictator" pressed for yet more power. And in mid-1934 Hitler was willing to give it. Chancellery archives suggest that when the Reichsbank president approached Hitler at the height of the foreign exchange crisis, in late June 1934, he sought personal control over the Reich Chamber of Commerce (RWK).[118] The RWK had been created in February 1934 by Schmitt's ministry as a (nominally) independent organization, designed to coordinate the work and provide a venue for corporate conflict resolution.[119] The more liberal Schmitt did not seek the formalization of cartels or their absolute subordination to the state.[120] Even accounting for the fluidity with which Nazis treated institutions, handing over the RWK to the Reichsbank was not straightforward. Appointing the Reichsbank president to run an organization subordinate to the Economics Ministry would only further blur the lines separating monetary and fiscal policies. Faced with the choice, Hitler decided to do away with the lines altogether.[121] At Bayreuth he gave Schacht "acting control" of the ministry. For the next three years, "acting" or not, Schacht's control over the German economy would be second to none.[122] And it would only deepen his centrality in the task of "transforming" Germany.

When discussing the blurred lines between fiscal and monetary policy, in modern days we usually assume that fiscal power takes over monetary affairs, generally to pursue cheaper credit. Yet in Nazi Germany the opposite was true: after years advocating for power and independence at the central bank, Schacht's system involved the central banker taking charge of fiscal matters, delivering an unprecedented level of control. Hence the banker got more than he bargained for at Bayreuth—or more likely that was his goal all along. After all, extreme concentration of power in German politics was in vogue during the summer of 1934. On August 2 the aged president of the Republic, Paul von Hindenburg, passed away. The *Reichskanzler* wasted no time: within an hour of Hindenburg's death, the Chancellery announced plans to do away with the office altogether, transferring all its duties to the Führer and disposing of the last vestiges of legal rule under the Weimar Constitution.[123] Meanwhile, with control over the Ministry, Schacht now had a formal Cabinet position and could interfere directly with businesses to reorient the German economy as he saw fit. His standing was further strengthened by Finance Minister von Krosigk's lack of real power within the Nazi hierarchy.[124]

Upon returning to Berlin Schacht asked one of his more liberal opponents, Secretary Posse, whether he enjoyed music. Puzzled by the question, Posse replied that he was indeed very interested but was no expert on the subject. "Neither am I," replied Schacht in a rare display of humility, soon to be corrected, "but I was at Bayreuth this weekend."[125] The implication was obvious: Schacht had Hitler's ear and Posse did not. When the government announced the fulfillment of Hitler's absolute dictatorship in the office of the Führer, Schacht's appointment to the economics portfolio was the next one on the list. It made the morning papers as an adjunct to the completion of Hitler's *Machtergreifung*— seizure of power. It was a telling sign of the banker's power over German economic affairs.

The *Financial Times* devoted but a short paragraph to the news, stressing that the new "economic dictator" would use his power to focus on the "knotty issues of foreign exchange and imports." Given the crisis, it was an understatement.[126] It goes without saying that not many other than Hitler were addressed as any kind of "dictator" in Nazi Germany. With Schacht's own seizure of power complete, foreign investors gave him the benefit of the doubt: German debt rallied on the appointment.[127] Thereafter the wizard-cum-dictator pressed on with his agenda of domestic centralization and aggressive foreign expansion. He declared that Germany would henceforth be unable to pay even the coupons for the Dawes and Young Plans, previously excluded from the debt moratorium due to their (implicit) preferred status.[128] In an interview with the *New York Times,* providing further details about this new affront to international creditors, Schacht described how economic decisions were now taken in Nazi Germany: "We handle all matters within my province as director of the economic life of Germany, right in my office—all matters that pertain to trade, industry, commerce, and banking." Only with regard to labor did Schacht admit to "confer[ring] with the [Labor]

Minister."[129] Finance Minister von Krosigk was nowhere to be seen. And the "acting" economics minister did not sound at all temporary.

Not for the last time, increased efficiency was the nominal justification for dictatorship. Yet Schacht's statements betray a particular distaste for plural decision making: "Everything works very smoothly and speedily [in Germany], much more than when we had politicians talking about everything under the sun and knowing little or nothing about anything, as we had here in the days of the old *Reichstag*." This allowed Schacht to nonchalantly declare Germany the "most democratic country in the world." When the *Times* asked for his thoughts on economic freedom, the banker—outwardly still a liberal, if tempered by pragmatism—became philosophical: "Economic freedom is abuse."[130] He could have added that his personal control was better.

Publicly Schacht justified centralization as an operational necessity rather than the ultimate objective of his designs. Even twenty years later he would justify his "system" as the only way for Germany to "go on" amid the shipwreck of globalization.[131] But unprecedented success and power further exacerbated authoritarian managerial tendencies that, as we have seen, were there all along. From the ministry the Reichsbank president developed a comprehensive system of state control over imports that depended on his staff; his excuse was that the state needed information to prioritize the "right" imports so as to avoid squandering limited foreign exchange.[132] Although Schacht was by no means the only individual in the Nazi hierarchy who determined import prioritization—with the Wehrmacht steadily rising in prominence— he was at the heart of the system, both by design and by execution. Indeed when foreign countries complained, they had to approach him—and nobody else.[133]

A new Reich bureaucracy with extensive access to business information developed executive power over foreign trade, in so doing altering the type of information businesses shared with government. These changes originated in tendencies started during the Great War and, to an extent, continued in the Weimar era.[134] Domestically an all-powerful Schacht deepened state oversight of industrial groups, cartels, and companies—all forced to register under this new system of government-controlled statistical reporting.[135] In the Third Reich, it was now clear, not all imports were created equal. The selective squeeze that followed hurt consumer products the most, threatening the recovery in civilian sectors such as textiles and small manufactures. Imports for expenditures held on, chiefly insofar as they were attached to armaments and select heavy industries such as IG Farben's synthetic fabrics and fuel programs, favorites among *Autarkie*-loving ministers.[136] It should have come as no surprise: Schacht's system was modeled on war management plans enacted during World War I to sustain the war effort in the midst of the effective Anglo-American naval blockade.[137] This was yet another case of Schacht "innovating" in the sense of taking up an existing program and refitting it to his authoritarian needs.

Eventually these policies were baptized Neue Plan (New Plan). Yet in stark contrast to Roosevelt's New Deal, Germany's priorities lay not in civilian development but rather in rearmament, which, I have shown, was at the heart of the recovery.[138] The Neue Plan was Schacht's brainchild. From his perspective it made sense: only from a position of relative strength could Germany achieve a change in its point of engagement with other powers. In the trade balance the policy worked: in 1935, 1936, and even 1937 Germany posted (small) surpluses that would have been unthinkable only years before. Much of this was due to the selective curtailment of imports, but Schacht's export promotion mattered significantly.[139] The balance of payments, of course, was another matter.

Stresemann's Atlanticist strategy was long gone in the foreign sphere. The idea of trading with those to whom Germany owed war debts in the hope that they would eventually come to appreciate the unsustainability of the Versailles system did not survive long in the Nazi era, though, as we have seen, a shift had been in the making—in no small part due to Schacht—since the late Weimar years. The Depression radically changed the foreign economic landscape. It can be argued that Schacht implemented an "anti-Atlanticist strategy." Having ceased foreign debt payments, Germany sought decoupling from its main trade partners. So Schacht's authoritarian system led to a considerable reorientation of German trade.

The message for mass consumption was different. In his August 1934 *New York Times* interview, Schacht had argued that, in trade terms, the ball was in the Americans' court: "It is up to the United States to see what can be done to promote the purchase of more German goods." At a time when the devaluation of the dollar made German imports hopelessly overvalued, what would happen if German exports to America did not grow substantially? "If the United States does not buy more, we will see to it that she sells us less."[140] Such trade controls led to a diversion of trade away from Britain and the United States, at a time when the British were increasing their regional trade with the Dominions through the imperial preference system and the U.S. protectionist withdrawal behind the devaluing dollar was still the only game in Washington.

The economic benefits of following this neo-*Weltpolitik* strategy could always be offset by political complications; they therefore required swift and decisive foreign economic diplomacy. First Schacht signed bilateral deals with the Dutch and Swiss, both of whom depended heavily on German industrial supplies but were also large export markets for Germany.[141] Then, and against all odds, he successfully persuaded Britain, his former ally in the heyday of cooperation with Norman's Bank of England, to abandon the united front with Washington over defaulted German debts. In a move that managed to outrage both politicians in Washington and financiers in New York, in 1934 Schacht secured a Payments Agreement with London that boosted German exports to the empire. For a time at least the United States was left alone in its opposition to Schachtian foreign economic policy.[142]

Seen from London—particularly from Threadneedle Street, the Bank of England's historic home—Schacht seemed far more preferable than the racialist, autarkic elements in the Nazi regime.[143] Meanwhile the banker's aggressive offensive continued. His staff brokered agreements with countries in the Balkans and Latin America to replace the sources of raw materials no longer purchased from Britain's empire.[144] As less developed countries promised Germany goods for its industries in exchange for its industrial produce, Schacht saw trade "decoupling" from the democracies as Germany's best way forward. The banker's finest biographer essentially agrees on this point; he goes so far as to call this strategy in the corners of Europe an "informal empire," adding that they could make Germany "embargo-secure" in the event of world war.[145]

Contemporary Anglo-Saxon commentators certainly noticed the imperial strand in Schacht's policy, but the democracies stood paralyzed as Germany made forays into the Balkans, striking deals to circumvent both the precarious state of Reichsbank finances and the marginality of the Reichsmark in the global financial system.[146] Undercutting its competitors, Germany offered discounts of as much as 50 percent below cash prices for (nominally overpriced) manufactured goods, provided the less developed countries were willing to pay for them in raw materials. Given the fresh memory of an international financial system crippled by currency and tariff wars, the local regimes were happy to oblige. This neomercantilist barter allowed manufactures to be exported to new destinations to replace old markets, while taking clear advantage of Germany's rising political clout. This was the essence of neo-*Weltpolitik*.

Yet the historiography has been short-sighted in limiting the application of this strategy to the Balkans.[147] Schacht's strategy was global in scope, even if it was adopted most readily in the less developed corners of Europe. A further instance that illuminates the alternative international trade sphere Schacht was seeking to create was the case of Brazil. The authoritarian government in Rio took advantage of its renewed trade ties with Germany to default on its foreign debt and release itself from FDR's vision of hemispheric free trade. Getúlio Vargas's administration would even attempt weapons purchases from Nazi Germany.[148] One could hardly get more disrespectful to the American Monroe Doctrine, and such policy was possible only because of close ties with resurgent Berlin. It was a point not lost on Secretary of State Cordell Hull, in those days the lone gunman of trade liberalism in the Roosevelt administration. Hull would seek to reverse the relative loss of U.S. influence through the 1934 Reciprocal Trade Agreements Acts.[149]

In its simplest terms, therefore, Schacht's overarching goal was to continue state-directed domestic growth while diverting German trade toward less powerful countries that could serve as markets for industrial output and a steady source of raw materials. This way he could circumvent powerful former trade partners and expand Germany's economic clout even while lacking formal cronies. Developing countries would come into Germany's trade sphere on terms far more beneficial to the Third Reich than to its developed rivals, whether it was the United States with its internal empire or Britain with its formal one. And there would be no question about Germany's now defaulted foreign debts. With "frankness bordering on cynicism which is characteristic of him," Schacht told the American Chamber of Commerce, "If Germany does not pay her foreign debts, she will not lose credit for that. . . . If I were permitted to compare small things with large ones, I might recall that Latin America was found worthy of credit after three or four successive failures."[150]

At a time when, as we shall see, Nazi Germany's first foreign military foray—the Spanish Civil War—was becoming an increasingly economic endeavor, Schacht was touring the Balkans to announce the wonders of his policies for the beleaguered region. In Belgrade he talked about the attractive symbiosis between German industry and the European periphery, and how it would (eventually) help develop the latter. "It would be quite wrong for the industrial states to set themselves against gradual industrialization of the agrarian countries," he said while trying to ingratiate himself with his audience. "The nature of agrarian exports would gradually change," he added, suggesting the progressive industrialization of the European periphery.[151]

Regardless of whether such a bright future materialized, in the meantime the primary production from the periphery would be safest if placed within the German economic sphere. What is more, political trends seemed to favor Schacht's strategies: "With a Radical Cabinet now ruling France," wrote a reporter for *Time* magazine in an article about German trade, "conservative or reactionary Balkan regimes look increasingly to Berlin." Ultimately "French heavy industry, which used to have Yugoslavia economically in its pocket, is gradually being frozen out."[152] Across the world other ambitious powers such as Japan emulated Schacht's strategies. If not the sole innovator, therefore, Schacht was the most successful exponent of this strategy—and with power over monetary and fiscal affairs he was at the very center of German economic policymaking.[153]

Government control under the "economic dictator" rose hand in hand with the relative importance of armaments in the German "economic boom." Although some scholars have called 1935–1936 "the respectable years" of the Nazi dictatorship, the relative importance of rearmament in the recovery only grew during the period.[154] And it did so considerably: between 1935 and 1938 armaments accounted for almost half of output growth, meaning it was crucial to lowering Germany's rate of unemployment. The original 1933 rearmament budget was greatly expanded between 1934 and 1936, to the benefit of Göring's Luftwaffe and Adm. Erich Raeder's Kriegsmarine. By choice or necessity, such was the quid pro quo in Schacht's bid for power.

In mid-1935, defying all estimates of what was economically possible for Germany, Hitler announced that the peacetime Wehrmacht would now have fully mechanized divisions featuring the state-of-the-art Panzer to follow the dictums of Heinz Guderian's "fast warfare" tactics.[155] The fundamental revision of the Versailles system continued unhindered between the collapse of internationalism on the one hand and the rise of appeasement on the other—facilitated by "Schachtian economics."[156] Germany would reengage the world from a position of power, but not necessarily one of isolation.

Although authoritarian control over the economy could ensure efficient use of scarce foreign exchange and international lobbying helped reorient foreign trade, a permanent supply of raw materials still eluded Schacht. German resource scarcity had been a structural feature of the Versailles system.[157] For a manufacturing behemoth without its own high-quality raw materials, a reliable and efficient global trade system was essential not just for growth but for the mere maintenance of living standards. Even before joining Hitler, Schacht had argued that this feature of the Versailles system all but assured a German backlash; the question was not *if,* but *when.* Now he was at the heart of such a reaction. As he put it to the Leipzig Spring Fair in 1935, "It is an error to speak of exact methods and immutable laws in economics. The economist must make possible what seems impossible."[158] Schacht was using his training and expertise at the service of Hitler's goals.

Yet a wider continental war was not necessarily the solution to Germany's shortage of raw materials—or so Schacht argued. He had been reorienting German trade not only to supply German industry with much-needed raw materials—everything from foodstuffs to compensate for inefficient agriculture to heavy industrial minerals to sustain industrial production—but also to exchange German industrial produce, underwritten by leverage Germany simply lacked in dealing with Britain or the United States. The ultimate rationale for this strategy was the increase of Germany's foreign power, which Schacht was knowingly funding through unprecedented military spending.

If Germany sought to challenge a Versailles system underwritten by Britain, France, and—effectively if not formally—the United States, it could not do so while depending on the United States and Britain for key imports and export markets. Throughout Schacht's career his vision of empire, as we have seen, was driven by an economic rationale.

As we have seen, this student of British mercantilism cared little about formal sovereignty. Rather the point of colonies in the post-1929 world was to procure raw materials without furthering dependence on trading partners via foreign exchange. This would solve the drain on reserves. At the very least, import growth would be kept in check. And in so doing Germany would create a "virtuous cycle" in foreign policy: projecting influence would further economic advantage, opening more markets and conferring it "power status," that unattainable goal in the Weimar years.

At the height of his power Schacht returned to the issue of colonies in ways far more tactful than Hugenberg. The central banker had been focused on the issue since well before the advent of the Nazis. Throughout he remained one of the most vocal advocates of returning Germany to its colonial "status"—so vocal that the issue had arguably cost him the Reichsbank once before.[159] Schacht seems to have had a more active role in economic foreign policy than the current historiography acknowledges.[160] The archival record suggests he was actively pursuing colonial policies from within the Party machine. In early 1935, at the zenith of his power, the official technically responsible for colonial policy, Gen. Franz Ritter von Epp, asked none other than the "economic dictator" to produce an economic policy paper in support of Germany's claims to colonies.[161] Schacht was more than happy to oblige. He penned a four-page paper supporting the view that colonies were the only way for Germany to achieve reliable access to raw materials without sacrificing its foreign exchange, meaning that these colonies would be brought within Germany's economic sphere, allowing either for barter or the circulation of German currency there. Interestingly Schacht attached a copy to a personal letter directed to the Führer, presumably to remind him of the significance of the issue. This is all the more surprising because Schacht's paper attacked the *Lebensraum* policy framework directly, a tenant of Hitler's *Mein Kampf,* claiming it would be "politically impossible" for Germany to expand to the east and displace the local populations.[162] Schacht's informal or economic imperialism, however, offered an alternative. The challenge helps delineate the sharp political rift between Schacht's vision for Germany as a more traditional imperial power, a neo-*Weltpolitik* strategy that would have been familiar to Wilhelmine imperialists, and the more radical combination of autarky, racial ideology, and pseudo-anthropology that was to underscore Germany's *Lebensraum* and its "drive to the East."

A Party policy paper published in 1934 further highlights this contrast. Simply titled "Colonies" and—importantly—signed by Hitler himself, the document was intended to instruct lower level party members of the party line on the issue of colonial expansion. Its trumpeting of *Lebensraum* politics could not have been starker: "More important than the importation of overseas products [from colonies] is the ability to feed the German people in Central Europe from their own ground and soil [*Grund und Boden*]."[163] In attacking such Party principles, Schacht was leading the way in believing, like other pragmatic Nazis and international observers, that when the Party's more dramatic ideological overtures clashed with economic feasibility, the latter would prevail. Had that not been the outcome before? Eventually Schacht was vindicated.[164] On March 28, 1935, the Führer acknowledged receipt of the paper with gratitude, while instructing his office to forward the letter to the Ministry of Propaganda, addressed to Secretary Funk, a rising character who none other than Schacht had introduced to Hitler.[165]

The policy battle within Hitler's Cabinet would go on, but until the late summer of 1936 it looked as if Schacht had prevailed—and decisively so. His justifications for Germany's return to colonial status as a worthy price to pay for peace in Europe found their way into policy well beyond his "dual mandate" at the Reichsbank and Economics Ministry. In fact they made it as far as the lectern of the ambassador to England, Joachim von Ribbentrop, who, despite his extreme views in other areas of policy, delivered a speech in December 1936 to the Anglo-German Fellowship on the issue. Its title succinctly summarizes the argument: "A Reasonable Colonial Solution Lies in Everyone's Interest: Germany Does Not Wish to Pursue Full Autarky." Ribbentrop essentially parroted arguments underwritten by the Schachtian economic framework being implemented back home.[166] *Lebensraum*, it follows, was not the preordained path of Nazi rule. In fact by the beginning of 1936 it was neo-*Weltpolitik*—as pushed and advocated by the "economic dictator" above all others—that dictated policy.

Colonies were not merely about acquiring raw materials without sacrificing foreign exchange in an age of protectionism. The symbiotic relationship between Germany and less developed countries had to go both ways: the developing country would have to generate demand for the goods the German economic rebound was producing. Problematically, much of Nazi Germany's new output was in the form of rearmament, a traditionally nonexport sector. As we have seen, the relative importance of rearmament in economic activity had grown significantly since 1933, a policy that Schacht underwrote. So Germany's economy was increasingly reliant on an industry that required foreign exchange to procure raw materials but failed to return it by exporting final products. It could therefore hardly be self-sufficient. The result was a progressive deterioration in Germany's overall terms of trade, indeed one that made the country's trade position unsustainable in the long term. In short, rearmament delivered jobs, but it could not deliver long-term stabilization without exports. Could it then force an eventual reordering of priorities?

Granted, it was Schacht who approved and funded Hitler's first rearmament plan, yet these plans had been revised upward repeatedly since. Other European governments had also moved to achieve full employment by similar means, providing further justifications for more armaments expenditure. By 1935 the 4.3 billion Reichsmark allocation that Schacht had agreed to finance only a year before had already been exceeded by at least 20 percent.[167] Escalation was to continue. Perhaps the most striking case is that of aircraft production. In the words of one Luftwaffe historian, the industry was "a child of the Nazis."[168] Technically Hermann Göring but more realistically bureaucratic mastermind Secretary Erhard Milch oversaw what can only be described as an explosion of German plane production: while the sector represented 0.2 percent of domestic GDP in 1933, it had risen to 1.6 percent by 1936.[169] It had grown by a factor of 8.

Around the time when Hitler decided to intervene in the Spanish Civil War, Germany's aircraft industry overtook automobiles in terms of total labor input. It employed 124,878 workers, a figure that rose rapidly from quarter to quarter.[170] It was almost entirely state-supported. In fact at times the Air Ministry took charge directly: Milch did not hesitate to remove Hugo Junkers from the direction of his eponymous company when they disagreed.[171] Around this time Willy Messerschmitt designed the impressive but costly Messerschmitt Bf 109 fighter. Even though he was also on bad terms with Milch, the design was so good that it won the ministry's prize in 1936; so infatuated was the Führer that he immediately ordered it into mass production.[172] So when Hitler announced a "new" Luftwaffe in 1936, over eight hundred new warplanes were already on active duty, a figure far beyond anything even the most war-mongering nationalist could have dreamed of before 1933.

By mid-1936 and in spite of Schacht's careful balancing, it was clear that such feverish rearmament could not be sustained forever, lest it completely destroy the careful economic rebalancing. To be sure, German industry was not facing an imminent growth crisis: every branch of the Wehrmacht could be relied upon for ever-increasing expansion. But the strain on both the government books and the Reichsbank's foreign exchange reserves was severe. Something had to give. Weaponry could do little to strengthen the country's export position within what remained of the international trade system. A Germany openly exporting weapons to its few allies was not practicable. Thus Schacht was stuck with a structural net importer as the economy's prime growth sector; before long he would need to reconcile the regime's persistence of rearmament with the realities of economic management. The produce of Hitler's Sparta would have to pay for itself.

All in all, economic policy in the first years of Nazism was built on a cyclical rebound that predated the regime and went on to achieve full employment. Yet the recovery remained heavily dependent on armaments at the expense of consumer sectors, including some traditional pillars of the German economy. Both internally, through authoritarian control, and externally, under the Neue Plan and the import-oversight system, the German economy was becoming increasingly state-sponsored and state-directed. Hjalmar Schacht was at the core of this process; indeed, as of 1934, and in terms of all monetary policy, trade strategy, and microeconomic management, Schacht was the main architect of the economic transformation of Germany.

Once in a position of strength, Schacht believed, a formidable Germany could capitalize on trade on its own terms. For their part Germany's competitors did not offer a united front against Schacht's second coming, thereby allowing his policies unprecedented success. Germany's new economic policy broke decidedly with the Atlanticist strategy of the Weimar era, seeking to return to a neo-*Weltpolitik* strategy. Schacht was certainly not the only neomercantilist in power in the Great Depression, yet it is hard to argue that he was not the most effective. His Germany was able to get away with such policies in the context of a lack of international coordination and cooperation. Of course causality could be argued the other way around, as he himself would later do: it was the international context that "forced" these policies onto Germany. Yet Schacht's second coming did not change the nature of his policies; their authoritarian direction and the projection of foreign economic power fit the banker's intellectual upbringing, work experience, long-term policy advocacy, and increasingly nationalistic tone.

In a way Schacht deserved his "wizard" *(Zauberer)* nickname: he had managed the alchemy of domestic industrial recovery, export promotion, import controls, and the continued avoidance of devaluation—to the benefit of Germany's dictator, an economically illiterate man with whom he found unprecedented favor. What is more, the trade deals Schacht brokered allowed Germany to acquire raw materials without sacrificing the little foreign exchange it had available. This found a way out of the 1934 crisis that had almost literally claimed the life of his predecessor. Schacht's pragmatism therefore allowed the Reichsbank to survive with radically fewer reserves than had been possible before. Perhaps the historiographic focus on the latter years of the Nazi economy as well as Schacht's defense at Nuremberg has helped obscure the centrality of Schachtian power. But if nothing else, Germany four years on from Hitler's accession to power was a radically different nation—and economically much of this had to do with the Führer's "economic dictator."

A few months after the remilitarization of the Ruhr and with appeasement on the rise in London and Paris, Hitler's increasingly self-assured regime embarked on its first foreign military adventure. Within months it would morph from a small-scope military project into a fully fledged colonial endeavor. Within the Schachtian economic system, it was crucial for Germany to find trading partners with abundant raw materials and in relative economic backwardness to complement a domestic economy running close to capacity but perennially short of inputs. Such partners would ideally be in need of the type of output Germany was so bent on producing at a time when the Nazi regime was not putting them to use. Sheer need could then allow for the fundamental goal of informal empire: allowing Germany to dictate the terms of its economic relationships. Where could that be achieved in mid-1936?

Hjalmar Schacht (left) during the German occupation of Belgium in World War I, working under Dr. Karl von Lumm (center), April 1915. Bundesarchiv.

A line outside a Berlin grocery store during the Weimar Republic's hyperinflation, 1923. Bundesarchiv.

Young Plan negotiations in 1924 in Berlin, featuring Reichsbank President Schacht (left), German Reparations International Commission member Owen D. Young (center), and Britain's Sir Robert Kindersley, February 1924. Bundesarchiv.

Schacht and the foundation stone for the new Reichsbank, May 5, 1934. Today the building is part of the Auswärtiges Amt, Germany's Foreign Office. Bundesarchiv.

Hitler and Schacht together at the ceremony laying the foundation of the new Reichsbank building, May 5, 1934. Bundesarchiv.

Economics minister and Reichsbank President Schacht speaks during a 1936 election rally at the bank, under a banner reading, "The Reichsbank stands firmly behind the Führer!" March 28, 1936. Bundesarchiv.

Tired Nationalist troops in harsh winter weather during the Battle of Guadalajara, a high point of the Republican Civil War effort, March 1937. Bundesarchiv.

Children walk among the Francoist troops occupying Bilbao in the resource-rich Basques after the city's capitulation, August 1937. Bundesarchiv.

Hermann Göring breaks ground at his steel conglomerate's operations in Hitler's home town, Linz, less than two months after the Anschluß, May 1938. Bundesarchiv.

Hitler meets Axis partner Benito Mussolini and Italian Foreign Minister Count Galeazzo Ciano at the Munich station, along with Hermann Göring and Heinrich Himmler, September 29, 1938. Bundesarchiv.

German air troops from the Condor Legion in northern Spain with a Messerschmitt plane amid Nationalist forces, 1939. Bundesarchiv.

After Franco's victory, German troops head for ships in the Spanish port of Vigo to return to Nazi Germany, May 1939. Bundesarchiv.

Hitler welcomes the Condor Legion with a parade next to its commander, Gen. Wolfram von Richthofen, and the Wehrmacht leadership, including Air Minister Hermann Göring, Adm. Erich Raeder, Gen. Walter von Brauchitsch, Wilhelm Keitel, and State Secretary Erhard Milch, June 1939. Bundesarchiv.

Hitler meets Francisco Franco at their only in-person meeting in Hendaye, France, October 1940. Bundesarchiv

Schacht imprisoned before the Nuremberg trials, 1945. Bundesarchiv.

chapter five

DAWN OF INTERVENTION

Colonies are necessary to Germany. We shall get them through
negotiation, if possible; but if not, we shall take them.

—HJALMAR SCHACHT, U.S. Embassy in Berlin, September 23, 1935

By most measures Hitler's supper on July 7, 1942, was nothing special.
It was served late, and the menu was characteristically spartan. The
Führer enjoyed his afternoon sweet cakes but reserved scant
military rations for supper, a display of humility that usually went
unnoticed by the more pompous Party leadership.[1] His guests went
along; being invited to share the table with the most powerful man in
Europe was a rare honor, even if not all in the Nazi establishment
enjoyed the exercise in sycophancy it usually involved.[2] The guest list
that evening featured military heavyweights: the head of the Supreme
Command of the Armed Forces, Wilhelm Keitel; his aristocratic
deputy, Alfred Jodl; the head of military intelligence (Abwehr), Wilhelm Canaris; and Ambassador Walther Hewel.[3] It was a predictable
lineup; Nazi Germany was then trying to defend the continental
hegemony that Blitzkrieg had delivered. Perhaps victory did not yet
seem unattainable to those who shared Hitler's table, but the balance
of forces was already unequivocal: Germany was pitted against Britain
and its empire, Soviet Russia, and, ever since Pearl Harbor, the United
States.[4]

Most crucially, the Eastern Front had turned. Unsurprisingly this was
the preeminent topic of discussion in those days, the greatest vulnera-
bility of Hitler's new political construct: Großdeutschland—Greater

Germany. Across a front that spanned hundreds of miles, the previous few weeks had been dismal for Nazi Germany. Field Marshall Wilhelm List failed to make progress against a larger, better-equipped Red Army. An enraged Hitler had since begun exercising his "leader prerogative" (*Führerprinzip),* which effectively meant personally calling even the smallest tactical shots of the eastern campaign.[5] This caused consternation among Wehrmacht men like Keitel and Jodl; yet it was but the latest step in a decade-long process of concentration of power that ultimately engulfed the military establishment that had once encouraged it.[6]

That evening Hitler's mind drifted from the East. Before dinner he had delivered a long diatribe about archaeology and deforestation.[7] Like most of Hitler's repetitive tirades, it would not have surprised a close reader of *Mein Kampf.*[8] Though at the time he was responsible for the most vicious exercise in empire building since Genghis Khan—including a genocide perpetrated on an industrial scale—Hitler was bent on discussing the "cultural degeneration" that "start[ing] to cut down trees without provisions for reforestation" led to.[9] He also decried the excavations going on all around Germany in search of pre-Christian Aryan symbols—a pet project of racialist ideologues like Walther Darré and SS supremo Heinrich Himmler. For his part, Hitler could not "help remembering that, while our [German] ancestors were making these vessels of stone and clay, over which our archeologists rave, the Greeks had already built the Acropolis."[10]

Hitler then steered conversation toward Spain. A former ambassador to Franco's Spain, Hewel, dwelled on how horribly poor Spain remained three years after the Civil War ended. He cited Franco's soldiers without guns or rank badges. Keitel continued in the same vein: he hypothesized that Hitler's honor guard during his meeting with Franco in Hendaye had been equipped with weapons so rusty they could have served only for show.[11] The entourage knew how to please their host. It was common knowledge in the Nazi hierarchy that Hitler had never forgiven Franco for failing to involve Spain militarily in the war, back when it seemed all but won.[12]

While others mocked Spain, Canaris remained silent. He could remember better times.[13] He was the only dinner guest who (allegedly) had also been present on another evening devoted to Iberian affairs, July 25, 1936, when, at Bayreuth and in the aftermath of a stirring *Siegfried,* Hitler decided to intervene in the Spanish Civil War.[14] The decisions of that momentous day all but determined the fate of the Spanish Republic; six years hence, in the throes of the world war, only disappointment remained. "Franco and company can consider themselves very lucky to have received the help of Fascist Italy and Germany in their first civil war," Hitler reasoned. "For, as the Red [Republicans] Spaniards never cease explaining, they had not entered into cooperation with the Soviets on ideological grounds, but had rather been forced into it . . . simply through lack of other support."[15] It was an astute observation that fits the evidence.[16] His central point was about something else.[17] "One thing is quite certain," he continued, "people speak of an intervention from Heaven which decided the civil war in favor of Franco. Perhaps so—but it was not an intervention on the part of the madam-styled Mother of God . . . , but the intervention of [Legion Condor chief of staff] General von Richthofen and the bombs his squadrons rained from the heavens that decided the issue."[18]

Blasphemy aside, who could disagree with the Führer? Though never in steady flows, men and supplies from Nazi Germany arrived at key times during Spain's war, first to prevent an early Nationalist collapse and then to drive them to victory. German intervention facilitated the transport of Franco's men in Morocco, including the Foreign Legion and the Army of Africa, in late July and early August 1936, and the key 1937 offensive against the Basques, whose effects on Guernica were immortalized by Picasso, and ensured the success of the final onslaught against Catalonia in early 1939. All in all, between ten thousand and fifteen thousand men sported Nazi swastikas on Iberian soil.[19] Even more significant was the supply of war matériel: around 150 state-of-the-art Messerschmitt 109s fighters, 63 Junkers Ju52 bombers, 125 Heinkel He51s, and 93 Heinkel He111s entered into combat in the skies over Spain, along with two hundred tanks and over a thousand artillery pieces, most crucially the celebrated 88mm anti-aerial gun. To anyone acquainted with World War II figures that count planes in the thousands and soldiers—as well as casualties—in the millions, these numbers may seem modest.[20] Yet to illustrate their importance in the Spanish theater of war, suffice to remember that when civil war broke out, there were around four hundred working airplanes in the whole country, most over a decade old and only a handful fit for military purposes. Spain was ill-prepared for any war, least of all one with itself.[21]

In the context of such backwardness, Nazi supplies of weapons and men, combined with the more numerous but usually less effective Italian supplies, were decisive to the outcome of the Spanish Civil War. Perhaps more important for our purposes, those amounts of weapons were also sizable for the Third Reich to provide to an essentially broke Franco at a time when the German economy remained far from its pre-Depression trend output.[22] Seventy years of historiography support the view that these supplies were decisive. Yet a more essential question emerges: What was Nazi Germany's motivation to deliver Franco's victory "from the heavens"?

Answering that question requires bringing together the two hitherto distinct narratives of this study: Spain's path to civil war and Nazi Germany's road to recovery under the stewardship of Germany's "economic dictator." Now that we are better acquainted with the economic and political situation in Germany in mid-1936, let us go back to the genesis of Nazi intervention. Franco's two emissaries to Hitler, Adolf Langenheim and Johannes Bernhardt, were fortunate. Though the Wagner festival at Bayreuth was always a highlight in Hitler's calendar, 1936 was special: it was not only the festival's sixtieth anniversary but also the fiftieth anniversary of King Ludwig II's death. To mark the occasion Hitler personally funded a new production of *Lohengrin,* an opera in which Wagner has Heinrich utter, "Now it is time, to defend the honor of the Reich." It was after *Siegfried,* however, that Hitler met Franco's emissaries.

Although there is still debate about who said what, it is possible to reconstruct not only Hitler's ultimate decision but also much of what was discussed.[23] If he was indeed there, Canaris knew Spain better than anyone in the room, Franco's emissaries included.[24] Perhaps there was another admiral present, but Canaris's inclusion would have made sense. Some sources suggest someone mentioned the possibility of bases in the Mediterranean, an idea Canaris devised during his many trips to Spain.[25] We know it was a key Italian goal and British concern, both in the Cabinet and the Royal Navy, throughout the conflict.[26] Göring would later testify at Nuremberg, "[I] urged [Hitler] to give support under all circumstances: firstly, to prevent the further spread of communism; secondly, to test my young *Luftwaffe.*"[27] This statement would dominate the historiography of intervention for decades. Yet other sources suggest that Göring was cautious at first.[28] Göring's chief preoccupation at Nuremberg was to preserve his self-aggrandizement for posterity. Beyond that the "anti-Communist" key in Nazi foreign policy was not fully developed in July 1936; it would grow in the coming months as the Axis with Mussolini strengthened. Others have argued that the move was a "logical" extension of Hitler's "quest for *Lebensraum*," but such a view is problematic inasmuch as Spain was not only not part of the ideological construct, but also, as we have seen, foreign policy seemed tilted toward *Weltpolitik* over *Lebensraum* objectives.[29]

War Minister von Blomberg seems to have agreed with Foreign Minister von Neurath's careful approach, a stance immortalized by the Wilhelmstraße memoranda Hitler chose to ignore.[30] The German legation in Madrid had sent a confidential report earlier that day predicting the rebellion would fail within days, if not hours.[31] It also argued that a Republican victory would all but assure an alliance with Russia, as well as further strengthening Prime Minister Blum of France.[32] This dispatch's conclusion is very likely to have reached Hitler, who had been briefed on the situation. Von Neurath's course of action was characteristic of his conservative bent and would have produced a foreign policy reaction similar to Britain's. Finally, given the speed with which matters surrounding economic exchange developed in the following hours, one could infer that someone, most likely Bernhardt, mentioned potential compensation for the matériel Franco had requested.[33] We do know that in spite of his business failures in the previous decade, Bernhardt was well acquainted with the import-export business. Ultimately a decision was made: "Support for the Generalissimo was agreed on in principle."[34] Thus began the Third Reich's first foreign military adventure.[35]

Wagner's grandiosity permeated Hitler's generosity: he provided Franco with more supplies than he had originally requested, including around twenty Junkers Ju52 transporters, six Heinkel He51S fighters, and artillery. This turned out to be the only initial shipment. In a move that almost drove the Spanish coup's main architect, Director Mola, to suicide, Hitler also decided German supplies would be sent to Franco, and no other leader. At best this ignored the military junta created under the leadership of Gen. Miguel Cabanellas hours earlier; Mola was part of it, but Franco was not.[36] It hardly mattered—and it is safe to assume Bernhardt and Langenheim had some sort of impact on this choice.

Hitler therefore immediately and irrevocably altered the internal dynamics of Nationalist leadership against the likes of Mola, Cabanellas, and Gonzalo Queipo de Llano, the eccentric rebel commander of Seville.[37] Ju52s were to be found airlifting Nationalist troops from Morocco as early as July 29. These were nothing short of crucial for Franco to overcome a Republican naval blockade weakened by internal rifts.[38]

Erhard Milch noted in a diary entry on July 26 that a special unit, code-named "W," had been created within the Luftwaffe to oversee the dispatch of war matériel and "volunteers" to Spain.[39] It is worth noting that Germans fighting in Spain would receive payment from the German government, never directly from Franco. In contrast, Franco would pay most of Italian soldiers' wages. Yet this was not just a state affair: upon returning to Morocco, Bernhardt set up a private company in Tetuán on July 31. The Compañía Hispano-Marroquí de Transportes (HISMA), approved by the local consul, was to be owned by Bernhardt and a former navy commander, Fernando Carranza, on Franco's behalf.[40] Ipso facto, Bernhardt would be in control as the preeminent Nazi representative for the duration of the Civil War. The humble company with scant starting capital would soon seek to monopolize transfers from Spain to Germany.[41] A few months later a complementary company was registered in Berlin, the Raw Material and Goods Buying Company (Rohstoffe-und-Waren-Einkaufsgesellschaft, ROWAK); its goal was to purchase from German private firms and export into Spain through HISMA. The lack of formal complaints from the Nazi economic hierarchy—which at the time responded to Schacht—at the very least suggests the setup was contemplated and likely agreed to in Bayreuth.

This system would quickly evolve into an effective dual monopoly on both sides of the trading relationship. It was a type of organization that fully fit the idea of privileged national champions expanding German economic influence abroad. Within the state-overseen structure of Schachtian industrial activity, ROWAK acted as a conglomerate of individual producers who, under bureaucratic control, colluded to export to Franco's Spain.[42] This was precisely the same structure introduced by Schmitt but radically reorganized by Schacht since his takeover of the Economics Ministry in 1934. An October 1936 memorandum by the head of the German Foreign Ministry Economic Policy

Department explained the system neatly: "Both companies have a monopoly of purchases and sales. If, for example, a German exporter wishes to deliver to Spain, he has to sell to ROWAK, which then resells to HISMA. [Von Krosigk's] Finance Ministry has extended ROWAK a credit of 3M *Reichsmarks* to start off. HISMA is said to have obtained Spanish credits."[43] Credit creation, along with special terms of trade and hefty commissions, followed suit. Though meager, those initial loans kicked off a new, radically different bilateral relationship between Germany and Spain than had previously existed.[44]

Hitler—and the world—learned about Mussolini's support for Franco through media reports detailing the destiny of crashed Savoia planes on the way to Morocco.[45] On July 30 the Führer dispatched Admiral Canaris to Rome to discuss Iberian intervention; this further suggests Canaris's close involvement in the project.[46] Hitler wanted coordination with Rome; this would be the first of many trips by Canaris in another growing bilateral relationship. Although Mussolini would soon be speaking about a "Rome-Berlin Axis"—forged in blood on Iberian soil—a closer relationship with Fascist Italy was not a Hitlerian priority when opting for intervention.[47] Indeed causation must be reversed: the Spanish adventure brought the fascist dictators closer together, after an initial rapprochement a year earlier over Mussolini's Ethiopian conquests. And in any event the Führer's strategy was subtler than il Duce's: there were elements of rising anti-Communism, reactionary solidarity, and purely strategic considerations.

On the last day of July eighty-five Wehrmacht men under Maj. Alexander von Scheele departed from a port in Hamburg aboard the *Usaramo,* headed to Spain. Time was of the essence.[48] Along with them went sixteen planes, anti-air defenses, and ammunition. They would be followed by at least three more shipments in the next three weeks, which avoided the naval blockade by docking in Portugal. After all, the Oliveira de Salazar regime in Lisbon eagerly supported the rebellion.[49] Their goal was the first major airlift in military history, one intended to prevent the collapse of the Nationalist war effort.[50] At first the Germans were not allowed to fly combat missions and would not let Spaniards service their equipment.[51] In keeping with the operatic tones of his post-Wagner decision to intervene, Hitler baptized the operation *Feuerzauber* (Fire Magic) after the third act of *Die Walküre.* At least the Führer's themes were consistent.

In the context of Schacht's economic model, intervention in the Spanish Civil War soon became a project driven by economic considerations. Less than two weeks into the Spanish Civil War and while the democracies' foreign offices struggled under French leadership to agree on a framework for nonintervention, an organization favoring state-sponsored companies was put in place to oversee Ibero-German trade. It was a Party venture, run through the Auslandorganisation.[52] This development would soon create frictions between the Party apparatus—to which Bernhard belonged—and Schacht's ministry. Those would be quickly overcome. More importantly, HISMA's registration is evidence that only a few days following Hitler's decision, there was a plan for compensation for fascist solidarity—in a way that took advantage of neo-*Weltpolitik* foreign expansion ideas.

For the time being shipments went in only one direction, from Germany to Spain, and there was little to no discussion about payment.[53] How could the Nationalists ever pay? They had no foreign exchange and no bullion whatsoever, not to mention an initial strategic disadvantage that only recently—in good part thanks to German support—they had begun to reverse.[54] On the Francoist side, dependence on German supplies was fully acknowledged. On August 19 the commander in Seville, Queipo de Llano, imposed the summary death penalty for smuggling or fraud, "including of course the export of capital."[55] The generals wanted to keep capital within Spain in order to avoid further peseta devaluation in international markets.[56] Soon thereafter the first Nationalist governing body, the Burgos Junta, extended Queipo de Llano's decree to all their territories. It also began confiscating private funds and bullion for the war effort; authoritarian Nationalist management would be surprisingly effective in the first two years of the war.[57]

More important, on August 27, in what a leading Iberian historian already saw as a product of early German pressures, the junta passed another decree, allowing Nationalist generals to seize minerals, industrial production, and foreign exchange for "the cause."[58] Unsurprisingly the measure targeted the production of raw materials from foreign-owned companies such as Rio Tinto, the large British-owned mining conglomerate, then squarely in Republican territory. Early in the Civil War Nationalist Spain therefore established an authoritarian control over its war economy that could be used to ensure the supply of matériel from abroad.[59] Beyond some affluent patrons like Juan March, there were not many other sources of wealth to tap.[60] But quite important for our purposes, as early as August 27, 1936, the Nationalists envisioned using Spain's natural wealth to sustain their war.[61]

While the generals focused on organization and the airlift, Spain's legitimate government was in disarray. Though the coup itself had failed, Azaña's Republic descended into internal chaos. Madrid was everywhere under pressure: regions like Catalonia nurtured unfulfilled desires of independence, while the revolutionary aspirations of anarchists and Communists hardly helped. Largo Caballero—still outside the government—toyed with supporting a full-on revolution.[62] Madrid's lack of control over the territory helped erode its initial advantage. Meanwhile left-leaning newspapers sought responsible parties for the "fascistic revolt"; on the fateful July 25 Barcelona's *El Socialista* even claimed, "All epitaphs should read: Here lies a victim of March's millions."[63] As it turns out, they were not all that far off.[64]

As we have seen, the short-lived Giral Cabinet attempted to purchase weapons abroad, repeatedly and in every way they could. Successive Republican administrations did so as well, including Largo Caballero's when he acceded to becoming premier of an "all Popular Front" government in October.[65] It is indicative of their isolation and desperation that they even sought to purchase weapons from Nazi Germany. The Republic asked the representative of the German airplane industry in Madrid to purchase "pursuit planes and bombers that are not too heavy."[66] The German diplomatic service—at last catching up with Hitler's interventionist mood—decided to delay and ultimately reject the proposal.[67] The Republic would then be forced to support its war effort by a gigantic smuggling operation, organized in Paris by de los Ríos. To have a jurist in charge of weapons procurement was a bit like the Hellenist in charge of the economics portfolio in the first Republican administration. Ultimately Madrid became dependent on Russia for war matériel, falling prey to Stalin's strategic interest—which, to say the least, was not aligned with the Republic's.[68]

Admiral Raeder of the Kriegsmarine tried and failed to persuade Hitler that the rebellion was doomed.[69] It did not matter that Raeder was the highest ranked navy officer since the legendary von Tirpitz; resistance to Hitler's Bayreuth decision was useless. At least the careful von Neurath managed to talk Hitler into adhering to the Non-Intervention

Committee (NIC) the French had been lobbying for before announcing a compulsory two-year military service in the Reich, an obviously militaristic measure bound to further strain relations with Paris and London in the aftermath of the Ruhr remilitarization.[70] According to some sources, on August 24 Hitler expanded his support for Franco beyond the airlift "as much as possible," stopping short of allowing Germans to engage in combat; it was likely a reaction to rumors pointing to increased Soviet involvement.[71]

By then Franco's men were making such good use of their state-of-the-art German war matériel that on August 27 the German chargé d'affaires in Madrid, Hans Voelckers, sent a telegram relating that on the previous morning aircraft had conducted an "aerial attack on Madrid and dropped bombs on the airports." Fully aware of their origin, Voelckers added a plea: "Please arrange that at least as long as *Lufthansa* [air] traffic is maintained no Junkers planes raid Madrid."[72] At the Wilhelmstraße Dieckhoff received the telegram alongside one from Lisbon, which proposed a logistical route involving Holland and Portugal so that the next batch of war matériel avoided all jurisdictions abiding by the NIC.[73] In hindsight the agent worried too much; Realpolitik, bureaucracy, and endless posturing would mire the effectiveness of the NIC for the next three years, not that it really mattered given British lack of interest.[74] While Europe drifted to world war, nonintervention would become the façade for the democracies' unwillingness to act against blatant breaches of international law.[75] In any event, through the work of Franco's brother Nicolás and others, Salazar's dictatorship in Lisbon was providing safe conduit for seaborne German men and supplies.[76] For all practical purposes, they were disguised as Portugal-bound. By the time the flow decreased under eventual British pressure, the Republican blockade of southern Spain was no longer effective. A direct maritime route for shipments had opened, soon to be patrolled by Italian vessels.[77]

By early September the airlift mission had been accomplished. But German men and planes remained in Spain; they now helped Franco consolidate in the South and plan a march on Madrid.[78] Italian "volunteers" and supplies also continued to pour in. The nature of the German intervention, however, began to change. This coincided with a visit from a representative of the Export Cartel for War Matériel, Eberhard Messerschmidt, who toured Nationalist Spain. The Export Cartel was one of the "civil" organizations now subordinated to Schacht's ministry that also worked closely with the Reichsbank, then in absolute control of German trade. Messerschmidt also visited Lisbon, where Nicolás Franco, under the pseudonym Fernandes Aguilar, worked to procure weaponry.[79] Messerschmidt's report upon completing his trip began by expressing delight with the performance of German aircraft.[80] Technically superior to anything the Republic had been able to procure up until that point, the Junkers and Heinkels that worried Voelckers in Madrid dominated the Iberian skies. The opening read like Göring's testimony at Nuremberg.[81] Yet the thrust of the report was devoted to HISMA and Bernhardt. First it relayed complaints from the German military commander, von Scheele, over issues of military communication between German troops and Franco. Apparently the Generalísimo believed that Scheele was merely "an employee of Herr Bernhardt," a statement suggestive of both Bernhardt's likely "mandate" at the Bayreuth meeting as well as his own self-aggrandizement.[82] More crucially Messerschmidt noted the lack of adequate compensation for German supplies: "It should not be overlooked that we must demand some value in return for our gifts. [A German representative] . . . induced Franco, over Bernhardt's opposition, to make deliveries of copper to us to begin with." Beyond any mirage of fascist solidarity, German long-term economic interest was very much present: "[Germans] must look ahead to our future interests, and I believe that now, while Franco is under certain pressure, is the moment for getting pledges from him with respect to our future economic and perhaps political influence."[83] It was a novel suggestion, one taken directly from the neo-*Weltpolitik* book. The initial focus may have been copper, but what matters more is that the representative of the Export Cartel was thinking along Schachtian lines: German intervention could be leveraged to its trading advantage, bringing Spain into Germany's trade sphere.

Perhaps better than any other German on Iberian soil, Messerschmidt sensed that the cost of intervention was rising. Once German involvement had outgrown the first batch of planes for airlift and morphed into a heavier, sustained operation involving regular bomber sorties and ground support, it became clear that German resources otherwise devoted to the domestic "defense" arsenal were now to be diverted to Spain. As we have seen, rearmament had been at the core of Germany's economic recovery. Despite a spectacular growth impact of weapons production underwritten by Schacht's Reichsbank, from a strictly economic perspective the new arsenals amounted to "final products." They were also hard to trade. "Gifting" them to Spain was an expensive exercise in solidarity. There was another way, and a particularly fitting one given the structural shortages in the German economy that the Schachtian trade system worked to counterbalance. Messerschmidt's report ended on a suggestive note: "Now would be the moment to assure ourselves [of] a basic [trade] treaty . . . which would lay down for a number of years to come what raw materials Spain is to deliver to us and to what extent Spain must buy manufactured goods from us." The point was clear enough: the dislocations of the Civil War could allow for a degree of economic penetration not otherwise achievable for resource-constrained Germany in Spain. Existing Neue Plan trade structures could deliver it. There was one caveat: the system would work "provided that Herr Bernhardt is now prepared to give up his role of Santa Claus."[84]

Such terminology did not go unnoticed in Berlin. In handwriting on a carbon copy of Messerschmidt's report, Gen. Helmuth von Wilberg noted, "Who allowed M[esserschmidt] to go to Spain in the first place? I did *not* want him there."[85] Yet as of September 1936, an important representative of Schacht's cartelized economy was arguing for a pragmatic use of Franco's utter dependency on Nazi support. In his view the domestic economic interest far transcended ideology. Despite von Wilberg's opposition, the policymaking apparatus in Berlin would soon be devoted to implementing, almost word for word, what he had suggested. Men like Messerschmidt argued that an arrangement was needed in order to deal with the considerable amounts of supplies being shipped to Spain, in order to make sure that the expanded intervention would no longer be a one-sided affair. Indeed, after a meeting in Berlin, Bernhardt did stop behaving like Santa Claus. Going forward his organization would act as the main vehicle for German pressures that soon began resembling a decidedly imperial relationship.

Franco's Nationalists utterly depended on German war matériel. Upon Göring's request, Deputy Führer Rudolf Heß promised to put the "entire *Auslandorganisation*" to the service of the cause. A major with Auslandorganisation links, Eberhard von Jagwitz, would perform so well in this capacity as managing director of ROWAK that he would later be promoted to undersecretary at the Ministry of Economics.[86] At the outset his operation faced two key logistical problems: first, supplies needed to get to Spain; second, he required foreign exchange from Schacht's ministry to be allocated for the operation. A fleet—mainly out of Hamburg—resolved the former, while a formal agreement with Schacht's bureaucracy addressed the latter. HISMA-ROWAK gained another seal of approval: as part of an internal agreement, the Economics Ministry refrained from sending a representative to Spain directly. This effectively allowed the privileged companies to operate independently and, effectively, in full representation of the state apparatus. Hence we can consider HISMA-ROWAK a "state-sponsored private duopoly," if only with stronger organizational ties to the Party than Schacht's traditional bureaucracy.[87] Shortly I will look into the concurrent power battles in Berlin at the time; the main point here is that the pressures were being exerted through privileged state-sponsored monopolies fitting the foreign economic policy of Nazi Germany as engineered by Schacht. The system was subsequently expanded from its original role to achieve a straightforward goal: obtain tangible economic penetration in Spain in areas that benefited economically constrained Germany. Canaris devoted much effort in reassuring Italy that the Germans sought no political advantage.[88] Economics were another matter.

At this relatively early juncture, no diplomatic or military aspect of intervention inhibited the economic structures being set up on both ends of the Ibero-German exchange. A member of the Sonderstab W division, Lt. Col. Walter Warlimont, pleased the Führer with his idea to unify all German troops in Spain into one division so as to avoid operational interference from Iberian commanders. It was one thing to deliver "victory from the heavens" for Franco's men, but quite another was to have Wehrmacht soldiers bossed around by Spanish commanders, whom, as a general rule, Germans did not respect. To be fair, Warlimont was a man of the Wehrmacht obsessed with power centralization and, eventually, Hitler's "Führerprinzip." After his September trip Warlimont recommended divorcing military leadership from responsibility for repayment and German economic penetration.[89] In the military field this led to the birth of the Condor Legion, which brought all German forces in Spain under a single command.[90] Led by generals Wolfram Freiherr von Richthofen and Hugo Sperrle, the Legion swiftly became an organizational and military success for the Nazis; it has since become inextricably associated with the bombing of Guernica, executed by the Legion with Italian aerial support.[91]

To Nazis in Spain, including Bernhardt's growing staff, their dual monopoly system had the potential to maximize the profits Germany could obtain from an utterly dependent Spain. In both German and Spanish archives some documents refer to the HISMA-ROWAK system as "temporary."[92] Yet it did not feel so on the ground. The focus of intervention had begun to change from a strictly military adventure to an operation where serious thought was devoted to compensation and integration into the growing German trade sphere.[93] Not everyone agreed with the means. Indeed some Economics Ministry staff resented the type of organizational independence HISMA achieved de facto under the stewardship of the Nazi Party and, more specifically, Göring's men. "The Economics Ministry would have preferred it if its own plans had been realized," wrote an officer in October. "After having been confronted with an accomplished fact [the creation of HISMA-ROWAK], however, it will await further developments."[94] It may not have been their first choice, but the ministry went with the system.

A key point, hitherto lost to the historiography focused squarely on developments in Spain without regard for German economic policy more broadly conceived, is that, regardless of who was ultimately in control, the HISMA-ROWAK system depended on Schachtian economic structures applied to the foreign sphere. First and foremost all economic exchanges were subject to governmental supervision through the close association between the state-sponsored "private" companies and the government. Moreover it effectively created a market for German industrial products, particularly but not exclusively war matériel, to be delivered in exchange for minerals, raw materials, and foodstuffs Germany so desperately needed to maintain its industry. This came at the particular juncture when it could be argued that the Nazi recovery was complete; the main worry in the Nazi economic elite—one that surely did not include financially illiterate Göring—was to avoid economic overheating and a rekindling of inflationary pressures.

Germany's challenge by late 1936 was that too much government investment had dampened individual demand while devoting industrial production to final goods (armaments) that spurred no further growth or activity. Spain was a key exception; hence the potential of economic penetration. The expansion of German influence in a relatively underdeveloped but resource-rich nation such as Spain could be achieved without sacrificing foreign exchange, just as in the Balkans. Last, but definitely not least, in Spain there would never be effective Spanish opposition to the "overvalued" Reichsmark and terms of trade.[95] The Spaniards did complain, as Abendroth and García Pérez have shown, about the generous commissions charged by HISMA. But little came of it.[96] The Nationalists simply lacked leverage in the exchange—and the Germans increasingly played their cards in full knowledge of such dependence. This was not a relationship of equals.

As early as the first days of September 1936, a Rio Tinto shipment of over two thousand tons of precipitate was redirected from London to Hamburg with the approval of the Nationalist leadership, the only caveat being that the receiving company neither requested it nor had the ability to process it.[97] This created some procedural complications in Hamburg, but the fact remained that Germany now had a new avenue for receiving much-needed foreign raw materials. And it did not require foreign exchange. It surely pleased Schacht's Reichsbank, critical as it was of lower-quality, domestically produced iron ore that was favored by supporters of full autarky. A few weeks later, after a trip to Spain by a chemicals expert from Schacht's chemicals supervisory office, a large-scale delivery system was set up through HISMA-ROWAK; almost immediately thereafter 200,000 tons of pyrites were requisitioned.[98] This was another crucial industrial input for the 1930s German economy.

According to British files, there was even an attempt by the Germans to procure Nationalist foreign exchange, presumably to prop up Reichsbank reserves. It was a meager amount.[99] But without foreign exchange, politically shunned by democracies, and in dire need of foreign credit to sustain a civil war effort, Franco had no real bargaining power. HISMA-ROWAK steadily strengthened its position as the predominant vehicle of a type of German influence in Spain that fits the framework of an informal empire.[100] This was a way to turn technically unproductive weaponry—the Third Reich's industrial product par excellence—into the key tool of informal empire. Rather than choosing between guns and butter in the domestic sphere, as early as September 1936 Spain took the opportunity to turn guns into butter.

By mid-October German aircraft had transported over ten thousand troops from Morocco, along with almost three hundred tons of supplies, plus the operations in the southern war theater. By early November the bleakest days of Franco's war effort had passed, in no small part due to German and Italian intervention.[101] Not so Mola's. Though both foreign ministries preferred to wait until Franco had conquered the capital before officially recognizing his government as Spain's "legitimate" one, Franco's assault on Madrid did not prevail.[102] The Nationalists did not pass—or at least not yet.

Franco's strategy subsequently changed focus: he deprioritized the takeover of Madrid and, interestingly, aimed for the resource-rich northern coast.[103] Despite the setback in Madrid, Rome and Berlin moved to recognize the Nationalists. This allowed for formal foreign relations to be established with Nationalist Spain. By the time official envoys were sent, the Germans' diplomatic mandate did not focus on political alignment; rather, it focused on economic penetration. The Third Reich's first official envoy to Franco, Gen. Wilhelm Faupel, told Hermann Sabath at the Foreign Ministry's Economic Office on November 25, 1936, that he "had received instructions from the Führer to concern himself particularly with the extension of commercial relations between Germany and the new Spain."[104] Hitler was at the very least personally interested in the expansion of German economic penetration in Franco's Spain.

Germans saw this task as time-sensitive, for Faupel thought it essential "to utilize the present favorable moment so that England, which was well provided with capital [Germany lacked], would not take the market away from us at a later stage."[105] The logic was clear: Germany ought to take advantage of the current window of opportunity to further its interests and build Spanish dependence beyond the Civil War. Faupel also expressed his gratitude for the fact that an economic expert had been specifically sent to the Spanish delegation in Burgos to counterbalance Bernhardt's influence.[106] As early as September HISMA had been officially elevated to the "representative of Germany's economic interests in Nationalist Spain."[107] In the context of Schachtian trade priorities in 1935–1936, these documents have an added weight: the focus on securing a constant and secure supply of raw materials for the purposes of heavy industry had found a new outlet. Although Schacht's imperial argumentations had been thwarted across great power capitals, Germany could find in Spain what Britain and France had denied it elsewhere. And this strategy—allegedly emanating directly from

Hitler—followed neo-*Weltpolitik* preoccupations rather than the *Lebensraum* framework. In this sense it seems consistent with the Schachtian policy on colonies, which was parroted by a wide variety of German government officials at the time.

In the previous decades and especially during the Weimar years, Germany had found it particularly hard to compete with British capital exports to less developed nations.[108] The British had remained the preeminent foreign investors and owners of Spain's key assets, mainly of the mineral variety.[109] Its wealth consisted of considerable supplies of iron ore (thus far in Republican hands), pyrites, mercury, and wolfram (essential for chemical industries). There was also wood and foodstuffs, of key importance for Germany. Britain was therefore the largest investor, with capital around $194 million, followed by France, with $135 million, and then the United States, with $80 million. Germany lagged far behind with $31.1 million.[110]

In the midst of the Civil War, however, the situation changed extraordinarily fast. The diplomatic constellation surrounding the Spanish Civil War made Franco dependent on German war matériel, and Bernhardt's HISMA and ROWAK in particular. Britain's government was both a member of the NIC and its host.[111] This helps explain why London put pressure on Lisbon to limit its help to Franco, while increasingly heeding calls from British capital for protection against the rising German economic clout.[112] What Faupel had in mind—perhaps the only issue on which he saw eye to eye with Bernhardt—was that without sacrificing foreign exchange, Spanish repayment for delivered supplies could be turned into German foreign investment in Spain so as to secure the kind of Iberian production the Nazi economy needed. It was a strategy that aimed at turning extraction of certain materials as payment into a longer-term investment project, one that could outlive the war. Far from simple compensation, this involved a long-term project for penetration with imperial overtones, if only informal rather than formal.[113]

The sectors to be targeted were, unsurprisingly, those most complementary to the burgeoning German economy: input products for capital goods and armaments—iron ore, pyrites, copper, wolfram[114]—and foodstuffs, an arena in which Germany was far from self-sufficient and in which there was a great need for expensive imported fertilizers.[115] The food sector's deficiencies had exacerbated disagreements between

Schacht and Darré, the racialist agriculture minister who was also a leading supporter of *Lebensraum*. Schacht often opposed devoting foreign exchange for imported fertilizers in order to prop up a largely inefficient sector, which Darré was set on reforming along ideological lines in a way that made little economic sense.[116] Spain, in short, could be brought into an informal Reichsmark sphere. Spain's decoupling from the democracies would therefore be not only political but also economic, materializing German hegemony in the European periphery in the process.

The fact that Spain was not industrialized and, generally, economically backward actually made the terms of trade more beneficial to Germany. Following the Schachtian trade model as applied at the time in Latin America and the Balkans, other industrial products could follow weapons into Spain.[117] A clearing agreement had been signed with the Republic back in March 1936, and the influx of weapons for the Nationalists greatly benefited the end balance for Germany. In this context German diplomats and HISMA-ROWAK sought to continue with the status quo and avoid any Spanish attempt to actually balance the trade deficit.[118] Sabath's boss at the Wilhelmstraße wrote that any future deal modifying the system should "give trade relations as favourable . . . as possible and to assure preference in the supply of those goods which are of special interest to them [Spaniards]."[119] It was a euphemism for weapons. In the coming months effective German pressures on the Nationalist leadership would prevent meaningful changes to the HISMA-ROWAK system, contrary to what Spaniards like Francisco de Agramonte, former ambassador in Berlin, sought.[120]

In an ironic twist of fate, Ritter's recommendation came right around the time the NIC began proceedings in London on the task of controlling the influx of foreign personnel and matériel into Spain. Military coordination with Rome notwithstanding, the idea of using war matériel as an effective tool of informal empire had already begun to take shape in Berlin power circles. At the time the reins of the economic power in Berlin were in flux, yet the project in Spain marched forward in strict adherence to Schachtian principles. The German weapons sent to Spain had begun to alter the direction of Spanish raw materials in favor of constrained Germany. Increasingly, on Iberian soil all other considerations seemed secondary.

chapter six

THE PRECIPICE

There has been time enough in four years to find out what we cannot do. Now we have to carry out what we can do.

—ADOLF HITLER, secret memorandum, September 1936

A round the time his preferred neo-*Weltpolitik* imperial strategies were successfully deployed in warring Spain, Hjalmar Schacht's "economic dictatorship" began to wane in Berlin. It was an ironic twist of fate for the man who had arguably done the most to "remake" the German economy, thus contributing to the consolidation of the Hitlerian dictatorship. His demise was the culmination of a Cabinet duel with one of the few men with a will for power more insatiable than his own: Hermann Göring.[1] By mid-1936 Göring was deputy head of the Party, head of the almost defunct SA, air minister, commander in chief of the Luftwaffe, and prime minister of Prussia, a title he was known to unwittingly shorten to merely "prime minister." And, as if that were not enough, he was also the highest authority on hunting and forestry, a responsibility he and the Führer took very seriously.[2] Like Schacht, he was an operator abroad. Some called him Hitler's *erste Paladin* (first paladin). Within Hitler's polycratic state—or, depending on one's historiographic perspective, his "chaos state"—Göring had a hand in every pocket of Nazi power.[3]

There was one exception: the economy was beyond Göring's reach. This was Schacht's fiefdom, managed through a "dual mandate" at the Reichsbank and at the Economics Ministry, where his "acting" control looked rather permanent. Back in 1931 the banker had first met Hitler at a dinner party thrown by Göring's (first) wife. From questionable election fundraising to even more questionable rearmament of Versailles, Schacht and Göring collaborated for years in the service of the same goal: consolidating Hitler's regime.[4] They both rose with the Führer, but by the time the Civil War raged in Spain, a gulf had emerged between them.

As was true for so many others, Schacht had little respect for Göring, who he believed exhibited "a complete lack of understanding of economics." Göring did not necessarily disagree.[5] Illustrative of their personal enmity is the chapter in Schacht's autobiography devoted to his bitter rival, which is scathing in tone, save perhaps for one point: "The choice of [Göring's] first wife is a particularly strong point in his favor."[6] It was Karin who had made Göring wealthy, allowing him to devote time and funds to the Nazi Party. Yet power deformed him; Schacht thought Göring's "ostentatiousness verged on the ridiculous. . . . Not only did he collect precious stones, gold and platinum jewelry in vast quantities, but he also wore them." The British ambassador agreed; at the time of Göring's second wedding, he wrote sarcastically, "Göring would seem to have reached the apogee of his vainglorious career: I see for him and his megalomania no higher goal . . . unless indeed it be the scaffold."[7]

As Broszat and Mommsen have explained in detail, there were many bureaucratic battles within the Nazi regime; indeed Hitler thrived in his role as the ultimate mediator. Yet this one mattered more than most. Though technically a matter of economics, the battle between Schacht and Göring is at the core of a decisive shift in the direction of the Nazi regime, a radicalization that not only changed the economic strategy, but also had profound implications for the regime's foreign policy and its projection of foreign power.

Around the time of the Berlin Olympics in August 1936, Schacht began advocating a slowdown in armaments production. As we have seen, armament goals had been modified several times beyond the (already gargantuan) June 1933 plan facilitated by his Reichsbank through what can only be described as "unconventional monetary policy." In effect Schacht had only increased the subordination of the Reichsbank to political power, a process that originated in the late Weimar Republic. The caveat was that in this case the central banker believed he was in control of political power, not the other way around.[8] For his work in advancing Nazi goals, "economic dictator" Schacht was given due credit. For instance, a display at the 1935 Nuremberg rally that Leni Riefenstahl captured in one of her documentaries, *Tag der Freiheit* (1935), celebrated the central bank and its president.[9] It had been through Schacht's economic program and his highly effective foreign economic strategy that the regime had the resources to achieve these rearmament goals, often masked as employment-boosting strategies. Such was the result of not only Mefo bills but also the Neue Plan, debt buybacks, radically overgrown industrial oversight, myriad controls, and export "schemes."

Yet Wehrmacht revisions to the planned military budgets only went upward, in a feedback loop closely associated with Hitler's increasingly aggressive foreign policy. Like economic protectionism years before, however, this had strategic consequences: increased German military spending spurred others into action. By 1935 Britain, France, Soviet Russia, and the United States were all increasing their military spending. On March 16, 1935, which Churchill judged to be a "momentous day," both France and Germany announced expansion of conscriptions.[10] Necessarily this meant that Germany's relative first mover advantage was eroding, as others caught up with pro-growth effects of weapons spending and foreign policy posturing. The sheer scale of Nazi rearmament, however, was unmatched.

Once recovery was accomplished, Schacht worried about the amount of outstanding credit in the economy and its future implications for inflation, a phenomenon far closer to public consciousness in Nazi Germany than it is today.[11] Of course Schacht had greatly contributed to credit growth in the 1930s, first through central bank overt and covert balance sheet expansion and later from the direction of the economics ministry. But increasingly, long-term investments focused on only one area of the economy. Weapons were "nonmarketable" goods that consumed imports but would not help the current account balance through possible export. In other words, increased weapons production would lead to a decrease in exportable goods, which, ceteris paribus, would decrease Germany's trade balance. The exception was, of course, Spain.[12] Eventually that would compromise the Reich's living standards. The expansion of the weapons sector could not be carried on ad infinitum. Unless, of course, Germany was prepared to make use of those weapons militarily as well as diplomatically. There is only so much weaponry needed for determent.

With full employment achieved and the output gap closed, domestic inflationary pressures were on the rise.[13] By 1936, in fact, the German economy was experiencing a shortage of skilled workers, leading to wage increases often concealed from the authorities. Three years into the regime, for instance, Darré's ministry became very concerned about the wage differential between agricultural and industrial workers, which led to some anticapitalist proposals.[14] What some have considered Schacht's "conservatism" here can only be ascribed to a more thorough understanding of economic forces than other members of the Nazi elite enjoyed; a tax on urban excess demand made little economic sense. Financial repression—through controls and taxation—could prevent an inflationary crisis for some time, but not forever.[15]

Hence Schacht argued for a policy shift. Was there hope for such a change? With his dictatorship consolidated and his power absolute, Hitler had gone on the foreign policy offensive in early 1936. He defied the Locarno treaties and remilitarized the Rhineland. The German government couched remilitarization as a direct response to a Franco-Soviet treaty; excuses aside, the move caused deep consternation.[16] Yet it elicited no military response from the democracies; indeed the British seemed disturbed not by the end but only by Hitler's means. "[The German government] have thus not by that action produced a result, so far as the demilitarised zone itself is concerned, which we were not prepared ultimately to contemplate," wrote British foreign secretary Eden in a confidential report to the Cabinet when the remilitarization was a fait accompli. "It is the manner of their action . . . which we deplore"[17]—not the action itself. Eden did worry that Hitler's gamble decreased Britain's margin for maneuver ahead of discussions for a "general European settlement": "Such negotiations are now inevitable, but we shall enter them at a disadvantage."[18] Paris was anything but reassured.[19] Even a few months later former prime minister Lloyd George defended Hitler's actions: "[In light of the Franco-Soviet Pact] . . . if Herr Hitler had allowed that to go without protecting his country he would have been a traitor to the Fatherland."[20] Mussolini, too busy with his African campaigns, did not lift a finger to defend Locarno.[21]

The Rhineland remilitarization was Hitler's greatest foreign policy triumph ahead of his intervention in Spain. "Great are the successes that Providence has let me attain for our Fatherland," he told an en-raptured Reichstag on March 7, 1936. "In these three years, Germany has regained its honor, found belief again, overcome its greatest economic distress and finally ushered in a new cultural ascent."[22] The implication was clear: the Versailles humiliation was no more. The Führer also declared Germany's "equality of rights" completed and renounced any further territorial claims. Rhetoric suggested there was at least some hope for a policy change.

The concepts of "equality of rights" surely pleased nationalists like Schacht; it fulfilled their wildest Weimar dreams. And it was in this context that the "economic dictator" believed it necessary to cease expanding armaments production, shifting growth to other economic sectors that had lagged behind. The key was to produce goods that could be exported to Germany's growing economic sphere of influence so as to address the country's chronic foreign exchange weakness—a goal that concerned his Reichsbank directly. Such a shift would avoid making the economy too dependent on weapons and in the process deescalate the international situation.[23] There was a more immediate economic risk: a policy shift would also reduce the risk of a return of the damaging balance of payments crisis that had given him control of the ministry.[24] On Christmas Eve 1935 Schacht refused a raw materials request by the war minister while making his worries explicit: "It is of course far from my mind to modify the support I have given for years to the greatest possible rearmament, both before and after the seizure of power. It is my duty, however, to point out the economic limits that constrain any such policy."[25] The export of weapons to places like Spain could ease constraints but could not be easily replicated elsewhere, lest the regime armed potential adversaries. Perhaps it was not necessary to thwart existing plans—which in itself could trigger a severe fiscal contraction—but it was definitely necessary to cease adding further armaments-driven stimulation. In short, the economic dictator needed an "exit strategy" for unconventional monetary and fiscal stimulus.

Such was the context in which Schacht resisted a further expansion of rearmament, fearing more unproductive investments would exacerbate inflationary pressures while eroding the hard-won advantages in the international trade sphere.[26] "Germany's rearmament had to fit into the framework of the New Plan—or break it,"[27] he would later write. His authoritarian controls over the economy could do only so much to backstop the inevitable. Meanwhile profits on private balance sheets accumulated.[28] Some of these were being used to pay down debt through international buybacks, but the inflationary threat was latent.[29] None other than the pliant Prussian Finance Ministry complained as early as 1936 that "inflation is already with us."[30] In light of unpleasant Weimar memories, a rise in prices threatened not only the stability of the Reichsmark but, potentially, the regime itself.[31]

In spite of Hitler's statements and Schacht's caution, the pace of rearmament in 1936 showed no signs of slowing; in fact the opposite was true. In spite of his rhetoric, Hitler ordered the expansion of the Luftwaffe to include more all-metal plane divisions, planned the beefing up of the Westwall French border defenses under Autobahn head Fritz Todt, and expanded Wehrmacht divisions yet again.[32] Unsurprisingly the military establishment celebrated the moves.[33] So did supporters of the *Lebensraum* school, for whom armaments signaled the possibility of crafting a formal empire for a new, expanded, Greater Germany. Not so Schacht. Internationally Hitler's continued aggressiveness in the aftermath of the Rhineland remilitarization did not go unnoticed, and Schacht found the international community more hostile to the regime, with fewer new markets prepared to open up to Germany.[34] And as checks on anti-Semitic outbursts during the Olympics gave way to new, Party-sponsored attacks, the delicate balance with Britain and France deteriorated further.[35]

Almost simultaneously discussions between France, Britain, and the United States gathered speed on an eventual stabilization of world currencies. The goal that had eluded the democracies since 1931 was suddenly in sight. Paradoxically this newfound willingness to engage was at least in part furthered by the political desire to contain Schacht's Germany.[36] The trade implications of a united front were dire for Germany, a possibility lost neither on the Reichsbank staff nor its president.[37]

Reservations and warnings were the last thing a triumphant Hitler wanted to hear. At the time the Führer's daring foreign policy was paying off handsomely. Three months after the Rhineland episode, success followed in Spain with the backing of the Francoist war effort, and so did a dawning alliance with Mussolini—all of which boosted Hitler's confidence.[38] With domestic power increasingly concentrated in his office and competing bureaucracies "working toward the Führer," Hitler's focus was almost exclusively devoted to foreign policy. Enabled by dithering in Paris and London, and in spite of rhetoric, the remilitarization of the Rhineland was only the beginning of Hitler's challenge to the continental balance of power. Yet the man tasked with steering the economy toward strategic rearmament and recovery was now recommending a change of focus to preserve the victories of his neo-*Weltpolitik* economic strategies.

Not so Göring. Though he was anything but an economist, he propounded what Hitler wanted to hear.[39] He was, after all, an expert in the internal Party politics Schacht derided.[40] Göring could not make substantive changes to Schacht's economic framework other than rejecting the banker's desire for a slowdown. But he had Hitler's ear and a new area to add to his extensive portfolio. Consistent with Party ideologues far more heterodox than Schacht, Göring held economics to be ultimately a matter of will: inflation could be kept down by government pressure and absolute control of prices and wages, expanding Schacht's industrial oversight systems if necessary; heavy industry could be kept growing by guaranteeing profits for businessmen, or, failing that, outright coercion; and exports could be maximized, by force if necessary. Years later, when total war dawned, Reichsbank vice president Kurt Lange synthesized it thus: "In an authoritarian state there can be no inflation."[41] What sounded good as subservient policy was not factually accurate; indeed, authoritarian states often suffer far higher inflation rates than democratic states with more independent central banks.[42]

Göring's plans involved no revolutionary insight from behavioral economics; the ultimate purpose of "will" applied to the Nazi economy was to make policy consistent with the strategic goals of *Lebensraum*. In direct contrast to *Weltpolitik* advocates like Schacht, supporters of *Lebensraum* conceived of a "final war" as inevitable destiny.[43] This implied a specific economic path: in spite of constraints and perhaps because of them, Göring favored further autarky as a path to ever increasing war preparedness. Reduced reliance on foreign markets would yield the necessary stability to weather the war that would give Germany control of the "world island" at the heart of Eurasia.[44] "I do not acknowledge the sanctity of any economic law," he later declared, only Hitler's will. "What the Führer has said is decisive: Economy must always be the servant of the nation and capital must be the servant of industry."[45]

Simply put, Göring wanted Nazi Germany to be ready to create a formal empire. This was the "logical" justification for his support for ever-rising expenditures in armaments and military infrastructure. It came in stark contrast with the goal of material well-being to be facilitated through a strong international position of power and economic imperialism through formal or informal colonies—the aim of Schacht's neo-*Weltpolitik* designs. If the objective were to prevail where Wilhelmine Germany had so spectacularly failed, then the Schachtian economic system was necessary, but not sufficient. Only *Lebensraum* could suffice. Everything would have to make way for that goal—including, if necessary, Germany's economic dictator.

A master of political maneuvering who had managed to survive the many purges of "old Party men"—more often than not because he was behind them—Göring moved fast.[46] In April 1936 he obtained control over the procurement of raw materials and foreign exchange as "special commissioner." The result was increased internal competition, even if Hitler often chose the path of duplication of managerial responsibilities. Though this represented an intrusion into Schacht's fiefdom, the banker acquiesced, likely under the assumption it was a propaganda issue.[47] "Friendly co-operation with the new agency was necessary and even possible," Schacht told his staff.[48] Göring's military discipline could perhaps help a foreign exchange situation that remained dire. It could also put checks on Party corruption, an issue that long disturbed Schacht.[49] Soon the Nazi apparatus beamed with the sacrifices for the Commissioner's goals. "A little girl sent Göring a golden bracelet," a sycophantic biography recounted. "It was her dearest and most precious possession, left to her by her mother who had died. The child wanted to give the best she had."[50]

This was not enough. Behind Schacht's back Göring commissioned reports on the economic situation, with implicit support from the military and other heterodox voices like Wilhelm Keppler, who distanced himself from Schacht's caution.[51] One of the reports backfired spectacularly: Carl Goerdeler, a veteran of *Deflationspolitik* and a leading conservative voice within the regime, sharply criticized Schacht's economic management, only he did so from the opposite perspective.[52] In a secret, daring memorandum, he argued that Germany had a unique opportunity to return to liberalism: it should drop Schacht's Neue Plan, reapproach the democracies, devalue the Reichsmark, and trust that exports would recover. The devaluation strategy would necessarily put a check on rearmament, making Wehrmacht imports too dear.[53] A series of internal Reichsbank studies at the time also recommended decelerating the rate of rearmament from within Schacht's central bank, but Goerdeler's was a far more orthodox adjustment than even the central banker proposed.[54] The Reichsbank did not call for an outright change in the authoritarian economic management—not least because of its control-obsessed president.[55] The mere mention of such policy options was heresy in Nazi Germany; on his copy of Goerdeler's memorandum, Göring wrote vitriolic comments—"Nonsense"; "What cheek!"—and forwarded a copy to Hitler's Berchtesgaden retreat.[56] Göring approved of Schacht's economic authoritarianism; if anything, he wanted more of it, not a return to liberalism. Other reports were more pliable.

Then Göring set up a parallel structure to the Economics Ministry with goals more extreme than those in Schacht's methodical designs. He aimed to implement a Four-Year Plan.[57] This involved Göring's interpretation of directives outlined in a top-secret memorandum on the gearing of the economy for large-scale war that Hitler dictated at Berchtesgaden.[58] Only four copies were made and none of them entrusted to Schacht.[59] To be fair, this new economic program did not imply a qualitative change in Nazi economic policy. After all, armaments had been central to the recovery Schacht oversaw and, to a large extent, directed.[60] Yet Hitler's writing implied a key quantitative leap against Schacht's explicit recommendations: far from cooling off armaments production, the Führer unleashed all constraints on the Wehrmacht.[61]

The document itself deserves a close look.[62] Hitler began from his usual worldview, addressing the "struggle for existence" in *Mein Kampf*–reminiscent language: "Even the idealistic ideological struggles [*Weltanschauungskämpfe*] have their ultimate cause and are most deeply motivated by nationally [*völklich*] determined purposes and aims of life." He went on to identify Germany's "destiny" in the Western struggle against Bolshevism: "Germany will, as always, have to be regarded as the focal point of the Western world in face of the Bolshevist attacks." Save for Germany and Italy—an addendum that reflected the

Axis—other states were "infected" by the twin demons of Marxism and democracy.

Hitler now saw a Bolshevist showdown as inevitable and its timing unpredictable. It was an important ex ante assumption from which to drive economic policy. Because of the Manichaean nature of the looming conflagration, Nazi state management ought to adapt: "In face of the necessity of defence against this [Bolshevist] danger, all other considerations must recede into the background as being completely irrelevant." From that axiomatic premise flowed unconstrained rearmament: "If we do not succeed in developing the German *Wehrmacht* within the shortest possible time into the first Army in the world, in training, in the raising of units, in armaments . . . Germany will be lost! . . . All other desires must therefore be unconditionally subordinated to this task. For this task is life and the preservation of life. . . . Nor will posterity ever ask us by what methods or by what concepts . . . we achieved the salvation of the nations, but only *whether* or not we achieved it."[63] It was an ominous preview of what was to come.

Moving onto economics, Hitler enumerated Germany's familiar constraints: overpopulation, lack of resources and foreign exchange, impossibility of stockpiling ahead of war, a potential naval blockade. He also outlined the successes of the past three years in terms of rising standards of living. The aim was unequivocal: "The only solution lies in extending living space of our people and/or the sources of its raw materials and foodstuffs. It is the task of the political leadership one day to solve this problem."[64] As we have seen, Schacht did not necessarily disagree with this goal. The question was how exactly this "solution" would be achieved: empire, to be sure, but what kind?

Hitler presented a clear dichotomy on private capital: "Either we possess today a private industry, in which case it is its task to rack its brains about production methods, or we believe that the determination of production methods is the task of the State, in which case we no longer need private industry." The Führer was therefore outdoing Schacht in terms of authoritarian control, favoring an extremely autarkic turn: synthetics production would rise, domestic ore production would rise, and costs mattered less than will. Industry would have to follow.

And yet a point that is usually lost is that Hitler still understood that full autarky was not economically feasible: "I consider it necessary that now, with iron determination, a 100 per cent self-sufficiency should be attained in all those spheres where it is feasible, and that not only should the national requirements in these most important raw materials be made independent of other countries but that we should also thus save the foreign exchange which in peacetime we require for our imports of foodstuffs. Here I would emphasize that in these tasks I see the only true economic mobilization." The memorandum concluded with two connected "tasks": "I. The German army must be ready for action [*einsatzfähig*] within four years. II. The German economy must be fit for war [*kriegsfähig*] within four years."[65]

It is beyond doubt that members of the *Lebensraum* school generally and Göring specifically influenced Hitler's drafting—and that the end product surely pleased them.[66] When describing it in public, Göring proclaimed, "It is for *your* empire and for *your* country which you yourselves have re-created and conquered. It is a question of the honor of Germany and the security of German life!"[67] Propaganda aside, this was the materialization of "Nazi will" in the economic sphere; it implied that civilian well-being could not be a priority in the face of existential danger.[68] "Economic life may remain free only so long as it is able to solve the problems of the nation," the Führer would argue a few months later. "If it cannot do so then it must cease to be free."[69] Although he personally lacked a formal appointment, Göring and his Four-Year Plan organization redoubled efforts to increase autarkic goals. In many areas they went far beyond what even Hitler had envisioned. His growing team began to focus on iron and coal as key ingredients to sustain not merely German industry in its "reprocessing role"—to borrow Schacht's economic terminology—but to wage war.[70] The ideas underlying the plan had been discussed during the summer of 1936, precisely around the time Hitler decided to intervene in Spain.

To put it mildly, Schacht saw this strategy as infeasible. When he heard about Hitler's intention to talk about it at the 1936 Party Conference, he approached Colonel Georg Thomas, a pragmatic ally of his within the military hierarchy. "If we now shout out abroad our decision to make ourselves economically independent, then we cut our own throats," he warned.[71] Germany did not have the domestic resources for the kind of self-sufficiency envisioned by the *Lebensraum* school. Also many of the technologies Hitler praised in his memorandum could not achieve the required scale in the required timeframe. And of course any further moves toward autarky would jeopardize the existing realignment of European trade he had carefully designed. This time, however, Schacht was alone; accurately reading the political climate, Thomas did not intercede.[72] "The lack of understanding of the Reich Economics Minister and the resistance of German business to all large-scale [*Großzügigen*] plans prompted me to compose this memorandum at Berchtesgaden [at the Berghof]," Hitler told Armaments Minister Albert Speer when handing him a copy of the memorandum eight years later.[73]

New priorities dawned. Returning to Berlin from Berchtesgaden, Göring summoned a meeting on September 4, one he declared—with characteristic humility—"of greater significance than any that had preceded it."[74] There he read Hitler's memorandum out loud, "gloating over Schacht's humiliation." A ranking Prussian official lamented that Herbert Backe at the Agriculture Ministry had missed the meeting: "Today we witnessed the most beautiful day in our economic history." Another supporter of *Lebensraum,* Hermann Reische, telephoned his (and Backe's) boss, Darré, a sworn enemy of Schacht's. Reische told Darré that Göring had "read out a devastating letter . . . [and] Schacht just sat there, baffled and impotent." Henceforth Schacht's Reichsbank and his Economics Ministry would no longer be the unchallenged core of German economic policymaking. With this new strategy, issues that worried Schacht and his supporters—the interrelated threats of inflation, labor shortages, industrial constraints, stability of the currency, inefficiency of synthetics production, and others—would all be controlled by government suasion and, when necessary, direct state management.[75] Hitler's fundamental assumption was that economics could behave like foreign policy, where aggressiveness had forged a new reality.

For the purposes of posterity, Schacht would take credit for the plan's positives. "Whatever was successfully accomplished with the Four-Year Plan," he would haughtily write, "was nothing but the continuation of measures I had inaugurated as Minister." There was something to the claim, but the difference was crucial: "Now, however, everything was rushed and exaggerated." As the plan developed under Göring, two problems dawned: sustainability and efficiency. "The extraction of benzine from coal [synthetic fuel] had been organized by me. . . . The wholesale cultivation of staple fibers had been set on foot, thanks to the steps I had taken. . . . The extension of mining operations, too, had

been tackled by me." For once, however, the "wizard" had been politically outmaneuvered.[76]

On these points Schacht echoed arguments from his traditional allies: German business.[77] Generally the heads of German industry were
anything but pleased with Göring's desire to be personally involved in
private production.[78] This was not merely an issue of import oversight
or goal setting.[79] Following the expropriation model Milch had applied
in the air industry with Junkers, Göring did not hesitate to push businessmen out of the way to achieve the plan's goals. To an extent this
was mandated by Hitler's memorandum, but Göring took it upon himself to exercise the power. More often than not the main beneficiary
was Göring himself.[80]

That was the genesis of the Hermann Göring Works (Reichswerke
Hermann Göring, RWHG), which in years to come would become
the largest steel conglomerate in the world.[81] Only a few months earlier Göring had boasted, "My department is not economics. I have never
been a director or on a board of directors and shall never be. Except
for the flower pots on the balcony I have never cultivated anything."
Will, however, would provide. "But I am ready with all my heart and
soul, and with firm belief in the greatness of the German nation [Volk]
to devote all my energies to this mighty task [Four-Year Plan]."[82] Schacht
meanwhile despised the means as much as the ends: "RWHG always
operated at a loss and was constantly demanding more credits from the
Reich, none of which had the least chance of ever being paid back. . . .
the thing swelled up to an enormous and utterly top-heavy growth,
with stupidity, corruption, and fraud writ large all over it."[83]

Schacht was down, but not quite out. The battle for economic power
in Berlin would not alter the structure of a bilateral exchange that still
answered to neo-*Weltpolitik* principles that underpinned Schacht's foreign economic strategy. After all, why fix something that was not
broken?

Nazi business in Spain was anything but broken. The Party-sponsored
company on the ground, HISMA, continued its advance through pressures on the Nationalist leadership. It applied a program directly derived from Schacht's goals of trade diversion and informal empire. The
adventure in Spain could not sit well with extreme autarky advocates;
if anything it pointed to Germany exporting resources it would have

a hard time replacing. It did, however, point to a possible avenue for further continental expansion without forcing an existential struggle leading to large-scale war.

As German demands on the Spanish leadership rose, underpinned by the inequality of the relationship, challenges were bound to arise. On January 12, 1937, the first official envoy to the Franco regime, Wilhelm Faupel, warned that German influence over the Nationalist leadership might soon wane. Because he conceived of influence on a relative basis, Faupel worried about a recent escalation in the number of Italian troops in Spain. Indeed following Mussolini's decision to hasten the end of the conflict, there had recently been a true explosion of Italian Fascists on Spanish soil.[84] The Germans continued to supply Franco, but Faupel worried the difference in commitments could translate into the political sphere: "The fear cannot be dismissed that our political influence . . . will fall to a second place [behind Italy]." Perhaps aware of the interests in Berlin, his reasoning drifted to economics: "Our interest [is] to conclude negotiations about economic and compensation questions before this [Italian] development has become clearly apparent." In a note from the Reich Chancellery accompanying the document, none other than Hitler himself ordered that Faupel's suggestion should be "acted on as soon as possible."[85] But when the German envoy discussed financial matters with an Italian peer on the military side, he reported back to Berlin that the Italians had gotten nothing concrete out of Spain beyond extremely vague promises. This would become a defining feature of Italian intervention.[86] What is more, Faupel estimated the Italian government had already spent over 800 million lire on intervention, and at least 200 more would be required. As we shall see, this a gross understatement of total cost. But Germany, Faupel acknowledged, had chosen a different path: "We have obtained far more in this respect through HISMA."[87]

It should not have been a surprise: the HISMA-ROWAK system created effective pressures on the upper echelons of Nationalist leadership through direct contacts with Franco and his closest clique. These pressures were effectively based on the unevenness of the bilateral relationship—and they paid off. As recent estimates make clear, German and Italian transfers made up almost the same amount the Republic had access to thanks to its vast gold reserves.[88] What is more, through draconian management and a peg, the Nationalists were able to contain inflation in their zone—a rare feat in civil wars and in particular a stark contrast to Republican Spain, which had to pay for its foreign supplies in gold.[89] According to some estimations based on company balance sheets, Rio Tinto alone provided between 16 and 24 percent of the total transfers of raw materials sent to Germany to compensate for supplies.[90] What is more, in early January 1937 HISMA communicated to local pyrites producers that German needs would amount to 1.2 million tons for the year, a figure expected to rise going forward. This would drastically and invariably reduce shipments to other locations; no matter how one interprets the data, the main loser was Britain.

Unsurprisingly the British-owned conglomerate did not stand still. As they saw Nationalist Spain decoupling from its traditional dependence on British capital, they warned London. Rio Tinto leadership complained repeatedly, urging action against creeping German economic hegemony even as they fulfilled Francoist orders.[91] It should be noted that company executives understood very clearly how the HISMA-ROWAK dual monopoly worked.[92] They furthered their economic argument by pointing out what these minerals would turn into. Sir Auckland Geddes, chairman of Rio Tinto wrote to Eden's Foreign Office, "The economic and strategic importance of these British-owned mines in Spain has not escaped the attention of the Spanish Insurgents [Nationalists] or their masters—Germany and Italy—all of whom are using every means to exploit and consolidate their present situation in a manner most detrimental to Great Britain."[93] His paper ended with a daring suggestion: if Eden's diplomacy did not manage to stop these shipments to Germany, then the Royal Navy should. The implication was clear: the "masters" forced this decision upon the Nationalist leadership. It was an astute reading of the situation.

An increasingly worried Foreign Minister Eden agreed with Geddes's assessment at a Cabinet meeting on March 8, 1937. Eden suggested the navy be used to reassert British power and prevent the export of pyrites to Germany. Yet First Sea Lord Chatfield opposed him, warning that this use of the navy might provoke war with the dictators.[94] An avid Francoist, Chatfield still worried about the security of strategic assets in Spain, not least Gibraltar. Amid the tension, Nicolás Franco agreed to give Rio Tinto a small foreign exchange allowance of £10,000 every month; this assuaged some concerns even if it did not alter the reorientation of Iberian trade.[95] The Francoist quid pro quo for support required that the Nationalists assent to a new hegemonic economic power: Germany over Britain.

HISMA's Bernhardt had clearly changed his ways since the days when Messerschmitt likened him to Santa Claus, with transfers agreed on principle and minerals already sailing to Hamburg. It remains an issue of contention whether the agent in Spain always intended to transition to a more exploitative system, yet as of late 1936 Bernhardt's behavior fit Messerschmidt's neo-*Weltpolitik* suggestions.[96] A memorandum prepared for a February 1937 conference on German-Spanish economic relations in Berlin confirmed this point. It came in the context of a debate about whether to continue with the HISMA-ROWAK duopoly or give in to Spanish requests to broker a clearing treaty that could potentially limit German industrial penetration in the Spanish economy.[97]

Though the report acknowledged that "too much" pressure on Franco could become counterproductive, it recognized the "undeniable success of HISMA-ROWAK, which have succeeded through their relations with General Franco in placing Germany ahead of all other countries in Spanish trade and in directing raw materials available in Spain primarily to Germany." Informal pressures worked. The Germans readily accepted that Franco's Nationalists "would rather sell these raw materials to other countries against foreign exchange." But they remained dependent on Nazi supplies, and leveraging this dependence in the trade sphere yielded tangible results. "To guarantee delivery of Spanish raw materials to Germany requires steady pressure on the Franco Government."[98] There was not even a semblance of equality in the bilateral relationship.

This imperial, mercantilistic strategy could be effective only in the context of Germany's new trade system, designed to disengage the country's economy from Britain and the United States and replace them with less developed countries of the likes of Spain. Profiting from the dislocations created by the Civil War amounted to a neo-*Weltpolitik* strategy of informal imperialism. In this sense Bernhardt and HISMA-ROWAK's behavior echoed Schachtian trade strategy in other undeveloped markets, from Latin America to the Balkans. Contemporaries were not unaware of such connections.[99] Schacht's personal power struggle with Göring notwithstanding, everyone in Berlin was in agreement about Iberian policy. From the Foreign Ministry, Ambassador Karl Ritter reported, "President [of the Reichsbank] Schacht himself had fully agreed with the proposal [to maintain trade structures]." Despite previous hesitation, ROWAK's Jagwitz took envoys from the Economics Ministry to Spain for negotiations regarding future concessions and further German penetration into the Spanish economy. This move de facto acknowledged the role of Schacht's organization in the setup of investments in Spain aiming to cement German hegemony beyond the Civil War.[100] Never more clearly, the Schachtian foreign trade framework came together with Franco's dire needs to maximize the potential extractive benefit for the German economy, and all without sacrificing scant foreign exchange.

Because of his utter dependence on German supplies and war matériel, Franco was therefore forced into rationally suboptimal foreign trade decisions—yet they were the only sensible ones within the constraints of his political economy. While decisive victory over the Republic eluded Franco, in considerable part due to Russian supplies flowing to the Republic, German influence over the Nationalists became hegemonic.

The Nationalists understandably wanted to preserve their raw materials for other markets where they could obtain dollars or pound sterling. But the Germans made sure that did not happen: they wanted something in exchange for support. Schacht's staff at the ministry then agreed that there would be no clearing agreement with Spain. This does not suggest the Spanish "called the shots" of an inherently uneven bilateral relationship.[101] And as we shall see, this contrasted starkly with Italian behavior. Although it has been largely overlooked in the histories of the Third Reich's economic and trade policy, German hegemony in Spain was far stronger than in the Balkans or Latin America, and the leverage was exercised to fullest effect in the supply of the weapons Franco so desperately needed. It was a textbook example of Schacht's preferred imperial strategy.

While Franco's troops continued a slow advance against the Republic, German diplomats sought to turn de facto economic hegemony into de jure benefits. This would entrench Germany's hegemonic position beyond the Civil War. To that effect two key documents regarding future Spanish-German relations were signed in Salamanca in 1937. On March 20 Faupel and Franco signed a protocol that stated, "Both Governments will constantly consult with one another on the measures necessary to defend their countries against the threatening dangers of Communism." Anti-Communist rhetoric notwithstanding, German commercial interests had a central place in the Concordat: "Both Governments are agreed in their desire to intensify the economic relations between their countries as much as possible." Though this first line amounted to little more than usual diplomatic parlance, the deal betrayed German interest in Iberian raw materials: "In this manner [Germany and Spain] reaffirm their purpose that the two countries shall henceforth cooperate with and supplement one another in economic matters in every way."[102] This rhetoric of complementarity and symbiosis had specific connotations for Spain: it meant that the relatively underdeveloped country would provide for the needs of German industry even if that were not the most efficient trading partner. The similarity with Schacht's "peaceful penetration" strategy in the Balkans is striking.[103]

Meanwhile in Berlin the Four-Year Plan developed its own bureaucracy.[104] Its goal was to change the direction of the German economy in the service of the *Lebensraum* school of formal, racialist control rather than with the *Weltpolitik* tradition of economic hegemony and informal empire.[105] In the context of Göring's rising role in economic affairs, it could still be argued—and indeed it has been argued—that German interest in Spain was primarily political, and not economic.[106] A Francoist victory had the potential to establish the type of united front against Communism that had been part of Hitler's strategic calculation back in July 1936, strengthening the fascist grip on the Mediterranean and effectively surrounding a French Republic that was, at best, uneasy of its British ally.

Yet documents detailing negotiations in Spain between Nazi and Francoist officials underscore the extent to which economic motives had eclipsed all others in the Spanish theater. Hitler's support for Faupel's economic-focused strategy is telling. The centrality of economic concerns was particularly evident in the German reaction when Spanish delegates pressed for a trade treaty in mid-1937, effectively threatening to dislocate the HISMA-ROWAK quasi-monopoly.[107] On May 13, 1937, Economic Policy Director Ritter sent the Burgos Embassy a confidential telegram arguing that it had become clear that the Spanish junta "[insisted] strongly upon the conclusion of a clearing agreement." Clearing agreements were nothing unusual at the time. Following the collapse of the international trade system, states seeking to benefit from trade without jeopardizing their current account position would conclude bilateral agreements on the quantities of commodities they were willing to trade with one another.[108] In fact Schacht had already used such agreements to promote barter trade with the less developed countries of southeastern Europe and Latin America. Such agreements played a crucial role in the Schachtian attempt to ensure German manufacturing could remain extrovert without diminishing minuscule foreign exchange reserves at the Reichsbank. As an added benefit, they ensured that German trade could be expanded without relying on Anglo-American credit lines. A multiyear agreement to institutionalize bilateral trade could have ensured that the present terms of trade were extended beyond the end of the Civil War, thus not endangering Hitler's nascent shadow empire. Given Franco's dire need for war matériel, the conclusion of a clearing agreement on such terms was certainly well within the Wilhelmstraße's room for negotiation. What is more, the nature of clearing agreements guaranteed a certain volume of orders over multiple years. The purchasing party could at any point recommend an increase in the quantity of goods through further negotiations, but it could not decrease its own exports unilaterally.

Spanish businessmen and Franco's staff were eager to get Bernhardt's HISMA out of their way. No one could blame them; as dependent as Franco was on German support, he wanted to rid himself of the "imperial" agent on the ground. The conclusion of a clearing agreement, then, made ample sense: the Spaniards would rid themselves of HISMA's institutional control, Germany would assure its bilateral trade ties with Spain remained advantageous, and both sides could do without the unnecessary commissions HISMA-ROWAK charged to replicate preexisting government functions.

Yet the perception of German interest blocked any moves in the direction of clearing. "We must have a guarantee," Ritter demanded, "that big transactions in raw materials and essential foods are reserved to HISMA-ROWAK as hitherto." He strongly recommended Faupel exercise pressure directly on Franco, treating the future dictator as little more than Nazi a puppet: "Call General Franco's attention particularly to the fact that in the past few months it was only through the preferential use of the proceeds of Spanish exports through HISMA-ROWAK which made it possible to finance an important part of the Spanish orders for war matériel in Germany."[109] Faupel toed this rather direct line with discernible imperial overtones. The document was even more explicit regarding whose interest was at stake in the dual monopoly: "We knew very well that HISMA-ROWAK was not very popular with the Spanish exporters and importers . . . [and] the same was true of German exporters and importers. They, too, assailed the present monopolistic position of HISMA-ROWAK. From the private business standpoint of these interests, this was to a certain degree comprehensible." But Ritter—like other Nazi officials—resisted changes: "We should reject the one-sided views of such special interests."[110] The state's interest in Spanish raw materials was paramount—and it involved turning down Nationalists requests. So, contrary to what Franco's Nationalists desired, the dual monopoly held on: it remained a key priority to preserve the hegemonic trade position that Francoist material dependence had created.

Political influence would maximize returns through the state-sponsored champion that could keep the Spanish market dependent on German capital goods, particularly those that allowed for conquest.[111] It was precisely what Schacht's 1926 speech to the Colonial Association had envisioned and his later policies as "economic dictator" had institutionalized—even if his enemy within the Cabinet, a man who instinctively favored a different type of colonial endeavor, was ultimately in charge of the Party apparatus implementing the policies.

The hegemonic role in Spain's economy mattered more to German officials than sovereignty; the type of control exercised on Iberian soil was never formal, even if some Republican reports detailed German territorial ambitions in Morocco, most likely as a ploy to involve London or alienate Rome.[112] Yet when compared to the formal Nazi empire, this informality of Nazi control in Spain made "imperial" pressures on Franco far cheaper and easier to manage than the alternative, hardly imaginable given the balance of power at the time. Ultimately, however, Schacht's neo-*Weltpolitik* strategy had an important caveat: though informality made hegemony easier and attainable without triggering large-scale war, it also made it ultimately reversible, particularly if a quest for *Lebensraum*—as discussed simultaneously in Berlin—were to be unleashed.

chapter seven

THE SHADOW EMPIRE

Said Göring, give me four years, and you'll see from the
shackles of money I'll set industry free.

—SCHACHTIAN RHYME, late 1937

In early 1937 Schacht penned an article for the prestigious *Foreign Affairs* in which he outlined Germany's colonial demands. It was not a
novel argument; but it was timely. At a time of ever-rising continental tensions, it was a piece of German propaganda aimed at an Anglo-
Saxon audience.[1] It remains one of the best examples of the neo-
Weltpolitik vision of empire. Although Schacht's policymaking power
was now openly challenged by the Four-Year Plan organization, the
"economic dictator" still pushed his agenda to expand economic hegemony abroad. This vision, involving a Germany that would leverage its economic might rather than seek formal territorial expansion, was losing influence within the higher echelons of Nazi
leadership; ever since Hitler's memorandum the previous September,
supporters of *Lebensraum* had had the upper hand. Former allies in
business and the military establishment abandoned Schacht when he
argued for a slowdown in armaments production. Facing trouble at
home, the banker turned abroad—just as he had done in the late 1920s.

Schacht's argument began along familiar lines, laying out the essential conflict between the aspirations of autarkists and global prosperity,
even in a context of diminished international trade. "Before the [Great]
war, Germany's world investments were in round figures 12,000 million

dollars, the profits of which could be used to buy raw materials all over the world. The markets where raw materials were procured were completely free. . . . All the important countries were on the gold standard, and this provided a sure basis for commercial calculations."[2] He was overstating how much Germany had actually profited from its colonies.[3] And yet "all these elementary principles of international trade and intercourse have now disappeared." In a world of protectionism, Germany was handicapped.

Such rhetoric was uncharacteristic of Nazi policymaking in one key respect: references to the prewar Wilhelmine era were scant in the 1930s, particularly in such laudatory tones. "Commercial treaties are concluded only for brief periods, and in their place have come quotas and restrictions, to say nothing of constant increases in more effective tariffs."[4] In the aftermath of the Great Depression, international trade had declined drastically, with severe consequences not only for high value-added exports but also for the supply of foreign raw materials. Schacht's system had allowed Germany to recover and maneuver around international trade imbalances. The banker argued it was reasonable that the countries affected most—that is, the countries with fewer raw material supplies in their homeland or within their trade sphere—would seek to mitigate their foreign dependence. It was a logical reaction to trade closure. At the time liberal voices saw autarkic behavior as self-fulfilling and primarily the fault of aggressive movers like Germany. The banker's reasoning also implied that those with extensive access to raw materials within their own "economic sphere" would be the first ones to abandon the prevailing international financial architecture. After all, they had alternatives that his Germany did not.

Schacht's targets were the usual suspects: the unable (Britain) and the unwilling (the United States) financial hegemons. "The British devaluation would never have had the success which it achieved if Great Britain had not been able to bring the monetary system of the Dominions onto the same basis as her own," Schacht reasoned. The point was that Britain did not have to face higher commodity prices because it could force its empire to accept a lower exchange rate within the sterling system; the main victims of beggar-thy-neighbor devaluation were competitors like Germany. A country with foreign debts that could not be devalued was in a particularly vulnerable position—and that was a feature of the Versailles system both Hitler and Schacht had worked tirelessly to destroy. What is more, "France could never have used her colonial empire so successfully if it had not been administered under the same monetary system as the mother country."[5] Like in the late 1920s, Schacht was attempting to legitimize German claims to colonies as a pressing matter of economic and monetary policy, not sovereignty or race.

We can also see Schacht's *Foreign Policy* article as a way to relegitimize his position after Göring's Four-Year Plan coup. It was not immediately obvious that either his Cabinet position or the Reichsbank presidency qualified Schacht to speak on matters of foreign policy, yet this was an arena where his international reputation made him influential in ways that his Cabinet peers were not. The banker's demands followed his traditional reasoning that there be "territories under German management and included in the German monetary system. All the other questions involved—sovereignty, army, police, law, the churches, international collaboration—are open to discussion."[6] This is clear evidence that he did not care about formal sovereignty in the same way as Haushofer, Darré, and other supporters of *Lebensraum* did.[7] It was trade that mattered most—and that would be the vehicle for domestic stability and international power.

In early 1937, therefore, Schacht still conceived of a return to the colonial arena as a potential political safety valve: acquisition of markets for Germany would simultaneously check the pressure on Germany's eastern borders and provide another avenue for domestic growth. It would also allow Germany to develop the 1935–1936 Neue Plan trade system to impose hegemonic power in European markets, replicating and expanding existing trade deals in southeastern Europe and Latin America. This in turn could put a limit on the Four-Year Plan and its supporters. The connection between preferably informal empire and a more stable Germany is reinforced by Schacht's stark warning at the close of the piece, one that—even if Hitler had never seen it—amounted to the neo-*Weltpolitik* answer to the Führer's memorandum: "[The German colonial problem] is simply and solely a problem of economic existence. Precisely for that reason the future of European peace depends upon it."[8]

At the time the minister and Reichsbank president was not merely playing journalism. During these tense months of Berlin power politics

and trade negotiations, a series of secret reports by a Spanish Republican agent in France described conversations with Schacht across European capitals. In Paris, Stockholm, and Brussels their discussions
directly addressed the economic nature of the German project in
Spain—and did so in a way that directly addressed Schacht's foreign
economic concerns. The context was complex. The structure of continental alliances was fast-moving, with Hitler, Mussolini, Leon Blum's
Popular Front, Stalinist Russia, and the British National Coalition
shifting their positions. In London, Neville Chamberlain replaced
Baldwin as prime minister in late May 1937.[9] In Paris, Blum, who instinctively (or quite rationally) distrusted Hitler, was stuck between a
desire for assertiveness and vacillation across the Channel.[10] As we have
witnessed with regard to the July 25, 1936, decision not to arm the
Spanish Republic, France's foreign policy position was a conundrum.[11]
Meanwhile the Soviet Union had greatly escalated its supplies to the
Republic, though Stalin was extracting his pound of flesh for it.[12]

On April 17, 1937, Schulmeister, a secret agent code-named after
the celebrated Napoleonic spy, reported encouragingly to Madrid that
Nazi support for Franco's Nationalists seemed "to be on the descending
curve."[13] It was neither the first nor the last time Republican agents
would advance such hopeful readings.[14] Schulmeister argued that the
cooling off was a direct consequence of Franco's resistance to further
German economic penetration; this reticence had led Germans to backtrack on promises of military support. The agent claimed to have been
privy to troop withdrawal discussions featuring Schacht and a well-
connected American businessman, Norman Davies. The government
in Madrid must have seen this as a particularly auspicious development
considering Schacht's standing and the fact that the internal disagreements within the Nazi establishment remained, as far as we know, private.[15] Any reversal in Nazi support for Franco had the potential to
change the balance of forces in the Civil War, in spite of recent Francoist advances in the resource-rich Basque region.[16] In the absence of
the Condor Legion and Nazi supplies, Republicans could stop the Francoist advance and, in the aftermath of a surprising victory in Guadalajara in March 1937, even stage a counteroffensive.[17]

What transpired in Schacht's subsequent meetings with Schulmeister
seemed even more auspicious for Spain's legitimate government. According to the Republican agent, Schacht appeared "happy to solve the

[Spanish] conflict in an economically advantageous way [for Germany]." Schacht went even further: he expressed "willing[ness] to engage in a commercial agreement with Republican Spain."[18] Perhaps Franco was resisting further economic penetration too strongly, so much so that a strategic shift in German policy was conceivable. The alternative was that Schacht was attempting to craft his own foreign policy with regard to Spain.

This document suggests that, aware as he was of Germany's constraints and his own challenged position in Berlin, Schacht saw intervention in Spain from an economic vantage point. Strategic concerns were secondary, and ideology did not feature at all. According to the Republican agent, Schacht ventured that, "if things were to be resolved well, Germany could absorb almost all [of Spain's] agricultural production."[19] At least in what he chose to share with the Republican agent, Schacht's main interest was Spain's continued contribution to the German economy. Importantly, however, he was less focused on raw materials for armaments production—such as the minerals HISMA's staff primarily pressed for—and more focused on the foodstuffs that cost his Reichsbank precious foreign exchange. As long as German economic preeminence was respected, Schacht presumably did not care about the details of intervention—or even the ultimate outcome of the Spanish Civil War. This was a rather extreme claim on Schacht's behalf; any such fundamental change in foreign policy would have required Hitler's explicit approval.[20] Was he acting alone? It is impossible to know for certain; yet these attempts at parallel diplomacy fit squarely with the preoccupations of the envoys representing his ministry and, to an extent, the Auswärtiges Amt (Foreign Office): to maintain Germany's newfound economic hegemony in Spain.

The foreign policy context of these discussions is especially instructive. Ever since August 1936—around the same time Göring became involved in the economy—Schacht had become personally engaged in bilateral negotiations with Blum's government. These were at the very least partially endorsed by Hitler. At their August 28, 1936, meeting, for instance, the French premier had expressed a desire to negotiate a commercial agreement with Germany. "I am a Marxist and a Jew," Blum had said, "but we can arrive at nothing if we set up ideologies as insurmountable barriers."[21] Conversations were tricky; Schacht insisted on his preferred mode of (economic) negotiation: bilateral over multilateral.

This was, it must be said, also Hitler's preferred way to conduct foreign policy. But the French premier was open to an agreement that would address Germany's perceived structural economic weaknesses.

France's Entente allies were not only aware of the meeting but were also briefed in detail.[22] In a long telegram to Eden's Foreign Office, Ambassador George Clerk complained from Paris that Nazi Germany "did not make use of normal [foreign policy] methods," while acknowledging Schacht's domestic power: this was "not the first time feelers of this kind were put through Dr. Schacht."[23] What is more, Schacht had briefed and obtained approval from Hitler for his offers in Paris, even if he lacked any "formal" foreign policy mandate.[24] Working toward the Führer had always worked for him. The crucial point, however, was that Schacht saw a "European settlement" as dependent on economic concessions for Germany and its access to raw materials.

When Blum argued that "it hardly seemed that the possession of a colony could be of such great importance to the German economy," Schacht responded that "a return to the colonial sphere" was a sine qua non. From Schacht's writings in the previous two decades, we know that this "colonial sphere" concept did not depend on formal sovereignty. In exchange for those outlets, Germany could acquiesce to a reduction of armaments as well as a "general settlement" with Britain and France. While he saw a direct agreement with Russia as impossible, Schacht envisaged practical ways to diffuse tensions through "indirect guarantees."[25] It could not be denied the meeting with Blum went well. "I am ready to begin the conversation immediately," he concluded. This time around, the French were forthcoming. A close confidante of Blum, André Blumel, later claimed negotiations advanced far more than was previously assumed.[26]

Yet an agreement never materialized. Eden refused to lend support to any colonial settlement along Schacht's lines. In a personal note to "my dear Minister" Delbos, the British foreign secretary believed his Cabinet "colleagues" would not feel comfortable "carry[ing] these discussions further until they are in possession of a more complete and detailed appreciation of the attitude of the German government."[27] Eden insisted on official channels: "discussions . . . through the diplomatic channel to prepare a Five Power conference."[28] Committed to the type of multiparty summit that had failed before (London) and would fail again (Munich), Eden rebuked Schacht's unorthodox rapprochement.

His opposition ran deeper: Eden also alluded to a speech he had given in July at the Commons against too many concessions to Germany in the colonial sphere. If the point were not clear enough, two weeks later Eden sent two communications in the same day to avoid "showing ourselves too eager for agreement" with Germany, which "applied also to the initiative of Dr. Schacht."[29] Even before this letter, such intransigence on German desires did not mean, however, the British government was ready to fully abandon the strategy of economic appeasement.[30] London's support for German "moderates" was not without its limits.[31]

Eventually Hitler rejected Britain's call for a new conference and Blum's desire for multiparty talks.[32] Increasingly, in the foreign sphere, "the Führer acted and the rest reacted."[33] Undaunted the Reichsbank president returned to Paris in March 1937. Blum welcomed him once again.[34] It was presumably during this trip that Schacht met Schulmeister in person and discussed German intervention on Iberian soil. On May 14, 1937, furthermore, in a technically off-the-record conversation between Schacht and a Republican emissary, the banker speculated on what it would take to get Germany out of Spain, linking an increasingly economically focused intervention to a wider economic settlement. He returned to the imperial framework that he had long advocated: "In the first place, colonies. And colonies where we can extract raw materials and in which our currency can circulate."[35] A few months later, with foreign policy tensions again running high, Schacht argued for a location where the economic power Germany wielded de facto in Spain could be awarded de jure and, one might add, with Anglo-French blessings.[36] It was not as if the public in Britain or France was not used to such arguments; the polite 1920s Weimar-era discussions about colonies had given way to far more anxious debates. British and French audiences in the 1930s were routinely bombarded with war-mongering literature. For instance, in the preface to the early 1939 volume *The Nazi Claims to Colonies,* First Lord of the Admiralty Duff Cooper wrote, "Germany wants colonies for one reason and one reason only. She wants them in order to strengthen her strategic position and thus assist her to secure the dominion of the world."[37] Ultimately British intransigence on the colonial issue remained unchanged, dooming both Blum's negotiations and Schacht's hopes.[38]

During these meetings with Republican agents, Schacht ventured a justification for the German involvement in favor of Franco. "Nobody knows . . . how we got dragged into this Spanish adventure," he told Schulmeister with false naïveté. "We started simply as businessmen and providing war materials not only to Franco, but also to the other side."[39] Such statements are dubious, particularly considering Hitler's Wagner-inspired decision to supply Franco and only Franco within the Nationalist camp, of which Schacht and his bureaucracies (both at the Reichsbank and at the ministry) not only knew about but also explicitly approved.[40] It may have been a purposeful lie, after all. After arguing that he had initially resisted intervention, just as the Foreign Ministry had, Schacht made a promise: "Germany will negotiate with France and Britain its full withdrawal from Spain, in exchange for very concrete concessions, mostly of [an] economic order."[41] Preserved in President Azaña's files, these documents underscore how much the primary goal of German involvement in Spain had changed since the evening of July 25, 1936. They also suggest a hitherto unknown Schachtian alternative foreign policy path in Spain, one that would have maintained the focus on economic profit.

By early 1937 the main driver of German involvement was economic in nature, linked to the Nazi regime's domestic priorities. The HISMA-ROWAK dual monopoly remained beyond Schacht's direct grasp even though it took advantage of a foreign economic strategy that he, above all others, designed and directed.[42] Schacht's desire for more oversight on the organization may well have rested on his political aims in Berlin, at a time when his power was being eroded. Bernhardt had effective operational independence on Iberian soil, meaning his finances were opaque at best.[43]

The management style of HISMA operations in Spain collided with Schacht's obsessive control.[44] Not so Göring. The latter rarely missed a chance to abuse his position in order to expand his fortune; it was an issue that preoccupied him at Nuremberg, though little else did.[45] In a classic example, the Göring Fund for the Arts (Kunstfonds) was financed by mandatory contributions taken from the wages of all the employees under his purview. This nonprofit organization's goal was art—only it would have been more fitting to call it a "Fund for Göring." After all, it set out to acquire artwork for the minister's many homes, themselves often financed by private companies and government budgets.[46] It was not merely top officials who benefited from corruption: embezzlement was rampant throughout Göring's many fiefdom, and nowhere was this more apparent than in the organization that shadowed Schacht's ministry. Although Göring, as Four-Year Plan plenipotentiary, banned black markets (an interesting theoretical concoction in and of itself), his employees were reluctant to enforce it because they profited from it.[47] A few months after the occupation of Norway, for example, a German Relief Organization (Deutsches Hilfswerk) was set up in Oslo as a simple front for the transfer of loot to Party officials.[48] As we shall see, such thinly disguised looting would become a central tenet of the Nazi formal empire, in addition to standard corruption in the "civilian" administration of occupied territories.[49]

It should therefore come as no surprise that HISMA-ROWAK, an exotic state-private hybrid in the Spanish theater, was reluctant to disclose the final destination of its sizable profits. HISMA's official auditor was convinced that Bernhardt was accumulating massive amounts of personal profit from the company and dedicated his life to collecting evidence against him.[50] Given Göring's peripheral involvement in HISMA and the inherently corrupt nature of his organizations, it is certainly not a stretch to ascribe at least part of the political pressure to maintain the HISMA-ROWAK dual monopoly as personal rather than national economics. In any event, corruption was one of the issues that most irritated Schacht about the Party hierarchy generally and Göring specifically.

A likely reason Schacht's negotiations with the Republic never prospered was that, as had happened in late 1936, Franco gave in to German demands. In stark contrast to what his economic delegation had requested in early 1937, the Nationalist leader duly withdrew the demand for a clearing agreement with Germany. He also stopped complaining about the HISMA-ROWAK dual monopoly that made German power in the Nationalist economy hegemonic. The reason is obvious: he simply could not do without Nazi war matériel. Under the strains of war, the symbiosis so favored by the Germans made sense to Spain's Nationalists as well. Franco even went as far as to apologize for his delegates "exceeding instructions" in their arguing for the clearing agreement that would have undermined HISMA's dominant role. In Spain it was business as usual.[51]

German demands on the Nationalist leadership multiplied. In mid-July 1937 Ambassador Faupel and Franco's foreign minister, Gen. Francisco Gómez-Jordana, signed a secret protocol sealing the agreement against Spanish interests; though, as per German desires, a trade agreement was put off, the governments promised in "binding form their mutual endeavor to advance commerce between their countries . . . [and their] earnest desire to assist one another to the greatest possible extent in the delivery of such raw materials, foods, semi-finished and finished products as are of particular interest to the recipient country."[52] The importance of this clause for the resource-constrained German economy is clear enough. This was a direct German imposition, brought about by imperial pressures. While weapons and men continued pouring in from Germany, Spain's outstanding debt to the Reich soared. And through HISMA Spain's Nationalist government relinquished a considerable foreign exchange and, more important, its natural wealth and foodstuffs—high-quality ores, pyrites, and other minerals—for Germany's industrial needs.[53]

Back in Berlin, Göring's Four-Year Plan organization did its best to contribute to economic growth; duplicating existing positions, its bureaucracy grew exorbitantly.[54] More than ever Schacht was convinced that Göring's goals could not be reconciled with a stable economy. The program threatened to change from rearmament in the service of economic development to economic development only insofar as it funded rearmament. The logical conclusion of such policy was dangerous: Germany would have to find bigger outlets for its production than a limited civil war like Spain's, where its policies of power projection and economic hegemony were at the time quite successful.

All paths led to the Führer. Over the past few months Hitler and Schacht had had disagreements regarding the pace of rearmament and the birth of the Four-Year Plan. Since late 1936 Schacht had identified the Four-Year Plan office as a bureaucratic enemy, instructing his staff not to take orders from it.[55] This bureaucratic battle was elevated to Hitler repeatedly in late 1936 and 1937, around the time of Schacht's failed negotiations with Republicans and in France.[56] One of these discussions was featured in Albert Speer's postwar memoirs; the Führer's favorite architect remembered a day when Schacht and Hitler became entangled in a private discussion on the pace of rearmament. Speer counted it as one of the few times before the war when Hitler lost his self-control.[57] He could hear them both from another room at Hitler's Berghof retreat.[58] "The dialogue grew increasingly heated on both sides and then ceased abruptly," Speer wrote. "Furious, Hitler came out on the terrace [of the Berghof] and ranted about this disobliging, limited minister who was holding up rearmament."[59] Göring's role must have come up. By then War Minister von Blomberg was sending increased funding requests for rearmament directly to Göring—not to Schacht.[60] Eventually Hitler managed to reassure Schacht, allegedly appealing to his ego and closing with a personal touch: "But Schacht—I'm fond of you."[61] Far from making a choice, the Führer allegedly urged an understanding be found. Could one be found?[62]

On August 5, 1937, Schacht wrote to Göring that his Four-Year Plan priorities did not make economic sense. "You can't bake bread or cast cannon from securities," he wrote condescendingly. Schacht judged Göring's plans to be highly inefficient. He also asked his opponent to take over ownership of the results if he continued to insist on favors to his organizations and cronies: "I declared to you months ago that uniformity is indispensable in economic policy. . . . I have previously stated that I consider your policy on matters of foreign exchange to be wrong and I am not able to share responsibility for it." He also appealed to Hitler: "The excessive requisitioning of raw materials and labor for public buildings, armaments, and the Four Year Plan threatens to bring about a decline in our export trade." Hitler knew that exports were of crucial importance to the country's financial health—unless imports could be curtailed even further than they already were under Schacht's extensive internal control system. He also appealed to the Führer's memories of the 1934 crisis, and implicitly the memory of Weimar's hyperinflationary chaos: "I wish to make it perfectly clear that if there is a decrease in foreign exchange accruing to us through exports, it stands to reason that the supply of raw materials will also slow down and this will lead to further gaps in our provision for buildings, armaments, and the Four Year Plan."[63] This argument challenged Göring's strategy of ever-increasing rearmament. In economics, unlike in Nazi politics, will alone did not suffice.

While Schacht was fighting for his political survival, the economic penetration and commodity flow that German intervention had materialized in Spain was in demand in Berlin.[64] In the larger context, however, preeminence in Spain and the Balkans was not quite enough if Schacht's calls for a reorientation fell in deaf years. The Reichsbank president had come to believe the domestic economy was destined for inflation, collapse, or both. By late 1937, confronted with the reality of Göring's grasp for economic power, however, Schacht worked toward the Führer yet again. "There can only be one head of Economic Affairs," he wrote on October 8, 1937. "Who that head is to be, you, *mein Führer,* must decide according to the measure of your confidence in the abilities and loyalty of the person appointed."[65] Perhaps there was a reason Schacht placed abilities before loyalty in the letter.

With German business coming under further pressure to comply with Göring's production goals, Schacht opted for the same path he had taken in the late 1920s: better an early exit than the collapse. Once again he explicitly warned of repressed inflation in an economy tilted too far toward unchecked armament production. Shortages in both materials and labor were by then obvious.[66] This time around, Schacht closed his missive with a sardonic verse: "Said Göring, give me four years, and you'll see / from the shackles of money I'll set industry free / Here's Schacht as hostage in the interim, / If I should bolt, you can strangle me." In his note to the Führer he remarked pithily that the rhyme presented "a prospect which—speaking personally—fails to attract me."[67] It was hard to forget the fate of the regime's purge victims.[68]

A few weeks later Schacht officially lost control of fiscal matters. On November 28, 1937, Göring formally became (acting) minister of the economy and plenipotentiary of the war economy. It was the end product of what American prosecutors at Nuremberg appropriately synthesized as a "clash between two power-seeking individuals."[69] But Schacht was not quite out. He retreated to being nothing more or less than president of the Reichsbank; he also remained minister without portfolio.[70] He had furnished the man who now sidelined him with the structures and recovery that made rearmament, along with the Spanish adventure, possible. Given Göring's lack of fundamental understanding of economics, it is wholly unsurprising that changes in actual structure, rather than degree, were not forthcoming.[71] Schacht believed that Göring not only jeopardized economic sustainability but also risked a wider war. Paradoxically a key backer of *Lebensraum* had sidelined the most successful proponent of neo-*Weltpolitik* at a time when the imperial model favored by the latter conception of empire was tangible on Iberian soil. Upon entering Schacht's office at the ministry, Göring allegedly asked, "How can one indulge in great thoughts in such a small room?"[72] He then placed a call to the Reichsbank president: "Herr Schacht, I am now sitting in your chair!" It was the kind of hubristic line that Schacht himself would have uttered to a humiliated opponent.

Göring's Nazification of the Economics Ministry did not change basic trade and economic policy structures; domestic authoritarianism continued, as did bilateral trade deals under the Neue Plan. In light of these developments in the political economy of the regime, the famous Hossbach memorandum of November 1937—a key German foreign policy document outlining Hitler's expansionism—can be read through a different lens, at least with regard to the Spanish Civil War.[73] In attendance were the main military and economic decision makers save Schacht: Hitler, Göring, von Blomberg, Raeder, von Neurath, and Gen. Werner von Fritsch. The meeting outlined Hitler's plans for formal empire closely mirroring *Lebensraum* thought. The document also explicitly refers to the strategic advantage of a long war in Spain: Hitler directly argued that "[German] interest lay more in the prolongation of the war in Spain."[74] Both German and Spanish archives are filled with complaints, filed around this time, in which Nationalist commanders protested through their ambassador in Berlin about Republican troops sporting German supplies.[75] Could it be that, months after Schacht's contacts with Schulmeister, the Nazis were actually selling weapons to the Republic? The evidence is contradictory: Republicans did purchase German weapons, but Nazi officials insisted it was only through a Dutch "weapons dealer." The Spaniards, at least as far as the documents indicate, believed them. It is unclear whether they had a choice.[76] In truth the weapons seem to have been manufactured in Greece from a producer with a German license.[77]

Ever the crowd-pleaser, Göring suggested at the meeting the "liquidation of military undertakings in Spain."[78] But Hitler rejected the idea. A protracted war in Spain, in which Germany remained involved, would serve its interests strategically by diverting French and British interest. It is safe to infer that the continuation of hostilities would also serve to deepen German economic penetration in the Iberian economy. As we shall see, this contrasts starkly with concurrent Italian preoccupations about their level of expenditure in Spain. But the German-Spanish trade system was then at its zenith, allowing Germans to provide weapons and get goods and assets in exchange. Dependence on the Third Reich was only bound to rise. The Hossbach conference also specifically dealt with the German shortage of iron ore and food-stuffs, the two key areas of focus in Spain.[79] Spain alone would never be able to make up for all of Germany's deficiencies, yet informal empire was making a key contribution. Yet Hitler moved in a different direction; his eagerness to gamble and risk full-on conflagration is what led Gen. Ludwig Beck to say Hitler's remarks were "crushing [*niederschmetternd*]."[80]

Reading the transcripts critically, one could argue the conference may actually have vindicated Schacht's more rational approach toward rebalancing the economy. In spite of the Four-Year Plan goals, Hitler had to face the fact that it was not possible to achieve *Autarkie* in food-stuffs (given growth patterns and Darré's policies) or ores (given ever-rising armaments production). These constraints have led some historians to argue that war in 1939 was necessary to hide the economic imbalances.[81] Rather than changing course, Hitler pressed on. And in so doing he increasingly relied on men who, like Göring, believed in the triumph of will over economic reality. When von Neurath approached Hitler in January 1938 to discuss the strategy outlined in the Hossbach memorandum, the conservative diplomat argued that many of Hitler's goals could be achieved, but only in time. Hitler's response was that they had no more time: Germany was headed for war.[82]

The destiny of those who attended the Hossbach conference was indicative of the regime's internal radicalization.[83] Only two months later, the messy "Fritsch-Blomberg affair" sidelined the two highest-ranking Wehrmacht leaders, who were accused of homosexuality and marrying a woman with a past, respectively.[84] It was after this affair that Walter Warlimont—of Condor Legion fame—altered the structure of the armed forces by creating the Oberkommando der Wehrmacht. Effectively superseding the War Ministry and promoting generals less critical of Hitler's rule, the OKW made military decisions more directly subordinate to the Führer.[85]

This fundamental shift at the core of the Nazi regime also translated into the foreign policy establishment. Radicalization permeated far and wide. On February 4, 1938, Hitler had von Neurath replaced by Joachim von Ribbentrop.[86] Von Neurath—who, along with his deputy Dieckhoff, had been so weary of Franco's pleas for help in the wake of the Civil War—had long wanted out of the Cabinet. Yet he had wished to leave his "anomalous and burdensome position to almost anyone other than Ribbentrop."[87] The "former champagne merchant," as he was often referred to, was fervently devoted to Hitler. According to a pithy Goebbels, however, he had "bought his name, he married his money, and he swindled his way into office."[88] The contrast with his aristocratic, conservative predecessor was stark. Mussolini later complained Ribbentrop belonged to the "category of Germans who are a disaster for their country," for he "[talked] about making war right and left, without naming an enemy or defining an objective"—and that was coming from Mussolini.[89] Schacht was not the only one on the way out; along with him went the last remnants of traditional conservatism from the Nazi Cabinet. Zeal remained.

Nazi internal politics had little bearing on the mechanics of intervention in Spain. Nothing would alter the economic focus of the Spanish endeavor.[90] With each Francoist conquest came more German-bound shipments of raw materials, from tungsten to iron ore, diverting trade away from Britain and France.[91] HISMA's corporate expansion was similarly rapid: it opened branches in the major cities that fell to Franco's armies, particularly when it came to the resource-rich North.[92] Far from Berlin politics and close to the war front, an economic empire was taking root in Francoist Spain.

On November 4, 1937, the Burgos Embassy sent a secret memorandum to the Wilhelmstraße that outlined an important debate for the bilateral relationship.[93] Dictated by Bernhardt himself, it complained about a new Spanish mining law limiting foreign ownership of Iberian mining assets to 25 percent of total capital.[94] Bernhardt had been accumulating mining rights since the outbreak of the war, cleverly transforming imports of German war supplies into direct investment in the Spanish economy. The means—as well as Bernhardt's style—had often annoyed German government officials, starting with Messerschmitt, but no changes were made. When the Spaniards complained, they were pushed aside. Bernhardt's moves foresaw foreign direct investment without using foreign exchange or bullion, setting the bases of an informal empire that transcended the trade dislocations of the Civil War. And mining rights, it must be noted, were often taken directly from under the noses of the British and French, who had long delayed recognizing Franco's government because of their governmental commitment to nonintervention.[95] Yet now Francoist authorities threatened to take it all away by reinstating national ownership over those assets.

In all fairness the law was consistent with the nationalist and traditionalist ideology of a nascent Francoist dictatorship. It was also the closest Franco's men had come to active resistance against German economic hegemony.[96] The terms of the report—as well as the formal and informal complaints elevated to Foreign Minister Gómez-Jordana and Nicolás Franco—illustrate the German reach in Francoist headquarters. As per usual Bernhardt was clear about his objectives: "It is clear to us that the Montana project [German ownership of undeveloped Spanish mines, referring to the Spanish Montaña, literally 'mountain'] constitutes the whole aim and purpose of our assistance in Spain." So much was, at this stage, clear. "The objective of our economic interest in Spain," he continued, "must be the deep penetration into the main sources of Spanish wealth, namely agriculture and mining. Whereas the products of agriculture fall in the share of the German Reich more or less without effort, since the Spaniards are forced to find a market, the mining problem is of tremendous importance in every respect."[97] The report spells out neo-*Weltpolitik* objectives as clearly as Schacht's speeches did. The implication was that the only way to preserve German access to mining raw materials was to divert trade; given the international situation, prices, and foreign exchange, those materials would not go to Germany if the Spaniards were allowed to trade freely. Most likely they would go to Britain, as had been the case before the Civil War.

No doubt Bernhardt worried about his role as an effective viceroy in Spain; a bad outcome in the negotiations, or indeed the success of rising British influence over Franco, could jeopardize his position.[98] The tone of the attached description of the Montaña project, originally involving ownership of no fewer than seventy-three mines all over Spain and Morocco, was even more confrontational: "[Germany] must make it evident to the leading figures in Nationalist Spain that Germany is engaged in an economic war and thus is also at war." Bernhardt therefore borrowed from the regime's rhetoric and concluded on a disingenuous comparative note: "Just as Germany immediately sent her help to her Spanish partner . . . Germany has a claim to immediate deliveries by Spain for her own economic war."[99] Through ownership, preferably executed without using foreign exchange, he could assure that Spanish natural wealth continued to go to Germany in the aftermath of war, regardless of which market was ex ante preferable to Spain. HISMA would remain at the core of the Iberian economy. But unlike on previous occasions, the disagreement over Montaña escalated. Throughout 1938 the mining ownership issue would come close to monopolizing German-Spanish relations.[100]

Almost simultaneously HISMA underwent an internal transformation aimed at diversifying its operations, becoming the Sociedad Financiera Industrial Limitada (SOFINDUS).[101] This German-controlled Iberian venture was meant to provide the sort of umbrella vehicle for all assets acquired during the Civil War that served German needs at home; acting as a holding company, it sought to own not only mines but also farming, trucking, and even clothing businesses. The farming sector was interestingly diversified: hides, wool, furs, even wine. Eventually it would also be proposed to expand SOFINDUS into banking to cement its power in a future Francoist reconstruction; it would have amounted to a Nazi-sponsored development bank for German informal empire in Spain. In this sense HISMA evolved into a fully fledged state-sponsored imperial company set up to operate freely and profitably once the war in Spain had ended.[102]

When Faupel's replacement, Ambassador Eberhard von Stohrer, met with Franco in Burgos on July 6, 1938, he had promising news. Despite relatively calm statements from London and Washington, tensions ran high in Prague and Paris in the aftermath of the Anchsluß. Consistent with his Hossbach strategy of lengthening the Spanish Civil War, the Führer had approved a comprehensive restocking of the Condor Legion. These were supplies Franco had been begging for, almost literally.[103] Yet von Stohrer did not limit himself to delivering that news. He also took care to bring up German intentions of owning the mines that, under the new law, were to remain domestically owned. He did so in language that reminded Franco of his dependent position.[104] Franco also dutifully promised to make exceptions for German ownership as soon as he could.[105] But he did not stop there. He also labeled as "unbridled enemy propaganda" the claims that his Nationalist war effort was dominated by the fascist powers.[106] In light of his behavior, it is not difficult to imagine why "enemy propaganda" spread those views.

After over two full years of civil war, Franco was nearing victory.[107] Some of the most respected historians of the conflict have claimed that he was delaying victory in order to eliminate his enemies and further his personal power.[108] German interests, as understood by Hitler, did not necessarily oppose a longer war. Yet Franco managed to annoy

Berlin on an issue beyond mine ownership: political alignment. Afraid of a late British and French intervention in a war that still raged on, Franco rushed to declare Spain's neutrality hours before the hastily organized Munich Conference in September 1938.[109] It fell to Marquis de Magaz, Franco's verbose ambassador in Berlin, to endure the ensuing complaints. Although Hitler had mentioned on at least two occasions his strategic desire to maintain Spain "benevolently neutral" in the event of war, in the aftermath of Munich the German diplomatic hierarchy chastened Franco's rushed neutrality announcement.[110] In order to prevent further alienation, Magaz suggested that the Generalísimo write a letter explaining himself to Hitler directly. After all, "although these men make diplomacy with guns, they are quite susceptible to flattery." Magaz mentioned this idea to his superiors on at least three occasions, but nothing came of it.[111]

When negotiations for more war supplies resumed, however, German officials no longer tried to conceal their primary concern: economic penetration.[112] Far from asking for further ideological alignment, they brought up mine ownership yet again. During a private meeting State Secretary Count Ernst Weizsäcker obliquely told Magaz that Germany "expect[ed] Spain to show us its gratitude with some compensation of economic character we have been awaiting for some time." This led the ambassador to conclude a report to Franco on a gloomy note: "I do not know what kind of economic prerogative he had in mind, though you can be sure they will be ambitious."[113]

Bernhardt even traveled to Germany to press on the mining issue. "The visit to Berlin of Mr. Bernhardt to negotiate the deliveries of war materiel may have put this whole issue around the compensation to HISMA," wrote Magaz. "I would not be surprised if he wanted this organization to continue after the end of the war, and that he brought up the mining question again, so intrinsically related to HISMA." Some days later, in a meeting with Condor Legion commander von Richthofen, Magaz wrote to Madrid, "The root of this retrospective indignation is economic and what Richthofen expressed is the cause of present disinterest." Even the Condor Legion leadership understood the economic prerogative. Only after the economic discussion did Richthofen mention "a moral cause [going back to the neutrality declaration], more or less justified, that we must vanish."[114]

In the aftermath of Munich, Schacht's Reichsbank tried once more to change the direction of German economic policy. Perhaps it was the banker's swan song from the upper echelons of Nazi power.[115] In a momentous internal memorandum, the Reichsbank described a plausible new path for German economic policy: from unbridled rearmament to more balanced growth, effectively the transformation from the "current war economy to a peacetime economy."[116] The alternative was dangerous: monetary expansion for ever-higher rearmament led to the "inflationary creation of money," labor squeezes furthered wage pressures, and exports once again languished. Echoing a warning from Schacht to Hitler a few months before, the Reichsbank worried about a potential balance of payments crisis that would also handicap foreign policy; the internal stability of the regime would no longer be guaranteed.

Rather than further undermining it, it was now imperative to have the Reichsbank "underpin not an expansive power politics, but a policy of peaceful reconstruction." The central bank could taper its intervention in the economy; it could carefully withdraw excess liquidity and redirect credit while a reduction in "nonmarketable goods"—a euphemism for armaments—shifted demand away from the state and into other sectors. This would avoid a hard landing. Politically too this would have implications: it would sideline the Four-Year Plan and Göring's aggressive autarkic goals that had unbalanced Schacht's constructs. "This task is difficult . . . however, it is also possible," the report concluded.[117]

Schacht made the argument for rebalancing publicly on October 15, 1938, even though the Reichsbank continued to float long-term government bonds to finance rearmament. In his view informal empire, projected through economic power and implemented through trade deals and aggressive diplomacy, remained far preferable to the possibility of war. What he did not know, however, was that the day before Göring had approved a new "gigantic [armaments] program compared to which previous achievements are insignificant" at an Air Ministry conference.[118] The plan followed Hitler's personal directives; the new orders only further turned up the dial on rearmament. Far from appeasing Hitler, the actual consequence of the Munich Conference was a further radicalization of Nazi rearmament aims.[119] Closely averting war did not mean peace. Rather the economics of German war readiness made conflagration into a logical policy conclusion. Though this profoundly worried Schacht, it did not bother Göring. For the acting minister, competition for continental resources made war a matter of *when*, not *if*. A month later, on November 29, Schacht gave a speech crediting economic policy for the German foreign policy that had delivered the Sudetenland and Anschsluß.[120] Even then hubris was powerful. Privately, however, Schacht would reiterate these rebalancing arguments in early 1939, including at a conference with Hitler and through Reichsbank reports urging a change in policy direction. But his private worries fell on deaf ears.[121]

At that time no less than 30 percent of German final economic output was in the armaments sector. Spanish raw materials would be instrumental to these designs. But would they come? At the time steady supplies from HISMA seemed secure. With the continent still at peace and Spain still at war, German hegemony in Spain was intact. Franco soon yielded to Nazi demands. In a memorandum on December 19, 1938, the Spanish Foreign Ministry formally accepted German ownership in five companies that went far beyond what the Nationalist mining law formally allowed.[122] These ventures controlled almost all of the mining developments originally known as the Montaña project, and all Spanish nationals involved were mere representatives of German capital and, consequently, of Hitler's interests. Four of the companies would be located in mainland Spain and a fifth one, Mauritania, in resource-rich Morocco. This implied that the wealth of Spain's last colonial outpost would also be put to work to German benefit. To call this a "vocation" for empire is an understatement.

Some scholars have focused on the mines' relatively small absolute size and that none were wholly owned by Germany. Yet ownership percentages hardly mattered from the perspective of resource extraction. In a truly colonial setting, as long as laws were written with exceptions to accommodate German desires, there was no need for full ownership.[123] In fact as early as July 9, 1938, Bernhardt had written in a secret note that Germany could control all relevant mining exports with capital participation as low as 40 percent.[124] On most of the ventures, therefore, the Germans had achieved more than was strictly necessary to assure their produce would be directed toward the economic hegemon and nowhere else.

HISMA's structure was embryonic for a reason: Spanish debts would allow Germany to compensate for the fact that Anglo-French investments in Spain had been considerably larger than Germany's before the Civil War and would grow HISMA into the largest vehicle of investment and extraction in the country.[125] As part of the payment for the outstanding debts with Germany, the Nationalist government also agreed to provide local funding for the launch of operations by the new HISMA-controlled companies, which complemented state funds transferred from Berlin to Bernhardt. This allowed for certain compensation for Germany's relative financial weakness, Schacht's long-standing chimera now formally inherited by Göring. Consequently not even the establishment of directly controlled companies to exploit Spain's natural wealth would require the use of German foreign exchange; such was the extent of Spain's dependence. There was no choice but to oblige.[126]

HISMA had therefore turned into a German offshore investment vehicle. By late 1938 SOFINDUS had been moved from Portugal to Spain and planned further expansions far beyond mining: from winemaking (Hermanos Scholtz in Málaga) to vertically integrated transport (Transportes Marion in Salamanca) to logistics (Nova in Salamanca). Tensions between Bernhardt and official Foreign Ministry representatives notwithstanding, Ambassador von Stohrer sent a rather self-congratulatory year-end report to Berlin. At times the document reads much more like a corporate quarterly filing than a foreign policy report. In it von Stohrer outlines how virtually every single issue of contention in the previous year had ultimately been resolved according to German wishes. It stands to reason this self-congratulation described a bilateral relationship that resembled the type of German economic dependency hitherto ascribed only to the Balkans and Central Europe. Of all of the German embassies, the Burgos Embassy was one where matters progressed, sooner or later, to the Third Reich's economic benefit.[127] Could anything alter the pattern of economic penetration by Germany into the Spanish economy?

As it turns out, it could. Yet before turning to the world war period, another intervention highlights the uniqueness of the German economic designs and execution in Spain. Franco was dependent not only on German intervention but also on Italian support. Fascist support for the Spanish rebellion predated the failed coup d'état that triggered civil war. And Mussolini spent far more resources than Hitler in his very own Spanish adventure. Yet none of the hegemonic benefits materialized in the context of Schacht's foreign economic strategy translate to Italy. Particularly when contrasted with Germany's, Italy's adventure in Spain was an expensive way to keep up a façade—that of Italy as a great power.

chapter eight

"HATEFUL TO GOD AND TO HIS ENEMIES"

Incontanente intesi e	Forthwith I comprehended,
certo fui	and was certain,
che questa era la setta	that this the sect was of the
d'i cattivi,	caitiff wretches
a Dio spiacenti e a'	hateful to God and to His
nemici sui.	enemies.

—DANTE, *L'Inferno*, III, 61–63

fter almost two decades in power, Benito Mussolini's inner circle had witnessed many a crisis by 1939. But few were more taxing than the months between the Munich Agreement in September 1938 and a second Czech crisis the following March. Despite il Duce's bombastic role as "peacemaker" in Munich, continental politics did not progress as he expected. Nazi belligerence only escalated further and "European peace"—a concoction that necessarily ignored the ongoing Spanish Civil War—seemed increasingly like a precarious mirage. In March 1939 Count Galeazzo Ciano, Mussolini's son-in-law and Italy's precocious foreign minister, was particularly anxious even while surrounded by positive news.[1] In Spain Franco prepared to march on Madrid, a goal that had eluded him for two years. In Ethiopia the Italian "civilizing mission" moved forward.[2] Ciano did not lose sleep over Italy's many continental antagonists—France, Britain, the Soviet Union, or even the dwindling Republic—but was anxious about Germany, unequivocally its closest ally.[3]

The anxiety was well-founded. On March 14 news reached Palazzo Chigi, the imposing home of Ciano's ministry overlooking Marcus Aurelius's imperial column, that Hitler's Wehrmacht had marched into Bohemia. Czechoslovakia was no more, and with it went Chamberlain's delusion of "peace in our time." "The Axis functions only in favor of one of its parts," Ciano complained privately, "which tends to acquire overwhelming proportions, acting entirely on its own initiative, with little regard for us."[4] Italy had been kept in the dark. The situation hardly changed when Prince Philip of Hesse, Hitler's personal go-between with Mussolini, arrived to make excuses.[5] Hesse cited Czech refusals to demobilize and incriminating contacts with Stalin. "Such pretexts may be good for Goebbels's propaganda, but they should not use them when talking to us," Ciano wrote scathingly. "[We] are guilty only of dealing too loyally with the Germans."[6] Mussolini stiffened when Hesse warned against any "large action" in response—a euphemism for an Italian annexation: "In case of war with France we shall fight alone, without asking Germany for a single man."[7] Later Ciano reflected, "It is useless to deny that all this concerns and humiliates the Italian people." So a further annexation was the answer: "It is necessary to give them [Italians] satisfaction and compensation: Albania." As soon as the Spanish Civil War came to an end, the Fascist leadership would deliver it.[8]

When Hesse left, "unhappy and depressed," Mussolini confessed his reluctance to relay the news even to the sycophantic Fascist press. "Italians would laugh at me," he worried. "Every time Hitler grabs a country he sends me a message."[9] By evening depression had given way to resignation. "We must, after all, take the German trick with good grace." Mussolini then turned to Dante's immortal verses to justify his volte-face: Italy could not afford to be "a Dio spiacenti e a' nemici sui [hateful to God and to His enemies]."[10]

Il Duce had a point. After the League of Nations drama over the invasion of Ethiopia, Italian-German intervention in the Spanish Civil War, the formation of the Axis and the anti-Comintern Pact, his acquiescence to the Nazi takeover of Austria (Anschluß) in March 1938 and Munich in September, Mussolini had thrown Italy's lot in with Hitler's Germany. The following June the Italian dictator would double down on that gamble when, seduced by the spoils of seemingly unstoppable Blitzkrieg, he declared war on France and Britain. In the long run, however, the strategic choice would doom his Fascism.

If Ciano was right about one thing, it was that the Axis did not work equally for its partners. A similar conclusion could have been drawn from the experience of the two countries' first alliance, the one sealed over their decisive intervention in the Spanish Civil War. In stark contrast with Germany's self-serving and economically driven goals, Italy shed more blood and treasure in Spain. Yet it got little in return. As is the case with German intervention, it is hard to argue against the importance of Italian involvement in Franco's war effort.[11] Italian supplies may have been less cutting-edge than Germany's, yet what it did not provide in quality, Italy more than exceeded in quantity: over six hundred planes and a thousand artillery pieces.[12] No fewer than seventy thousand Italian men, formally "volunteers," saw action on Spanish soil in what came to be known as the Corpo di Troppe Voluntarie (CTV).[13] Given that scale of intervention, it is unsurprising that scholars talked about an "undeclared Italian invasion" of Spain.[14]

Shortly after the end of Fascism, Mussolini's former ambassador to Spain, Roberto Cantalupo, published a melancholic memoir of his mission. Regretting the lives lost, he argued that Italy had become trapped in a vicious cycle of Iberian loss and escalation.[15] The historiography of the Civil War agreed with this argument, arguing for the primacy of ideology for Mussolini.[16] Thomas supports this view by citing the private reasons Mussolini gave his wife, Rachele, as well as his ideas about "shaping" Fascist character through conflagration: "When the war in Spain is over, I shall have to find something else."[17] A classic Puzzo study implicitly agrees, reinforcing the importance of Fascist troops for Franco.[18] In 1975 John Coverdale published an illuminating volume that saw intervention as a bid for international status as well as continuation of Mussolini's long-standing anti-Republican policy. Italy sought to defend Fascism in Spain, even when they did not see Franco as an ideal vehicle for it.[19] Economic considerations were secondary at best.

The intervention in Spain did become a rare point of agreement between two opposing schools when Italian historiography undertook a reassessment of the Fascist era.[20] Despite their deep differences, Alexander de Grand and Renzo de Felice agree on the scant advantages derived from Mussolini's adventure in Spain.[21] As a corollary to the unproductive German alliance, De Grand devotes but a short paragraph to the "minimal . . . short-term" economic benefits in Spain, ultimately failing "even to serve as a stimulus for further Italian rearmament."[22] In 1993 Vincenzo Giura published a more thorough analysis, drawing from unpublished Italian documents but failing to link the intervention to wider Fascist policy and the German alliance.[23]

The purpose of contrasting German and Italian interventions is to underscore the uniqueness of the Nazi project on Iberian soil. Not unlike the German commitment, Fascist involvement in Spain spiraled. Although Mussolini always chose to prioritize the mirage of Italian imperial largesse, there were men within his administration who tried to make Italy benefit economically from its transfers to Spain, or at least recoup the investments. Among them Filippo Anfuso and Felice Guarneri, the chief of staff at Ciano's ministry and the minister of foreign exchange, respectively, stand out. Yet their efforts were generally weak, uncoordinated, and late. Ultimately intervention in Spain not only brought Italy closer to Germany but also tied the Fascist government to a larger, better developed, and increasingly aggressive "partner" that rarely behaved as such.

An Italian "invasion of Spain" would have been unthinkable when Benito Mussolini was born.[24] Around the turn of the century parliamentary democracy had developed into an oligarchic system dubbed "Giolittian reformism" after Prime Minister Giovanni Giolitti, who argued for gradualism in the aftermath of a "unification" process that had actually resembled a conquest.[25] Giolitti ruled over a demographic revolution, characterized by rapid urbanization and a "great sprout" in manufacturing. He maintained power with a careful balance of authoritarian control in the South and protective tariffs to buy off industrial elites. In foreign affairs Italy pursued a "case-study of dishonesty" to avoid static alliances.[26]

Bourgeois aspirations found outlets in nationalism and imperialism.[27] Benito Amilcare Andrea Mussolini first followed his father into the Socialist ranks, where he became devoted to overthrowing Giolitti's system.[28] Yet an early passion for war distanced him from traditional pacifists. Irreverent, impassioned, and intellectually restless, he argued for intervention in World War I as editor of the Socialist outlet L'Avanti. Forced out, and financed by pro-war industrialists, he soon reappeared as the founder of Il Popolo d'Italia, a newspaper that became the seedbed for his nascent ideology. Torn between the Leninist aspirations of militant Socialists and the trumped expansionist dreams of nationalists, the Giolittian system crumbled. The forces of revolution and reaction were unleashed; as in Restoration Spain, reaction would prevail and do so, paradoxically, through a former Socialist.[29]

The key backing for Mussolini's Fascio di Combattimento did not come from cities but from agrarian organizations in the depressed countryside.[30] It was therefore a constituency analogous to that which lent Hitler its earliest electoral support.[31] The Fascist movement soon grew into an amalgam of disillusioned war veterans, nationalistic students, and reactionary landowners.[32] A year later, and with financial backing from industrial elites weary of Socialism, Mussolini orchestrated a masterful public relations coup: he marched on Rome and into government.[33]

Once in power Mussolini strengthened the executive and developed a personal myth. Everything from needless memoranda to key policy programs required the characteristic *M* scribbled on them for approval. His movement underwent a profound transformation when the quasi-revolutionary aspirations of the agrarian right were abandoned for Italy's traditional pillars of power: crown and galero. Long gone were the anticlerical and republican promises in the streets of Milan, where Socialists like the young Mussolini had promised to "hang the last Pope with the guts of the last King."[34]

Fascism had no ex ante economic platform.[35] As part of a maneuver to secure industrial support, Mussolini made Alberto De Stefani finance minister.[36] His classically liberal program, which brought rapid growth and international respect for the authoritarian regime, was far removed from the policies we associate with fascist economic management today. In a momentous speech at the Fascist Congress in Naples, De Stefani expressed his belief in capital accumulation and budget balancing as the way to make up for emigration and further develop Italian industry. He proposed a "productivistic" approach toward business, which effectively meant leaving it alone.[37] Spending was cut, mainly by firing almost a hundred thousand public sector employees, and some taxes were axed. To implement a program of "economy, work, and discipline," Mussolini got more powers from Parliament.[38] In his Italy political dictatorship and economic liberalism seemed like viable bedfellows. Yet in the mid-1920s the prospect of a Weimar-like hyperinflation haunted a regime cut off from international capital markets.[39] Despite public spending limits, De Stefani's rapid industrial development combined high growth with high inflation. In the political sphere, the assassination of the young, charismatic Socialist leader, Giacomo Matteoti, moved the regime further from the rule of law. It also silenced opposition.[40] It was a harbinger of totalitarianism.

In the economic sphere change came from within, with banker and industrialist Giuseppe Volpi replacing De Stefani.[41] A new economic program involved tighter controls on state spending, more trade protectionism, and the seduction of foreign investors—particularly Wall Street—to refinance Italy's (already) sizable foreign debt.[42] The following October a landmark deal was struck in Washington to refinance World War I debts and access markets in an issue floated by J. P. Morgan.[43] The next step in the path to pre–World War I financial normality was reestablishing gold convertibility.[44] Two late 1920s policies became symbols of Fascist economic management: the Rocco laws and the "Quota 90." The former, named after an obsequious justice minister whom Mussolini called "the legislator of the Fascist revolution," effectively outlawed political dissent. Lockouts and strikes became illegal, while Fascist trade unions were now responsible for "representing labor." In theory this was a step toward Fascist "corporatism," where top-down control promised better organizational outcomes than unbridled competition between labor and capital. Rocco argued that Fascism did "not abolish the individual . . . but subordinates him to society, leaving him free to develop on lines that will benefit [his] fellow men."[45] In its third way between capitalism and Socialism, the regime promised to spawn a "new breed of men," a concept that had almost negligible racial implications, at least in the 1920s. In practice Fascist principles applied to industrial organization meant labor was oppressed—and ruthlessly so.

The so-called Quota 90 involved an aggressive revaluation of the Italian currency, the lira: 90 lire to the British pound. Its goal was boosting credibility and alleviating high inflation. Since a speech in Pesaro announcing the "battle of the lira" on August 18, 1926, Mussolini had intertwined Italy's currency with his popularity: "From this square to all the world I say I will defend the lira to the last breath, to the last drop of blood."[46] Rhetorical flourish aside, an overvalued exchange rate became a symbol of government status just as it did in Britain a year before. And, like in Britain, the economic consequences of such policies were disastrous. Despite the benefits it could accrue in terms of foreign debts, Italy's trading partners, creditors, and even the central bank opposed the revaluation; the peg was simply too high, making the country helplessly uncompetitive in international markets.[47] Growth suffered. And yet, in Mussolini's Italy appearances weighed more than economic facts.[48]

The deflationary effects of the Quota 90 ensured that Italy did not have much boom for the Depression to bust. As could have been expected, the fall in both external and internal demand caused unemployment to rise considerably before 1929.[49] Though Italy did not necessarily fare worse than the rest of Europe in the Depression, industrial production still fell by a third between 1929 and 1932, and did so from a low base. In this context unemployment tripled as the government imposed across-the-board cuts.[50]

It was then that Fascism jettisoned economic orthodoxy. At first the regime turned inward. Semiofficial *enti* and *instituti* were formed to favor corporatist production. Inspired by German cartels, Italian industrialists were encouraged to participate in *consorzi,* decreasing competition. The Industrial Reconstruction Institute, modeled after Herbert Hoover's Reconstruction Finance Corporation, aimed at sustaining production in the face of an avalanche of private defaults.[51] The resulting deep penetration of the state in the economy would long outlive the Fascist regime. Henceforth industrial production and prices were micromanaged by syndicates, the Confindustria association of business (which remains a staple of modern Italy), and il Duce himself. The regime also pushed for the expansion of public works and welfare programs to kick-start growth.[52] As elsewhere in Europe, the seeds of the welfare state were planted.

Predictably these measures made a mockery of budget discipline: the deficit grew sevenfold between 1930 and 1933, and the public roster almost doubled. Following the 1931 banking crisis, the Fascist government also stepped in to bail out its banking system, which in effect gave the government a central role in domestic finance.[53] Financial crisis exacerbated centralization, autocracy, and financial heterodoxy. But courtesy of the regime's effective propaganda, many around the world were impressed by Rome's "third way." "Italy has become a Mecca of political scientists, economists, and sociologists," wrote an émigré Harvard professor in 1936.[54]

On the trade front Italy sought retaliation for its main partners' protectionism.[55] Mussolini's government imposed trade restrictions and exchange controls, alienating Italy from its traditional markets. "Buy Italian" became a belligerent slogan.[56] Emulating German policy at the same time, Rome sought to expand trade with less developed countries. By the end of 1934 Italy had signed bilateral clearing deals with Hungary, Bulgaria, Romania, Yugoslavia, Turkey, and Germany, and partial ones with Argentina and Chile.[57] But the Italian industrial base was far more limited than Germany's, as were its trade successes.

Never enthralled by economics, Mussolini was fascinated by different victories. The fascist worldview implied that "remaking man" could be achieved only by spilling blood in the service of a "fascist collective"—as opposed to "capitalist individual"—ideal. As the Depression deepened, Roman imperial references multiplied: Mars entered the pantheon of Fascist gods. It did so with a bang.[58] Official documents confirm that preparations began in late 1933 for the Fascist invasion of Ethiopia, one of Africa's last independent states.[59] An offensive hoped to unite that territory with Somaliland in a power play that pitted Italy against British interests.[60] Success would give Italy economic and political control over a vast, contiguous African territory with considerable economic potential. Or so was the plan. Italy returned to a period of economic growth around the time preparations were made to forge a (larger) "place in the sun."[61] Beyond dispute, the Fascist drive for colonial expansion was seen then as a profitable endeavor in terms of natural wealth to be acquired as well as domestic industrial production in war-related industries.[62] The evidence from other European countries seemed to confirm this perspective. Only after 1945 would these views change.[63]

The Ethiopian war further weakened the feeble League of Nations.[64] The British and French were unwilling to break relations with Mussolini, whom they had successfully relied upon to contain Hitler a year before to protect Austrian independence.[65] This strategy led to the Hoare-Laval plan, a precursor of appeasement that sought to save diplomatic face while giving Italy a free hand.[66] Mussolini spun it as a triumph. When leaked, opinion across Europe rightly perceived it as a betrayal of Ethiopia.[67] Almost reluctantly the League imposed economic sanctions, curtailing Italy's access to the Balkan markets.[68]

Two months before the beginning of the Spanish Civil War, on May 9, 1936, Mussolini appeared for a speech before half a million Italians. Only a week earlier contracts had been signed in Rome promising funding and supplies for Iberian conspirators. Overlooking a refashioned Via dell'Impero from his favorite balcony, the dictator explained that the Italian state had ceased to simply be a monarchy: after "fourteen years of irrepressible energy and discipline of youth," it was now an empire.[69] King Victor Emmanuel III, sleepless after staring at an African map all night, was now king of Italy and emperor of Ethiopia. Although the preferred historical analogies were Roman, echoes of Victorian Britain were not too distant. Mussolini reserved for himself the title "Founder of the Empire." Though uncorroborated, the rumor was that the king had toyed with the idea of naming him prince, but Mussolini declined, fearing some old Fascists would disapprove. Regardless, tributes to the new Augustus multiplied: Mussolini was now genius, statesman, Caesar.[70]

It was none other than poet-cum-politician Gabriele D'Annunzio who had revived the imperial rhetoric il Duce appropriated: "Even if the coast of Tripoli were a desert, even if it would not support one peasant or one Italian business firm, we still need to take it to avoid being suffocated in *mare nostrum*."[71] In the aftermath of victory, the aged poet wrote to the politician who had fulfilled his unrealized dreams: "You have subjugated all the uncertainties of fate and defeated every human hesitation. . . . You have nothing more to fear."[72] The Italian economy, however, struggled after an expensive, difficult war. The budget deficit was so extreme that Italy was forced to go off the gold standard and devalue 41 percent to regain competitiveness. And yet a 1937 pamphlet detailed the "economic development" that Fascist rule had allegedly brought to Ethiopia, the heart of "Italian East Africa."[73] Conquest and colonization were veiled in *mission civilisatrice* terminology: "At the moment of Italian occupation, Ethiopia was in a state of disintegration . . . suffering from a paralysis which had endured for centuries, thus preventing the vast resources of Ethiopia from being developed for the benefit of mankind." Yet one nation had intervened to right this wrong: "Italy was obliged to begin everything from the very beginning . . . and within two years [it] has laid the foundations of a new civil and economic system."[74] Tellingly for a time of broken international trade, the pamphlet's first page featured an illustration of the raw materials Italy could procure from Ethiopia. Then it detailed the workings of the new empire: state-sponsored banks, industrial conglomerates, migrant labor, and the introduction of the lira.[75] This last move had allowed Mussolini's overworked foreign exchange minister, Felice Guarneri, to reduce allocation of foreign exchange for certain raw materials. Yet it was no game changer: the glittering empire could not be relied upon for key industrial inputs. In what can be seen as a preview of the Spanish intervention, the African empire cost far more resources than it generated, with the war alone costing 12 billion lire.[76] And yet Mussolini saw it as the "greatest colonial war in all history."[77] If only reality had matched the propaganda.[78]

In the context of sanctions, Hitler's Germany served as deus ex machina: it provided Mussolini with a diplomatic lifeline in the midst of continental isolation.[79] Leaving behind their Austrian disagreements, the dictators came together over Italian rights to empire, thwarting French desires to drive Rome away from Berlin. Such rapprochement proved a smart gamble for Hitler's anti-League policy, conducted—like the Spanish decision—increasingly outside the structure of von Neurath's Auswärtiges Amt. The Italian economy by 1936 had promising outlets for expansion but suffered from similar limitations on strategic raw materials, foreign exchange, and markets as its newfound ally.

Mussolini did not take time to consolidate. Instead he jumped on another opportunity to assert Fascist power, this time in the western Mediterranean. When Francoist envoy Luis Bolín offered payment guarantees against whatever supplies Italy could provide to the Nationalist war effort, Ciano responded, "*Mister* Bolín, *Mister* Bolín, the eventuality of those payments has not even crossed our minds." Intervention was not a matter of money, for "if we did what you suggest . . . we would become active belligerents in a civil war."[80] As it turns out, Bolín's self-aggrandized account was incorrect; contracts that involved financier Juan March detailed payments in exchange for promised supplies for the rebellion. It is almost inconceivable that a date for the uprising had not been discussed.[81] And yet, when rebellion materialized, Mussolini dithered. Only on July 25, following a call from the exiled Spanish king, further financial backing, and sensationalistic news about Blum's eagerness to help the Republic, did Mussolini give his blessing. Thus Savoia-Marchetti aircraft joined the Junkers airlifting Francoist troops from Morocco.[82]

Italy and Germany had independently agreed to support Franco when the Quai d'Orsay formally proposed a policy of nonintervention to make up for Prime Minister Blum's volte-face from his stated desires to arm the Republic. At the time and in secret, Abwehr head Adm. Wilhelm Canaris and his Italian counterpart, Gen. Mario Roatta, discussed providing supplies in "roughly" equal amounts.[83] Such bilateral meetings had been an innovation created by the Abyssinian crisis.[84] Yet Spain forced even closer collaboration. On August 7, as the continental press roared with news of French supplies being smuggled into Spain, Rome shipped twenty-seven fighter planes, twelve anti-aerial guns, and five tanks. They were destined for the southern front, where Nationalists were making headway from rebel-held Seville. By the end of August 1936, at another rendezvous, Canaris and Roatta agreed to share details of their Iberian involvement, coauthoring a memorandum that detailed every last machine gun sent.[85] The agreements stipulated a preference for Franco over all other generals in Nationalist Spain, which matched Hitler's July 25 decision. This only strengthened Franco's grip on power, even though—as we have seen—he was not part of the original Junta. It involved a change of focus from prerebellion contracts in Rome. Preempting Italian designs for Mediterranean bases, Canaris proposed a clause abandoning all territorial claims over Spanish territory.[86] Ciano eventually agreed, relieved to hear there would be no German demands on Morocco. Yet, as we have seen, German efforts in Spain by this time were already shifting toward economic rather than territorial goals. As diplomatic contact between Rome and Berlin intensified in the following two months, shipments to Spain grew: Rome sent more tanks, planes, and supplies.[87] But how much intervention could Italy afford? Few countries in Europe were spending as much on foreign war without a clear economic strategy underpinning it.[88]

Money aside, Mussolini also sent Arconovaldo Bonaccorsi, known as Conte Rossi, an eccentric and fanatical Fascist, to Majorca to fight off a Republican invasion.[89] The mission was accomplished in two weeks, yet Rossi remained. Delusions of grandeur ensued: not only did Rossi rename the island's main avenue Via Roma, but he also toured the island daily in an Italian coupe with his confessor "hunting for Reds." He wore a large white cross on his neck while declaring to pious Majorcan elites that he required "a woman a day."[90] Eventually he overstepped the mark: by trying to establish a Majorcan trade monopoly with Italy, he managed to annoy the powerful March family. Following loud complaints in Rome from an original financial backer for the rebellion, il Conte was eventually recalled.[91]

Ironically, while Rossi "conquered" Majorca, Italy joined the Non-Intervention Committee, which began proceedings in London. Italian and German delegates worked to prevent any significant resolution from passing. And Soviet and British delegates, for different reasons, acquiesced.[92] "Each move of the NIC [was] made to serve the rebellion," wrote U.S. Ambassador Claude Bowers. "[The] committee was the most cynical and lamentably dishonest group that history [had] known."[93] It was not a wholly unfair characterization.

In Rome little changed in practice; support for Franco only intensified and with it military coordination with Berlin. In October Ciano established a naval guard under Capt. Giovanni Ferretti guaranteeing all naval traffic to Nationalist ports, a move that was beyond the logistical reach of the German Kriegsmarine.[94] This gave logistical alternatives for both troops and soon for raw materials. Shipments could now get beyond the dwindling Republican blockade in ways other than through Oliveira Salazar's Portugal. It was a response to a German request, which in retrospect fit economic motivations: the Italian naval guard was not there just to guarantee military deliveries.[95]

Armed with Italian and German supplies, Franco attacked Madrid in late November. The city's defenders held on. All the same, on November 19 Italy joined Germany in recognizing Franco's as Spain's legitimate government. The *Guardian* speculated that the announcements had been coordinated.[96] The fascist powers also confirmed the departure of diplomatic envoys to Nationalist headquarters in Burgos. A week later, and after intense negotiations led by Ciano's chief of staff, Filippo Anfuso, the Fascists and the Nationalists rushed a treaty. Unlike Germany's concurrent dealings, the main focus of the document was political: "The Fascist Government and the Spanish Nationalist Government will maintain close contacts with each other, and will concert their actions on all questions of common interest, particularly on those concerning the Western Mediterranean . . . and will lend each other mutual support in the effective defense of their common interests."[97] Astonishingly the fourth article called for the abolition of League of Nations Article (16), accused of being "full of grave dangers to peace."[98] There were also vaguer economic promises, more weakly worded than

German documents: "[The signatories] believe it is of value to lay down . . . the method to be adopted for the exploitation of their own economic resources, particularly raw materials, . . . [and] develop as much as possible all forms of economic relations and sea and air communications."[99] Together with a provisional, limited clearing agreement signed three days before and modeled after those agreed upon with the Balkans, Anfuso's treaty foresaw raw materials flowing from Spain to Italy to at least partly compensate for the cost of intervention. Potential for Italian compensation in Spain did exist; beyond promises, however, the Italian experience was radically different than Germany's.[100]

Economic compensation and penetration were simply not Fascist priorities in Spain. When Franco's push to take Madrid failed, Mussolini sought more military control.[101] Ciano organized a Spanish Office within his ministry to centralize command and "all requests from the military mission in Spain" less than a week after Anfuso's treaty.[102] While Germany pressed Franco to obtain permanent economic concessions, Rome doubled down militarily: it sent more than ten times the men in the Condor Legion. Their objective was political: to act decisively in Franco's war and strengthen the regime's reputation as a major European power. Propaganda spoke of shaping "Fascist character."[103] So a test in total war loomed. Four days into his job, the new head of the office received a note from Mussolini ordering three thousand Fascist volunteers be sent to Spain "in order to put some backbone into the Spanish Nationalist formations."[104] At the time, the Nationalist leadership wanted well-trained German and Italian troops for strategic assaults and all the air power they could get; the value of thousands of zealous Fascist militias answering to Rome was dubious at best. That is perhaps why, upon hearing Mussolini's plans, Franco wondered out loud, "Who requested them?"

Just as he was in no position to reject German economic demands, Franco was in no position to turn down troops. Italian shipments soon outgrew anything Anfuso had foreseen. By February 1937 there were forty-nine thousand Italian troops on Iberian soil, to be organized into the Corps of Voluntary Troops.[105] Of the four divisions put under Roatta's command, three comprised Fascist recruits—appropriately baptized God Wills It, Black Arrows, and Black Pens—and a fourth, the Littorio, which stemmed from the Italian Army.[106] The demographics provide insight into recruitment: they were overwhelmingly young and from impoverished southern Italy, where unemployment was very high. These men were attracted by the mercenary promise of a salary for service abroad. A sample of volunteers was reported to have an average of more than three children each, without much income to speak of.[107] So the *Manchester Guardian* was not wrong when it argued, "Italians have no desire to go and fight [in Spain] . . . , but thousands have volunteered . . . for the sake of the pay."[108] Subsequently Germany increased its supply shipment to largely match matériel from Rome; not so troops.

British Foreign Secretary Eden continued attempting to steer Italy away from Berlin, a goal also shared by Paris. Eden struggled to "normalize" Italian relations personally, often by approaching Ambassador Dino Grandi directly.[109] On January 2, 1937, in spite of gargantuan Fascist commitments in Spain, an Italian-British modus vivendi was announced.[110] It came to be known as the "Gentlemen's Agreement," though British diplomats worried that "exchange of assurances might be a better title and less likely to raise a smile."[111] The architecture of foreign relations generally and British responses to the dictators specifically put France in an awkward position, raising fears of isolation in Paris.[112] The Anglo-Italian agreement promised to maintain Spain's territorial integrity and avoid all postwar annexations, a key strategic concern of the Royal Navy.[113] This may have defeated the intentions of zealots like Rossi, but it was a diplomatic coup for Mussolini; it kept a door open to a long-term deal with Britain even while relations with Berlin blossomed. It gave Italy options.[114]

On Iberian soil, however, "Italian invasion" struggled. After the failure to take Madrid came the tragedy of Guadalajara. This Francoist offensive, led by Italian troops, turned swiftly into a Republican counteroffensive, fortified by Soviet military supplies and international brigades. On March 18, 1937, through a combination of bad weather and misguided tactics, Roatta's men withdrew. It was perhaps the Second Republic's finest military hour.[115] The international press blasted reports of the Italian reversal. In a dispatch to the United States, Ernest Hemingway wrote enthusiastically, "It is hard to overemphasize the importance of this battle, where native Spanish battalions, composed mainly of boys untrained last November, not only fought stubbornly in defense with other better-trained troops, but attacked in a complicatedly planned and perfectly organized military operation. . . .

Brihuega will take its place in military history with the other decisive battles of the world."[116] The *New York Times* went as far as to compare Mussolini's Guadalajara to Napoleon's Bailén, the 1808 battle that changed the course of Bonaparte's Spanish campaign.

Infuriated, Mussolini escalated even further. He ordered massive new shipments of men and supplies.[117] Barely a week after Guadalajara, this newfound bravado of the Fascist leadership had consequences as far as London, where the French delegation at the Non-Intervention Committee complained explicitly about Italian intervention. In a "very urgent" telegram to Berlin, the German ambassador wrote that Paris "would not allow [herself] to be treated in such a cavalier manner, as if she were a second-rate state."[118] According to the Quai d'Orsay, the Italian behavior amounted to a "serious danger to the [continental] peace."[119]

Not for the last time Mussolini disregarded French complaints. He even went as far as to publish an unsigned article in *Il Popolo d'Italia,* arguing that the world had misinterpreted Guadalajara. "Of the 40 kilometers gained in their advance, the [Italian] Legionaries retained 20 at the end of the battle. . . . What was then the 10-day battle of Guadalajara?," he asked rhetorically. "A victory. An authentic victory."[120] The coexistence of such words with Italian participation at the NIC is astonishing. There is no doubt that in the aftermath of Guadalajara, Fascist intervention became more closely intertwined with Italy's international reputation. In contrast to the more careful Auswärtiges Amt, Hitler did not seem to mind; heavy Italian involvement in Spain allowed the Führer more room for maneuver elsewhere, and, as it turns out, it had no tangible effects on Germany's economic hegemony in Spain.[121]

While Mussolini fretted about "status," others in Rome worried about cost. The total bill for involvement in Spain increased greatly, not least due to Italy's gargantuan troop commitments in Spain less than a year after the conclusion of the Ethiopian war. Anfuso and Guarneri, the foreign exchange minister, were most concerned.[122] Anfuso's diplomacy had attempted to check expenditures while setting the stage for some sort of repayment. The liberally minded Guarneri, a remnant from the old liberal days of early Fascism, was bent on reminding il Duce that Italy simply lacked the resources to sustain his great power foreign policy. In Ciano's diaries, almost every single appearance by

Guarneri is followed by expressions of doubt from both the foreign minister and Mussolini, who accused him of "needless pessimism."[123] On November 27, 1937, for instance, Ciano reported that he found in a British intercept "evidence of Guarneri's doubts regarding the financial situation." Was he a traitor? Ciano wrote, "The Duce told me that he is watching him, given the Confindustria environment he comes from."[124] Guarneri was a man of big business. In order to criticize the illiberal moves toward closure, dirigisme, and increasingly economic autarky, Guarneri would later compare Italy's strategy to Germany's: "Schacht had opened the German economy to a period of full recovery which, assisted by the game of alliances, had created many benefits in terms of exports."[125] But Italy did not enjoy such benefits because of Mussolini's choices; compared to Germany, Italy pursued more extreme autarky and committed itself to relatively larger military undertakings given the size of its economy.[126] The former directly led to lower exports, while the latter drained scant foreign reserves through military investments. And the promised spoils of war never quite materialized as advertised.

Guarneri's worries permeated the 1937 treaties with Spanish Nationalists. The official excuse for signing new deals was the recognition on both sides that Anfuso's original accords could not cover the greatly increased levels of Italian aid. By then it was obvious the war would continue for months, if not years.[127] The treaties represented clear efforts to offset the foreign reserve drain created by the Spanish supplies, most of which required raw materials beyond the humble "lira sphere." It was effectively a variation of Schacht's "import problem," except that Italy's commitments were relatively larger and its economy far smaller than Germany's.[128]

Others in the Fascist leadership worried, too. Vincenzo Fagiuoli, president of the state-sponsored conglomerate Italian Society of Fertilizers (SAFNI), negotiated a preferential treaty for Italy with the Francoist authorities, signed in mid-April 1937.[129] The agreement stipulated that Spain would pay around 150 million lire per year on a debt that was estimated, at the time, at around 2 billion lire. This represented a sevenfold increase in the annual payments from Anfuso's accords months before. Although the agreement has been interpreted as a major Italian triumph, the higher Spanish payments were largely consistent with augmented Italian men and supplies since late November. The Nationalists were promising to pay more, but only because Italy was spending so much more in their war.[130] This was no breakthrough in debt re-payment, nor did it imply the stabilization of Fascist expenses. Beyond recognized debt, Fagiuoli managed to include transfers of at least 75 million lire in merchandise in the treaty before the end of the year, focusing on ores, wool, and hard currency.[131] Though almost insignifi-cant when compared to the total size of Italian investments, the Burgos archives confirm that Guarneri's ministry pressed hard to fulfill that provision.[132]

When discussing compensation, however, the Nationalists refused to make any concessions about ownership. This contrasts with the German progress through the HISMA-ROWAK system. As much was acknowledged by German ambassador Wilhelm Faupel upon receiving a confidential report detailing economic concessions to Italy on Jan-uary 12: "We have obtained far more [than the Italians] in this [eco-nomic] respect through HISMA."[133] With regard to in-kind transfers, Italians did receive sporadic shipments from Spanish mines, including Rio Tinto. Yet the size of transfers to Italy was minuscule; they did not even begin to cover expenses.[134]

The Republican military victories of mid-1937 forced Nationalists to ask Rome for even more help. The request was so large that Anfuso traveled to Burgos to discuss it with Franco directly.[135] There, he man-aged to tone down requests while ensuring that at least a quarter of the total would be paid for in foreign exchange and raw materials so as to minimize the drainage on Italian supplies that could not easily be replenished. Nicolás Franco expressed doubts about this arrangement in consideration of Nationalist Spain's almost nonexistent foreign ex-change. Concurrently and through HISMA, the Germans were taking over an ever-larger percentage of trade in goods that conceivably could have been sold in the international market for hard currency. German advantage thus implied Italian disadvantage. So Anfuso echoed Fagi-uoli: he suggested direct ownership of mines, which the Italians would have more than gladly received as payment. But the Spaniards politely dodged the suggestion.[136]

They would try again. When Nicolás Franco visited Rome in August 1937, the Italians sought to involve Fagiuoli's SAFNI and a bank consortium with the hope of leveraging loans and centralizing control over Spanish-Italian economic exchanges. This suggests that a year into the war and after a gargantuan ramp-up in intervention directed by Mussolini and Ciano, members of the Fascist government tried to move closer to a HISMA-ROWAK model. The Fascist administration more broadly conceived was more interested in payment than "fascist solidarity" at a rate the country could not afford. Led by the Bank of Rome, a bank consortium would lend Franco 250 million lire, which he could then use to purchase war matériel from Italy.[137] But did financial engineering change anything? SAFNI would also oversee all future transactions and agree on prices with Nationalist companies, thus helping offset the cost of war matériel.[138] Italy had found a way to get some of its investment back—at least theoretically. Meeting with Mussolini, Franco fretted about the "massive" shipments from the Soviet Union; while the Italian leader declined surface vessels for the Nationalists, he did commit to better patrolling of Turkish coasts.[139]

Although it was his signature on the latest accords, Ciano's mind drifted away from economics. As Franco's troops conquered the mineral-rich Basques, all of Ciano's diary entries on Spain dealt exclusively with political and military developments.[140] In stark contrast, Nazi representatives at the time rushed to open HISMA offices in the North. On August 25, 1937, for instance, Ciano celebrated: "Santander fell today under the fire of our [CTV] Legions. . . . I think back to the days of Guadalajara. Many were really frightened at that time. . . . But we kept the faith."[141] Two days later he made it clear which Iberian spoils he cared about most: "I cabled [CTV commander] Bastico, tactfully, to obtain the flags and cannons taken from the Basques. I envy the French, [Napoleon's] *Galerie des Invalides,* and the Germans, the Military Museum." After all, "no painting is worth a flag taken from the enemy." Ciano would get his flags, but the war was not yet won—and meanwhile the bill kept growing. British Cabinet documents confirm that London was well aware of Italy's rising financial difficulties; in a report discussing Fascist threats on Egypt, it was noted that Italy did not seem to be replenishing imported fuel supplies "for financial reasons."[142] The Spanish drain only added to Italy's difficulties.

In early 1938, when Nicolás Franco arrived in Rome to once more ask for help, an intransigent Guarneri awaited him. The minister's position was clear: no more supplies would be shipped before an agreement was reached on payment terms. Negotiations reached an impasse.[143] International tensions escalated due to Hitler's designs for Austria and

Czechoslovakia, so much so that even Ciano entertained doubts about how much Italy was spending in Spain. On March 26 he wrote in his diary, "I discussed the 1938 consignment [of weapons] with Nicolás Franco. They ask for a billion's [lire] worth of goods, with payment in kind, or almost, and very chancy. . . . We give blood for Spain. Is that not enough?"[144]

Payment in kind was not even assured. Francisco Franco got personally involved. "I request your able collaboration and effective support for the solution of these [financial] problems," he wrote directly to Mussolini. Franco wanted il Duce to help "overcome the obstacles and the difficulties that such requests always encounter in administrative organisms." Then he resorted to flattery: "In their severity and legitimate defense of the public interests, [negotiators] become obstinate, and need to be spurred on by the political genius of someone who, like yourself, directs the destiny of an empire."[145] Adulation worked. Overruling Guarneri, Mussolini instructed the deal be closed despite the Spaniards' "chancy" ability to pay. He who directed the "destiny of an empire" ignored the more cautious voices in his government.[146]

The Italian compensation system was a broken one not only when compared with the contemporary Nazi ones but also in terms of the absolute price and quality of Iberian spoils. For instance, in July 1938 Nationalist authorities needed forty aircraft engines from Fiat and Caproni to restock their fleet and regain aerial superiority.[147] Yet a debate between the SAFNI and Franco's men arose over Spanish exports to Italy. Guarneri's ministry refused compensation in iron ore at the exchange rate offered by the Spaniards, which made the crucial raw material almost as expensive as it would have been in the international market.[148] What was the point of the sacrifice? Eventually the Spanish envoy acknowledged in a secret memorandum to Burgos, "I do not think we can get the exchange at those prices."[149]

Quality also became an issue. Italians were adamant that their supplies come from Rio Tinto mines. Yet the Spaniards had already committed that production, a very large percentage of which went to none other than Germany. Eventually a deal was brokered guaranteeing some future production: the Nationalists promised 100,000 tons of Rio Tinto pyrites. Once again the contrast with Germany was stark: at the time Bernhardt's men planned for the development of their own mines, the Montaña project, in clear violation of the existing Nationalist mining law.[150] All Italian attempts at ownership had been either ignored or politely rebuffed. Not so Germany's. If one considers how much they were being forced to relinquish through Bernhardt's HISMA-ROWAK and Germany's aggressive diplomacy, it was sensible for Franco's men to do everything they could to avoid further depleting their natural wealth. Once again Italians delivered; but, constrained by German demands, the Spaniards rarely reciprocated.[151]

The winds of wider war blew stronger than ever when the Spanish Civil War finally came to an end in 1939. It was in this context that negotiations began in Rome to settle the gargantuan war debts that Nationalist Spain had accumulated. Although the absolute amounts were nothing prohibitive when compared to world war figures, they were still sizable—and had clear impacts on Italy's own war preparedness. Even then, however, Fascist leadership disregarded economic considerations for political purposes. Having steered Franco into passing a fascistic labor law in late 1938 reminiscent of the Rocco laws, Mussolini and Ciano sought to add Spain to the Anti-Comintern Pact, which had strengthened their alignment with Nazi Germany.[152] But negotiations between Burgos, Berlin, and Rome progressed slowly. Influenced by his need for more supplies to advance on stubborn Madrid, Franco ultimately agreed to join. On March 31, 1939, a day before the official end of the war, Franco secretly adhered to the Anti-Comintern Pact.[153]

In the coming months, however, the Francoist government avoided large payments or agreement on a debt payment plan.[154] Back in Rome it was time for a proper accounting; a confidential report sent to Ciano's ministry finally confirmed Guarneri's pessimism: Italian intervention in Spain had cost over 8 billion lire.[155] Depending on which estimate one chooses, this represented between 6 to 8 percent of Italian GDP.[156] To provide a modern comparison, the Brown University "Costs of War" project estimated in 2013 that the total cost of the U.S. war in Iraq cost 2.2 trillion 2013 U.S. dollars. This is roughly equivalent to 1.3 percent of GDP per year of engagement, less than half the comparative weight of the Italian intervention in Spain.[157] Meanwhile Spanish transfers of raw materials and foreign currency during the war had accounted little over half a billion lire, meaning little over 5 percent of the total, direct Italian expenditure. And this figure did not include further costs like pension benefits for war veterans, needed in spite of the charade of "volunteers" for foreign consumption.[158] Although the investment had been large—at least four times larger than what was originally envisioned in 1936—Italy had little to show for it. The contrast with German ownership of mines, companies, and the larger transfers secured by Bernhardt's HISMA-ROWAK dual monopoly is obvious enough.

In the following months Franco sought to seduce Mussolini into showing his imperial largesse yet again. In 1939 il Duce personally intervened to defer Spanish repayment and then condone debts. Barely a month before Hitler unleashed his Wehrmacht on Poland, for instance, Ciano had sent a short note to Franco dated August 21 stating, "Duce gives six more months to the payment of 300 M[illion] lire due on the 21st of the current month."[159] After the war Guarneri complained, "The results [of the Spanish intervention] were scarce, and not even distantly comparable to the human sacrifice and material transfers that Italy had withstood in order to support the Francoist cause." The behavior of Franco's men, eager to maneuver from a position of relative strategic weakness and lack of resources, is logical. Guarnieri's main antagonist remained his boss: "We [Guarneri and his ministry] had to concentrate our best efforts to prevent Mussolini from giving in to his desire of appearing magnanimous with regards to existing debts."[160] Once more calls for caution fell on deaf ears. On May 8, 1940, a new accord between Rome and Madrid forgave over 3 billion lire since Italy recognized "the great struggle of reconstruction and its friendly commitment to her [Spanish] needs."[161] The Spanish strategy of relying on Mussolini's generosity to avoid pressures prevailed. The remaining 5 billion lire were to be paid through a deferred plan lasting no less than twenty-five years. Given Italy's context and Germany's hegemony, to call Fascist behavior "generous" seems like a gross understatement.[162] Franco would fully settle all debts with Italy only in 1967—a tad too late to aid Mussolini in his world war.[163]

In late 1938 Guarneri had written a succinct but significant introduction to *Economic Spain: Today and Tomorrow,* in which he sought to underscore the importance of economics-focused analyses: "The knowledge of specific market economies is an essential premise for an intelligent . . . policy of commercial expansion abroad. . . . [This book] makes a precious contribution to our knowledge of the Spanish market, which Italy must closely follow and study for the possibilities of the day after tomorrow, when victory—to which the youth of the *Littorio* [army] division has given so much energy and blood—will have given Spain back its order and work discipline."[164] Yet far from profiting from its vast investment in blood and lire in Spain, Italy had fallen victim to its dictator's misguided economic strategies and, indirectly, Germany's unequal, self-interested, and imperial control of Franco. Consequently Italy was left with scant "possibilities for the day after tomorrow." Indeed the exercise in great power politics only exacerbated Italy's financial problems, diminishing its war preparedness. Even without a looming world war, the high expenditures in Spain could have been justified only in "strategic" terms—and given the way the Axis alliance worked, even those results were meager indeed.

All this was the result of shortsighted policy. During the Depression the Fascist government adopted a decidedly aggressive foreign policy, which affected its finances in a number of important ways. It resulted in an inward move toward autarky. The grandiose expansionism meanwhile led directly to the battlegrounds of Ethiopia and Spain. At least in part to keep up the mirage of Italian strength, Mussolini and Ciano made decisions with regard to Spain that went against Italy's economic best interest: they committed too many men, too many supplies, and too much foreign exchange to an Iberian adventure for which they neither received nor required repayment. Succinctly, il Duce put prestige over profit.

Another type of intervention was possible. Powerful but ultimately secondary men in the Fascist administration—Anfuso, Guarneri, Fagiuoli—worked hard to have Italy profit from its investment in the Francoist war effort, or at least to offset its costs. Their failure had important consequences for Italian financial and military preparedness in the looming war. As Roatta would later declare, "Italy's material poverty cannot be invoked as the sole reason for our lack of military preparedness [in World War II], for in the fascist period huge sums were invested in so many other projects."[165] Spain stands out among those.

Ultimately, as Ciano wrote in March 1939, one part of the Axis behaved with "little regard for the other." He could have seen it coming well before the second Czech crisis if he had bothered to focus on finance rather than flags. The intervention in Spain was more revealing than the lack of communication over the destiny of Bohemia: Germany had used its size and might far more effectively than Italy, extracting tangible benefits from Franco's dependence. While Mussolini worried about his reputation, the Schachtian principles that underlay the HISMA-ROWAK system laid the basis for peacetime dependence of the Spanish economy. And when Italian technocrats were given a chance to attempt a more favorable arrangement, they were too weak and too late.

And yet il Duce was right about one thing: by mid-1939 Italy could afford to be "hateful to God and to His enemies." In fully aligning himself with Nazi Germany, Mussolini by early 1939 had made his choice.[166] The "hour of irrevocable decisions," as he called the declaration of war on June 10, 1940, had come long before that. That is perhaps why he made only a half-hearted attempt to convince Franco to join in the war during their meeting in the town of Bordighera, in spite of Hitler's requests.[167] Even his later letters to Franco did "not wish to hasten in the least the decisions" the Spanish leader would fail to make on behalf of "the two victorious Axis Powers."[168] In fact even at the height of the Axis's military successes, the Italian government fretted about the implications of the realignment of European economies to fit Berlin's designs.[169]

Simply put, Nazi Germany's interest was not Fascist Italy's interest, and that became painfully clear in Rome as the world war dragged on. Nothing had much changed since the first days of an alliance forged on Iberian soil. It was for good reason that in December 1940 Hitler claimed that defeat for Rome "had the healthy effect of once more compressing Italian claims within the natural boundaries of Italian capabilities."[170] After small engagements in France, Mussolini's forces fared even less well in the Balkans, moving Hitler to invade Greece to "save" the campaign. If a first world war had given birth to Fascism, a second one would put an end to it.

chapter nine

THE FORMAL EMPIRE

In earlier times things were simpler. In earlier times you pillaged.
He who had conquered a country disposed of the riches of that
country. At present, things are done in a more humane way. As for
myself, I still think of pillage, comprehensively.

—HERMANN GÖRING, August 6, 1942

By early 1939 the informal empire that Mussolini never sought was
tangible for Nazi Germany. The scale of Nazi ambitions is perhaps
best illustrated by the many industries in which the nascent and
increasingly diversified SOFINDUS conglomerate planned investments. What a leading Spanish historian called a "vocation for empire"
was, in truth, the reality of informal hegemony: from mines and farms
to trucking and logistics, Bernhardt and his staff were involved. Their
goals were inextricably linked to Germany's economic needs. By then
Berlin was taking in the lion's share of Spanish trade: no less than
three quarters of all exports.[1] In spite of tensions between Bernhardt
and official state envoys, the German Embassy in Burgos ultimately
defended HISMA; diplomats under Ambassador von Stohrer recognized how effective dual monopoly had been. As we have seen, Nationalists had repeatedly tried—and failed—to alter how exchanges
operated. Spain remained poor and at war; a German intervention that
was radically different from Italy's yielded a "special relationship" with
Berlin underpinned by a project of investment and resource extraction
to "compensate" for investments and set out the framework for the

long-term control of the Iberian economy. Indeed on Spanish soil German economic motivations had overshadowed other concerns.[2] The German goal on the ground was now to perpetuate economic hegemony, keeping Spain within Germany's trade sphere. This was consistent with neo-*Weltpolitik* foreign economic policy in countries as distant as Yugoslavia and Argentina.[3] The unequal relationship between Spain and Germany betrayed the "neocolonial character" of German policy.[4] Yet the destiny of this "shadow empire" was inextricably intertwined with Hitler's wider foreign policy. Would informal empire suffice?

This question would be answered by decisions over the economy and rearmament that were up to the Führer; informal empire was not enough. The Cabinet radicalization that sidelined Schacht and favored Göring between late 1936 and early 1939 implied a policy move toward formal empire. This project began in earnest in central Europe, with the Austrian Anschluß and Czechoslovakia's dismemberment. Appeasement fed it. The invasion of Poland led to war with France and, to Hitler's surprise, Britain as well in September 1939. Occupation, annexation, and extermination followed what was, at least at first, a rapid succession of German military victories. Yet it was this quest for *Lebensraum* that undid Hitler's shadow empire in Spain, and six years later, Nazi Germany itself.

German territorial expansion began well before the end of the Spanish Civil War.[5] While Bernhardt and von Stohrer in Spain worked to expand HISMA into SOFINDUS to cement German hegemony, Hitler once again raised the stakes. As we have seen, Hitler was more directly in charge of military decisions after the birth of the Oberkommando der Wehrmacht, yet his distrust of the military establishment did not dissipate.[6] Meanwhile Schacht's replacement in the Economics Ministry and von Neurath's at the Foreign Ministry removed opposition to ever-higher military expenditures.[7] The Führer was less constrained than ever before.

An opportunity for aggression presented itself barely a month after von Neurath's replacement; the Austrian crisis was to be transformative for the regime. The fascist but anti-Nazi Austrian premier, Kurt Schuschnigg, scheduled a surprise plebiscite on union with the Reich on March 9. In what the *Economist* described as a "bold step . . . tilted toward the government," Schuschnigg invited Austrians to vote for a "free and German, independent and social, Christian and united Austria."[8] Göring had been encouraging such a union for years, yet this had been the root of tensions with Mussolini before the Spanish Civil War.[9] Hitler had grown restless. With moderating forces out of power, his fixation on crafting a Greater Germany, an idea easily traceable to *Mein Kampf,* underscored a drive for formal expansion.[10]

Hitler denounced Schuschnigg's plebiscite, suggesting it violated the terms of a previous agreement, even if he had effectively achieved all his formal demands. But what Hitler wanted were not his demands.[11] He then issued an ultimatum favoring Arthur Seyß-Inquart, a Nazi lawyer whom Schuschnigg had been forced to accept as interior minister. With Chamberlain's Britain noncommittal, Schuschnigg decided to resign. Austrian president Wilhelm Miklas, however, resisted. Seyß-Inquart himself harbored doubts.[12] Ultimately everyone—Schuschnigg, Seyß-Inquart, even Miklas—gave in. And yet the Wehrmacht invaded all the same. The German military was far from ready for war, but there was no war: when troops crossed the border on the morning of March 12, Austrian crowds greeted them. An American journalist commented sardonically that the invasion violated the terms of Hitler's own ultimatum.[13] Unlike in 1934, Mussolini acquiesced: "The Duce is pleased and tells [Prince] Hesse to inform the Führer that Italy is following the events with absolute calm."[14] This led to an unusually effusive response: "I will never forget [Mussolini] for this, never, never, never, come what may."[15]

There was no ex ante plan. Only in his native Linz did Hitler decide for "total Anschluß," implying full Austrian annexation and integration into the Reich. A month later a rubber-stamp plebiscite—to this day a preferred mode of authoritarian legitimization—received support from 99.7 percent of Austrians. The numbers were suspicious.[16] As remains the case in Eastern Europe today, referenda held under military occupation are not quite legitimate. Yet anecdotal evidence does suggest that Austrians were generally supportive; Hitler had successfully appropriated what was once a dream of the left on the eve of defeat in 1918.[17] Union materialized long-held pan-German dreams that transcended traditional party lines.[18]

Seyß-Inquart promulgated a law subordinating Austria to the Third Reich. As early as March 17, two days after Hitler spoke in Vienna, the Reichsmark was circulating in Austria. Foreign exchange reserves were sent to Schacht's (empty) Reichsbank coffers. Austrian reserves were considerable: 782 million Reichsmarks, 345 million of which were official reserves, the rest from private sources.[19] This inflow more than doubled Reichsbank reserves. Practically they allowed for a trade deficit larger than any since 1929, freeing Schacht's Reichsbank, at least temporarily, from almost constant balance of payment concerns. Concurrently Schacht incorporated the Austrian National Bank into the Reichsbank and his "aggressive speech" discussing the success of Anchsluß ended with an oath of personal allegiance to Hitler and, if that were not enough, three emphatic, "Sieg Heils."[20] Austrian economic integration proceeded relatively swiftly thereafter.[21] The Nazis eliminated import duties on agricultural machines by mid-April; they introduced the Reich turnover tax on May 1 as a first step toward a full tributary harmonization.[22] "The economic frontier," noted the *Economist* on April 26, "is gradually disappearing."[23] Tellingly, the article was already featured in the newspaper's "Germany" section.

The ubiquitous Göring received yet another commission. He visited Austria to announce a reconstruction plan that focused, unsurprisingly, on rearmament. After a bloodless Anschluß, preparations for a different type of annexation marched on. Göring's speech was a masterpiece of Orwellian doublethink: "Austria is free, but belongs once again to the Reich."[24] Actually Austria lost all independence; at first it was made a province (Ostmark) and later subdivided into smaller units to weaken the centrality of Vienna. Indeed the "the two-thousand-year-old supra-national metropolis" was not even singled out as one of the five key cities in Greater Germany for infrastructure projects.[25] Hitler's native Linz, however, was.[26] Austrian jurisprudence was likewise subordinated. The process was swift and attacks on minorities—chiefly Jews and Austrian nationalists—proliferated.[27] Himmler's SS took the reins of the "purification" agenda.[28] 1938 vintage maps already reflected Germany's formal expansion.

Austria was not enough. Around the time of the Vienna crisis, Hitler encouraged a Sudeten German leader to make demands that the Czechoslovakian government would find unacceptable. Another border faced tensions, which eventually led to the Munich Conference. While Nationalist Ambassador Magaz struggled to justify Franco's hastened neutrality announcement, on November 21 the Reich annexed the Sudetenland.[29] Munich humiliated Czechoslovakia not only diplomatically but also economically: it ceded 40 percent of Czechoslovakian industrial capacity, including coveted armaments factories, and 55 percent of its coal production.[30] Forsaken by the democracies, Czech president Edvard Beneš resigned, paving the way for a more pliable successor. In March 1939 the Germans took over the rest of the country.[31] Such was the result of the "second Czech crisis," which led Mussolini—through Dante's immortal verses—to question the Axis forged over collaboration on Iberian soil.

On paper the Czechoslovakian Army had enough divisions to stand up to the Wehrmacht; yet once again no war broke out. The Germans pressured President Emil Hácha to "invite" German occupation; after all their eyes were already on a new target.[32] The destiny of Czechs was entrusted to the same Ministry of Interior team that had dealt with the legalities of the Anschluß.[33] Among them stood out Wilhelm Stuckart, a prolific theorist of Nazism who was quickly becoming a specialist in the practice of territorial annexation.[34] Like Austria before it—but this time through a "Führer decree"—Czechoslovakia ceased to exist, replaced by the Protectorate of Bohemia and Moravia and a puppet Slovakian Republic.[35] Stuckart's "constitution" was at best confused, proclaiming both the protectorate's independence and its dependence on the Reich. It echoed Göring's description of Austria's fate. In reality the Führer ruled the protectorate at will, a right he would later exercise.[36] The Czechs retained a local administration, yet their dependence was as absolute as Austria's. A new system of dual citizenship gave automatic rights to Germans residing in the protectorate, but it did not work the other way around; henceforth Czechs were second-class citizens.

Economic integration into the Reich proceeded as fast as Austria's; before the protectorate's constitution was finished, Göring's steel conglomerate was already after Czech production.[37] The goal was, once more, the growth of military preparedness. Requisitions were sizable: Czech horses were essential for a Wehrmacht that was far from the fully mechanized war-making machine of popular imagination.[38] The monetary situation was complicated by the prescient Czech decision to send their reserves abroad. But the Bank of England agreed—via the Bank of International Settlements—to return Czech gold to the protectorate. They never got to Prague. Courtesy of the hard work of a diligent Economics Ministry official on whom Schacht had relied to negotiate trade deals, Helmuth Wohlthat, the gold went straight to the Reichsbank.[39] The total annexation influx was 360 million Reichsmarks, a net addition of around 35 percent of existing reserves at Schacht's Reichsbank.[40] From the perspective of central bank reserves, therefore, empire provided relief.[41] And, notwithstanding his aforementioned private concerns, Schacht was never one to pass up a chance to take credit in public: "From the beginning the Reichsbank has been aware of the fact that a successful foreign policy can be attained only by the reconstruction of the German armed forces."[42] Like he had in the late 1920s, even at this stage he continued to behave as if he were the Reichsbank.

With rump Czechoslovakia, Hitler crossed another border: for the first time the Nazis formally took over a territory where ethnic Germans were not a majority, revealing the vacuity of previous Nazi arguments.[43] Acutely aware that the world's eyes were on Prague, Hitler appointed von Neurath as protector, a relatively conservative choice that was at least partially a signal to foreign audiences. Changes on the ground were nonetheless "revolutionary."[44] Racial tensions escalated, again stoked by the SS.[45] Acute observers saw through this, not least a young George Kennan, who, stationed in Prague, considered his work at the time to be "child's play."[46] How long would peaceful Nazi empire last?

While Hitler advanced in Central Europe, the Spanish Civil War finally came to an end: Franco marched into Madrid and on to victory. Nationalist alignment with the Axis was such that two important treaties were signed the week before the end of the War. On March 27 Spain signed the Anti-Comintern Pact. It became the first country to do so since Japan, Italy, and Germany had created the anti-Moscow alliance.[47] On the very last day of the war, March 31, Franco signed a Treaty of Friendship with Germany. This agreement built upon the 1937–1938 formal treaties and signaled future priorities.[48] It stipulated Spain's "benevolent neutrality" in the event of a wider war. Articles 8 and 9 dealt with economics, expanding the focus of German economic penetration into the reconstruction effort. Any reading of the Treaty strongly suggests that the Third Reich—and not Britain or France, historically the biggest investors in Spain—was expected to be the central force behind Spanish reconstruction.[49] Despite a truly dire financial standing, Franco still moved farther from the democracies and toward

Berlin. In what can only be understood as a reaction to alignment with Berlin, the British Foreign Office blocked an essential loan to Madrid.[50] The political allegiance of Franco's New Spain was clear enough—and it had equally obvious financial consequences.

It was not just politics. Although the war was over, another battle dawned for Franco's regime. Notwithstanding the direct ownership of the Montaña project mines beyond what Spanish law had allowed, the wartime transfers of raw materials shipped back to Hamburg, and all the talk of anti-Communist "fascist solidarity," Nationalists in Spain and at the Berlin Embassy continued to worry about the German dual monopoly that had so blatantly subordinated Spanish production to German needs. They also worried about "the debt": the repayment of thus far unquantified large expenses incurred by Germany on Spanish soil not covered by HISMA's exports. Unlike poorer Italy, Germany never seriously considered forgiving Spanish debts. Quite the contrary: Ambassador von Stohrer argued on April 14 for "psychological" measures that could appeal to the vanity of Spanish leaders obsessed with the "triumphant" Nazi regime.[51] The ambassador also advocated rethinking the SOFINDUS investment vehicle, thus making German imperial power in Spain "softer."

An Economics Ministry delegation prepared a key trip to Spain. German envoy Sabath previewed the negotiating tactics: Spaniards "are to be treated chivalrously" lest they feel "we are demanding payment for the shedding of German blood." And yet he suggested mentioning German personnel expenses—meaning the Legion—as a negotiating tactic, but "compensation from them is not to be demanded." Last, "Italians are not to be offended."[52] Two months behind schedule but appropriately for the summer season, on June 12, a German delegation arrived in San Sebastián; it included all the senior economic officials who had developed economic relations during the Civil War: Sabath from the Auswärtiges Amt; Friedrich Bethke, de facto director of ROWAK; and the commercial attaché in Madrid, Enge.[53] Its leader was none other than Wohlthat, one of Schacht's key trade negotiators.[54] Wohlthat's schedule those days suggests that though the Economics Ministry leadership had changed, Spain's role within a budding Reich imperial system remained; before arriving in Spain, he had negotiated an oil deal with Romania in March. Since Schacht's trade deals in the Balkans, Romania had become an integral part of the Nazi informal empire; over 50 percent of its trade was with Germany and, as of the Wohlthat-negotiated deal, there was a coordinated five-year development plan.[55] In the words of IG Farben's Max Ilgner, the goal of the Romanian deal was "to increase [German] exports by playing an active role in the industrialization of the world."[56] Interestingly, later Wohlthat was stationed in Prague to oversee the integration of the Czech industrial base into the Reich, and after Spain he traveled to London to negotiate (successfully) the return of Czech gold reserves.[57]

The Wohlthat-led German delegation toured war-torn Spain. Although they considered a possible adaptation of the dual monopoly, the officials stressed the importance of German economic hegemony and Spanish supplies for German industry, where most of Spain's exports were now destined. The Spanish Civil War had radically changed the direction of Iberian trade.[58] On the Spanish side, by contrast, an internal government report argued that now that the Civil War was over, "there is no reason why we should be forced to accept an economic *diktat*."[59] Franco's men were unsurprisingly eager to change the nature of their relations with their closest ally and sponsor.

Logistically, however, Spain lacked the basic statistical data needed to negotiate a normalization of economic relations. The Germans strongly opposed any change that would make exchanges more equal.[60] Wohlthat and his team imposed their will: the SOFINDUS system was maintained until a "fuller agreement" was reached. The latter was of course nowhere close. Bernhardt's team was happy with the result, a sign it was not ideal for Spain. Although some authors have claimed that this result owed much to the political proclivities of Spanish leaders, it seems clear from their own language that they understood how much the dual monopoly hurt their economic standing. Yet German hegemony meant there was little they could do about it.[61] The end result of this "imperial tour" was therefore tilted toward German benefit. It would get worse for Spain: following the trip, German diplomats took up "the debt," their ultimate Civil War lever to further expand their burgeoning informal empire.

In Eastern Europe, meanwhile, tensions escalated even further. Germany's 1918 humiliation was perhaps nowhere more obvious than in Poland's Prussian possessions. Such territories were crucial to *Lebensraum* "theorists."[62] With Austrian and Czech territories secure, Hitler looked to Warsaw. Relatively new minister von Ribbentrop proved to be a skillful negotiator in seducing Stalinist Russia; Moscow was as pragmatic and self-serving as it had been during the Spanish Civil War. Thus Nazi Germany and Russia eventually signed an unexpected nonaggression pact.[63] Echoing Bonaparte, Hitler spoke privately of a "continental bloc" linking Fascist Italy, Russia, and even Japan pitted against Britain and the United States.[64]

This time, however, invasion unleashed war.[65] When German troops crossed the border into Poland on September 1, 1939, Britain and France honored their treaty commitments. The twenty-eight days of Blitzkrieg were a success for the Wehrmacht, but the Polish Army fought bravely.[66] As soon as occupation materialized, the usual bureaucratic disputes erupted. The Wehrmacht attempted to exercise control over civilian administrators—a category that usually involved too many Nazis to please the military leadership—and SS "task forces" *(Einsatzgruppen).*[67] To no avail: Hitler's orders allowed unprecedented liberty to the Party and the SS in the management of the occupied territories.[68] When Gen. Johannes Blaskowitz tried to punish SS members for extreme violence, Hitler rebuked him, calling him "infantile" and "out of order."[69] In early October the Führer issued a pardon for German excesses; with this carte blanche, retaliations against acts of Polish resistance escalated further.[70]

Four months earlier than originally planned, the Werhrmacht was sidelined in occupation management in favor of Party men. This would soon become a staple of war-time management. The policy applied in particular to the eastern territories that were integral to the *Lebensraum* ideological construct.[71] Yet formal Nazi empire lacked consistent rules.[72] Territories were left to the destiny of whoever ran them; some were lucky, most were not. This was a novel strategy: it represented a radical departure from the experience during the Great War, when the silent dictatorship's General Government in Poland was run exclusively by the military command.[73]

Like Austria and Czechoslovakia, Poland as such ceased to exist. The Polish Corridor and Pomerania were annexed into the Reich; as per von Ribbentrop's secret treaty clauses, Russia occupied a broad swath of eastern Poland. The remainder became the General Government, with Krakow as its capital. Unlike in the Slovakian puppet state or the local administration of the Czech protectorate, Poles were placed under the leadership of a "racially aware" administration. Its leader, Hans Frank, was eager to set the standard for Nazi imperial management.

Frank himself pointed out the differences in treatment during a visit to the Czech protectorate: "There were large red posters in Prague announcing today that seven [Czechs] had been shot. If I wanted to hang a poster for every seven Poles that have been shot then all the forests in Poland would not suffice in order to produce the paper necessary."[74] Extreme corruption and even more extreme violence characterized the rule of a man who became known—for the worst reasons—as "the King of Poland."[75]

In the absence of a formal peace treaty, the disappearance of Poland created a legal quandary. This legal limbo bothered the Auswärtiges Amt staff, but it scarcely mattered to the Führer. Although the analysis of these decisions has focused historically on what they meant for the Final Solution, they also had important economic implications. The zloty currency kept circulating in the General Government, stamped as of 1940 by a new authority. With greater intensity than in either Austria or Czechoslovakia, the Polish invasion was characterized by plunder. Berlin did not mind: Hitler and Göring repeatedly argued that the rank and file of German troops deserved spoils. But not indiscriminately: the best assets were reserved for the Party leadership.

At first Frank implemented an uneconomic and unsuccessful but racially inspired drive to keep the Poles out of most jobs. As the war dragged on, however, Polish labor had to be brought into the Reich economy, increasingly across the border into Germany proper.[76] As genocide was perpetrated at an industrial scale all over eastern Europe, more than a million Poles became forced labor in the Reich.[77] Foreign workers—with Poles as the largest single source—would rise to 19 percent of the Reich workforce, a staggering number even by today's globalized standards.

In Spain the Nationalist leadership had expected war. What they had not expected was the Ribbentrop-Molotov Pact.[78] After their subscription to the Anti-Comintern Pact as well as a three-year war at least partly justified as "a fight against Reds," Spain's economic hegemon had suddenly found a modus vivendi with Stalinist Russia. Ribbentrop-Molotov involved the partition of eastern Europe and the supply of grain and other raw materials from Russia to Germany, at least in part to sustain the grossly inefficient strategies of Agriculture Minister Darré.[79] In Madrid, however, it caused deep consternation.[80]

As soon as Hitler's war began in earnest, the Anglo-French economic blockade presented gargantuan logistical problems for continued exports to Germany.[81] The echoes of the Great War were loud.[82] Yet unlike during that war, Spain's economy in 1939 was far more closely tied with Germany's than Britain's; as we have seen, three years had completely altered Spain's economic role in Europe.

Then there was "the debt." The topic of German expenditures during the Spanish Civil War had been broached twice before. In May 1939, when the Condor Legion left Spain, Germans had left behind equipment coveted by Franco's regime, including around seventy-five (used) war planes, mostly Heinkel 101s and Messerschmitt Bf 109s, the Legion's fighting workhorses.[83] An agreement had been reached about price, including a wear-and-tear discount of 35 percent. This was comparatively straightforward. In June–July 1939, however, during Wohlthat's tour and negotiations, the German delegation considered Civil War debts a "cardinal" issue for future commercial relations; they were left to a separate commission.[84] It was then that the Germans first presented their full demands to the Spanish leadership; this involved repayment for acknowledged expenses, a new set of expenditures the Spaniards did not recognize (but had no way to dispute), and an assessment of Spanish raw material and foreign exchange remittances to Germany (almost all via HISMA). The Germans also undervalued the Iberian war-time contributions to the German economy.[85] Madrid was thus presented with a bill detailing all kinds of expenditures; as a negotiating tactic, the full expenses of the Condor Legion were sometimes discussed, leading the Spanish to argue that such an approach would have turned the legionnaires into outright mercenaries.[86] In mid-1939 the German total was 359 million Reichsmarks, a colossal sum.[87] A considerable problem for the Spaniards was that German sources and Bernhardt's HISMA had kept the accounting. Bookkeeping had not been a Francoist priority.[88]

Torn apart by a thirty-month-long civil war, Spain was in no position to honor these obligations.[89] After 1945 Franco would complain that Spain had already relinquished all available foreign exchange to Germany, along with a considerable amount of natural resources that could have been sold to Spain's more traditional customers.[90] This would suffice to establish German hegemony over the nascent regime. During the July 1939 negotiations, however, the Spanish delegation at first com-

plained that they had expected a "political answer" to these issues—
meaning they wanted the same treatment they had received from Italy.
They should have known better. Then they complained they had already paid much in kind and foreign exchange during the civil war.

Negotiations reached an impasse, so the issue of debt was still outstanding when the invasion of Poland triggered war. Wohlthat returned
to Spain in November 1939 to negotiate a new agreement, to be signed
in December. By then Germans had a new, crucial preoccupation: to
keep commercial channels open despite the Anglo-French naval
blockade.[91] It was around this time that the Germans sent their first
full report of "war debts," presumably to further their negotiating leverage. The Spanish goals meanwhile had not changed: they wanted
to minimize repayment and once and for all replace the HISMA-
ROWAK dual monopoly.

What had changed was Madrid's assessment of its own best interests
as well as its ability to pursue them. First off, there was better technical expertise in the Iberian delegation led by José Pan de Soraluce.[92]
Spanish historians have argued that the Iberian resistance was due to
the imposition of commercial concerns over political ones.[93] Yet such
a view ignores the wider geopolitical developments. The beginning of
world war had completely altered a bilateral relationship that had not
seen any Spanish freedom of action in three years. First, Wohlthat arrived in Spain for a shorter period and with a much-reduced delegation.[94] Second, the Germans saw no easy logistical way to keep control
over Spanish exports in the context of the blockade.[95] Perhaps most crucially, with war raging on the Continent it was not plausible for Germans to argue that the agreement should be part of a fuller commercial treaty. The Germans now required much more cooperation from
the Spaniards to get raw materials to their industrial centers and around
the blockade. Recall the German concern about the sustainability of
raw material supplies in the event of war going back to the early years
of the regime. And yet Wohlthat tried to maintain the previous
arrangement.

Constrained by the exigencies of war, German negotiators pushed
a banking license for SOFINDUS, to be funded by the Spanish government as an advance payment on debts, so as to be able to create credit for
German companies on Iberian soil. In a first, the Spaniards rejected
this idea. Instead the Francoist government revived the interministerial

treaty commission, an entity that had been sidelined for years in negotiations with Germany. It unanimously voted to seek "freedom" from
Germany for economic relations with other countries.[96] Months earlier any such resistance would have been unthinkable.

Two confidential agreements were eventually signed.[97] Wohlthat
conceded in December that the dual monopoly would no longer be
the exclusive medium of exchange, at least for the duration of Germany's war.[98] In the Reich the treaties were rightly interpreted as a
Spanish victory, so much so that Göring called a special meeting the
following March at his residence in which he rebuked Wohlthat in front
of a variety of his colleagues.[99] The seasoned negotiator responded that
they had few alternatives if they wanted to maintain the commercial
exchange in spite of the Anglo-French blockade. On this point the rest
of the group seems to have agreed; now at war, Germany needed the
continued provision of high-quality iron ore, wolfram, mercury, and
foodstuffs, along with anything that could be extracted from a now
freer Spain.[100] As for "the debt," the Spaniards had merely promised to
"look into" the amounts, bills, and exchange rates used to calculate
the total liability. In the following seven months the Spaniards made
no further payments in foreign exchange.[101] Suddenly time was on Franco's side.

A further sign of Germany's weakened position was that Spain moved
to normalize other economic relations. Asserting their newfound
freedom, Franco's regime, which had resisted any connection with the
democracies just months earlier, signed commercial treaties with both
France and Britain in early 1940.[102] From the German perspective, this
violated the 1937 promise that Spain's first comprehensive agreement
would be with the Third Reich, but from the Spanish point of view
the agreements signed by Wohlthat and his team had already "fulfilled"
that obligation. Legalism aside, Franco was freer to seek counterbalancing contacts with Germany's enemies. Like their resistance to further economic penetration, this Iberian volte-face would have been im-
probable before the invasion of Poland; with Spain at peace and
resource-constrained Germany at war, Franco could continue to resist.

What makes the new Spanish stance so remarkable is that in the wider
foreign policy arena German power was still in the ascendancy. During
the so-called phony war, the Nazi empire grew almost unwittingly.

The Danish government's declaration of war had no sooner reached Germany on April 9, 1940, than the Danes were forced to capitulate. It was perhaps the briefest military campaign in history.[103] Control of Danish airfields and routes was essential for a preemptive attack on Norway, launched that very day. Aided by its terrain and an Anglo-French expeditionary force, however, Norway resisted.[104] Control of those territories was essential from an economic as well as a strategic perspective: it would allow unfettered access to high-quality ores from Narvik.[105]

The subsequent administration of both territories was dissimilar. The Danes were managed with the least possible oversight: without an overbearing viceroy, permanent civilian staff, intervention from the Wehrmacht, or even a sizable SS involvement. The German ambassador, Cecil von Renthe-Fink, became a "Reich plenipotentiary," while the political system was left with a degree of independence that eluded other occupied territories.[106] This "light touch" not only served as political window-dressing at a time when the destiny of Norway and the Low Countries was undecided but also ensured that the Danes kept producing what Nazi Germany needed most from them: dairy and other primary goods.[107] Surrounded by occupied territories, however, foreign policy independence was out of the question. So Danes acquiesced to German hegemony and integration into its economic system.

The destiny of Norway could hardly have been more different. Having resisted for longer than most—the most, in fact, of any invaded country, save Soviet Russia—Hitler once again personally sidelined the Wehrmacht. His choice of Rhineland local party chief Josef Terboven as *Reichskommissar* did not bode well for Norwegians; it was further complicated by the existence of a local pseudo-Nazi party with close—if complicated—ties to the German Nazi Party.[108] Judging by their electoral performance before the war, National Samsling (NS), the party led by Vidkun Quisling, was anything but popular. In the aftermath of King Haakon VII's exile to London, however, Terboven unilaterally abolished the monarchy and established a government made up almost exclusively of NS members. This move did not endear him to the population. The same applied to the puppet government established under Quisling in 1942.[109] The London *Times* coined the use of *quisling* as a synonym for Nazi collaborator; the term has proven far more popular than Quisling ever was.[110] The years of occupation saw martial law, mass executions, and concentration camps. It was highly unusual for a Nazi leader to disgust Goebbels by his treatment of occupied peoples, but Terboven somehow managed.[111]

Belgium and the Netherlands provide further examples of the haphazard nature of formal Nazi imperialism. In Belgium the occupation began with massive looting, condoned by the Nazi leadership.[112] The Reich swiftly annexed the territories lost in Versailles—Eupen, Malmédy, and the village of Moresnet—via a Führer decree on May 18.[113] Meeting the king in late 1940, Hitler was vague about the country's future: Belgium would "occupy a position of some sort within the economic and political cooperation with the Reich."[114] It was not to be a simple occupation. From a management perspective, however, the strategy was not dissimilar to the one followed during the Great War, in which Schacht had gotten his first taste of both public service and empire. With the exception of the annexed territories, the Wehrmacht remained in control throughout the war under Baron Alexander von Falkenhausen, an old-school *Kaiserreich* type whose cousin had run the occupation during World War I.[115] Perhaps that is why the economic integration of Belgium went relatively smoothly: looting stopped, business orders poured in from Germany, and Belgian business leaders were quick to integrate their production into the Reich industrial core.[116] Even though production had fallen below 1939 levels, the Germans were not deterred; the economic pie might have been smaller, but the Reich took a considerably larger slice. Exports to Germany had priority, and after December 1941 exports to other occupied territories were technically banned to divert even more trade toward the Reich proper.[117] In spite of currency controls, however, inflationary pressures built up, driven by the artificially weak exchange rate of the franc against the Reichsmark that furthered German purchasing power. It was another World War I déjà vu.[118]

In the Netherlands the "Rotterdam blitz" echoed Guernica: resistance against the Wehrmacht ended swiftly on May 14, 1940. Against the wishes of the military establishment, the administration of occupied Netherlands was entrusted to the Nazi Party.[119] Yet Anschluß veteran Seyß-Inquart implemented a type of occupation radically different from Terboven's in Norway. Hitler had encouraged the Austrian to seek collaboration, particularly given the need to access raw materials from the unoccupied Dutch Empire. The man *Time* called "Germany's handy man for disciplining captured countries" proved to be a careful, effective exploiter.[120] Inspired by suggestions from Schacht's old ally at the War Ministry, General Thomas, he resisted looting and mass requisitions. Instead he took a more decentralized approach.[121] His so-called *Auftragsverlagerung* policy involved letting local producers fulfill orders from German businesses, which had effective priority over all others. By 1940 they accounted for 14 percent of Dutch GDP. *Auftragsverlagerung* was arguably the closest the formal Nazi empire ever came to informal empire, meaning that control was less violent and arbitrary as well as more rooted in economic incentives for the local population. Dutch unemployment decreased so rapidly that Seyß-Inquart boasted to a Party outlet that he had solved in half a year what the Dutch government failed to do over a decade since the Depression.[122] This policy was certainly more economically efficient than Göring's looting and the more systematic exploitation displayed after 1942.

By mid-1940 Hitler's focus was on France, which had not mounted an aggressive campaign.[123] During the winter of 1939–1940 he sent workers back to factories so as to avoid a severe impact on the overheated economy, where the shortage of labor remained acute.[124] Meanwhile forced labor into the Reich began to grow not only from annexed territories but increasingly from occupied territories.[125] The German invasion, codenamed *Fall Gelb*, advanced faster than even the Wehrmacht had expected; the French, badly organized and questionably led, did not resist for long.[126] By May 23 the British Expeditionary Force and some of the best French troops had been encircled; the Dunkirk evacuation is remembered in Britain as a triumph, when in reality it was the salvage operation at the end of what Churchill appropriately called "a colossal military disaster." A French armistice followed on June 22.

Because of its size and importance, France would be a key test for German imperialism. Three weeks after the armistice, on July 15, Franco-German frontiers were readjusted back to the 1871 borders. Alsace, Lorraine, and three other French departments (Moselle, Bas-Rhin, and Haut-Rhin) were henceforth fully integrated into the Reich.[127] Under some of the same men responsible for the Austrian and Czech "integrations," these territories were to be Germanized "within ten years." The Nazis took these goals very seriously.[128] As of early August, statistics in the regions became indistinguishable from those in the rest of the Reich. On August 16 the Reichsbank published a report on the economy of Alsace-Lorraine. It seems obvious the report had been in the works since before the invasion.[129] France was divided. There were two occupied areas—one under German military command and a tiny one under Italian control, a fitting symbol of Mussolini's role in Hitler's plans. Then there was Marshal Pétain's Vichy government, which eventually administered the rest of France.[130] Pétain's fascistic "New Order" worked only within German-imposed constraints. The *Economist* editors were right to point out there were three Frances: "one occupied, one muzzled, and one exiled."[131]

Without a proper peace treaty, however, France's ultimate destiny was unclear.[132] From an economic perspective, France was a prize bigger than all the other occupied territories put together. Göring—whom General Thomas, echoing Schacht's similarly condescending remarks, addressed as "not an economist"—behaved characteristically: he oversaw massive looting in luxury and industrial goods.[133] This fit his conception of France as a "defeated nation."[134] Thereafter he focused on adapting French airplane factories for Luftwaffe production, a goal that was aided by France's extensive aluminum industry.

As elsewhere, German soldiers in France received occupation currency *(Reichskreditkassenschein)* to be used for their expenses.[135] The central bank (Banque de France) was forced to issue corresponding francs and to charge the French government for the cost. This implied a generous occupation subsidy; such monetary expansion in a growing economy fed inflation. France suffered: the overvaluation of the Reichsmark against the franc was extreme, surpassed only by the exchange rate with the Greek drachma.[136]

Logistically the exploitation of the crown jewel in the German Empire proceeded through levying egregious occupation costs that had little to do with actual Wehrmacht expenditures. These had been "negotiated" by an economic delegation under Hans Hemmen that resisted Göring's more brutal approach in favor of "lighter" management. Eager to maintain good relations with Pétain's regime, the Wehrmacht and von Ribbentrop's Auswärtiges Amt supported it. Göring complained about the "humane" way the French were treated; he also professed nostalgia for outright "pillaging."[137] But even the "moderate" Wehrmacht had taken no less than eighty-one thousand tons of copper from France, Belgium, and the Netherlands immediately after the successful invasions. In all, 13 billion francs' worth of raw materials would be taken from France.[138]

As leading economic historians of the period have argued, however, the lack of certain key resources in the occupied territories and the lack of access to their imperial possessions (applicable to France and Belgium) severely limited what Germany could hope to gain from its glittering continental empire. This meant that the resources that could be obtained from what remained of Germany's informal empire—principally Spain but also the Balkans—were still essential. The longer the war, the worse Germany's resource handicap became.[139]

Blitzkrieg on French soil brought Mussolini into the war. But it did not bring in a far more cautious Franco, who was desirous of "tranquility."[140] Yet the Generalísimo was tempted all the same. In a September 16 meeting between von Ribbentrop and Ramón Serrano Suñer—Franco's brother-in-law, soon to be the Spanish foreign minister—the Germans offered French Morocco to Spain in exchange for belligerence, as long as Germany could have bases and, perhaps most crucially, formal mining rights.[141] In order to fulfill the Spanish military's centuries-long North African obsession, Franco wanted control of Gibraltar and Oran as well. As we have seen, these aims directly addressed Royal Navy preoccupations since the beginning of the Spanish Civil War. Franco invited Hitler to meet.[142]

In mid-1940 Berlin authorized Bernhardt to write a letter to Franco directly, expressing eagerness to continue economic exchanges while the Iberian government "analyzed" war debts. Bernhardt's focus was on the commercial debts in a masked attempt to unblock negotiations. At the time German formal control over western Europe was, other than in Spain, absolute.[143] In the process the preeminence of SOFINDUS was reasserted as a vehicle to turn Spanish debts into productive investments for Germany. Writing on July 5, a week after France's capitulation, Bernhardt complained to Franco that not enough raw materials flowed to Germany, while promising further "military cooperation"—meaning new matériel for the regime—if exports recovered.[144] The final amount was not prohibitive since the "commercial" debt "from Spain to HISMA" was only around 15 million Reichsmarks. Bernhardt's intervention was initially successful with the Spanish leadership. And yet this time around, the Spanish bureaucracy in charge of foreign exchange created impediments for SOFINDUS investments.[145] At the time Germans wanted to use existing war debts to pay for fruit imports, a choice that underscores the importance of Spain in the German trading system beyond the industrial needs of "the war economy."[146] In this sense the focus is reminiscent of Schacht's during his secret Republican contacts.

Germans complained once again about the Iberian war debts. This time the Spanish government understood it could delay no longer, and agreed to send a delegation to Berlin to audit bills. Yet they would take until the following September to finish. On October 20 the Führer took a train to the South of France on the way to the Spanish border. There he met French prime minister Pierre Laval, who sought better relations between the Vichy regime and Nazi Germany.[147] Hitler suggested at least some of France's colonial possessions would become German after the war, but that did not deter the eager Laval.[148] Hitler and von Ribbentrop were encouraged: they favored Vichy France as a potential ally over Francoist Spain.

Three days later Hitler arrived in Hendaye to meet Franco, whose train was late.[149] On the French side of the border, this was the closest the Führer had ever been—and ever would be—to Spain. Franco opened the conversation by expressing gratitude for Nazi intervention in the Civil War; yet he had come to ask a hefty price for military support in Hitler's war. Eager to avoid the French Empire siding with De Gaulle's Free French government in exile, Hitler did not have that much to give.[150] The Führer offered Gibraltar if Spain joined a "wide front" against Britain, but it was clear he did not want to antagonize the French. Franco enumerated his extensive demands. Hitler stood up, irritated, and threatened to leave.[151]

Talks nonetheless continued. When he finally left, Hitler was heard saying, "There's nothing to be done with this man."[152] Later that month in Florence he would famously complain to Mussolini that he would rather have his teeth pulled out than talk to Franco again. For his part, Franco told Serrano Suñer, "These people are intolerable. They want us to come into the war in exchange for nothing."[153] Hitler's later meeting with Pétain went far better than that with Franco. During the long train ride back to Germany, Hitler pressed on Wehrmacht heavyweights Jodl and Keitel that the coming summer would be an ideal time to move against Stalin.[154] An invasion of the Soviet Union, code-named

Barbarossa, was therefore Hitler's strategic answer to two intertwined failures: to woo Soviet foreign minister Molotov into a new arrangement and to subdue Britain.[155] Whether Hitler's attitude would have been different if Franco had been more forthcoming than Pétain is impossible to ascertain.[156] What we do know is that Hitler's almost concurrent dispatch of German agents to Romanian oil fields, an old bastion of his South Eastern economic empire, led a jealous Mussolini to launch a unilateral invasion of Greece. It would prove to be a ruinous move.[157]

After Hendaye, Spain redoubled efforts to assert its newfound freedom. At a meeting attended by both Franco and Serrano Suñer, the Generalísimo instructed his men to delay any agreement on German war debts. Franco commented that there would likely be "far more beneficial" ways to settle a bill "incurred in the fight against communism" after the wider war ended. In a cable to Berlin, Ambassador von Stohrer speculated that Franco wanted to treat the debts in a "global peace conference." Franco hoped a victorious Hitler would simply forgive the Civil War debts.[158]

In light of such instructions, debt negotiations stalled. Constrained by war needs as well as the blockade, SOFINDUS lacked funds to develop investments and expand its role in the reconstruction economy. In a counterfactual world without Hitler's ever-growing military commitments—soon to include the Soviet Union—a different projection of power in peacetime Spain would have been likely. As it was, however, Bernhardt could only hope to develop the investments he had already secured without new funds. A provisional agreement over existing debts was reached in Berlin only on February 28, 1941, through a protocol signed by Wohlthat on behalf of Germany and Ginés Vidal for Spain. The Spaniards did recognize a debt total in this document, yet they insisted on a "global reduction."[159] Franco hoped Mussolini's debt forgiveness would act as a precedent for Hitler. But that was wishful thinking. In stark contrast to pre–world war Ibero-German relations, the Nazis began to see themselves as unable to achieve what they wanted—and yet they did not budge on debts. Having achieved at least a nominal agreement on the amount (including a small hike, presumably due to new expenses or interest),[160] officials in Berlin decided to wait until after the success of Barbarossa to press Spain on the debts;

they maintained their focus on the flow of crucial raw materials instead.[161] The golden days of informal empire, when Germans demanded and the Spanish obliged, were decidedly over.

Delayed by untimely interventions in Yugoslavia and Greece, the Wehrmacht invaded the Soviet Union on June 22, 1941. Goebbels noted it was the same day Napoleon had chosen for his ill-fated invasion 129 years before; keenly aware of the historical parallel, Hitler commissioned "experts" to claim Bonaparte had actually invaded on June 23.[162] Only in light of Britain's dogged resistance did Hitler return to the "crusade against Communism"; after all, ideological aversion had not impeded the 1939 Ribbentrop-Molotov Pact. Barbarossa was a colossal military offensive undertaken by 3 million troops; like Napoleon's, its beginning was auspicious.[163] *Lebensraum* imperial thinking permeated it. "What India was for England, the eastern territory will be for us," Hitler declared in his military headquarters a month later.[164]

When Barbarossa failed to achieve decisive victory, however, management of the formal empire changed radically. Goebbels did not speak of "total war" before 1943; all the same, economic data suggest a more systematic exploitation of western occupied territories began far earlier, in late 1941. Before this turning point the *Auftragsverlagerung* system first implemented by Seyß-Inquart in the Netherlands had been imported into Belgium and Denmark.[165] As we have seen, a system reminiscent of informal empire techniques allowed for collaboration with local elites and businesses in the running of occupation.[166] Yet the Eastern Front demanded an amount of resources that this system simply could not muster.

In late 1941 economic and financial controls were once again tightened in Germany, gearing the country for a longer war.[167] Some accounts have put a "turning point" in December 1941, when it became obvious that Barbarossa was not the resounding success it first seemed to be.[168] As early as August, however, General Thomas considered closing down 40 percent of Dutch industry—despite an ongoing production boom—in order to remedy Germany's coal shortages, a strategic deficiency exacerbated by France's import needs.[169] Thereafter Germans redoubled efforts to import labor into the Reich to take advantage of higher domestic productivity. At least temporarily slave labor boosted production. "Increased exploitation" took until into 1942 to apply to the French economy, but it was vicious when it did.[170]

Nazi ideology and, more important, Hitler's leadership style contributed to the management bottlenecks in the empire, which were coupled with repression of the lower classes.[171] The Führer's state has been described as a "government without administration."[172] Scholars have referred to this style as "polycratic," meaning there were multiple, often overlapping pockets of power within. The inevitable bureaucratic infighting that resulted ensured all sorts of decisions were elevated to the dictator. Key moments in the history of the Third Reich—the Night of the Long Knives, the remilitarization of the Rhineland, the establishment of Schacht's "economic dictatorship," intervention in the Spanish Civil War, the Four-Year Plan, Schacht's sidelining, the Anschluß, the invasion of Poland and eventually Barbarossa—involved decisions that were, ultimately, Hitler's alone. After the defeat at Stalingrad, to borrow Bracher's classic phrase, leadership began to turn from polycratic to "chaotic."[173] Frick's Interior Ministry seemed to acknowledge as much in a 1942 report: "It is one of the most characteristic organizational principles of National Socialism that tasks of great political priority . . . are assigned not to agencies with clearly defined competencies, but to a trusted individual furnished with sweeping powers."[174] This fundamental issue with decision making was problematic not only in the military establishment that Warlimont's OKW revolutionized but also in the economic arena.[175]

Far from the "economic dictatorship" Schacht led between 1934 and mid-1937, a plethora of economic decision makers competed for finite resources and control. There was Göring, himself "not an economist," and his grand Four-Year Plan; General Thomas at the OKW; and the Economics Ministry staff, now under a more pliable Walther Funk, who eventually took charge of the Reichsbank. If that were somehow not enough, Hitler personally expanded the role of "plenipotentiaries" in the economy; he made Fritz Todt responsible for munitions, and, after Todt's death in early February 1942, the architect Albert Speer succeeded him as minister of armaments and war production. The positions were run separately from the military command, the Economics Ministry, and even the Four-Year Plan administration, duplicating (or, to be precise, quadruplicating) orders and bureaucratic infighting. Each answered to Hitler directly. Schacht's point about the need for ultimate responsibility in economic decision making in his 1938 letters to the Führer seemed, in retrospect, justified. Collaboration, so sought-after in occupied Europe, was never a feature of the upper echelons of Nazi rule.

Never one to be left behind, Göring created his own plenipotentiaries. Although Paul Pleiger was a far more capable manager than his boss, his commission over the Reich's coal supply led to bottlenecks.[176] Corruption always featured prominently in Göring's enterprises.[177] With plunder and exploitation on the rise, productivity fell. Paradoxically when Hitler needed it most, the formal empire ended up producing less. This was at least partly a result of production bottlenecks and resource shortages, but labor productivity fell in France and other occupied territories as the war dragged on. War weariness, demoralization, and outright resistance increased, as did public perception of the futility of the Nazi war effort.[178] This did not stop Berlin from demanding ever more resources: the Reich requisitioned 19 percent of French national income in 1940, almost 21 percent in 1941, and 36.6 percent in 1943, their last full year in control of French territory.[179] Strained natural resources, organizational chaos, and falling productivity of the post-Barbarossa Nazi formal empire in the West vindicated alternate modes of continental hegemony.

Going back to Poland's General Government, the East was always different. Economic decisions were always secondary to a racial project that became ever more radicalized by the proximity of the war front.[180] Hitler's "India" was not one where Germany merely exercised political and economic control. Rather it was one where "Nazi colonization" demanded the outright extermination of non-Germanic peoples.[181] The early excesses in annexed territories and Frank's General Government eventually developed into the Final Solution, a project viciously—and programmatically—executed as of 1942.[182] Those who welcomed the invading Wehrmacht as liberators from Soviet oppression in 1941 changed their mind swiftly, as soon as the true, murderous colors of German Empire became evident.

Barbarossa led to a period when Franco sought to ally himself closer with Hitler, while still asserting a level of independence that had not existed prior to September 1939. In the first, successful months of German invasion of the Soviet Union, Spain paid its commercial balance in cash—and to Bernhardt.[183] It was the only time there were no delays in the process. Internal documents from Francoist ministers betray the motive for swift payment: Franco and his closest clique believed Hitler would prevail over Stalin.[184] Barbarossa also fit the Francoist ideology far better than the Ribbentrop-Molotov Pact ever did. In keeping with this anti-Communism, the Spanish government sent the División Azul (Blue Division) to the Eastern Front. Around forty thousand Spaniards fought in the Volkhov riverfront and the siege of Leningrad between mid-1941 and late 1943, unwittingly brought into a war of annihilation for Nazi *Lebensraum*.[185] At the time Madrid insisted on new military supplies from Nazi Germany. Once again Franco wanted planes, guns, artillery. At various times and well into 1943, Franco promised these supplies would be used to defend Spain from a potential Allied invasion.[186] The Führer had not forgotten Hendaye. In the midst of its impossible two-front war, furthermore, Germany could not afford the same resources it had once deployed in Spain. And Franco continued to dither on repaying the old war debts.

As the war dragged on, Spain became an important supplier of another key resource that Nazi Germany lacked: labor. Franco sent workers to Nazi Germany, and his government obtained a further reduction of its outstanding debts through "discounts" on these workers' wages.[187] The Francoist leadership therefore benefited directly from this quasi-slave labor, which the Germans insisted on training themselves.[188]

Yet by this time Francoist Spain depended heavily on some strategic Allied supplies. Chief among them was oil, one of those resources that U.S. industry gave Franco on credit during the Civil War. Heavily constrained, particularly after Barbarossa, Nazi Germany was not an alternative source for these supplies. Yet most of Spain's foreign trade was still tilted to Germany and its formal empire. According to 1944 data, 39.2 percent of all Spanish exports went to Germany proper and another 30 percent to German-occupied territories. Although German informal empire was no longer tangible on Iberian soil, trade integration remained: Spain was a key German source of raw materials from ores to foodstuffs, including ammonia, nitrogen, and war manufactures like uniforms and parachutes.

As we have seen, the loss of German hegemony in Spain predated the turning tides of war. Still tied to Germany commercially but essentially freed from the German economic hegemony, Franco's government sought to balance the Axis with the Allies as the war dragged on. At a few instances during the Civil War, Franco attempted to counter

German impositions with renewed British contacts. This was successful only seldom and did not really alter the trade and policy domination by Germany, a key consequence of the Spanish Civil War.[189] Well into World War II, however, rising U.S. influence added to British counterbalancing. This would eventually lead to a confrontation with Franco—and set the stage for the international ostracism of Spain that followed Allied victory.

On November 14, 1942, President Roosevelt sent Franco a cordial public letter explaining the need for U.S. troops and matériel in North Africa to fight Gen. Erwin Rommel's Africakorps. Rommel's invasion of Egypt threatened British dominance of the Middle East and its supply channels.[190] After mentioning U.S.-Spanish "friendship" three times in the first sentence, Roosevelt highlighted the benefits of cooperation: "Spain has nothing to fear from the United Nations."[191] Though he welcomed FDR's letter publicly and privately, Franco did not alter his relations with the Third Reich. Just two days before, in a letter from Foreign Minister Francisco Gómez-Jordana to his ambassador in Berlin, Franco had ordered the ambassador to "seek for Spain (the only nation in the world which openly and sincerely professes her friendship for the Third Reich) war materiel, free of charge, in order to resist the Allies."[192] Franco's militaristic regime still desired cutting-edge weaponry as insurance and, in stark contrast to the past, it wanted it gratis.

It was wolfram exports to the Axis, however, that triggered a crisis symbolic of the dusk of German influence and the dawn of U.S. influence. Starting in mid-1943 the State Department had been pushing for a wolfram embargo that would stop Germany from furnishing this crucial raw material from Spanish mines.[193] With the second highest melting temperature of any element, wolfram was instrumental for the production of rocket engines, at the core of the technological breakthroughs eagerly publicized by Speer's Ministry of Armaments.[194] No "miracle weapon" would save the doomed Nazi war effort, but the United States still struggled to limit Germany's access to the key resource. Unsurprisingly Spanish foreign minister Gómez-Jordana resisted: "An embargo of wolfram would mean a break with Germany because Germany would not tolerate it."[195]

In spite of British hesitation, Carlton J. H. Hayes, the U.S. ambassador to Spain, advocated for economic sanctions to punish Franco's economic ties to the Axis: "So long as our economic supplies to Spain particularly of petroleum are furnished as nearly automatically as at present I fear he [Franco] will continue to believe he can maintain his present attitude [of steering the middle course] without penalty from us." In words that echoed those uttered by Germans a few years earlier the ambassador concluded, "By far our strongest weapon is the economic weapon."[196] Oil supplies to Franco were eventually cut for long enough to get the dictator's approval for a wolfram export cap. It was thanks to British mediation that an agreement was reached.[197]

German resource isolation intensified as its armies began to lose ground. When the Allies advanced, Franco too became more isolated. In 1945 Roosevelt wrote a telegram to Hayes's replacement in Madrid anticipating the end of European hostilities. FDR, who had come to regret his lack of support for the Spanish Republic, was not as welcoming as he had been in 1942: "Having been helped to power by Fascist Italy and Nazi Germany, and having patterned itself along totalitarian lines the present regime of Spain is naturally the subject of distrust. . . . Most certainly we do not forget Spain's official position with and assistance to our Axis enemies at the time when the fortunes of war were less favorable to us." Roosevelt's was, if anything, an understatement. "There are many things which we could do and normally would be glad to do in economic and other fields to demonstrate that friendship [with the Spanish people]. The initiation of such measures is out of the question at this time, however, when American sentiment is so profoundly opposed to the present regime."[198]

The San Francisco Conference echoed this sentiment when a Mexican-sponsored resolution excluding Spain from the United Nations was passed by acclamation.[199] The same applied in Potsdam, where Churchill and Stalin supported Roosevelt's desire to isolate Franco.[200] For his part, Don Juan de Borbón, the exiled Bourbon heir to the Spanish throne, had issued the Lausanne Manifesto on March 19, 1945, denouncing fascism and criticizing Franco's close ties with Nazi Germany and Fascist Italy.[201] The dictator's rule in the last months of World War II became markedly antimonarchist because of an emerging rift with those who favored another Bourbon restoration.[202]

While Franco's repression machine quelled domestic dissent, his ambassador in Washington acted defensively. Juan Cárdenas, none other than the duplicitous ambassador in Blum's France at the beginning of the Civil War, cited Roosevelt's 1942 letter to Franco amid a much-massaged treatment of Nazi relations in a letter to the secretary of state. His closing, however, betrayed reactionary tendencies: "Spain, in short, will unfalteringly maintain its rights and is ready to isolate itself from those who may have such an impaired conception of international relations among peoples."[203] Thereafter, the regime manipulated statistics to underplay how much it had contributed to the German war effort, in particular with respect to wolfram exports; it also made as few references as possible to effectively stolen remittances of Spanish workers laboring in Nazi Germany.[204]

Nonetheless international ostracism did materialize. In February 1946 the French Cabinet unilaterally closed its border and cut off all trade with Spain in reaction to the summary execution of anti-Franco dissidents.[205] The regime had tried to show a better face, but Franco remained Franco. Simultaneously the French administration pressured its British and U.S. allies to pursue a similar blockade. Before he penned his "Long Telegram," the U.S. chargé d'affaires in Moscow George Kennan wrote about Soviet designs in Spain, "Politically as well as strategically Russians recognize in Spain a key territory in which it is highly important for them to win influence."[206] If Allied isolation led to a new civil war, as Hitler had once predicted, then a Communist Spain could well emerge victorious. After all, since late 1945 Communist-dominated *maquis* groups had renewed armed struggle against Franco's regime.[207]

In the Tripartite Declaration of March 4, 1946, the Allies declared, "As long as General Franco continues to rule Spain, the Spanish people cannot anticipate full and cordial association with those nations of the world which have, by common effort, brought defeat to German Nazism and Italian Fascism, which aided the present Spanish regime in its rise to power and after which the regime was patterned."[208] Opposition to Franco became a central tenet of U.S. policy until the Eisenhower administration, when anti-Communism trumped concerns about anachronistic fascism and led to the establishment of military bases on Iberian soil in 1953.[209] Only then did the Francoist regime begin to reverse a disastrous economic policy modeled after Nazi *Autarkie*.

The decline and fall of Germany's informal empire in Spain began when Hitler launched his bid for *Lebensraum,* unleashing world war in the process. The birth of Nazi formal empire put an end to the uneven relationships that had given Germany economic hegemony over the nascent Francoist regime, a shadow empire forged through the decisive German intervention in the Spanish Civil War. After the failed summit in Hendaye, the same Spanish state that had created legal exceptions to accommodate German demands created impediments for resource extraction. That is not to say that Germany did not obtain some benefit from its relationship with Spain, for it continued to import the raw materials it needed to keep up the war effort. Yet the terms of engagement were radically different and far less advantageous to Germany: hegemony was gone. Eventually British and U.S. involvement further curtailed Spain's economic ties to Nazi Germany, even though Francoist ideology clung to pseudo-fascism. This led directly to Franco's international ostracism, one that would be maintained until at the very least 1953.

By September 1, 1939, the tables had turned for good. Crafting the exploitative, genocidal, and ultimately ephemeral empire for which we remember the Nazis required burying the informal one on Iberian soil.

conclusion

INTEGRATED EUROPE

He was also told of [Roman] battles . . . and what [the Romans]
did in Spain to get possession of the silver and gold mines there.
By planning and persistence they subjugated the whole region,
although it was very remote from their own.

—1 Maccabees 8: 1–3

O nly Europe's political consolidation can bring about an intensifica-
tion of the whole economic life in the European sphere and eliminate the disturbances and tensions that so far have prevented the
fruitful co-operation," wrote Europe's most powerful economic official. In a pamphlet ominously titled *The Economic Future of Europe,* he
described a bright tomorrow: "The European economies can be developed to a much higher degree and the[ir] yield increased materially
by co-operation that is based on logic." The goal was straightforward:
"It will be necessary to bring about a consolidation of the common
economic bond between the peoples of Europe. This will be made possible by closer co-operation in all spheres of economic policy." He then
explained the rationale for such ever closer integration: "Economic
solidarity in European countries should make it possible to uphold
European economic interests more effectively against other corresponding groups in the world economy."[1]

Such ideas are mainstream today, when an increasingly postnational
European Union guarantees a common market for twenty-eight nations from Latvia to Portugal and an evolving monetary union of eigh-

teen states managed by Europe's most federal institution, the European Central Bank. But it was hardly so in the summer of 1940, when *The Economic Future of Europe* was penned by Walther Funk, Hjalmar Schacht's successor at the Reichsbank and the Ministry of Economics. A lethargic journalist who had once edited the *Berliner Börsenzeitung,* a leading German financial newspaper, Funk had been introduced to Hitler by Schacht before the Nazi seizure of power.[2] In words that echoed his predecessor's nationalistic economic framework, Funk continued, "European countries today recognize their natural trade partner. . . . Germany's potential economic power is so great that she has, besides the ability to produce her own war requirements, sufficient capacity to produce export surplice [*sic*]."[3] Less than a month after the armistice with a humiliated France, on July 20, 1940, the minister announced an economic New Order to reconstruct war-torn Europe.

What kind of integrated Europe did the Nazis dream of? At a press conference in Berlin following the armistice with France, Funk predicted that Schacht's bilateral trade treaties would eventually give way to multilateral deals with centralized clearing in Berlin. Schacht's Depression-era goal of decoupling Germany from Britain and the United States would thus be achieved. In the process Germany would become the undisputed core of Europe. Its economic leadership would not be contested. "By concluding long-term trade agreements with European countries," Funk explained, "it is intended that the European economic systems shall adapt themselves to the German market by a system of production planned far into the future."[4] Centrally planned rationalization and specialization would be directed—and dictated—from Berlin.

The New Order would ensure that: "[Countries] will be able to secure for themselves a safe and steady market for many years ahead."[5] The void left by the apparent failure of classical liberalism after the breakdown of globalization would be filled by German economic theory.[6] Some building blocks existed already: political alignment, economic dependence, and foreign policy subservience were rewarded in Denmark and the Netherlands, where elites profited from German industrial orders with comparatively little oversight.[7] The German logic implied that Britain and the United States, with their imperial preference and gold hoarding, respectively, could not offer a compelling alternative. While Britain struggled, Funk reasoned, the Nazi state was "able to keep her house, and be it remembered it is a much enlarged house, in order." A *Pax Germanica* would "guarantee Greater Germany maximum economic security and the German people maximum consumption in commodities."[8] Coming from a man who had thrived in Goebbels's Ministry of Propaganda, Funk's economic New Order constituted a calculated public relations offensive: under German rule reconstruction would yield European union.

Hitler was more cautious. Never particularly interested in economics, he preferred to keep his long-term plans vague.[9] He cared little for financial architecture, preferring talk of actual architecture instead: colossal squares, gargantuan train stations, and majestic monuments occupied his mind.[10] Perhaps only in that respect did the Führer share Funk's vision of a German-led Europe standing up to the vastness of the United States, a central preoccupation of his since the days of his *Second Book*.[11] A few months earlier, on April 5, an unusually frank Goebbels had told the media, "If anyone asks how you conceive of the new Europe, we have to reply that we don't know. Of course we have some ideas about it. But if we were going to put them into words it would immediately create more enemies for us."[12]

On November 19, 1940, a dossier of (incomplete) press clippings detailing Funk's evolution of Schachtian economics landed on John Maynard Keynes's desk at the British Treasury.[13] Attached to it was a note from Harold Nicolson at the Information Ministry asking Keynes to counter Funk. "The dossier which you sent along with your letter seems to suggest we should do well to pose as champions of the pre-war economic status quo," began Keynes's reply a day later, "and outbid Funk by offering good old 1920–21 or 1930–33, i.e. gold standard or international exchange *laissez-faire* aggravated by heavy tariffs, unemployment, etc." That would not be enough. "Is this particularly attractive propaganda?" Keynes asked rhetorically. "If you think it is, [then] I am certainly not the man to put it across. . . . Obviously I am not the man to preach the beauties and merits of the pre-war gold standard."[14] It was his "barbarous relic," after all.[15]

Schacht and Keynes had known each other since at least 1922, when the British economist had planned the *Manchester Guardian*'s Reconstruction Supplements series.[16] Their contributors list includes some of the finest economic thinkers of Europe and the United States: Fisher, Pigou, Leffingwell, Lamont, Einaudi, Hilferding, Rathenau, and Schacht.[17]

When Schacht took the reins of the Reichsbank, Keynes was supportive of his stabilization efforts, most crucially the Dawes Plan.[18] The admiration seems to have become mutual in the late 1920s, when, lest we forget, Keynes also drifted toward economic nationalism. Following the failure of the World Economic Conference in 1933, Keynes delivered the Finlay Lecture at University College Dublin, titled "National Self-Sufficiency."[19] According to Keynes's leading biographer, it "seemed to swing the full circle from Adam Smith to Friedrich List, the German founder of economic nationalism; or, for the contemporary-minded, to Dr. Schacht, Nazi Germany's economic overlord."[20]

It is hence less surprising that Keynes was not too critical of Funk's Schachtian framework. "In my opinion about three-quarters of the passages quoted from the German broadcasts [about the plan] would be quite excellent if the name of Great Britain were substituted for Germany. . . . If Funk's plan is taken at its face value, it is excellent and just what we ourselves ought to be thinking of doing." Worthy advice followed nonetheless: "If [the plan] is to be attacked, the way to do it would be to cast doubt and suspicion on its *bona fides*. The point is . . . not what Funk purports to do is objectionable, but what he will actually do."[21] It was a characteristically astute observation. At a time when the Luftwaffe brought the war to London, Keynes had admittedly not devoted too much time to the postwar economic order. "No one I have yet seen has the foggiest idea of what [postwar economics] ought to be," he admitted to Nicolson.[22] Yet Funk's plan forced Keynes to start pondering it seriously, four years before the Bretton Woods conference recast the global financial architecture for the second half of the century.[23]

As it turns out, Keynes did have something to send Nicolson: a piece of economic propaganda he had produced earlier that year criticizing Nazi economic management. Its title, *¿Qué quiere decir el area?*, betrayed its origin: Keynes's pamphlet was requested, produced, and distributed by the British Embassy in Franco's Spain.[24] The purpose of the pamphlet—perhaps his first blueprint for the postwar order—was to argue that trading within Britain's "sterling area" benefited Spain far more than remaining within Germany's economic system. His key point was that, as early as 1940, Britain and its empire offered more to Franco's Spain than Nazi Germany did. It was an argument Schacht would have had to agree with; Germany still suffered from its recurring capital shortage, and all the conquests in the previous years had failed to overcome a severe lack of strategic raw materials: oil, coal, building stone, minerals from iron ore to wolfram, and of course food.

Franco's Spain did not have much of a choice before the advent of world war; the decisive German intervention in the Spanish Civil War created economic dislocations that the Germans wittingly and ruthlessly exploited to create informal control of the nascent Francoist regime. After 1939, however, Franco was freer to follow Keynes's advice: the advent of world war radically altered the balance of power, burying Hitler's Spanish shadow empire.

Nazi Germany's empire had many faces. In the East a racialist project driven and directed by the Nazi Party led to a barbaric exercise in extermination and the crassest forms of economic exploitation. In the West the haphazard nature of Nazi rule meant that different countries received different treatment. Much was left to the local personalities. After the failure of Operation Barbarossa in 1942, however, outright exploitation and labor conscription increased throughout Hitler's formal empire.[25] So too did terror and genocide. Unable to seduce and having reached the limits of coercion, the Nazi empire was, all in all, a catastrophic failure.[26] Yet its failure was not a foregone conclusion when the Nazis came to power in 1933. Brutal exploitation was certainly not the preferred mode of projecting international power during the Nazis' first foreign policy adventure.

As Gallagher and Robinson once observed, "It would clearly be unreal to define [British] imperial history exclusively as the history of those colonies coloured red on the map."[27] No map ever included Spain as part of Hitler's empire. Nor did any map of the British Empire include Brazil or Argentina in the late nineteenth century. The purpose of these pages has been to argue that the German intervention in the Spanish Civil War constituted a project of informal imperialism inspired by Hjalmar Schacht, the lead economic architect of the Nazi recovery. Schacht's was an alternative vision of German hegemony in Europe, one that favored *Weltpolitik* over *Lebensraum*.

The opportunity for Germany was born out of Iberian decline. Spain's decades-long duel with itself led to a nasty, brutish, protracted civil war. The Nationalist rebellion that ignited it was not only uncoordinated but also largely unsuccessful; the generals sparked the social revolution they had sought to prevent. Broke and divided, their rebellion seemed doomed. In order to prevail against Spain's legitimate government, they needed the tools of modern warfare the country had not been able to afford for decades. The diplomatic decisions of July 25, 1936 made fascist intervention the primary determinant of the war's outcome. In what has rightly been called "a world war in miniature," it was fascist intervention that allowed for Nationalist victory.[28]

The dictators, however, did not embark on their Spanish adventures for ideological or strategic considerations alone. Mussolini followed his traditional Mediterranean policy. Antibolshevism and balance of power—along with Wagnerian bravado—informed Hitler's decision to overrule a more careful and conservative Auswärtiges Amt. In a matter of weeks Reich diplomats, economic policymakers, and the Nazi Party began a long quest to profit from the economic and political dislocations created by the Civil War. For all its poverty, Spain remained resource rich—and a resource-starved Third Reich seized its chance.

On Iberian soil it fell to Nazi Party functionaries to craft informal empire. Most of them in fact answered not to Schacht but to Göring, who managed to outmaneuver Schacht politically in late 1937.[29] Yet the project was possible and profitable not because of Göring but because of Germany's "economic dictator" and the economic system he was building. Schacht was the main architect of a Nazi economic system. His policy framework—monetary stimulus, concealed but extensive rearmament, economic decoupling from Britain and the United States, trade diversion toward less developed countries where Germany could leverage its force, veiled export promotion, controversial debt management, exchange and trade controls, and unprecedented state oversight of industry—delivered the weapons and dictated the priorities of German officials operating in Spain.

In less than three years Germany eclipsed two centuries of Anglo-French dominance in Spain, suggesting that Spain was a more successful testing ground for informal empire than better-known targets of German influence in the Balkans, central Europe, and even Latin America. Controlled by Bernhardt on the Nazi's behalf, HISMA became a Reich-sponsored vehicle for a form of hegemony; this, as it turns out, was a type of vehicle for which Schacht had advocated. The goal was economic symbiosis, whereby Germany exchanged the product at the core of its economic recovery (armaments) for control and, eventually, ownership of Spanish raw materials.

The "economic dictator" of Nazi Germany was powerful indeed; but his vision was always contested. While he argued for clearing agreements as the basis of long-term German economic hegemony, effectively securing countries' roles within Germany's trading sphere, Göring and other Nazis favored sustaining a domestic boom that by 1937 was becoming too dependent on armaments. More than a turf war between two hubristic men, this was a battle between two conceptions of German power. The first was *Weltpolitik,* focused on international markets and informal control; in the post-Wilhelmine period, Schacht had been one of its key supporters. The second, *Lebensraum,* favored a formal empire, located in the East and involving a type of colonial resettlement that would require at the very least a massive relocation of local populations and at the most unprecedented genocide. *Lebensraum* promised "essential living space," a concept intertwined with racialist interwar pseudo-science. The war of annihilation in turn necessitated unprecedented levels of economic self-sufficiency—autarky—at least for the "transformative conflagration," another glorified concept in *völkish* ideology generally bereft of traditional economic considerations.

From his education as a disciple of List's school of the "national economy" to his experience in Kaiserreich-occupied Belgium; from his first term at the Reichsbank to his experience at 1920s international conferences, Schacht embodied the *Weltpolitik* tradition. Like Keynes, Schacht was convinced that the shipwreck of globalization was not temporary. Germany's salvation therefore lay in the pursuit of its own, strategic self-interest. Unilateralist and aggressive, Schachtian economics was not the only nationalist economics in Europe—but it was arguably the most successful. For Schacht, decoupling from Britain and the United States would allow an assertive Germany to craft its own, alternative economic and political hegemony over Europe. This conception of power did not require formal control; as he consistently argued on the perennial question of colonies, sovereignty mattered less than market access and natural resources.

With his unprecedented dual mandate over economic and monetary policy, Schacht was at the heart of German economic policymaking between 1933 and 1937. He imposed comprehensive control over the German economy and crafted a network of bilateral trade deals that projected power beyond Germany's borders. This "modern equivalent of barter" was particularly useful for a nation devoid of foreign exchange reserves and armies but equipped with a highly productive industrial sector. Lacking colonies, Germany would obtain inputs in exchange for its industrial produce. Through subsidies Schacht pushed overvalued German goods, and through clearing he dispensed with the lubricants of global trade—gold and hard currency—that his Reichsbank lacked.

Although it has been consistently ignored in the discussions of Nazi Germany's political economy, Spain was unlike the other targets of Schachtian trade policy. In contrast to Latin America or the Balkans, Franco's Nationalists needed precisely the products Hitler's Sparta was so keen on producing. It exported its theoretically unproductive military output in exchange for strategic raw materials—including iron ore, pyrites, wolfram, and foodstuffs—that fed back into the German economy. Far from doing Spain a fascist favor, Germany pressed first for economic benefits and eventually direct ownership. While Britain, France, and the United States remained aloof, HISMA-ROWAK became a state-sponsored (if corrupt) vehicle for investment in Spain and German hegemony. This approach differed materially from—and arguably undermined—Fascist Italy's own intervention.

During the Civil War the economic symbiosis between Spain and Germany worked, to the detriment of not only Spain's more traditional trading partners, but also Mussolini's Italy, Franco's other sponsor. Raw material and foreign exchange transfers led to long-term investments on Spanish soil, as the German authorities sought to deepen trade reorientation by acquiring assets in Spain. Schacht's part-time foreign policy interventions underscored what the Reich wanted to get out of a dependent Spain. This was anything but a relationship of equals. As the British representatives of Rio Tinto kept reminding the Foreign Office, resource-extraction in Spain helped Nazi Germany become better prepared for war. Perhaps more crucial was the effort to cement Germany's central role in the Nationalist economy far beyond the end of the civil war.

Yet the onset of World War II wrecked Germany's shadow empire in Spain, allowing Franco a freedom of action that he had lacked before. Although scholars like Leitz and García Pérez have been quick to call the German project in Spain a "failure" when looking at the 1936–1945 period as a whole, a different conclusion may be reached by narrowing the focus. All Nazi projects were failures by 1945. But between 1936 and 1939 Germany reversed more than two centuries of

Anglo-French economic hegemony. At the end of its Civil War, the Francoist regime was friendly, pliable, and utterly dependent on Nazi diktats. The contrast with Fascist Italy could not be starker. A Germany constrained in resources had become Spain's most important trading partner. It would remain so well into the war. And without a wider war, it is highly likely that such dependence would have continued beyond when it did.

This leads us to the key question: Why was Schacht's framework abandoned? Why was informal empire, as crafted in Spain as in the Balkans, not enough? The answer is partly political, partly ideological. Paradoxically, around the time his foreign trade model was succeeding in Spain, Schacht's star waned in Berlin. The Spanish project can thus be placed within an internal radicalization that saw other, more traditionally conservative German leaders—men like von Neurath, Goerdeler, even von Blomberg—ousted from the Reich's leadership. Men with a stronger commitment to Nazi ideology came to the fore.[30] In contrast to Schacht, ideologues like Himmler and Darré believed the extension of informal control over other territories would not solve Germany's problems permanently.[31] In Bernd Wenger's formulation, however, their gamble on war "involved risks so great that they defy rationalization in terms of pragmatic self-interest."[32] The "war of the world" had a fundamentally different character from anything Schacht had contemplated. This was the essence of Hitler's leadership. Rather than economic preeminence in the *Weltpolitik* tradition that prevailed under Schachtian management until 1937, it was the goal of racially recast *Lebensraum* that dominated thereafter.

After 1939 Schacht was politically disowned. Though he remained minister without portfolio until well into the war, he was neither consulted on nor informed of Hitler's decisions.[33] A leading historian has suggested he attempted to defect to the United States in 1939.[34] Allied troops in 1945 found him at Dachau, where he had been sent after Claus von Stauffenberg's attempt to assassinate Hitler in July 1944. It was at Nuremberg that Schacht would see his bitter rival once again. During the trials, Allied soldiers showed the banker to a prison cell with two bathtubs. One was reserved for him, while in the other lay an oversized, naked Göring busily washing himself. "Sic transit gloria mundi!" Schacht reflected. [35]

★   ★   ★

On April 22, 1942, some weeks before the dinner party at which he boasted about his decisive role in the Spanish Civil War, Hitler devoted one of his diatribes to financiers. Reminiscing about disagreements with Schacht, he wondered, "Seeing that the whole gang of financiers is a bunch of crooks, what possible point was there in being scrupulously honest with them?" Schacht had fatally underestimated the man through whom he aspired to remake Germany. "The method [of not disclosing one's intentions] was also to the advantage of the financial experts themselves;" the Führer continued, "for if things should go wrong, they would then be in the position to justify themselves in the public eye by claiming they had not been told the truth."[36] This was precisely Schacht's defense at Nuremberg, where he claimed, as in his questionable autobiography, that Hitler "would have found other methods and other assistance; [since] he was not a man to give up."[37] Calling Schacht "the façade of starched respectability," U.S. prosecutor Robert Jackson insisted that the banker was "part of a movement that he knew was wrong, but was in it just because he saw it was winning."[38] It was a fair characterization of a hubristic man driven by an insatiable thirst for power. Yet neither naked opportunism nor enabling Hitler's rearmament was considered worthy of capital punishment. Perhaps it was not that Schacht was innocent, only that, as he allegedly told a visitor, for the trials to seem legitimate, someone had to walk out alive.[39] Thereafter Schacht would be found advising emerging market governments, running his own banking business, and somehow finding the time to stoke fears of inflation by criticizing the "easy money" policies of the Reichsbank's successor, the *Bundesbank,* in the 1960s.[40]

Schacht's Faustian pact with Hitler yielded not only massive rearmament but also an informal projection of German economic power that promised more enduring results than the ultimately self-defeating, suicidal quest for *Lebensraum.* In light of the evidence that German informal empire in Francoist Spain was in many respects viable, a different version of an "integrated" Europe becomes all too easy to imagine, buried though it has been for seven decades.

APPENDIX
Economic Data

Figure A.1 Weimar Hyperinflation and "Schachtian" Stabilization: German Marks vs. U.S. Dollar, 1922–1926
Source: Global Financial Data.

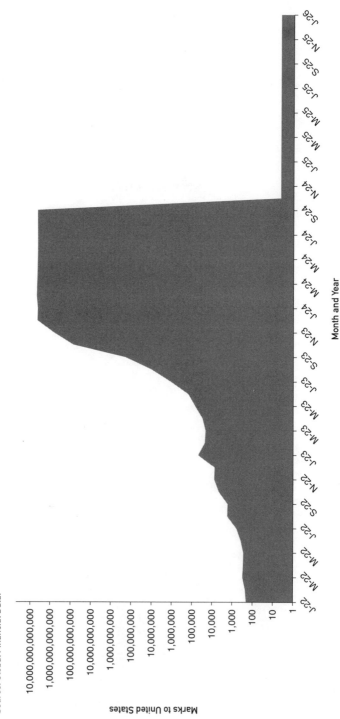

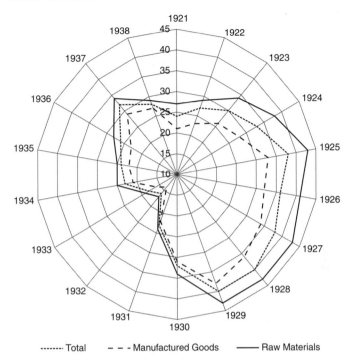

Figure A.2 The Shipwreck of Globalization: World Exports by Year,
1921–1938 (1953 = 100)
Source: United Nations.

········ Total   – – – Manufactured Goods   —— Raw Materials

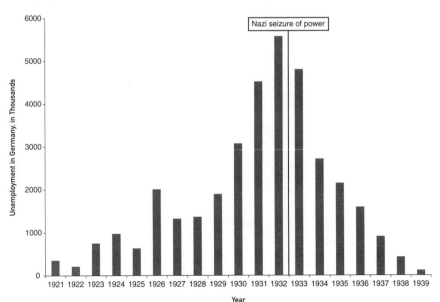

Figure A.3 The Jobs Crisis and the Seizure of Power: German Unemployment,
in Thousands, 1921–1939
Source: Statistisches Jahrbuch.

Figure A.4 The Constant Pressure: Reichsbank Foreign Currency Reserves,
1924–1940
Source: Statistisches Jahrbuch.

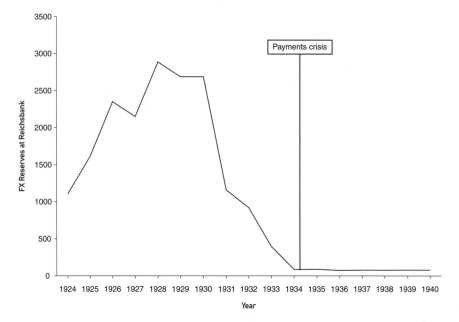

Figure A.5 German Imperial Symbiosis I: Destination of Spanish Exports, 1935–1938
Source: Banco Exterior España.

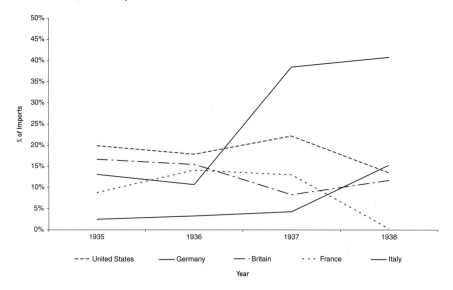

Figure A.6 German Imperial Symbiosis II: Source of Spanish Imports, 1935–1938
Source: Banco Exterior España.

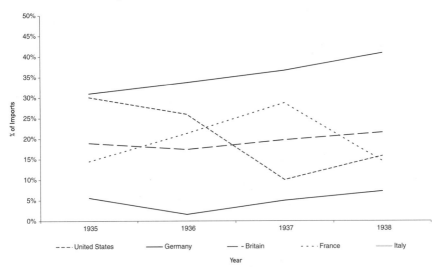

Figure A.7 Empire for Less: Cumulative German and Italian Interventions Costs in Spain, in Million Pesetas
Source: Banco Exterior España.

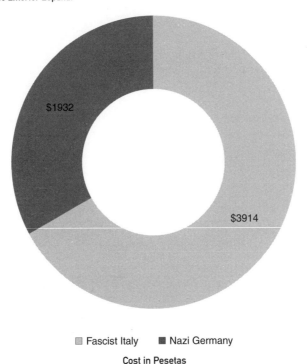

NOTES

Unless otherwise noted, all translations are my own.

INTRODUCTION

1 "España es diferente." Manuel Fraga Iribarne, a founder of the Partido Popular and Franco's long-standing minister of tourism and information, is credited for the slogan.

2 Pierpaolo Barbieri, "From UN Outcast to U.S. Partner: Steering Francoist Spain toward the Economic Miracle," *Hemispheres: The Tufts Journal of International Affairs*, no. 30 (2009): 89–128.

3 The Spanish language has around 400 million native speakers, second only to Mandarin and ahead of English. Winston Manrique Sabogal, "Lo que hay que saber del español," *El País*, November 27, 2010.

4 Arturo Pérez Reverte has called the Civil War a "conflict that is narratively exhausted." "Clarín," *Revista Ñ*, November 23, 2012.

5 Among others, Lorca was close to José Antonio Primo de Rivera, founder of the fascistic Falange. See Ian Gibson, *The Death of Lorca* (Chicago, 1973).

6 "Garzón investigará la represión franquista y abrirá la fosa de Lorca," *El País*, October 16, 2008.

7 Nieves Galindo, in Silvia Pisani, "Investiga el juez Garzón la muerte de García Lorca," *La Nación* (Buenos Aires, Argentina), October 17, 2008.

8 Reed Brody, "The Dismal Assault on Baltasar Garzón," *Guardian*, April 13, 2010.

9 The European extradition battle energized Chilean magistrates. Eventually the Chilean Supreme Court revoked Pinochet's immunity and international inquiries further undermined his legacy by revealing hidden bank accounts in the United States and Hong Kong. These accounts invited questions—pertinent in many a Latin American government—about private corruption in a regime obsessed with "public virtue."

10 He requested the death certificates of thirty-five high-ranking Francoist officials. "El juez Garzón abrirá 19 fozas," *ABC*, October 16, 2008.

11 Jaime Sartorius, "La Ley de Amnistía no ampara el Franquismo," *El País*, March 15, 2001.

12 Preston's account of the first years of Juan Carlos's rule is unrivaled: Paul Preston, *Juan Carlos: A People's King* (London, 2004).

13 Anna Cuenca, "Justicia española sentencia el fin de la carrera del juez Baltasar Garzón," *AFP*, February 9, 2012.

14　Human Rights Watch, "El proceso contra Garzón supone una amenaza a los derechos humanos," January 13, 2012.

15　The Partido Popular was founded by the Francoist minister of "España es diferente" fame. "Garzón pide al Constitucional que anule la decisión sobre su condena," *El País,* July 19, 2013.

16　Thomas Catan, "Generalísimo Francisco Franco Is Still Dead—And His Statues Are Next," *Wall Street Journal,* March 2, 2009.

17　Ley de la Memoria Histórica. "Ley 52/2007, de 26 de diciembre, por la que se reconocen y amplían derechos y se establecen medidas en favor de quienes padecieron persecucióno violencia durante la guerra civil y la dictadura," *Boletín Oficial Español,* no. 310, l.22296, 2007.

18　Diana Rodríguez, "El Gobierno retira la estatua de Franco en Nuevos Ministerios," *El País,* March 17, 2005.

19　Sabrina Vidal, "'Me expreso mejor en la lengua que me prohíben'—Musica," *Diario de Mallorca,* June 6, 2006.

20　"Dedicado a Antonio Machado, Poeta."

21　Separated from his brother, the poet had remained active in war-torn Spain; first in Valencia, then in Barcelona, he wrote some of his best verses while escaping the advance of Franco's Nationalists.

22　Antonio Machado, *Soledades* (Exeter, U.K., 2006).

23　For a translation, see Miguel Hernández, *The Selected Poems of Miguel Hernández,* translated by Ted Genoways (Chicago, 2001), 350.

24　"Papá Cuéntame Otra Vez." Though Serrano is the performer, the song itself was written by his brother.

25　"Sous les pavés, la plage."

26　Much great historical work—by Angel Viñas, Ronald Radosh, Stanley Payne, and Paul Preston—on the plight of the Republic has been published in the past two decades. In particular see Viñas's now classic studies, including *Franco, Hitler y el Estallido de la Guerra Civil: Antecedentes y Consecuencias* (Madrid, 2001). See also his excellent Republican trilogy: *La Soledad de la República* (Barcelona, 2006), *El Escudo de la República* (Barcelona, 2007), and *El Honor de la República* (Barcelona, 2009).

27　Building on the traditional work of Overy, Milward, and Barkai, among others, Adam Tooze and others have significantly updated our understanding of Nazi economic policy in the past decade. Adam Tooze, *The Wages of Destruction: The Making and Breaking of the Nazi Economy* (London, 2006). See also Avraham Barkai, *Das Wirtschaftssystem Des Nationalsozialismus: Ideologie, Theorie, Politik, 1933–1945* (Frankfurt, 1988) and Alan Milward, *War, Economy, and Society, 1939–1945* (Berkeley, 1977).

28　Mark Mazower, *Hitler's Empire: How the Nazis Ruled Europe* (New York, 2008); Alan Milward, *The New Order and the French Economy* (Oxford, 1970) and *The Fascist Economy in Norway* (Oxford, 1972).

29　For a different perspective, see Christian Leitz, *Economic Relations between Nazi Germany and Franco's Spain: 1936–1945* (New York, 1996). For a Spanish doctoral dissertation with enlightening documentary evidence building on Viñas's original research, see Rafael García Pérez, *Franquismo y Tercer Reich* (Madrid, 1994).

30　Henry A. Kissinger, "The White Revolutionary: Reflections on Bismarck," *Daedalus* 97, no. 3 (1968): 888–924.

31　This perspective generally contradicts the main (German) readings of Nazi intervention, which until only a few years ago remained mired in Cold War rhetoric.

From the West, see Manfred Merkes, *Die Deutsche Politik Gegenüber Dem Spanischen Bürgerkrieg, 1936–1939* (Bonn, 1961); from the East, Marion Einhorn, *Die Ökonomischen Hintergründe Der Faschistischen Deutschen Intervention in Spanien 1936–1939* (Berlin, 1962). See also two key works updating the previous work and focusing on the key architect of German exploitation on Spanish soil: Hans-Henning Abendroth, *Hitler in Der Spanischen Arena: Die Deutsch-Spanischen Beziehungen Im Spannungsfeld Der Europäischen Interessenpolitik Vom Ausbruch Des Bürgerkrieges Bis Zum Ausbruch Des Weltkrieges 1936–1939* (Nuremberg, 1970) and *Mittelsmann Zwischen Franco und Hitler: Johannes Bernhardt Erinnert 1936* (Marktheidenfeld, 1978).

32 For a central proponent of this argument, see Robert H. Whealey, *Hitler and Spain: The Nazi Role in the Spanish Civil War, 1936–1939* (Lexington, Ky., 1989).

33 This is a perspective largely ignored in the latest academic biography of Schacht as well as Tooze's economic history of Nazism. For the biographical perspective, see Christopher Kopper, *Hjalmar Schacht: Aufstieg und Fall Von Hitlers Mächtigstem Bankier* (Munich, 2006). There are also many gaps in Schacht's famous autobiography: Hjalmar Horace Greeley Schacht, *76 Jahre Meines Lebens* (Munich, 1953). See also Heinz Pentzlin, *Hjalmar Schacht: Leben U. Wirken E. Umstrittenen Persönlichkeit* (Berlin, 1980); John Weitz, *Hitler's Banker* (Boston, 1997)

34 This fits a framework outlined by Ian Kershaw, *Hitler: 1936–1945: Nemesis* (London, 2000).

35 On Nazism as religion, see Michael Burleigh, *The Third Reich: A New History* (New York, 2000).

36 Ismael Saz, *Mussolini Contra La II República: Hostilidad, Conspiraciones, Intervención (1931–1936)* (Valencia, 1986).

37 Mario Luciolli, *Mussolini e l'Europa: La Politica Estera Fascista* (Florence, 2009); Fulvio D'Amoja, *La Politica Estera Dell'impero: Storia Della Politica Estera Fascista Dalla Conquista dell'Etiopia all'Anschluss* (Padova, 1967).

38 Angel Viñas, "La connivencia Fascista con la sublevación militar otros éxitos de la trama civil," in *Los Mitos Del 18 De Julio,* edited by Francisco Sánchez Perez (Barcelona, 2013), especially 79–182.

39 Whealey synthesizes this point in the conclusion of *Hitler and Spain.*

40 Coverdale's classic history of Italian intervention does not focus nearly enough on the strategic implications: John Coverdale, *Italian Intervention in the Spanish Civil War* (Princeton, 1975). The best source on this issue is a concise Italian account, largely ignored by the historiography: Vincenzo Giura, *Tra politica ed economia* (Napoli, 1993), especially 90–94.

41 Galeazzo Ciano, *Diary 1937–1943* (New York, 2002), entry of March 14, 1939, 200. For a note on the source, see Chapter 3, n1.

42 John Gallagher and Ronald Robinson, "The Imperialism of Free Trade," *Economic History Review, II,* 6, no. 1 (1953).

43 See for instance Harold James, *Making the European Monetary Union* (Cambridge, Mass., 2012).

44 See Michael Burleigh, *The Third Reich*; Götz Aly, *Hitler's Beneficiaries* (New York, 2007). See also Ian Kershaw, *The Nazi Dictatorship* (London, 1993), especially 40–47; Adam Tooze, *Economics, Ideology and Cohesion in the Third Reich: A Critique of Goetz Aly's "Hitlers Volksstaat,"* translation of a *Dapim Lecheker HaShoah* essay, September 2005, courtesy of the author.

45 Mazower, *Hitler's Empire,* especially 2–15.

46 Milward, *War, Economy, and Society,* 14; Tooze, *Wages,* especially 532–33. The logical conclusion of this idea, basically that the German economy needed war in

1939, can be found in Timothy Mason, "Innere Krise und Angriffskrieg 1938/1939," in *Wirtschaft und Rüstung am Vorabend des zweiten Weltkrieges,* edited by Hans Volkmann (Düsseldorf, 1975).

47 For that view, see Rafael García Pérez, *Franquismo y Tercer Reich,* 71–74; Christian Leitz, *Economic Relations,* especially chapter 5.

48 Ramón Pérez-Maura, introduction to *La Guerra Civil en sus documentos* (Madrid, 2004), 394.

1. TWO SPAINS

1 Atocha was also the location of the 2004 terrorist bombings in Madrid, called "11-M" in reference to the date.

2 "Este museo no es el más extenso, pero sí el más intenso." The alliteration works far better in Spanish.

3 Agustín Benito Oterino, "La Luz En La Quinta Del Sordo: Estudio De Las Formas y Cotidianidad," Universidad Complutense de Madrid, 2004.

4 There is great controversy regarding the painting's name. Like the rest of the period's paintings, they were not formally titled by Goya (or their name was never found). Some have titled it "The Duel," while some Spanish sources from the nineteenth century call it "The Galicians."

5 Miguel de Unamuno, "Hispanidad," in *Síntesis,* 6: 305–10 (Buenos Aires, 1927). Machado has several couplets fitting the theme of "two Spains" in his eclectic *Proverbios y Cantares:* "There is a Spaniard that wants to live / and begin does he, / between a Spain that dies / and another one that yawns." Antonio Machado, *Proverbios y Cantares,* in *Poesias completas de Antonio Machado* (Madrid, 2006), nos. 52, 8.

6 There is debate as to where the famous statement originated, yet it was definitely used at the time in reference to Spain. To commemorate the wedding of Philip's daughter to the Duke of Savoy, the Italian poet Giovanni Battista Guarini wrote, "Altera figlia / Di qel Monarca, a cui / Nö anco, quando annotta, il Sol tramonta" (Proud daughter / of that monarch to whom / when it grows dark [elsewhere] the sun never sets). Later Francis Bacon referenced it: "Both the East and the West Indies being met in the crown of Spain, it is come to pass, that . . . the sun never sets in the Spanish dominions." Francis Bacon and Basil Montagu, *The works of Francis Bacon, lord chancellor of England* (Carey, 1841), 438.

7 Famously the Treaty of Tordesillas divided the New World between Portugal and Spain under the auspices of the Church, giving the empires a mandate to "Christianize while conquering."

8 For the popularization of this idea, see Paul Kennedy, *The Rise and Fall of the Great Powers* (London, 1988).

9 *Los fusilamientos de la montaña del Príncipe Pío* (1814).

10 Lynch's new biography of San Martín synthesizes the flow of enlightened ideas. John Lynch, *San Martín* (London, 2009).

11 For the key source making this argument, see François-Xavier Guerra, *Modernidad e independencias: Ensayos sobre las revoluciones hispánicas* (Madrid, 1992).

12 In French, "Ils n'ont rien appris, ni rien oublié." The saying is usually attributed to Prince Talleyrand.

13 For data, see Javier Cuenca, "Ingresos netos del estado Español, 1788–1820," *Hacienda pública española* 69 (March–April 1981), 183–208. See the useful graphical display in Miguel Ángel López Morell, *La casa Rothschild en España* (Madrid, 2005), 42.

14 See François-René Chateaubriand, *Mémoires D'Outre-Tombe* (Paris, 1999); this translation is Jean d'Ormesson's.
15 Niall Ferguson, *The House of Rothschild* (New York, 1998), 141.
16 Alejandro Pérez, *Artículos de Mariano José de Larra* (Barcelona, 1983).
17 The First Carlist War took place during the regency of Isabella's mother, Maria Christina of the Two Sicilies. There were "statues" (shorter constitutions) in both 1934 and 1937, as well as a new Constitution in 1937. See Jordi Canal, *El carlismo: Dos siglos de contrarrevolución en España* (Madrid, 2000).
18 The term is untranslatable but comparable to the liberal land reforms of the Risorgimento. See Gabriel Tortella, *El Desarrollo de la España Contemporánea* (Madrid, 1995), 43. Gaspar de Jovellanos, a central figure of the Iberian Enlightenment, had written a report about land reform in 1795, which the Inquisition sought to ban: Gaspar de Jovellanos, *Informe de D. Gaspar de Jovellanos en el expediente de Ley Agraria* (Bordeaux, 1820). For a modern account, see Francisco Martí Gilabert, *La desamortización española* (Madrid, 2003).
19 Josef Becker and Michael Schmid, *Bismarcks Spanische "Diversion" 1870 und der Preussisch-Deutsche Reichsgründungskrieg* (Paderborn, 2003).
20 Edgar Holt, *The Carlist Wars in Spain* (Boston, 1967), 243.
21 Alexandre Dumas, among others, disagreed. His conservative political leanings notwithstanding, he wrote of republican Spain, "Hier, ivre de bonheur, il me fut impossible de retenir les larmes qui par instants coulaient sur mes joues; il me semblait que je voyais les yeux ouverts le plus beau rêve de ma vie—la République Universelle." In Gerald Brenan, *The Spanish Labyrinth* (Cambridge, U.K., 1960), 15, n2.
22 Sandhurst, Britain's preeminent Royal Military Academy, remains a leading institution of military training.
23 Raymond Carr, *Spain, 1808–1975* (Oxford, 1982).
24 Néstor Luján, *Cuento de cuentos: Origen y aventura de ciertas palabras y frases proverbiales* (Madrid, 1993), 222–23.
25 "Son españoles los que no pueden ser otra cosa." He also penned a retrospective on his Restoration. See Antonio Cánovas del Castillo, *Historia de la decadencia de España* (Madrid, 1910) and *La Restauración Monárquica* (San Lorenzo Escorial, 1978).
26 A key Liberal project was the Institute of Free Learning, judged by modern economists to be one of very few distinctly Spanish ideas that positively impacted the country's development. For one history of the organization, see Carlos Algora Alba, *El Instituto-Escuela de Sevilla (1932–1936)* (Seville, 1996).
27 The Pacto del Pardo formalized the power-sharing agreement. See Robert Kern, *Liberals, Reformers, and Caciques in Restoration Spain, 1875–1909* (Albuquerque, N.M., 1974), especially 67–69.
28 Adolfo Posada, *Estudios sobre el régimen parlamentario en España* (Madrid, 1891), 28–30, cited in Brenan, *Spanish Labyrinth,* 4.
29 Ibid., 5–7.
30 See Paul Preston, *The Coming of the Spanish Civil War* (London, 1994), 74–120.
31 The *New York Times* oddly eulogized his murderer. "Angiolillo Died Bravely," *New York Times,* August 22, 1897, 5.
32 Angel Ossorio y Gallardo, *Julio de 1909, declaración de un testigo* (Madrid, 1910), 13.
33 For an overview of the period, see Stanley Payne, *Politics and the Military in Modern Spain* (Stanford, 1967), chapter 10.
34 For a good comparative study focused on foreign policy, see Gustavo Palomares Lerma, *Mussolini y Primo De Rivera: Política exterior de dos dictadores* (Madrid, 1989).

35 See Leandro Alvarez Rey, *Bajo el fuero militar: La dictadura de Primo de Rivera en sus documentos* (Seville, 2006), 200–202. For a history of Primo's alliance with the most reactionary elements of Spanish society, see Carmelo Adagio, *Chiesa e nazione in Spagna: La dittatura di Primo de Rivera* (Milan, 2004).

36 Hugh Thomas, *Spanish Civil War: Revised Edition* (New York, 2001), 49.

37 According to an interesting linguistic analysis by Prados de la Escosura, economists' favorite words to describe this period in Spain are *stagnation, failure,* and *backwardness.* See Jaime Vicens Vives, *Manual de historia económica de España* (Barcelona, 1965); Leandro Prados de la Escosura, *De imperio a nación* (Madrid, 1988), 15, 239–41; Jordi Nadal, *El fracaso de la revolución industrial en España* (Esplugues de Llobregat, 1975), 293–96; Nicolás Sánchez-Albornoz, *España hace un siglo: Una economía dual* (Madrid, 1977), 36. For comparisons, see Gabriel Tortella, "Atraso y convergencia: El desarrollo de la España contemporánea en el contexto de la Europa Mediterránea," in *El sistema financiero en España,* edited by Martín Aceña (Granada, 1999); Ramón Tamames, *Estructura Económica De España* (Madrid, 1986), 4–10. An important if solitary exception is David Ringrose, *Spain, Europe, and the "Spanish Miracle"* (New York, 1998), especially 387–97.

38 Tortella, *Desarrollo,* 10–12, 70–75.

39 Sánchez-Albornoz, *España hace un siglo,* 26.

40 For a detailed statistical analysis, see chart 3.5 in Gabriel Tortella et al., "Producción y Productividad Agraria," in *La modernización económica de España,* edited by Nicolás Sánchez-Albornoz (Madrid, 1985), 76. Maddison's data concur, in Angus Maddison, *The World Economy* (Paris, 2006).

41 By the time of the Republic, farms of less than twenty acres amounted to over 99 percent of all holdings. See Michael Seidman, *The Victorious Counterrevolution* (Madison, Wisc., 2011), loc. 214.

42 The number of enrolled students per 1,000 children was 104.1 in the 1880s, then decreasing by around 17 percent to 85.9 in the 1910s. See Tortella, *Desarrollo,* 85.

43 Lars Sandberg, "Ignorance, Poverty and Economic Backwardness in the Early Stages of European Industrialization: Variations on Alexander Gerschenkron's Grand Theme," *Journal of European Economic History* 11 (1982): 675–98.

44 Prados de la Escosura, *De imperio a nación,* 28; Nadal, *El fracaso,* 226.

45 The See Rondo Cameron, *France and the Economic Development of Europe, 1800–1914* (Princeton, N.J., 1961). Also cited in Tortella, *Desarrollo,* 163.

46 See Tamames, *Estructura Económica,* especially "Conclusiones." As for the "pernicious" effects of openness, most authors refer to the sell-off of rights to exploit Spain's considerable mineral wealth. For Rothschild investments in Rio Tinto and other companies, see Guy de Rothschild, *The Whims of Fortune* (New York, 1985), 220–21.

47 See Tortella, "Prefacio" to Prados de la Escosura, *De imperio a nación,* 11–12.

48 For details on the period's commercial policies, see José María Serrano Sanz, *El Viraje proteccionista en la Restauración* (México, D.F., 1987); Prados de la Escosura, *De imperio a nación,* 22.

49 For an original comparison with Switzerland, a country with largely similar natural endowments, see Jean Bergier, *Histoire économique de la Suisse* (Lausanne, 1984). The *arancel,* the Spanish import tariff, had a long history across its empire. For instance, see José Manuel de Paz, *Sumario del arancel, aprobado por su Magestad* (México, D.F., 1723).

50 Once again most sources argue this, though each focuses on a different factor. See Nadal, "Conclusiones," in *Fracaso de la Revolución Industrial;* Tortella, *Desarrollo,* 379–80; Tortella, "Atraso y convergencia," 12–14; Vicens Vives, *Manual de historia económica,* 32–45; Sánchez-Albornoz, *España hace un siglo,* 6–13. Despite a similar conclusion, Prados de la Escosura blames the industrial sector itself the most, in *De imperio a nación,* 24. For the classic development theories, see Alexander Gerschenkron, *Economic Backwardness in Historical Perspective* (Cambridge, Mass., 1966); Walt W. Rostow, *The Stages of Economic Growth* (Cambridge, U.K., 1990).

51 De Larra, "All Saints' Day 1836."

52 In Prados de la Escosura, *De imperio a nación,* 25. Also Joseph Harrison, *An Economic History of Modern Spain* (Manchester, U.K., 1978), 54; Sidney Pollard, *Typology of Industrialization Processes in the Nineteenth Century* (Chur, Switzerland, 1990), 244; Clive Trebilcock, *The Industrialization of the Continental Powers, 1780–1914* (London, 1981), 363; T. Iván Berend and György Ránki, *The European Periphery and Industrialization, 1780–1914* (Cambridge, U.K., 1982), 140.

53 "Carthago delenda est," meaning "Carthage must be destroyed," was a common Latin political line at the time of the Punic Wars. Plutarch has Roman statesman Cato the Elder ending his speeches with variations of the phrase. See Charles E. Little, "The Authenticity and Form of Cato's Saying 'Carthago Delenda Est,'" *Classical Journal* 29, no. 6 (1934): 429–35.

54 José Ortega y Gasset, 'El error Berenguer," *El Sol,* November 15, 1930.

55 For details on Lerroux, see Ramón Serrano, *Alejandro Lerroux* (Madrid, 2003).

56 Thomas, *Spanish Civil War,* 41.

57 See reference in *Time,* June 29, 1931.

58 On the strike, see Álvaro Soto Carmona, *El Trabajo industrial en la España contemporánea 1874–1936* (Madrid, 1989), 423.

59 Manuel Azaña, *La velada en Benicarló* (Barcelona, 1939).

60 For the modeling of the Republic in action, see Seidman, *The Victorious Counterrevolution,* especially chapter 1. Seidman's previous social history of the Republic is also a worthy work: Michael Seidman, *Republic of Egos* (Madison, Wisc., 2002).

61 "En mi hambre, mando yo." Salvador de Madariaga, *España* (Madrid, 1931). The account was partly derived from the previous, riveting work by Madariaga in English.

62 Segura's letters are reproduced in full in Gonzalo Redondo, *Historia de la Iglesia en España, 1931–1939* (Madrid, 1993), 1: 142–46.

63 Cited in *Time,* May 18, 1931.

64 Ibid.

65 Cited in Brenan, *Spanish Labyrinth,* 36.

66 For reference, see G. M Godden, *Conflict in Spain, 1920–1937: A Documented Record* (London, 1937), 35.

67 For a detailed compendium of sources surrounding the Sanjurjada, see Stanley G. Payne, *Politics and the Military in Modern Spain* (Stanford, 1967), chapter 15. It was rumored a left-leaning prostitute had relayed to her republican clients the conversations her other, more conservative clients were having.

68 See Preston, *Coming of the Spanish Civil War,* 140. For another view, see Edward Malefakis, *Agrarian Reform and Peasant Revolution in Spain* (New Haven, Conn., 1970).

69 For a thorough yet obviously biased overview of the process, see *La Reforma Agraria en España* (Valencia, 1937).

70 Manuel Tuñón de Lara, *La España del siglo XX* (Madrid, 2000), 1: 469–71.

71 For a good account of Sanjurjo in Portugal, see César de Oliveira, *Salazar e a Guerra Civil de Espanha* (Lisbon, 1987), 114–16.
72 In January 1934 Largo Caballero formed a "pre-revolutionary committee," as if revolution could be staged by committee and from party headquarters. See the classic Stanley Payne, *Spain's First Democracy* (Madison, Wisc., 1993), 198–99.
73 See Miguel A. Ardid Pellón, *José María Gil Robles* (Barcelona, 2004).
74 For a recent history of the 1934 revolution, see Emilio García Gómez, *Asturias 1934: Historia De Una Tragedia* (Zaragoza, 2010).
75 For a very enlightening collection of original documents detailing the revolution and consequences, refer to the Harvard Western European Local History Preservation Microfilm Project, 01061: *La Revolución de Asturias: Documentos* (México, D.F., 1935). See also a very useful account of the confusion from "impartial witnesses" in *Revolución en Asturias: Relato De La Última Guerra Civil Por Un Testigo Imparcial* (Madrid, 1934).
76 José Gonzalo Flórez, *La Segunda República Española* (Madrid, 1997), 118, 120.
77 Luis E. Togores, *Millán Astray, Legionario* (Madrid, 2003).
78 For an analysis of their cult of death, see John H. Galey, "Bridegrooms of Death: A Profile Study of the Spanish Foreign Legion," *Journal of Contemporary History* 4, no. 2 (1969): 47–64.
79 The argument about Franco's repression is best made in the classic Gabriel Jackson, *The Spanish Republic and the Civil War, 1931–1939* (Princeton, N.J., 1965).
80 *El Liberal de Bilbao,* January 20, 1936.
81 Ibid.
82 Gabriel Jackson, *La República Española y la Guerra Civil* (Barcelona, 2008), 537–38.
83 For quotes on the newspapers of the time, including the monarchist *ABC* complaining about the "rabble" rumors, see Gonzalo Redondo, *Historia de la Iglesia en España, 1931–1939* (Madrid, 1993), 491.
84 Gil Robles at the Cortes, June 15, 1936.
85 José Antonio Primo de Rivera, *Obras completas de José Antonio Primo de Rivera* (Madrid, 1954). See his speech on October 29, 1933, at the Madrid Comedy Theatre.
86 Ibid.
87 Republican guard José Castillo had been shot down a day earlier, allegedly by a gang of José Antonio's Falangists.
88 There remain many questions surrounding the event, though most accounts agree the government was not aware of the reprisal against Sotelo. In fact, according to many sources, those men who had taken him from home had not planned to kill him. For what transpired in the car, a vital source is the account by Aniceto Castro from June 15, 1939, obtained during a dubious Francoist process.
89 José Antonio had been imprisoned during the elections under charges of weapons trafficking—a sure way to halt any possible Falangist coup d'état.
90 Preston has argued, convincingly, that the Sotelo murder finally pushed Franco to join, yet much remains unclear about Franco's actions immediately preceding the coup.
91 Thomas, *Spanish Civil War,* 203.

2. "TODAY IS SO FAR FROM YESTERDAY"

Epigraph: Antonio Machado was one of Spain's salient twentieth-century poets. He remained in Republican Spain, first Valencia, then Barcelona, and in France, where he died days before Franco's final victory. Antonio Machado, *Soledades* (Exeter, 2006).

1 See for instance, Paul Preston, *Las Tres Españas del 36* (Barcelona, 1998), 338–83.

2 Paul Preston, *Doves of War: Four Women of Spain* (London, 2002).

3 John O'Loughlin, Colin Flint, and Luc Anselin, "The Geography of the Nazi Vote: Context, Confession, and Class in the Reichstag Election of 1930," *Annals of the Association of American Geographers* 84, no. 3 (1994): 351–80; Richard Bessel, "The Nazi Capture of Power," *Journal of Contemporary History* 39, no. 2 (2004): 169–88; Courtney Brown, "The Nazi Vote: A National Ecological Study," *American Political Science Review* 76, no. 2 (1982): 285–302.

4 "¡No pasarán!" Her radio speech aired on July 18. Though she was referring to rebel sympathizers in Madrid, the line became popular during Franco's siege of the city in November 1936. The same cry was heard in London against the British Union of Fascists. It has also acquired a literary life, from J. R. R. Tolkien's *Lord of the Rings* to Umberto Eco's *Foucault's Pendulum*. For the original address, see *La Guerra Civil en Sus Documentos* (Madrid, 2004), 32–36 (henceforth *Documentos Españoles*).

5 The latest accounts emanating from pioneering work from Aceña, Martinez Ruiz, and Pons Brias confirm this "initial advantage." Their focus is on early Republican military defeats, but those can only be understood in the context of fascist intervention. See Pablo Martín-Aceña, Elena Martinez Ruiz, and Maria A. Pons Brias, "War and Economics: Spanish Civil War Finances Revisited," *University Library of Munich, Germany, MPRA Paper*, no. 22833 (2010), especially 25–26.

6 The Popular Front government had relocated both Mola and Franco.

7 Viñas provides a great overview on this point, though highly critical of what he describes as "anti-Republican" historical accounts. Angel Viñas, *El Escudo de la República* (Barcelona, 2007).

8 The best estimates for the balance of forces remain Lord Thomas's. Hugh Thomas, *The Spanish Civil War* (New York, 2001), chapter 19.

9 His memoirs, focused on his experiences in government long before the Civil War, were published by Nationalist presses in 1937: Emilio Mola, *Memorias* (Barcelona, 1977).

10 Esteban Gómez, *El Eco de Las Descargas: Adiós a la Esperanza Republicana* (Barcelona, 2002), 85.

11 Bank of International Settlements, *Sixième rapport annuel,* November 5, 1936. See also Angel Viñas, *El Oro de Moscú* (Barcelona, 1989), 12–13.

12 Pablo Martín Aceña, *El Oro de Moscú y el Oro de Berlín* (Madrid, 2001).

13 Richard Burdekin and Farrokh K. Langdana, "War Finance in the Southern Confederacy, 1861–1865," *Explorations in Economic History* 30, no. 3 (1993): 352–76.

14 The methods by which this control over the navy had been secured would hurt the Republic soon thereafter. Burnett Bolloten, *The Spanish Civil War: Revolution and Counterrevolution* (Chapel Hill, N.C., 1991), 49.

15 Fernando Schwartz, *La internacionalización de la Guerra Civil Española* (Barcelona, 1972), 38.

16 One of the planes crashed and two were forced to land in French Morocco, which provided Paris with irrefutable evidence of Italian intervention. After the airlift the Ju52s were retrofitted for bombing. Edward Homze, *Arming the Luftwaffe* (Lincoln, Neb., 1976), 182–90.

17 José Gomá Orduña, *La Guerra en el aire* (Barcelona, 1958), 45.

18 See Gerald Howson, *Arms for Spain* (London, 1998), 36.

19 Ibid., 43.

20 Louis Fischer, *Men and Politics: An Autobiography* (New York, 1941), 354.

21 Original reproduced in Allison Peers, ed., "Documents of the Civil War," *Bulletin of Spanish Studies* (Institute of Hispanic Studies at the University of Liverpool), 13, no. 52 (1936): 192.

22 See Diego Martínez Barrio, *Memorias* (Barcelona, 1983), 242–63.

23 At the time, the Ministry in Spain was filled with intercepted telegrams from abroad from different offices declaring their support for the rebellion. These papers were later collected and added to the so-called Archivo de Azaña in the Barcelona Archives, at the Ministerio de Asuntos Exteriores in Madrid. See Archivos de Azaña, box (b.) 88 (henceforth, Archivos Españoles).

24 Jean Lacouture, *Leon Blum* (New York, 1977), 305.

25 *Documents Diplomatiques Français 1932–1939 (11 Avril–18 Juillet 1936)* (Paris, 1963), Document 283, 786.

26 André Delmas, *A gauche de la barricade* (Paris, 1950), 110.

27 The famous case of Alfred Dreyfus, the Jewish French Army officer convicted of a crime he did not commit, exposed deep social fissures (and anti-Semitism) in the Third Republic. From politicians to novelists, from filmmakers to philosophers, "L'Affaire" led to Manichaean divisions: people were either Dreyfusards or anti-Dreyfusards. For Blum's unashamedly political recollections, see Léon Blum, *Souvenirs sur l'affaire* (Paris, 1935).

28 Lacouture, *Blum*, 54.

29 A proto-fascist, Charles Maurras was a royalist and ultraconservative Nationalist author and founder of the movement Action Française. For the wider context, see Jean-Pierre Azéma and Michel Winock, *Histoire de l'extrême droite en France* (Paris, 1993).

30 *L'Echo de Paris,* March 23, 1936.

31 See Barry Eichengreen, *Golden Fetters* (New York, 1992), 138.

32 *Le Populaire,* May 4, 1936.

33 Clara Malraux, *Le Fin et Le Commencement* (Paris, 1972), 16.

34 Debate between Léon Blum and Marceau Pivert, May 5, 1936. See reproduction in Lacouture, *Leon Blum,* 246–47.

35 Vallat would be director of the Committee on the Jewish Question during the Vichy years. This translation is Martin's. Benjamin Martin, *France in 1938* (Baton Rouge, La., 2006), 52.

36 *L'Humanité,* June 13, 1936.

37 Government stability was not a hallmark of the Third Republic. Blum was the Third Republic's 114th prime minister in just over sixty years, averaging almost two per year.

38 Cot had steadily drifted to the left since his 1933 trip to the Soviet Union; to this day there remains some debate about whether he had become a secret agent of the Kremlin at the heart of the French government, though documents do not seem to support this view.

39 Sabine Jansen, *Pierre Cot: Un Itinéraire politique du Radicalisme au Progressisme* (Paris, 2000).

40 According to evidence Cárdenas gave Lord Thomas in the 1970s, however, he remained loyal to the Republic for a few more days. It is a questionable assertion, to say the least.

41 Homze, *Arming the Luftwaffe,* especially chapter 3, covers Republican deliveries.

42 Cot would go ahead with nationalizations some months later, as France caught up on Nazi rearmament.

43 For the last-minute planning of the meeting in London, see CAB/23/85, U.K. Cabinet Memoranda, 1935–1937 (or 1937–1939) Cabinet Papers, National Archives, Kew, especially 133.

44 Treaty of Versailles, Articles 42, 43, 44.

45 Cited in Alan Bullock, *Hitler: A Study in Tyranny* (New York, 1962), 137.

46 The perspective from France was that Britain was simply "unreliable." See Nicholas Rostow, *Anglo-French Relations, 1934–36* (London, 1984).

47 Robert Young, *In Command of France: French Foreign Policy and Military Planning, 1933–1940* (Cambridge, Mass., 1978), especially 121–25.

48 Keith Middlemas and Anthony John Lane Barnes, *Baldwin: A Biography* (London, 1969), especially 1023.

49 Reproduced in French in *Documents Diplomatiques,* Tom. III, Doc. 20, 46.

50 All high commissioners and ambassadors to the United Kingdom are technically accredited to the Court of St. James, which remains the "senior palace of the Sovereign."

51 Cited in Lacouture, *Leon Blum,* 307.

52 *Les événements survenus en France de 1933 à 1945: Témoignages et documents recueillis par la Commission d'enquête parlementaire* (Paris, 1952), 257. In his memoir Eden mysteriously omits the line.

53 Stone details how Eden changed his mind only in mid-1937, too late for the Spanish Republic. Glyn Stone, *Spain, Portugal and the Great Powers, 1931–1941* (London, 2005), 53–54.

54 Little makes the interesting argument that, at that particular time, the British Cabinet fretted more about Communism than Nazism, and this had an impact on the 1935 general election. Douglas Little, "Red Scare, 1936: Anti-Bolshevism and the Origins of British Non-Intervention in the Spanish Civil War," *Journal of Contemporary History* 23, no. 2 (1988): 291–311. See also Middlemas and Barnes, *Baldwin,* especially 823–24.

55 *Les événements survenus en France,* 257.

56 James Marshall-Cornwall et al., eds., *Documents on German Foreign Policy 1918–1945, from the Archives of the German Foreign Ministry,* Series D, 1937–1945, vol. 3: *Germany and the Spanish Civil War 1936–1939* (Washington, D.C., 1950) (henceforth, *German Documents*), Doc. 3, 4, n1. For two key sources on these documents, see Hans-Jürgen Döscher, *Das Auswärtige Amt Im Dritten Reiche: Diplomatie Im Schatten Der "Endlösung"* (Berlin, 1987); Norbert Frei, *The German Foreign Office and the Nazi Past: Report of the Independent Historians' Commission* (Berlin, 2011). Dieckhoff, acting head of the Foreign Office (Ministerialdirektor), had also swiftly referred the information to Prince Bismarck in London so he could discuss it with Eden. On July 23, however, Dumont at the Reich Foreign Office had been able to contact only Achilles, the clerical officer (Kanzler), at their mission in London.

57 Little, "Red Scare, 1936," 293–94.

58 Viñas, *El Escudo de la República,* chapter 8, especially 321–29.

59 The covers of *Paris-Soir* and *L'Intransigent* are reproduced in François Fontaine, *La Guerre d'Espagne: Un deluge de feu et D'images* (Paris, 2003), 26–28.

60 *German Documents,* Doc. 23.

61 Young, *In Command of France,* 128–30.

62 *L'Action Française,* July 22, 1936.

63 M. D. Gallagher, "Leon Blum and the Spanish Civil War," *Journal of Contemporary History* 6, no. 3 (1971): 56–64.

64 *Documents Diplomatiques,* Doc. 28, 56. Time of arrival: 15:00 Paris time.

65 For his later account of these tempestuous years, see Albert Lebrun, *Témoignage* (Paris, 1945).

66 The Delbos position owed much to his allegiance to Eden across the Channel, as detailed in new research by Stone: Glyn Stone, "Yvon Delbos and Anthony Eden: Anglo-French Cooperation, 1936–38," in *Anglo-French Relations Since the Late Eighteenth Century* (Abington, U.K., 2009), 165–86.

67 Admiral Darlan, dispatched to London to confer with Lord Chatfield, First Sea Lord, was not encouraged. He dryly informed Blum that should French intervention lead to war, "France could not count on British support." See Gallagher, "Léon Blum and the Spanish Civil War," 60.

68 Stone, *Spain, Portugal and the Great Powers,* 50. See also Young, *In Command of France,* 128.

69 This was consistent with his evolving ideology. See Jansen, *Pierre Cot.*

70 Stone, "Yvon Delbos and Anthony Eden," 167.

71 De los Ríos seems to have argued this point explicitly. See Gallagher, "Léon Blum and the Spanish Civil War," 63.

72 Ibid.

73 *German Documents,* Docs. 15 and 17 are useful examples of this.

74 This implied the "success" of the policy of nonintervention as advocated by London, which I address below. See Stone, *Spain, Portugal and the Great Powers,* especially 57–62.

75 Pierre Cot, "Nationalisation d'industrie aeronautique," in Cot Papers, July 1936 (but mistakenly cited as 1937), cited correctly in Herrick Chapman, *State Capitalism and Working-Class Radicalism in the French Aircraft Industry* (San Francisco, 1991), notes. See also Pierre Cot, *Triumph of Treason* . . . (London, 1944).

76 Dante Puzzo, *Spain and the Great Powers* (New York, 1962), 241.

77 A young Toynbee oversaw a volume of *Survey of International Affairs* on the Spanish war and devoted a very detailed chapter 2 to breaches in nonintervention. Arnold J. Toynbee, ed., *Survey of International Affairs* (London, 1925–1937), 2: 10–23.

78 This is Gallagher's conclusion in "Blum and the Spanish Civil War," 64. Though for slightly different reasons, Stone and Lacouture agree.

79 See Archivos Españoles, b. 36, Docs. 2–17 for de los Ríos's reports to Madrid. For Malraux's role in the war, see Paul Nothomb, *Malraux en Espagne* (Paris, 1999).

80 Enrique Moradiellos, "British Political Strategy in the Face of the Military Rising of 1936 in Spain," *Contemporary European History* 1, no. 2 (1992): 123–37.

81 Rostow, *Anglo-French Relations,* especially 162.

82 Stone concludes the British national government decided to "stand aside and let events take their course." Stone, *Spain, Portugal and the Great Powers,* 26. For the Foreign Ministry perspective, the best source is Stone, "Yvon Delbos and Anthony Eden," 165–86. See also Gallagher, "Léon Blum and the Spanish Civil War," 64.

83 W. N. Medlicott et al., eds., *Documents on British Foreign Policy,* second series, vol. 17 (London, 1979) (henceforth, *British Documents*). See chapter 7, Doc. 4, 7.

84 Middlemas and Barnes, *Baldwin,* 954.

85 *British Documents,* p. 5. See my earlier discussion in this chapter of Eden's warning to Blum. It was expressed in a meeting that was supposed to take place with all leaders in attendance.

86 *British Documents,* Docs. 15, 16. The document focused mainly on the personal situation of Oliván, the Spanish ambassador in London, a personal friend of Eden's. See Doc. 17.

87 This is a contested issue, beginning with Baldwin's son's appraisal of the situation back in 1955, written almost as a direct attack on Churchill. Whatever he did in private, Baldwin surely did not advocate rearmament during the general election. This was smart politics given the Labour and Liberal opposition. A. J. P. Taylor, *English History, 1914–1945* (London, 2005), 377.

88 Thomas Jones, *Diary with Letters* (London, 1956); Ian Kershaw, *Hitler 1936–45: Nemesis* (London, 2000), 4.

89 Stone, "Yvon Delbos and Anthony Eden," especially 185–86.

90 This seems to be confirmed by a relatively new biography of Eden: D. R. Thorpe, *Eden: The Life and Times of Anthony Eden First Earl of Avon, 1897–1977* (London, 2011).

91 An interesting new study details Salazar's role in propaganda: Alberto Pena Rodríguez, *O Que Parece É: Salazar, Franco e a Propaganda Contra a Espanha Democrática* (Lisbon, 2009).

92 Ministério dos Negócios Estrangeiros Portugal, *Dez Anos De Política Externa (1936–1947): A Nação Portuguesa e a Segunda Guerra Mundial* (Lisbon, 1961), vol. 3, Doc. 20 (henceforth *Portuguese Documents*). See also Moradiellos, "British Political Strategy," especially 129, n17.

93 This expression refers to the so-called Aliança Luso-Britânica, in place since the Treaty of Windsor in 1386.

94 *Portuguese Documents,* vol. 3, Doc. 23.

95 Saz deserves credit for this document. See Ismael Saz, *Mussolini Contra la II República* (Valencia, 1986), 204–5.

96 Italy would later dream about its own bases in the western Mediterranean. Simon Ball, *The Bitter Sea: The Struggle for Mastery in the Mediterranean, 1935–1949* (London, 2009), especially chapter 1.

97 Winston Churchill, *The Gathering Storm* (London, 1948), 168.

98 Foreign Office, Private Foreign Office Papers of Sir Anthony Eden, FO/954/27A, 1, National Archives, Kew, U.K. Writing from Chartwell, Churchill thanked Eden for a copy of *Twelve Days* and communicated that his bookseller would be sending *Uncle, Give Us Bread.*

99 Jones, *Diary with Letters,* 231. See also Rostow, *Anglo-French Relations,* 245–47.

100 Hugo García, *The Truth about Spain! Mobilizing British Public Opinion, 1936–1939* (Brighton, U.K., 2010), especially 80–81.

101 FO/954/27A, 1.

102 García, *The Truth about Spain!,* 81.

103 Philip Williamson, *Stanley Baldwin* (Cambridge, U.K., 1999), especially chapter 1. On the effect of the massacres and the critical view of at least British and Argentine emissaries, see Viñas, *El Escudo de la República.*

104 The 1935 naval agreement between Germany and Britain, in which the Nazis agreed to limit the expansion of the Kriegsmarine to around 35 percent of the size of the British Navy, implicitly acknowledged a German navy far beyond Versailles's stipulations. Mark Alch, *Germany's Naval Resurgence, British Appeasement, and the Anglo-German Naval Agreement of 1935* (London, 1977).

105 Though, as a whole, the autobiography is self-serving, the resignation letter to the Cabinet is reproduced in Anthony Eden, *Facing the Dictators* (Cambridge, Mass., 1962), 689.

106 Douglas Little, *Malevolent Neutrality* (Ithaca, N.Y., 1985); Tom Buchanan, *England and the Spanish Civil War* (Cambridge, U.K., 1997), 39. I have not been able to corroborate such evidence from other archival sources.

107 See Puzzo, *Spain and the Great Powers,* chapter 4.

108 Chatfield, a decorated Great War officer, was first sea lord between 1933 and 1938. See T. A. Heathcote, *British Admirals of the Fleet 1734–1995: a Biographical Dictionary* (Barnsley, U.K., 2002), 42.

109 Gibraltar would become a crucial issue in Francoist relations with Britain, but also a point of leverage with Hitler. Paul Preston, "Franco and Hitler: The Myth of Hendaye 1940," *Contemporary European History* 1, no. 1 (1992): 1–16. See also Angel Viñas and Carlos Collado Seidel, "Franco's Request to the Third Reich for Military Assistance," *Contemporary European History* 11, no. 2 (2002): 191–210.

110 Ralph Harrington, "'The Mighty Hood': Navy, Empire, War at Sea and the British National Imagination, 1920–60," *Journal of Contemporary History* 38, no. 2 (2003): 171–85.

111 Thomas details why Giral, formerly navy minister, gained the reputation of an "assassin of naval officers." See Thomas, *Spanish Civil War,* 216.

112 The Republic's lack of fuel would become an issue given the unilateral withdrawal of support by Texas Oil. For more on this, see below.

113 Robert Whealey, "Economic Influence of the Great Powers in the Spanish Civil War: From the Popular Front to the Second World War," *International History Review* 5, no. 2 (1983): 229–54.

114 The best source for this data remains Angel Viñas, *Política Comercial Exterior En España (1931–1975)* (Madrid, 1979). See also Stone, *Spain, Portugal and the Great Powers,* 26.

115 See Christian Leitz, *Economic Relations between Nazi Germany and Franco's Spain* (New York, 1996), especially chapter 3.

116 This is detailed in Leitz, *Economic Relations between Nazi Germany and Franco's Spain,* 129–34.

117 Toynbee, *Survey of International Affairs* (1937), vol. 2, chapter 4. Also see Marcel Acier, *From Spanish Trenches; Recent Letters from Spain* (New York, 1937).

118 On the "revolution within," see Bolloten, *The Spanish Civil War.* See also Preston, especially 276–83 in *The Coming of the Spanish Civil War.* See also Angel Viñas, *La Soledad de la República* (Barcelona, 2006), especially chapter 14. Viñas is critical of this view from the democracies, seeing it as subservient to their inaction. Like Preston before him, he argues that the right would have attempted a coup against the Republic sooner or later, given the reluctance toward compromise with the moderate left and its reformism.

119 Delbos arrived at this conclusion because of his stalwart commitment to the British alliance. See John E. Dreifort, *Yvon Delbos and the Quai d'Orsay: French Foreign Policy During the Popular Front, 1936–1938* (Lawrence, Kan., 1973), 84. See also Stone, "Yvon Delbos and Anthony Eden," 166–67.

120 Movements are detailed in *Los movimientos de oro en España durante la Segunda Guerra Mundial (R.D. 1131/1997, de 11 de Julio)* (Madrid, 2001). Also see Pablo Martín Aceña, *El oro de Moscú y el oro de Berlín* (Madrid, 2001); Ángel Viñas, *El oro de Moscú* (Barcelona, 1979).

121 For the original document as produced by the Non-Intervention Committee, see International Committee for Application of Agreement Regarding Non-Intervention in Spain, *The Legislative and Other Measures Taken by the Participating Governments* (London, 1936). For an accessible account of the wider context, see Antony Beevor, *The Battle for Spain* (London, 2006), 348–52.

122 It became a Francoist myth after the war. For a critical assessment, see Viñas, *El oro de Moscú,* 5–12.

123 For the seminal account with unparalleled access to the relevant Russian archives, see Ronald Radosh, Mary Habeck, and Grigori Nikolaevich Sevostianon, *Spain Betrayed* (New Haven, Conn., 2001).

124 Orlov in the *Senate Internal Security Sub-Committee,* part 51, 3434. Cite from Thomas, *Spanish Civil War,* loc. 8908.

125 *New York Times,* January 10, 1957. I owe this find to Thomas, *Spanish Civil War,* loc. 8908.

126 In the Soviet Academy's *International Solidarity with the Spanish Republic* (1974) planes and tanks are overstated by 30 and 105 percent, respectively, when contrasted to military archives. When calculating real cost of Republican purchases, it becomes clear that the official ruble exchange rate fixed at 5.3 to the USD was tweaked for the transactions. That way Spain charged $600 for a Maxim Soviet gun that would otherwise have been $283 or $25,000 for a 127mm gun that would have cost $9,433.96. See Howson, *Arms for Spain,* chapters 19–20.

127 Viñas, *El Escudo de la República,* chapter 4.

128 In *El Oro de Moscú,* Viñas cites as published a volume on the full works of Largo Caballero that remains unfinished. The document, dated December 22, 1936, was in a letter from the Spanish premier to the agent Rosenberg.

129 María Elizalde Pérez-Grueso, "Las Relaciones entre España y Estados Unidos en el umbral de un nuevo siglo," in *España y Estados Unidos en el siglo XX,* edited by Lorenzo Delgado Gómez-Escalonilla and María Elizalde Pérez-Grueso (Madrid, 2005), especially 19.

130 Leandro Prados de la Escosura, *De Imperio a Nación: Crecimiento Y Atraso Económico En España (1780–1930)* (Madrid, 1988), 220–21.

131 Albert Bushnell Hart, *The Monroe Doctrine: An Interpretation* (Boston, 1920), 78.

132 Pierpaolo Barbieri, "From UN Outcast to U.S. Partner: Steering Francoist Spain toward the Economic Miracle," *Hemispheres,* no. 30 (March 2009): 89–128. For original documents, see U.S. Department of State, Office of the Historian, *Foreign Relations of the United States, 1933–1945, Franklin Delano Roosevelt* (Washington, D.C, 1954) (henceforth, *FRUS*). See vol. 7: *Europe.*

133 The famous speech is reproduced in its entirety in Franklin Roosevelt, *Franklin D. Roosevelt and Foreign Affairs* (Cambridge, Mass., 1969), 3: 377 and Dominic Tierney, *FDR and the Spanish Civil War* (Durham, N.C., 2007), 26.

134 *FRUS,* Doc. 1193, 437–39.

135 Ibid., 437.

136 The document explains that phone and cable lines were being cut. See *FRUS,* Doc. 2174, 440.

137 Eleanor Roosevelt also allegedly pressed FDR to aid the Republic throughout the war. See Gabriel Jackson, "II República, New Deal, y Guerra Civil," in Delgado and Elizalde, *España y Estados Unidos,* 115–16.

138 See *FRUS,* Doc. 2207, 443–44, from Johnson in Madrid to Washington on the issue of refugees close to the embassy. Bowers repeatedly dispatched updates to Hull on this issue.

139 *FRUS,* Doc. 2190, 445–46.

140 *FRUS,* Doc. 2203, 445–46.

141 See *German Documents;* Jackson, "II República."

142 Many Americans, however, fought in the Civil War. Edwin Rolfe, *The Lincoln Battalion* (New York, 1974).

143 On Mexican involvement, see Mario Ojeda Revah, *México y La Guerra Civil Española* (Madrid, 2004).

144 Julio Tascón, "International Capital before 'Capital Internationalization' in Spain, 1936–1959," Working Paper, Harvard University Minda de Gunzburg Center for European Studies, especially 4, n1.

145 See Little, *Malevolent Neutrality,* 5–12.

146 Interview with Claude Bowers, Columbia University Oral History Project, 1954, 125–26. Also see Claude Bowers, *My Mission to Spain* (New York, 1954).

147 For one of the sources on this, see John Pollard, *The Fascist Experience in Italy* (New York, 1998), 96.

148 See Angel Viñas, "La connivencia Fascista con la sublevación militar otros éxitos de la trama civil," *Los Mitos del 18 de Julio,* edited by Francisco Sánchez Perez (Barcelona, 2013), 79–182.

149 Hughes-Hallett's majestic biography of D'Annunzio traces the emergence of many of these aesthetic and political trends with careful detail: Lucy Hughes-Hallett, *Gabriele d'Annunzio: Poet, Seducer and Preacher of War* (New York, 2013). For the official view, see Benito Mussolini, *La Dottrina del Fascismo: Con una Storia del Movimento Fascista* (Rome, 1934).

150 In 1933 Mussolini couched his defense of a "new man" against the "liberal" *Homo economicus:* "The economic man [*Homo economicus*] does not exist; an integral man exists, one that is political, that is economic, that is religious, that is a saint, that is a warrior." Benito Mussolini, *Quattro Discorsi Sullo Stato Corporativo* (Rome, 1935). For a lengthier discussion of that specific speech, see Alessandro Somma, *I giuristi e l'Asse culturale Roma-Berlino: Economia e politica nel diritto fascista e nazionalsocialista* (Milan, 2005), especially 221, n150.

151 For a contemporary view, see Wolfgang Scholz, *Die lage des spanischen itals vor der Revolution* (Dresden, 1932). Also cited in Stanley G. Payne, *A History of Fascism, 1914–1945* (Madison, Wisc., 1995), 132. See also Saz, *Mussolini Contra la II República,* especially 182–86.

152 See Thomas, *Spanish Civil War,* 129. For more on the corporatist turn, see Chapter 3.

153 Indeed this government would release Sanjurjo, who exiled himself in Portugal, then under the yoke of Salazar.

154 Viñas, "La connivencia Fascista," 185–88. Hence Viñas speaks of Fascist "connivance" in coup planning.

155 Ibid. He claims it is "almost impossible" that Pedro Sainz Rodrigues, the Spaniard chiefly responsible for the negotiation of the contracts, did not tell the Italians about the possible chosen date.

156 Azaña wrote in his diary, "I will send him [Franco] to Baleares so that he will be farther away from temptations." Manuel Azaña, *Memorias íntimas de Azaña* (Madrid, 1939), 310.

157 Franco carried a letter explaining he was headed to the mainland to "crush the rebellion." But at this point his intentions were the very opposite. The best detail of the eventful *Dragon Rapide* trip led by British captain Cecil Bepp can be found in Thomas, *Spanish Civil War,* chapter 13, figure 6. Bepp was later decorated (several times) by Franco.

158 Bepp's descendant, Nicolas du Châtel, in correspondence with the author, June 24, 2008. Gil Robles also argued this in his postwar memoir. See also José María Gil Robles, *No Fué Posible La Paz* (Barcelona, 1978), 780.

159 The note is reproduced photographically in the biased Luis Bolín, *España: Los años vitales* (Madrid, 1967). Franco apparently prioritized Rome verbally.

160 Ricardo de la Cierva, *Historia esencial de la Guerra Civil Española* (Madrid, 1996), 155.

161 "Quiero ver al Duce." Bolín, *España,* 177. Franco's order is reproduced on p. 193, and it also carries the signature of Sanjurjo.

162 Ciano's father had been a distinguished Italian naval officer in World War I, which gave the new movement added legitimacy.

163 Introduction in Galeazzo Ciano, *Diary* (New York, 2002), 3–7.

164 Bolín, *España,* 181.

165 Ibid., 183.

166 A proper account of March's involvement is lacking, and the files at his foundation are unsurprisingly scant with regard to this period. The Spanish presses, however, produce plenty of journalistic material on March. For instance, Sánchez Soler has called the uprising "Juan March's best and riskiest investment." Mariano Sánchez Soler, *Los Banqueros de Franco* (Madrid, 2005), especially 7–25.

167 Viñas, "La connivencia fascista," especially 85–90.

168 Javier Tusell, *Franco y Mussolini* (Barcelona, 2006), 9–15; Romano Canosa, *Mussolini e Franco: Amici, Alleati, Rivali* (Milan, 2008).

169 The British High Command insisted on not considering Italy a potential adversary at the time. Little also details how the British fought to get Italians on board on the policy of nonintervention in the days after July 25. Little, "Red Scare," 300.

170 This is a point well made by Moradiellos, "British Political Strategy," 132–37.

171 See Puzzo, *Spain and the Great Powers,* 231–45.

172 Figures from Thomas, *Spanish Civil War,* appendix 7, 985. The figures are largely consistent with other estimations, particularly Viñas's in *Política Comercial.*

173 A possible exception to this was a botched attempt to take over Austria in 1934, which Mussolini had resisted.

174 Kershaw, *Nemesis,* 6–8.

175 Gerhard Weinberg, *The Foreign Policy of Hitler's Germany: Diplomatic Revolution in Europe, 1933–36* (Atlantic Highlands, N.J., 1994).

176 Max Domarus, ed., *Reden und Proklamationen, 1932–1945* (Würzburg, 1962), 596. This is a period that Kershaw has termed "Ceaseless Radicalization." See Kershaw, *Nemesis,* 1.

177 Reproduced in Thomas, *Spanish Civil War,* 343. See also Stanley G Payne, *Franco and Hitler: Spain, Germany, and World War II* (New Haven, Conn., 2008), 47.

178 The request involved the Marquis of Quintanar and a German official (Killinger). *German Documents,* Docs. 2, 5.

179 Though Mola was part of the Junta, its director was Gen. Miguel Cabanellas.

180 Beyond Bernhardt's dubious account, Franco's writings seem to suggest this much was true. Luis Suárez Fernández, *El General De La Monarquía, La República y La Guerra Civil: Desde 1892 Hasta 1939* (Madrid, 1999), 332.

181 Angel Viñas, *En Las Garras Del Águila: Los Pactos Con Estados Unidos, De Francisco Franco a Felipe González (1945–1995)* (Barcelona, 2003), 394. Viñas, however, repeatedly claimed that little of what Bernhardt said after World War II could be trusted. Ángel Viñas, in correspondence with the author, August 23, 2008.

182 A junior captain, Francisco Arranz, joined the Germans. Viñas has speculated that Franco did not send Beigdeber because he believed the mission would be unsuccessful. I am not so sure.

183 Stops were made in the Canary Islands, Morocco, Seville, and Marseilles before landing in Berlin.

184 Though "Wilhelmstraße" remains a common way of referring to the German Foreign Ministry, most of the key Third Reich ministries were located on the street. While the Foreign Office was at the former Reich president's palace, which Minister von Ribbentrop would later refurbish lavishly, on Wilhelmstraße 73, the Finance Ministry, the Propaganda Ministry, and Hitler's Chancellery were on the same street. In modern Berlin it is home to the Agriculture Ministry, the Finance Ministry, and the British Embassy.

185 *German Documents,* Doc. 58. Three days earlier Dieckhoff had received Count von Welczeck's memorandum about French intentions to help the Republic.

186 Ibid., note C1. The minister is generally seen to have started to lose power within the regime; some authors go as far as to argue that Hitler already wanted to get rid of him. See John Louis Heineman, *Hitler's First Foreign Minister* (Berkeley, 1979), especially chapter 8.

187 Alfred Heß file, Bundesarchiv Lichterfelde, Berlin. Original citation in Angel Viñas and Carlos Collado Seidel, "Franco's Request to the Third Reich for Military Assistance," *Contemporary European History* 11, no. 2 (2002): 191–210.

188 Viñas and Carlos Collado Seidel, "Franco's Request," especially 202–3. Given his experience, Viñas is understandably wary of the self-aggrandized Bernhardt versions in the 1970s, though claims about Bernhardt's admission that he had indeed lied about that Bayreuth meeting have not been confirmed by available documentary evidence.

189 Friedhelm Burbach, former Bilbao consul general, was an important figure later given honors by the Francoist regime. We can extrapolate that he likely helped to convince Bohle to go against the Wilhelmstraße. The Heß brothers and Burbach met at the Evangelisches Paedagogium in Bad Godesberg. We owe the school connection to Viñas. See Viñas and Collado Seidel, "Franco's Request," 203. The Heß connection is present only in Abendroth's account; it is missing in most of the English and Spanish accounts of the meeting, though few question it was Hitler's decision that ultimately settled the matter. Kershaw's recent Hitler biography cites the right information. See Hans-Henning Abendroth, *Hitler in der Spanischen Arena: Die Deutsch-Spanischen Beziehungen Im Spannungsfeld Der Europäischen Interessenpolitik Vom Ausbruch Des Bürgerkrieges Bis Zum Ausbruch Des Weltkrieges 1936–1939* (Nuremberg, 1970), 474–75.

190 Both Göring and Hitler had been at the performance. Most sources suggest Göring was far more careful than he would later argue at Nuremberg.

191 Erich Raeder, *Mein Leben* (Tubingen, 1956), 2: 80–81.

192 There remains some debate about who exactly was in the room when the decision was taken. Some doubt whether Canaris was there given the elusive reference to his rank and not surname.

193 Angel Viñas, *Franco, Hitler Y El Estallido De La Guerra Civil: Antecedentes Y Consecuencias* (Madrid, 2001), 34–39.

194 It is worth noting that all German men fighting in Spain would receive payment from the Nazi government, and never directly from Franco. Along with Italian troops, they got a small wage supplement.

195 Although I disagree with his economic analysis of intervention, Whealey's political analysis is remarkable. Robert Whealey, *Hitler and Spain: The Nazi Role in the Spanish Civil War, 1936–1939* (Lexington, Ky., 1989), especially 132.

196 Ibid.

197 A Nazi term Richard Evans translates as "forcible-cooperation." See also Karl Dietrich Bracher, "Stages of Totalitarian Integration," in *Republic to Reich: The*

Making of the Nazi Revolution; Ten Essays, edited by Hajo Holborn (New York, 1972), 109–28.

198 Kershaw, *Nemesis,* especially xxxvii–xxxix.

199 This omission underscores the effective lack of respect for the diplomat and the formal foreign policy apparatus despite their "elite" class connection. *Völkischer Beobachter,* July 27, 1936, cited in Angel Viñas and Carlos Collado Seidel, "Franco's Request to the Third Reich for Military Assistance," *Contemporary European History* 11, no. 2 (May 2002): 191–210, especially 205.

3. THE RISE AND RISE OF HJALMAR SCHACHT

1 Brigitte Hamann, *Winifred Wagner: A Life at the Heart of Hitler's Bayreuth* (London, 2005), especially chapter 3.

2 Speech delivered on June 28, 1934.

3 Norbert Muhlen, *Der Zauberer: Leben und Anleihen des Dr. Hjalmar Horace Greeley Schacht* (Zurich, 1938), 162. Translation here is Adam Tooze's, *Wages of Destruction* (London, 2006), 71.

4 Tour recounted in *Time,* August 6, 1934, of which Schmitt was on the cover, even if he was already on the way out in Berlin. Selling in the international market below costs to achieve other ends is what economists refer to as "dumping."

5 Particularly for an economy as tilted toward foreign trade as Germany's, the recovery in imports signaled a revival in activity.

6 See the classic Barry Eichengreen, *Golden Fetters: The Gold Standard and the Great Depression, 1919–1939* (New York, 1996).

7 We can conclude that through an extrapolation of forward exchange rates. *Economist,* August 11, 1934, 8.

8 Schmitt was Hitler's second economics minister. See Willi Boelcke, *Die Deutsche Wirtschaft 1930–1945: Interna des Reichswirtschaftsministeriums* (Düsseldorf, 1983), 64–67. His predecessor, Alfred Hugenberg, was also in charge of food and agriculture before they were made into a separate ministry under the racial ideologue Walther Darré.

9 Former chancellor von Schleicher (and his wife) were gunned down, even if they had nothing to do with the SAs. The role of the Sturmabteilung, created in 1921 as a sort of Hitlerian private army modeled after Mussolini's blackshirts, has long been debated. By 1934 their populist, revolutionary rhetoric under Röhm had made the SAs enemies in the Wehrmacht, as well as Himmler's Schutzstaffel (SS). After the purge they continued to exist but dwindled in importance. For the purge in context, see the classic Joachim Fest, *Hitler: Eine Biographie* (Frankfurt, 1989), 460–65.

10 For a detailed history, see Hans Hellmut Kirst, *Die Nächte der langen Messer* (Hamburg, 1975).

11 Close associates of Vice Chancellor Von Papen were also murdered. In a broadcast Reichstag address Hitler accused SA leader Röhm of attempting a putsch. When Röhm was offered a pistol to kill himself, he is said to have responded, "If I am to be killed, let Adolf do it." William Shirer, *The Rise and Fall of the Third Reich: A History of Nazi Germany* (Greenwich, Conn., 1960), 221.

12 Hjalmar Horace Greeley Schacht, *Confessions of "the Old Wizard": Autobiography* (Boston, 1956), 132.

13 For his hesitation, see Schacht, *Autobiography,* 265. See also Ulrich Völklein, *Geschäfte mit dem feind* (Hamburg, 2002); Norbert Mühlen, *Der Zauberer* (Zürich, 1938), 14.

14 In the American press the name lasted a long time: "Germany: Schacht Trapped," *Time,* March 15, 1926; "Power Politics: Smoke and Fire," *Time,* July 31, 1939. For European sources, see *Schacht in der Karikatur* (Berlin, 1937), especially 50–53; Mühlen, *Der Zauberer.* Note also the title of Schacht's autobiography, *76 Jahre meines Lebens,* first translated into English in 1956 as *Confessions of "the Old Wizard."*

15 For the hopeful tone with which Schacht's ministry was expected, see *Economist,* August 11, 1934, 8.

16 Hugenberg was a crucial figure in the first year of the regime, as well as German nationalism more generally. For more on him in English, see John A. Leopold, *Alfred Hugenberg: The Radical Nationalist Campaign against the Weimar Republic* (New Haven, Conn., 1977).

17 The exception to this is of course the timely Tooze, *Wages of Destruction,* and the work of Albrecht Ritschl.

18 The complexity of the issue arose from the constitutional issues linking the duchies of Schleswig and Holstein to the Danish Crown and the German Confederation. Bismarck first made the Danish king relinquish all rights to Austria and Prussia, to then turn Schleswig-Holstein into a German province in 1866.

19 For details on the Danish Crisis, see Erich Eyck, *Bismarck and the German Empire* (London, 1950), 82–83, and the wonderfully researched Jonathan Steinberg, *Bismarck: A Life* (Oxford, 2011), 210–14.

20 Ahead of the Nuremberg trials, the *New Yorker* speculated that Schacht "had the distinction" of having been conceived in Brooklyn. See *New Yorker,* December 8, 1945, 24.

21 A relatively new biography of Schacht covers this point well. See Christopher Kopper, *Hjalmar Schacht: Aufstieg und Fall Von Hitlers Mächtigstem Bankier* (Munich, 2006), chapter 1.

22 Greeley ran—and lost—against Ulysses Grant in the 1872 election. A much weaker campaigner than he had been a newspaper editor, he was particularly hurt by Thomas Nast's vicious cartoons in *Harper's Weekly.*

23 Frédéric Clavert, "Hjalmar Schacht, financier et diplomate 1930–1950," PhD dissertation, University of Strasbourg, 2006.

24 Mühlen, *Der Zauberer,* 23.

25 Interestingly Schacht was in a procession for Bismarck while in Hamburg, which he comments on in his autobiography. The old chancellor's look made an impression on young Schacht, who latter commented, "I recalled again and again the penetrating, grave expression of the Chancellor's keen eyes. What had he tried to tell us by that look? A duty, a warning, a plea that we should not allow his work to be carelessly destroyed?" Schacht, *Autobiography,* 60.

26 Clavert, "Hjalmar Schacht, financier et diplomate."

27 The exception here is Kopper, *Hjalmar Schacht,* yet I do not believe the focus is sufficient. Siegfried Wendt, "Hasbach, Wilhelm," in *Neue Deutsche Biographie* 8 (1969): S. 17 f.

28 For Hegel's economics, see Gareth Stedman Jones, "Hegel and the Economics of Civil Society," in *Civil Society, History and Possibilities,* edited by S. Kaviraj and S. Khilnani (Cambridge, U.K., 2001); Pierpaolo Barbieri, "Minding the Liberal Gap," unpublished paper, Cambridge University, 2010.

29 Hasbach is regularly mentioned in early critiques of Smith. For instance, one British scholar who picks up on Hasbach's argument about the similarities between Hume's and Smith's concepts of "sympathy" is James Bonar, *Philosophy and Political Economy in Some of Their Historical Relations* (Sonnenschein, 1893), 180, n1.

30 See, for instance, Richard Kleer, *Role of Teleology in Smith's Wealth of Nations, History of Economics Review* (2000), 14–29.

31 David Reisman, *The Economics of Alfred Marshall* (Basingstoke, U.K., 1986).

32 This would later push its disciples into institutional analysis and eventually business schools in the United States.

33 For a salient study on the birth of *Homo economicus,* see Lev Menand, "Changing the World from a Point within It," unpublished thesis, Harvard University, 2009. Courtesy of the author.

34 In his (in)famous introduction to the German edition of his *General Theory,* Keynes begins by laying out the usual German rejection of the classical thinkers: "[German economics] has been skeptical and realistic, satisfied with historical and empirical methods and results which reject a formal analysis," which Keynes speculates will make it more likely for Germans to support his proposals. He continues, "I may, therefore, perhaps expect to meet with less resistance on the part of German readers than from English, when I submit to them a theory of employment and production as a whole which deviates in important particulars from the orthodox tradition. . . . How hungry and thirsty German economists must feel *having lived all these years without [a theory]!"* See John Maynard Keynes, *Allgemeine Theorie der Beschäftigung, des Zinses und des Geldes* (Munich, 1936).

35 The existence of a cohesive "historical school" has been a subject of debate, yet for our purposes approaching it as an entity of sorts is useful. For the critique, see Erik Grimmer-Solem and Roberto Romani, "The Historical School: A Reassessment," *History of European Ideas* 24, no. 45 (1998): 267–99. For the original works, see Wilhelm Hasbach, *Die allgemeinen philosophischen Grundlagen der von F. Quesnay und Adam Smith begründeten politischen Ökonomie* (Kiel, 1890) and *Adam Smith und die Entwicklung der politischen Ökonomie* (Kiel, 1891).

36 Mühlen, *Der Zauberer,* 6–7.

37 Hjalmar Schacht, "Der Theoretische Gehalt des englischen Merkantilismus," inaugural dissertation presented to the Philosophical Faculty of the University of Kiel (Berlin, 1900), 9.

38 See Allen Wood, "Editor's Introduction," in G. W. Hegel, *Elements of the Philosophy of Rights* (Cambridge, U.K., 1991), xxvii; Hegel, *Elements of the Philosophy of Rights,* especially 182–92. For List's classic, see Friedrich List, *Friedrich List: Das nationale System der politischen Ökonomie,* edited by Eugen Wendler (Baden-Baden, 2008).

39 Though List never credited Hamilton for his influences on protectionism and nationalist economics, it is worth noting that his ideas had not been developed before his 1827 trip to the United States, during which he seems to have been acquainted with Hamilton's essays. See Guy Callender, *Selections from the Economic History of the United States, 1765–1860* (Boston, 1909), 552; William Smith Culbertson, *Alexander Hamilton: An Essay* (New Haven, Conn., 1911). I am grateful to Charles Maier for pointing me in this direction.

40 Friedrich List, *Das nationale System der politischen Ökonomie* (1842; Berlin, 1982). See also Avraham Barkai, *Nazi Economics* (Oxford, 1990), 78–79.

41 Fernand Braudel, *Civilization and Capitalism, 15th–18th Century: The Wheels of Commerce* (San Francisco, 1992), 210. In his now-classic study, Braudel attributes the Elizabethan book to Sir Thomas Smith, adding pithily that the comment "sums up all we need know about the trade balance and perhaps all anyone has ever known." Examples of non-German, early mercantilists include Philipp von Hörnigk in Austria and Jean-Baptiste Colbert in Louis XIV's France.

42 The net international investment position (NIIP) forms part of a country's foreign balance sheet: the difference between its external assets and its liabilities. A positive NIIP implies the world owes the country, whereas the opposite is true for a negative NIIP.

43 See Clavert, "Hjalmar Schacht, financier et diplomate."

44 These arguments feature prominently in John Maynard Keynes, *A Treatise on Money* (London, 1930).

45 Originally a partial answer to modernization theory in social science, dependency theory argues for "unequal terms of trade" between a core of wealthy countries and a periphery of poorer ones. The latter group, usually producers of raw materials, cannot escape a cycle of poverty because of the inherent advantage the former obtain by selling finished products. See Enzo Faletto and Fernando Henrique Cardoso, *Dependency and Development in Latin America* (Berkeley, 1979).

46 Emanuel Leser, ed., *William Staffords drei Gespräche über die in der Bevölkerung verbreiteten Klagen* (Leipzig, 1895), as quoted in Schacht, "Der Theoretische Gehalt des Englischen Merkantilismus."

47 "The inhabitant of London could order by telephone, sipping his morning tea in bed, the various products of the whole earth, in such quantity as he might see fit, and reasonably expect their early delivery upon his doorstep," Keynes famously wrote of the prewar financial system in the nostalgic John Maynard Keynes, *The Economic Consequences of the Peace* (New York, 1919), chapter 2.

48 According to a historian taken by the Schacht myth, such personal conviction was built on the fact that "Schacht is a man of courage," who nevertheless "does not defend any principle irrespective of cost." This was a man who, after achieving prominence, began collecting his own caricatures in the media; he would have official presses publish a collection of his favorite ones: Hjalmar Schacht, *Schacht in Der Karikatur* (Berlin, 1937).

49 Though focusing on worse crimes than merely economic ones, the atrocities committed by the German Army in the first weeks of the war that so damaged its international reputation in the 1920s can be found in "Commission d'enquête sur la violation des règles du droit des gens, des lois et des costumes de la guerre," in *Rapports et documents d'enquête* (Brussels, 1921), especially vol. 1.

50 Schacht worked under von Lumm. Kopper, *Hjalmar Schacht,* especially 44–46.

51 Karl Richard Bopp, *Hjalmar Schacht: Central Banker* (Columbia, Mo., 1939), 11.

52 Schacht, *Autobiography,* especially chapter 16.

53 Though the histories of the bank detail its connections to Nazism, there is little on the period before. See *25 Jahre Genossenschafts-Abteilungen der Dresdner Bank: Ein Beitrag zur Geschichte des Deutschen Genossenschaftswesens* (Berlin, 1929), at the Harvard social history/business preservation microfilm project, Project 2a, 20630.

54 See Schacht, *Autobiography,* chapter 18, for his personal thoughts, surely tempered by time and his Nazi service.

55 For an interesting retrospective, see "Foreign News: Bigger? Better? Brighter?," *Time,* January 28, 1935.

56 Heinz Schröder, *Das Ende der Dolchstosslegende: Geschichtliche Erkenntnis und politische Verantwortung* (Hamburg, 1946). For Wilson's problematic idealism, see Thomas Knock, *To End All Wars* (New York, 1992).

57 Hjalmar Schacht, *The End of Reparations* (New York, 1931), 17.

58 Richard Overy, *War and Economy in the Third Reich* (Oxford, 1994), 6.

59 The reference is to the famous report on the thinking of von Moltke. See also Niall Ferguson, *The Pity of War* (London, 1999), 100. See also Christopher

Clark, *The Sleepwalkers: How Europe Went to War in 1914* (London, 2012), especially 526–27.

60 Zara Steiner, *The Lights That Failed: European International History 1919–1933* (London, 2005), 68.

61 The purpose of the gold linkage at a time when everyone had (temporarily) gone off gold was so that the Germans did not devalue their way through the debt. For the best gross domestic product (GDP) estimations, see Albrecht Ritschl, "Les reparations allemandes, 1920–1933: Une controverse revue par la theorie des jeux," REPEC, 1999; Albrecht Ritschl and Samad Sarferaz, *Currency vs. Banking in the German Debt Crisis of 1931,* CEPR, 2006; Filippo Occhino, Kim Oosterlinck, and Eugene N. White, "How Occupied France Financed Its Own Exploitation in World War II," *American Economic Review* 97, no. 2 (2007): 295–99.

62 Keynes, *The Economic Consequences of the Peace.*

63 Walter Landis, *An Engineer Looks at Inflation, Its Effects in Germany and France* (Charlotte, Va., 1933). See also Bopp, *Schacht,* 12.

64 Ferguson, *The Pity of War,* 428–35.

65 On inflation as "always and everywhere a monetary phenomenon," see Milton Friedman, *The Counter-revolution in Monetary Theory: First Wincott Memorial Lecture* (London, 1970).

66 For a selection, see Niall Ferguson, *Paper and Iron* (Cambridge, U.K., 1995), 356–59.

67 Schacht, *End of Reparations,* 33, 35–37.

68 For stimulating research on Keynes anticipating arguments of bounded rationality with his thoughts on the Conference itself, see William P. Bottom, "Keynes' Attack on the Versailles Treaty: An Early Investigation of the Consequences of Bounded Rationality, Framing, and Cognitive Illusions," *SSRN eLibrary* (n.d.).

69 Schacht, *End of Reparations,* 34.

70 Ibid.

71 Schacht, *Autobiography,* 229.

72 Tom Fergusson, *When Money Dies* (New York, 2010), especially 205–18.

73 Secondary issuing referred to private money, issued generally by German corporations and banks, which exacerbated the monetization of debts since they were used like money (though often with a discount). Schacht, *Autobiography,* 178–81.

74 John Parke Young, *European Currency and Finance: Commission of Gold and Silver Inquiry, United States Senate . . . Foreign Currency and Exchange Investigation* (Washington, D.C., 1925), 36.

75 For the most detailed account of the period that, like the above, places reparations at the core of the inflation issue, see Gerald Feldman, *The Great Disorder: Politics, Economics, and Society in the German Inflation, 1914–1924* (New York, 1993).

76 For the classic paper on this, see Thomas J. Sargent, "The Ends of Four Big Inflations," *NBER,* January 1, 1982, 41–98.

77 J. R. Wright, *Gustav Stresemann: Weimar's Greatest Statesman* (Oxford, 2002), 215, 444.

78 An earlier version of the solution was the Roggenmark, advocated by the powerful German agricultural lobby, which would have ultimately linked the currency to rye prices. The idea was dropped, yet it influenced the Rentenmark architecture. For other alternatives considered, see Schacht, *Autobiography,* 179–80.

79 Sargent makes this point, as well as agreeing with the centrality of reparations to the original Weimar deficits. Sargent, "The Ends of Four Big Inflations," especially 74–75.

80 Ferguson, *Paper and Iron,* 363.

81 Fergusson, *When Money Dies,* 123.

82 For a contemporary view from a journalist trained in political science (and a very friendly biographer), see Franz Reuter, *Schacht* (Leipzig, 1934).

83 Cited in John Weitz, *Hitler's Banker: Hjalmar Horace Greeley Schacht* (Boston, 1997), 76.

84 For innovations, see for example the speech Rudolf Havenstein, *Rede des Reichsbankpräsidenten Excellenz Dr. Havenstein in der Versammlung der Handelkammer in Frankfurt a.M. am 20. September 1917* (Berlin, 1917) at the Harvard Library Digitalization Project. For his views on war, see Ferguson, *Pity of War,* 136.

85 See the contemporary report of activities of Germany's American creditors during the war: Moritz Bonn, *German War Finance* (New York, 1916).

86 *Putsch* is essentially German for *coup d'état.* Along with most Nazi "old fighters," strongly nationalistic Erich Ludendorff, a World War I leader close in stature to Hindenburg, joined in. See Jordan Rudolf, *Der Hitler-Putsch Vom 8. November 1923: Der Hitler-Prozess–1924* (Bremen, 1986).

87 Mommsen provides a sine qua non account of this episode in Hans Mommsen, *Die Verspielte Freiheit: Der Weg Der Republik Von Weimar in Den Untergang 1918 Bis 1933* (Berlin, 1989).

88 The year 1924 may not have been great, but it was definitely much better for German business than 1923. See Sargent, "The Ends of Four Big Inflations," 77, and, for the contemporary view, see Young, *European Currency and Finance,* 39.

89 Schacht, *Autobiography,* 53–54.

90 Stephen A. Schuker, *The End of French Predominance in Europe: The Financial Crisis of 1924 and the Adoption of the Dawes Plan* (Chapel Hill, N.C., 1976), especially 292.

91 Charles Kindleberger, *The World in Depression* (Berkeley, 1986), especially 48. For a less academic view, see Liaquat Ahamed, *Lords of Finance: The Bankers Who Broke the World* (London, 2009).

92 Robert Long, *Fortnightly Review,* August 1, 1924. Cited from Weitz, *Schacht,* 79.

93 Dawes was writing in 1939. See Charles Dawes, *A Journal of Reparations* (London, 1939), 55.

94 For depressed trade data at the time, see Schacht, *End of Reparations,* 173–77.

95 Donald McCoy, *Calvin Coolidge: The Quiet President* (Lawrence, Kan., 1988), 330–42.

96 Walter Bagehot, *Lombard Street: A Description of the Money Market* (London, 1910), 4.

97 Robert Skidelsky, *John Maynard Keynes: A Biography* (London, 1983), especially vol. 2: *The Economist as Saviour 1920–1937.*

98 Cited in Andrew Boyle, *Montagu Norman: A Biography* (London, 1967), 188–89.

99 Debts were incurred, for the most part, before the United States entered the war in 1917. For the J. P. Morgan perspective, see Ron Chernow, *The House of Morgan* (New York, 1991), especially chapters 1–3.

100 Paul Warburg, cable to Owen D. Young, March 14, 1924, quoted in Stephen Clarke, *Central Bank Cooperation: 1924–31* (New York, 1967), 61.

101 See the original, Rufus C. Dawes, *The Dawes Plan in the Making* (Indianapolis, 1925).

102 It would be unfair to argue that contemporaries did not grasp the implications of this phenomenon. See, for instance, Joseph Stancliffe Davis, *The War Debt Settlements* (Charlottesville, Va., 1928).

103 Schacht, *End of Reparations,* 161, 162.

104 Robert Kuczynski, *Bankers' Profits from German Loans* (Washington, D.C., 1932), especially 139–41.

105 Norman had bypassed an established commission of experts in pledging help to Schacht (and opposing a Franco-Belgian proposal). In a letter to Fed chairman Benjamin Strong on January 7, 1924, Norman described Schacht's plan as the "last chance" for German stabilization. It is best described in the classic Clarke, *Central Bank Cooperation,* 58–59.

106 See Kuczynski, *Bankers' Profits,* 140, for his estimations.

107 For Schacht's opposition to the reparations promises, see Weitz, *Schacht,* 82. For a history of two positions, see Wright, *Stresemann;* Tooze, *Wages of Destruction,* 18–19. For the background to Stresemann's conflicts with industrialists, see the comparison between Stresemann and Briand in Charles S. Maier, *Recasting Bourgeois Europe* (Princeton, N.J., 1975), especially 387.

108 The full amount to be paid was left undetermined, yet the payments went down to 1 billion Reichsmarks, and then would rise as the German economy improved.

109 See Articles 118–56 of the Treaty of Versailles. Keynes, *Economic Consequences of the Peace,* 67–69. It could be argued, however, most of these colonies were not properly developed in the Wilhelmine era. See trade data in W. O. Henderson, *The German Colonial Empire, 1884–1919* (London, 1993), especially appendix, 132–33. See also original data in André Touzet, *Le problème colonial et la paix du monde* (Paris, 1937), 228.

110 Neither the speech nor his contacts with the Colonial Association are mentioned in Schacht's autobiography—or in others, for that matter.

111 For more on this, see Woodruff Smith, *The Ideological Origins of Nazi Imperialism* (New York, 1986), especially chapter 3. The phrase itself originated with Von Bülow, Bismarck's successor: "Mit einem Worte: wir wollen niemand in den Schatten stellen, aber wir verlangen auch unseren Platz an der Sonne." See *Fürst Bülows Reden nebst urkundlichen Beiträgen zu seiner Politik, Mit Erlaubnis des Reichskanzlers gesammelt und herausgegeben von Johannes Penzler* (Berlin, 1897–1903), 6–8.

112 Hildebrand has explained in detail how this answered to "mutual needs" within both organizations. Klaus Hildebrand, *Vom Reich zum Weltreich: Hitler, NSDAP und koloniale Frage, 1919–1945* (Munich, 1969), especially 149–52.

113 Smith, *Ideological Origins of Nazi Imperialism,* especially 52–78 (pre–World War I) and 196–201 (Weimar).

114 Particularly instructive is the W. J. Ashley introduction to the English edition of the book, published a year later; it illustrates not only a deep understanding of Neumann's intellectual background but also how his ideas were received in the United Kingdom while the war raged on. Friedrich Naumann, *Central Europe* (London, 1916), especially v–xvii.

115 The Treaty of Brest-Litovsk, sometimes referred to in interwar Germany as the "forgotten peace," was the peace treaty that ceased hostilities in the Eastern Front of World War I. Signed by the Germans and the new Soviet government in Russia, it effectively expanded the German Empire to cover the Baltic states and relinquishing Russian control of Finland and Poland. The territories governed by the Ober Ost therefore would now be either part of the formal German Empire or puppet states dependent on the Wilhelmine Crown. For more, see Golo Mann, *The History of Germany since 1789* (Harmondsworth, U.K., 1974), 560.

116 Vejas Liulevicius, *War Land on the Eastern Front: Culture, National Identity and German Occupation in World War I* (Cambridge, U.K., 2000), 252.

117 Hans Grimm also wrote a best-seller that was instructive in its conception of "a people without space," which its title directly references. Hans Grimm, *Volk ohne Raum* (Lippoldsberg, 1975).

118 Literally "blood and land." For an interesting study in the regime, see Matthias Eidenbenz, *Blut und Boden: Zu Funktion und Genese der Metaphern des Agrarismus und Biologismus in Der Nationalsozialistischen Bauernpropaganda R. W. Darrés* (Bern, 1993).

119 Volker Berghahn, introduction to *Quest for Economic Empire,* edited by Volker Berghahn (Providence, R.I., 1996), 12; Paul Kennedy, *The Rise of the Anglo-German Antagonism, 1860–1914* (London, 1980), 411–15.

120 Though rejected by the Junker class, by lowering barriers to foreign grain the kaiser's government had encouraged Russia and Austria-Hungary to provide Germany foodstuffs in exchange for better treatment of Prussian industrial products. Such policies stimulated continental market integration in favor of industrial interests. See Smith, *Ideological Origins of Nazi Imperialism,* 78.

121 Hjalmar Schacht, *New Colonial Policy—paper read by Dr. Hjalmar Schacht in the Berlin-Charlottenburg branch of the "Deutsche Kolonial-Gesellschaft" on March 24, 1926* (Berlin, 1929), 2, 3–4.

122 This is a point well-made by Kopper, *Hjalmar Schacht,* 295.

123 Schacht, *New Colonial Policy,* 7.

124 See also Kopper, *Hjalmar Schacht,* 296.

125 His definition of imperialism in the sentence quoted above represents "formal" imperialism in the form of direct political and territorial control. See Schacht, *New Colonial Policy,* 15. For the Hobson-Lenin debate, see J. A. Hobson, *Imperialism: A Study* (London, 1988); Vladimir Lenin, *Imperialism: Highest Stage of Capitalism* (Zurich, 1916), 2–10.

126 Schacht, *New Colonial Policy,* x, 1, 16.

127 Ibid., 7, 15.

128 See, for instance, Schacht, *End of Reparations,* 10.

129 Smith, *Ideological Origins of Nazi Imperialism,* 245–55.

130 Germany was allowed to join the League only in 1926.

131 Gustav Stresemann, *Vermächtinis* (Berlin, 1933), 2: 334–35, cited in Wolfe Schmokel, *Dream of Empire: German Colonialism, 1919–1945* (New Haven, Conn., 1964), 81.

132 Schmokel, *Dream of Empire,* 82.

133 Arthur Dix, *Weltkrise und Kolonialpolitik: Die Zukunft zweier erdteile* (Berlin, 1932).

134 John Gallagher and Ronald Robinson, "The Imperialism of Free Trade," *Economic History Review,* n.s., 6, no. 1 (1953): 1–15.

135 For two examples, see Panikos Panayi, *Weimar and Nazi Germany: Continuities and Discontinuities* (London, 2001), 297.

136 Hjalmar Schacht, *End of Reparations* (London, 1933), 33. Kindleberger makes the connection to Schacht's plea to Strong at the Fed for funding for long-term business investment only a year before. See Kindleberger, *World in Depression,* 27. The original reference can be traced to Lester Vernon Chandler, *Benjamin Strong* (Washington, D.C., 1958), 335.

137 Amos Simpson, *Hjalmar Schacht in Perspective* (The Hague, 1969), 31.

138 Schacht, *Autobiography,* 289–92.

139 *International Military Tribunals* (henceforth *IMT*), via Avalon Project, Yale University, *Volume* V, 131–32.

140 Succinctly, when an investor borrows capital to purchase an asset and the price behaves against its purchase, then the exchange is likely to ask for margin to cover

those loses. The situation is exacerbated in those cases in which there is no theoretical loss limit: if one buys a stock, the minimum price is 0, yet if one sells a borrowed stock, then there is no ceiling to the potential loss.

141 John Kenneth Galbraith, *The Great Crash, 1929* (Boston, 1961).

142 Cited from the original in Bopp, *Schacht,* 24.

143 Ibid.

144 See Feldman, *Great Disorder,* 425.

145 Adam Heinrich Müller, *Die Elemente der Staatskunst* (Berlin, 1809). For the reference, see Richard Werner, "Aspects of German Monetary Management and Development Economics and Their Reception in Japan," in *Economic Development and Social Change: Historical Roots and Modern Perspectives,* edited by George Stathakis and Gianni Vaggi (London, 2006), 127–29. It should be noted that List did not respect many of Müller's ideas, as pithily synthesized in, among others, Barkai, *Nazi Economics,* 56.

146 William Johnson Frazer, *The Central Banks: The International and European Directions* (Westport, Conn., 1994), 3.14, 215–16.

147 Schacht worked on a modified version of the real bills theory. See Harold James, "Die Reichsbank 1876 bis 1945," in *Fünfzig Jahre Deutsche Mark: Notenbank und Währung in Deutschland seit 1948,* edited by Deutsche Bundesbank (Munich, 1998), 29–89. Indeed Schacht remained supportive of this framework as late as 1964 during a lecture at the University of Wisconsin, which at least one scholar saw as a pillar of Bundesbank behavior in the postwar years, as well as its institutional skepticism of Keynesian monetary recommendations. See Frazer, *The Central Banks,* 216.

148 Werner, "Aspects of German Monetary Management," 128–29.

149 In Helmut Müller, *Die Zentralbank, eine Nebenregierung: Reichsbankpräsident Hjalmar Schacht als Politiker der Weimarer Republik* (Opladen, 1973).

150 Harold James, *The Interwar Depression in an International Context* (Frankfurt, 2002), especially 80.

151 For a non-German perspective, see Robert Donald, *The Polish Corridor and the Consequences* (London, 1929), 9–15.

152 Weitz, *Schacht,* 99; Schacht, *Autobiography,* especially chapter 32.

153 Interestingly the bank's official history ignores Schacht's role: http://www.bis.org/about/history.htm?l=2.

154 Schacht, *Autobiography,* chapter 32.

155 For the reparations agent in action, see Feldman, *Great Disorder,* 851–52.

156 "International: Snowden v. Europe," *Time,* August 19, 1929, 1.

157 Chernow, *House of Morgan,* 420–32.

158 *Time,* August 19, 1929, 3.

159 Schacht, *Autobiography,* 257.

160 For the Socialist's economic thought masterpiece, see Rudolf Hilferding, *Das Finanzkapital: Eine Studie über die jüngste Entwicklung des Kapitalismus* (Frankfurt, 1968).

161 For a diatribe against "politicians" and their debt habits, see Schacht, *End of Reparations,* especially chapter 8.

162 Bernt Engelmann, *Germany without Jews* (Toronto, 1984), 258.

163 Ben S. Bernanke, "The Macroeconomics of the Great Depression: A Comparative Approach," *Journal of Money, Credit and Banking* 27, no. 1 (1995): 1.

164 For the classic accounts, see Galbraith, *Great Crash;* Milton Friedman, *The Great Contraction, 1929–1933* (Princeton, N.J., 2008); Christina Romer, "What Ended the Great Depression?," *Journal of Economic History* 52, no. 4 (1992): 757–84.

165 Ben Bernanke and Kevin Carey, "Nominal Wage Stickiness and Aggregate Supply in the Great Depression," *Quarterly Journal of Economics* 111, no. 3 (1996): 853–83.

166 Barry Eichengreen and Jeffrey Sachs, *Exchange Rates and Economic Recovery in the 1930s,* National Bureau of Economic Research, May 1986; For a more general view, see Barry Eichengreen, *Golden Fetters* (New York, 1996), 22–23.

167 Harold James, *The End of Globalization* (Cambridge, Mass., 2001), 11.

168 Galbraith, *Great Crash,* 179.

169 Barry Eichengreen and Douglas A. Irwin, "The Slide to Protectionism in the Great Depression: Who Succumbed and Why?," *SSRN eLibrary,* July 2009.

170 The process fits squarely with the suggestive framework of economist Benjamin Friedman, who has underlined the effect of economic hardship on people's willingness to take on the often painful adjustments resulting from freer trade (or the continuation of open policies). See Benjamin Friedman, *The Moral Consequences of Economic Growth* (New York, 2005).

171 For the complications inherent in the new Young Plan mechanisms, see Albrecht Ritschl, *Deutschlands Krise und Konjunktur 1924–1934: Binnenkonjunktur, Auslandsverschuldung und Reparationsproblem zwischen Dawes-Plan und Transfersperre* (Berlin, 2002); Albrecht Ritschl, "Dancing on a Volcano: The Economic Recovery and the Collapse of Weimar Germany," in *The World Economy and National Economies in the Interwar Slump,* edited by Theo Balderston (New York, 2003), 105–42.

172 On the banks' capital positions, see Isabel Schnabel, "The German Twin Crisis of 1931," *Journal of Economic History* 64, no. 3 (2004): 822–71.

173 See Ritschl and Sarferaz, *Currency vs. Banking in the German Debt Crisis of 1931,* 1–3.

174 The "Borchardt controversy" has raged for over two decades on whether Brüning actually had any alternatives. Arguing that he did not are Knut Borchardt himself and the more data-focused Ritschl, in *Deutschlands Krise und Konjunktur.* See Knut Borchardt, *Wachstum, Krisen, Handlungsspielräume der Wirtschaftspolitik: Studien zur Wirtschaftsgeschichte des 19. und 20. Jahrhunderts,* Kritische Studien zur Geschichtswissenschaft (Göttingen, 1982), with whom I am inclined to agree. Against this position stands Hans Ulrich Wehler, *Deutsche Gesellschaftsgeschichte,* vol. 3 (Munich, 2003).

175 German big business also supported him. The point about the Social Democrats is well made in Henry Asby Turner, *German Big Business and the Rise of Hitler* (Oxford, 1985), chapter 4.

176 For a contemporary perspective abroad, see "Germany: Cabinet of Monocles," *Time,* June 13, 1932.

177 Wehler, *Deutsche Gesellschaftsgeschichte,* 3: 517–25.

178 The point is made by Harold James, *The Interwar Depression in an International Context* (Oldenbourg, 2002), 78.

179 *Akten der Reichskanzlei,* no, 502, October 2, 1931, 1782–83. Straumann claims the same argument was repeated at least once more, on October 27. See Tobias Straumann, "Rule Rather than Exception: Brüning's Fear of Devaluation in Comparative Perspective," *Journal of Contemporary History* 44, no. 4 (2009): 603–17, especially 607, n12. Straumann also convincingly argues that in Scandinavia as well as Switzerland the fear of inflation was paramount, as it was (per Borchardt) in Britain after the devaluation and (per Temin and Eichengreen) in France and the United States. See Barry Eichengreen and Peter Temin, "The Gold Standard and the Great Depression," *SSRN eLibrary,* June 1997. http://ssrn.com/abstract=226470.

180 Unsuccessful attempts to maintain overvalued pegs include Britain in 1992, Thailand in 1997, and Argentina in 2002. A rare successful attempt was Hong Kong in the aftermath of the Asian financial crisis to which Thailand and Malaysia succumbed.

181 It has been convincingly argued that wage rises in the late 1920s strained corporate profits.

182 For the best overviews, see Richard Overy, *The Nazi Economic Recovery* (New York, 1996), 12; Kindleberger, *The World in Depression,* 168–97. Straumann convincingly argues there was an anti-inflation consensus in the rest of the continent, including—following Borchardt's argument—post-devaluation Britain, where the Bank of England kept rates prohibitively high for six months after going off gold.

183 For the positive international views of Brüning, particularly in London government circles (and including the Bank of England), see William L. Patch, *Heinrich Bruning and the Dissolution of the Weimar Republic* (Cambridge, U.K., 2006), especially 161.

184 Charles P. Kindleberger, *Keynesianism vs. Monetarism: And Other Essays in Financial History* (Boston, 2006), 121.

185 See Luther Reichsbank reports in ibid., 122.

186 For one usage, see Wehler, *Deutsche Gesellschaftsgeschichte,* 3: 527.

187 Cited in Mühlen, *Der Zauberer,* 83.

188 "Schacht Shocks," *Time,* October 13, 1930. He also talked about changing the Constitution.

189 These were clearly politically motivated attacks since some of the generous discounting policies for collateral had been pioneered while he was at the helm of the Reichsbank. For the best treatment of this, see Bopp, *Schacht,* 26.

190 Ritschl and Sarferaz, *Currency vs. Banking in the German Debt Crisis of 1931,* 3–5.

191 Chapter 4 addresses the reparations moratorium that resulted from this crisis.

192 Hjalmar Schacht, *Das Ende Der Reparationen* (Oldenburg, 1931).

193 Indeed with Havenstein dead and Luther at the helm, Schacht was the only living former head of the Reichsbank, which gave him public respectability. For more details on his public activities, see Harold James, *The German Slump* (Oxford, 1986), especially 187.

194 Kopper does not develop why he considers Schacht's views on the current account implications of new colonial management as necessarily "erroneous." That same year, as we will see, Britain derived clear trading benefits from abandoning the gold standard along the Dominions and not alone. See Kopper, *Hjalmar Schacht,* 303.

195 See Schacht, *Autobiography,* chapter 38. Göring was deputy head of the Party. Thyssen would become a key industrial backer of the Nazis. See Shirer, *The Rise and Fall of the Third Reich,* 147. Early links with Thyssen and his personal funding of Strasser and Göring is described accurately in Richard Evans, *The Coming of the Third Reich* (London, 2003), 245.

196 See "Schacht Shocks" for a description. For more on the short-lived front, see Friedhart Knolle et al., *Harzburger Front von 1931* (Clausthal-Zellerfeld, 2007).

197 Turner, *Big Business and the Rise of Nazism,* especially 240–44.

198 Ibid. No mention seems to have been made about curtailing freedoms or destroying trade unions. This was a popular Hitlerian phrase, one that he would repeatedly use at the Reichstag once in power.

199 The source for this is an unpublished passage in the manuscript of Emil Hellferich's memoir. See Emil Hellferich, *1932–1946,* 14. For Schacht's later denials,

see testimony of July 21, 1947, in *IMT*, Vol. XII, 3943. Both cited from Turner, *Big Business and the Rise of Nazism,* especially 432, n64.

200 Hans Mommsen, *The Rise and Fall of Weimar Democracy* (Chapel Hill, N.C., 1998), 512.

201 Originally cited in Mühlen, *Der Zauberer,* viii.

4. "GIVE ME FOUR YEARS"

1 Hjalmar Horace Greeley Schacht, *Confessions of "the Old Wizard": Autobiography,* translated by Diana Pyke (Boston, 1956), 300, 303.

2 "Germany: Cabinet of Monocles," *Time,* June 13, 1932.

3 *Freiheit* is a loaded word, technically translatable to "liberty" and "freedom" yet heavy with historical connotation in German. The focus on rearmament from the beginning of the regime has been well established. See, for instance, United States Holocaust Memorial Museum Collection, Freiheit und Brot pin collection from the 1936 election.

4 For a contemporary view on the situation in state governments, see Emmanuel Hattemer, *Die rechtliche Beschränkung der Finanz- und Organisationsgewalt der deutschen Länder, insbesondere durch Sparmassnahmen des Reichs* (Bensheim, 1929).

5 Luther had been instrumental during Schacht's first appointment. By 1933 their personal relations were cordial but not friendly.

6 Adolf Hitler, *Hitler's Table Talk, 1941–1944: His Private Conversations,* edited by Hugh Trevor-Roper, translated by Gerhard L. Weinberg and Norman Cameron (New York, 1951; 2008), 432.

7 For the charter of the Reichsbank, see Reichsbank Files, BAL R2501, Bundesarchiv Licherfelde, Berlin (henceforth, German Archives).

8 I have found no supporting evidence for Hitler's claim in the archives, nor have others.

9 *Hitler's Table Talk,* 432.

10 Schacht, *Autobiography,* 303. See also 302 for negotiation, as told by Schacht.

11 Marc Hayford and Carl A. Pasurka, "The Political Economy of the Fordney-McCumber and Smoot-Hawley Tariff Acts," *Explorations in Economic History* 29, no. 1 (1992): 30–50.

12 Niall Ferguson, *The House of Rothschild: The World's Banker, 1849–1999* (London, 1999), 183.

13 Iago Gil Aguado, "The Creditanstalt Crisis of 1931 and the Failure of the Austro-German Customs Union Project," *Historical Journal* 44, no. 1 (2001): 199–221.

14 James's account of the system's interconnectedness is unparalleled: Harold James, *The German Slump: Politics and Economics, 1924–1936* (Oxford, 1986), especially "The Banking Crisis."

15 Isabel Schnabel, "The German Twin Crisis of 1931," *Journal of Economic History* 64, no. 3 (2004): 822–71.

16 Barry Eichengreen, *Golden Fetters: The Gold Standard and the Great Depression* (New York, 1996), 19, cf. 27. Eichengreen argues convincingly that the Reichsbank had few alternatives but that there was "more scope for monetary expansion" following controls.

17 Richhild Moessner and William Allen, "The Wave of Bank Failures Was Precipitated by a Run on the Viennese Bank Creditansalt," Working Paper No 333, Bank for International Settlements, Basel, December 2010.

18 Germany promised to keep up interest and amortization payments on foreign currency–denominated bonds. See "Finance Minister Dietrich Assures World

Germany Will Meet Private Debts," *New York Times,* January 1, 1932. See also Adam Klug, *The German Buybacks, 1932–1939: A Cure for Overhang?* (Princeton, N.J., 1993), 9, n6.

19 Frank Child, *The Theory and Practice of Exchange Control in Germany* (London, 1978); James, *German Slump,* especially 281–86.

20 Some interesting original sources are in Klug, *German Buybacks,* 9, nn8, 9, 10.

21 French intransigence was at least in part derived from the beneficial franc valuation against gold. See Kenneth Mouré, *The Gold Standard Illusion: France, the Bank of France, and the International Gold Standard, 1914–1939* (Oxford, 2002).

22 This gold "hoarding" has been well illustrated as a classic prisoner's dilemma. Douglas Irwin, *Did France Cause the Great Depression?,* Working Paper, NBER, September 2010.

23 William Janeway, "The Economic Policy of the Second Labour Government 1929–1931," PhD dissertation, University of Cambridge, 1971. I am grateful to Dr. Janeway for the manuscript.

24 *Economist,* September 26, 1931, 5.

25 Parliamentary Papers, *The House of Commons,* 1930–1931, Series 227, Vol. 1: 763.

26 See *Economist,* September 26, 1931, 4, for a somewhat surprised comment about the lack of panic, banking or otherwise, in London.

27 For the architecture, see Martin Daunton, "Britain and Globalization Since 1850: Creating a Global Order, 1850–1914," paper presented to the Royal Historical Society, November 26, 2006, 10–12.

28 Neil Forbes, *Doing Business with the Nazis* (London, 2000), 99.

29 *Economist,* May 20, 1933, 1061.

30 Carlos Diaz Alejandro, "Latin America in the 1930s," in *Latin America in the 1930s,* edited by R. Thorp (New York, 1984), 17–49.

31 Wallace Notestein, "Joseph Chamberlain and Tariff Reform," *Sewanee Review* 25, no. 1 (1917): 40–56.

32 J. M. Macaonnell, "After the Ottawa Conference," *Foreign Affairs* 11, no. 2 (1933): 331.

33 The United States opposed it. Ian Drummond, *The Floating Pound and the Sterling Area, 1931–1939* (Cambridge, U.K., 1981), 241–64.

34 For the internal debates in the United States, see Jean Edward Smith, *FDR* (New York, 2007), 328–30.

35 Roosevelt remained noncommittal toward the gold standard during the campaign; thereafter he was "agnostic" but sided against economic orthodoxy. Smith, *FDR,* especially 327.

36 For the finest proponents of hegemonic stability theory, see Charles Kindleberger, *The World in Depression* (Berkeley, 1986); and Barry Eichengreen, *Hegemonic Stability Theories of the International Monetary System,* CEPR Discussion Papers, September 1987.

37 See Patricia Clavin, *The Failure of Economic Diplomacy: Britain, Germany, France and the United States, 1931–36* (Basingstoke, U.K., 1996), especially chapter 4.

38 For the whole cast of characters, see Murray Newton Rothbard, *A History of Money and Banking in the United States: The Colonial Era to World War II* (New York, 2002), 464. For the instructive Fed notes, see http://fraser.stlouisfed.org /docs/meltzer/hardia0633.pdf.

39 Patricia Clavin, "'The Fetishes of So-Called International Bankers': Central Bank Co-operation for the World Economic Conference, 1932–3," *Contemporary European History* 1, no. 3 (1992): 281–311.

40 Clavin, *Failure of Economic Diplomacy,* 136.

41 Like other nationalists, Hugenberg agreed with Schacht's interpretation of the economic case for colonies. John Heineman, "Constantin Von Neurath and German Policy at the London Economic Conference of 1933: Backgrounds to the Resignation of Alfred Hugenberg," *Journal of Modern History* 41, no. 2 (1969): 160–88. See also Klaus Hildebrand, *The Foreign Policy of the Third Reich* (Berkeley, 1973), 34.

42 *Economist,* June 24, 1933, 1341.

43 Gerald Feldman, *Allianz and the German Insurance Business, 1933–1945* (Cambridge, U.K., 2001), especially chapter 2; Wolfe Schmokel, *Dream of Empire: German Colonialism 1919–1945* (New Haven, Conn., 1964), 90.

44 Heineman, *Constantin Von Neurath and German Policy,* 183.

45 By the end of June, Hugenberg's party was abolished.

46 Unsurprisingly his autobiography addresses only unemployment. Schacht, *Autobiography,* 198.

47 The best source for this remains Harold James, *The Reichsbank and Public Finance in Germany, 1924–1933* (Frankfurt, 1985).

48 *Hitler's Table Talk,* 433.

49 Cited in Adam Tooze, *Wages of Destruction* (London, 2006), 159.

50 Ibid., 54.

51 For cold war data, see Hamid Davoodi et al., "Military Spending, the Peace Dividend, and Fiscal Adjustment," *IMF Staff Papers* 48, no. 2 (2001): 290–316.

52 Hitler reprimanded von Blomberg for telling von Krosigk, who "did not need to know." The Finance Minister was never a central figure in the regime. See Hitler, *Table Talk,* 433.

53 *Trial of the Major War Criminals before the International Military Tribunal, Nuremberg, 14 November 1945–1 October 1946* (Nuremberg, 1947), via Avalon Project, Yale University (henceforth *IMT*), Schacht File, especially January 11, 1946, Morning Session, 131–35.

54 Richard Overy, *War and Economy in the Third Reich* (Oxford, 1994), chapter 2; David Landes, *Unbound Prometheus* (Cambridge, U.K., 1969), 440–46.

55 Schacht, *Autobiography,* 303.

56 For details on this complicated relationship, see Henry Turner, *German Big Business and the Rise of Hitler* (New York, 1985); Peter Hayes, *Industry and Ideology: IG Farben in the Nazi Era* (New York, 2001). For an overview, see Volker Berghahn, "German Big Business and the Quest for a European Economic Empire in the 20th Century," in *Quest for Economic Empire,* edited by Volker Berghahn (Providence, R.I., 1996).

57 Speech in Max Domarus, *Hitler: Speeches and Proclamations, 1932–1945: The Chronicle of a Dictatorship* (London, 1990), vol. 2, speech dated September 13, 1933.

58 Ibid., 1.

59 Schacht gives the figure of 90 percent unemployed in the construction industry, which seems overstated considering other sources. See Schacht, *Autobiography,* 302.

60 For a new take, see Nico Voigtlaender and Hans-Joachim Voth, *Highway to Hitler.* Working Paper. National Bureau of Economic Research, May 2014. http://www.nber.org/papers/w20150.

61 Fritz Todt, *Drei Jahre Arbeit,* 48, cited in Overy, *War and Economy,* 85.

62 First published in England in early 1936, only later in the year in German. In fact the idea of a multiplier of government spending belonged to Keynes's King's College colleague, Richard Kahn. See John Maynard Keynes, *The General Theory of Employment, Interest, and Money* (Basingstoke, U.K., 1936), especially book 3, chapter 10.

63 The complex line in question deserves a full reproduction to avoid all-too-common misinterpretations: "Trotzdem kann die Theorie der Produktion als Ganzes, die den Zweck des folgenden Buches bildet, viel leichter den Verhältnissen eines totalen Staates angepaßt werden als die Theorie der Erzeugung und Verteilung einer gegebenen, unter Bedingungen des freien Wettbewerbes und eines großen Maßes von laissez-faire erstellten Produktion." John Maynard Keynes, preface to *Allgemeine Theorie der Beschäftigung, Vorwort Zur Deutschen Ausgabe* (Berlin, 1936).

64 Albrecht Ritschl, *Deficit Spending in the Nazi Recovery, 1933–1938: A Critical Reassessment,* Institute for Empirical Research in Economics, University of Zurich, http://ideas.repec.org/p/zur/iewwpx/068.html.

65 The biggest advocate of this position, though also based on Ritschl's data, is Tooze, in *Wages of Destruction,* chapter 2.

66 See tables 2.1 and 2.2 in Overy, *War and Economy,* 70–71; Fritz Blaich, "Why Did the Pioneer Fall Behind?," in *The Economic and Social Effects of the Spread of Motor Vehicles,* edited by T. C. Barker (Basingstoke, U.K., 1987).

67 For a longer description, see Dan Silverman, *Hitler's Economy: Nazi Work Creation Programs, 1933–1936* (Cambridge, Mass., 1998).

68 Schacht later boasted about keeping rearmament a secret through Reichsbank maneuvers. For an example of a speech during the Sudetenland crisis, see *IMT,* Vol. II, chapter 16, Part 2, EC-369.

69 The issue was discussed at length at Nuremberg. See *IMT,* EC-436 and 3728-PS, specifically.

70 This point has been well made by both Barkai and James: Avraham Barkai, *Das Wirtschaftssystem des Nationalsozialismus* (Frankfurt, 1988), especially 156–57; James, *German Slump,* 377.

71 See Schacht, *Autobiography,* 317–18 for a description of the system. Also in Edward Homze, *Arming the Luftwaffe* (London, 1976), 183. See Schacht, *Autobiography,* 305.

72 *IMT,* EC-436.

73 Luis Jácome et al., "Central Bank Credit to the Government: What Can We Learn from International Practices?," IMF Working Paper, 2012.

74 For the theory on how Mefo bills would be redeemed, see Barkai, *Wirtschaftssystem des Nationalsozialismus,* 157; Kindleberger, *World in Depression,* 178.

75 Günther Frede and Wilhelm Treue, *Wirtschaft und Politik, 1933–1945* (Braunschweig, 1953), especially 13. Notwithstanding the "polycratic" nature of Hitler's regime, Schacht assumed an increasing share of economic power

76 See Schacht, *Autobiography,* 305, for his own calculations, largely consistent with Barkai. See also Richard Overy, *The Nazi Economic Recovery, 1932–1938* (New York, 1996), 7–9; Charles Maier, *In Search of Stability* (Cambridge, U.K., 1987), especially 70–90.

77 See BAL R2501 6440, and 6501, respectively, German Archives. The former is also cited in Tooze, *Wages of Destruction,* 43.

78 James, *German Slump,* 406.

79 For an interesting take on labor relations, see Ronald Smelser, *Robert Ley, Hitler's Labor Front Leader* (Oxford, 1988).

80 Gerald Feldman, *The Great Disorder: Politics, Economics, and Society in the German Inflation, 1914–1924* (Oxford, 1997), especially chapter 13.

81 The regime had refused to rescue local municipalities, leading many to default.

82 The argument is made in both Stephen Schuker, *The End of French Predominance in Europe* (Chapel Hill, N.C., 1976) and Nicholas Rostow, *Anglo-French Relations* (London, 1984).

83 In James, *German Slump*, especially 427, the author doubts the effectiveness of Schacht's tactics, but newer econometric analyses lend credence to the 1930s view that Germany used debt buybacks selectively to boost its exports. Klug, *German Buybacks*, especially 4–5.

84 *Economist*, May 20, 1933, 1061–62.

85 See Schacht, *Autobiography*, 314. It was widely known to contemporaries; for a critical view, see Norbert Muhlen, *Der Zauberer: Leben und Anleihen des Dr. Hjalmar Horace Greeley Schacht* (Zurich, 1938), 98–102.

86 On this issue he was borrowing Keynes's by-then famous formulation.

87 An example of this is the connection between Germany's default and Brazil's a few years later.

88 Muhlen, *Der Zauberer*, 34–37.

89 BAL R2501 6602, German Archives. Also in Tooze, *Wages of Destruction*, 52.

90 He was only partially justified. For data, see *Economist*, June 10, 1933, 1230–32.

91 Kindleberger, *World in Depression*, 260–63; Eichengreen, *Golden Fetters*, especially chapter 10.

92 Niall Ferguson, *Paper and Iron: Hamburg Business and German Politics in the Era of Inflation, 1897–1927* (Cambridge, U.K., 1995), especially 463–65.

93 Klug, *German Buybacks*, 2–3.

94 See Karl Bopp, *Hjalmar Schacht: Central Banker* (Columbia, Mo., 1939), 25–27, for a more detailed description.

95 For the full historical spread see Klug, *German Buybacks*, table 2.

96 James, *German Slump*, 433.

97 James Marshall-Cornwall et al., eds., *Documents on German Foreign Policy 1918–1945, from the Archives of the German Foreign Ministry* (Washington, D.C., 1950) (henceforth, *German Documents*), Series C, 1937–1945, vol. 2, Doc. 182, "Meeting of the Economic Policy Committee." See also Gerhard Weinberg, *The Foreign Policy of Hitler's Germany* (Atlantic Highlands, N.J, 1994), 44.

98 Klug, *German Buybacks*, especially 54–55. Buybacks were perceived to be successful at the time, with Schacht getting credit. These statistical findings contradict the effects of an overly skeptical debt buyback model in Jeremy Bulow and Kenneth Rogoff, "Sovereign Debt Repurchases: No Cure for Overhang," *Quarterly Journal of Economics* 106, no. 4 (1991): 1219–35. Klug believes buybacks served to reduce debt but not to promote exports.

99 BAK R4311/ 787, from a telegram dated June 23, 1934, cited in Klug, *German Buybacks*, 44.

100 Adolf Hitler and Henry Picker, *Tischgespräche im Führerhauptquartier 1941–1942* (Munich, 1968), 332.

101 Klug, *German Buybacks*, 23, misunderstands that the central bank was ultimately responsible for the policy, not the Economics Ministry.

102 For another take, see Michael Ebi, *Export um Jeden Preis: Die Deutsche Exportförderung von 1932–1938* (Stuttgart, 2004), 34–61.

103 *Economist*, June 10, 1933, 1230–32.

104 For a summary, see Christopher Kopper, *Hjalmar Schacht: Aufstieg und Fall von Hitlers mächtistem Bankier* (Munich, 2006), 192.

105 *Economist*, June 10, 1933, 1230–32.

106 For an essential synthesis, see Berghahn, "German Big Business," 4–37.

107 It may have been the Lutheran rhetoric that caught the employee's attention, but the entire passage is underlined in red in the Reichsbank's press archives. Werner Daitz, "Grundsätze der deutschen Außenhandelspolitik," *Berliner Börsen-Courier,* June 4, 1933, Reichsbank Pressestelle Archives, R 2501/2596, *Bundesarchiv Lichterfelde,* Berlin.

108 For a good study of Darré and Backe's agricultural policies, see Tooze, *Wages of Destruction,* 166–202.

109 Indeed, popularized "Blut und Boden" as an expression in Richard Walther Darré, *Neuadel aus Blut und Boden* (Berlin, 1930; 1941).

110 Herbert Backe, *Das Ende des Liberalismus in der Wirtschaft* (Berlin, 1938); Richard Walther Darré, *Um Blut und Boden: Reden und Aufsätze* (Munich, 1930).

111 The entire collection is archived in German Archives, R 2501/2596.

112 "Germany: Towards Autarky," *Economist,* September 26, 1936.

113 For a contemporary overview of the German economy with references to the synthetic programs, see "Germany: Wehrwirtschaft," *Time,* May 22, 1939.

114 German Archives, R 2501/2596, 187. The speech was published in *Germania,* March 17, 1934.

115 *IMT* files are full of such stories. See, for instance, *IMT,* Vol. II, chapter XVI.

116 Camille Loutre, *Gazette de Lausanne,* April 27, 1934. The original reads, "Un pays, grand transformateur de matières permières en produits fabriqués et suroutillé comme tel, doit-il, comme il le fait, pratiquer un protectionnisme agraire intégral?"

117 This characterization is inextricably associated with Bracher. See Karl Dietrich Bracher, *Adolf Hitler* (Bern, 1964).

118 German Archives, R43-II/324b, 15.

119 This was run under German Archives, Wirtschaftsführer Keßler. R43-II/324b, 1.

120 See Feldman, *Allianz and the German Insurance Business,* 2.

121 Ian Kershaw, *Hitler: Hubris* (New York, 1999), especially 580.

122 Tooze agrees, in *Wages of Destruction,* 78. Neither Kershaw nor Overy nor James disagree.

123 Technically, upon Hindenburg's death the office was supposed to be transferred to the president of the Reich's Supreme Court, pending new elections. A referendum two weeks later rubber-stamped the decision. For more, see Richard Evans, *The Third Reich in Power* (London, 2006), 213.

124 Von Krosigk had been appointed by the disgraced von Papen in 1932 and had remained in power under Chancellor Schleicher and then Hitler. Along with Hitler and Frick, he was the longest-serving Cabinet member in Nazi Germany. He was later tried and convicted in the Ministries' Trial. Decades later he produced an interesting memoir: Lutz Schwerin von Krosigk, *Memoiren* (Stuttgart, 1977).

125 Citation from Tooze, *Wages of Destruction,* 85.

126 "Hindenburg's Career," *Financial Times,* August 3, 1934, 9.

127 "German Loans Better," *Financial Times,* August 3, 1934, 1.

128 This was a position so stubbornly opposed that he eventually had to backtrack.

129 "Schacht Disavows Pledges on Loans," *New York Times,* August 26, 1934, 1 and inserts.

130 Ibid.

131 Hjalmar Horace Greely Schacht, *The Magic of Money* (London, 1967), 208–11.

132 This strategy further undermined the role of Finance Minister von Krosigk, usual collateral damage of Schacht's creeping power. Kopper describes this process in detail in *Schacht,* especially chapter 7.

133 For an example of Schacht's authoritarianism in negotiations involving the USSR, see Edward E. Ericson, *Feeding the German Eagle: Soviet Economic Aid to Nazi Germany, 1933–1941* (Westport, Conn., 1999), especially 18–19.

134 "Ueberwachungsstellen." This is a point made in Tooze's salient early study: Adam Tooze, *Statistics and the German State, 1900–1945* (Cambridge, U.K., 2001).

135 Philip Newman, "Key German Cartels under the Nazi Regime," *Quarterly Journal of Economics* 62, no. 4 (1948): 576–95.

136 Hayes, *Industry and Ideology,* especially chapters 4–5. Hayes makes the well-researched argument that Schacht gave businesses, in particular conglomerates like IG Farben, far more say in the way cartels were run.

137 Tooze, *Statistics and the German State,* 170–75.

138 See Schacht, *Autobiography,* 328. Schacht justified himself nonetheless: "Unfortunately, this Plan involved the creation of an extensive control machinery and [a] whole lot of officials, for which I expressed my deep regret."

139 For data, see table 6 in Overy, *The Nazi Economic Recovery,* 27.

140 Ibid.

141 German Archives, BAL 2501 2210.

142 For the British perception of relative victory, see Neil Forbes, *Doing Business with the Nazis* (London, 2000), especially 11.

143 Bernd Jürgen Wendt, *Economic Appeasement: Handel und finanz in der Britischen Deutschland-Politik 1933–1939* (Düsseldorf, 1971).

144 Kopper, *Schacht,* especially 294–305.

145 Ibid., 303.

146 "The Balkans: Schacht for Peace," *Time,* June 29, 1936.

147 Even Kopper is guilty of this omission. See Kopper, *Schacht,* especially 294–305.

148 Fine research on the sale attempt can be found in Christian Leitz, "Nazi Germany and the Luso-Hispanic World," *Contemporary European History* 12, no. 2 (2003): 183–96.

149 Stanley Hilton, *Brazil and the Great Powers, 1930–1939* (Austin, Texas, 1975), 71–85. Hull was then at work in the 1934 Trade Agreements: Kenneth Dam, *Cordell Hull, the Reciprocal Trade Agreement Act, and the WTO,* Brookings Institution, October 2004, 1–2.

150 P. Lucius, *Je Suis Partout,* Paris, December 15, 1937, 4. This was widely cited in the American press. See *Milwaukee Journal,* December 18, 1937, 1.

151 Schacht, *Autobiography,* 330–31.

152 "The Balkans: Schacht for Peace," *Time,* June 29, 1936.

153 Stephen Large, *Shōwa Japan: Political, Economic and Social History, 1926–1989* (London, 1998), especially 359–60.

154 As for the assertion regarding the "respectable years," see W. E. Hart (pseudonym), *Hitler's Generals* (London, 1944), especially 201–10; Weinberg, *The Foreign Policy of Hitler's Germany.* On the deficit, see Ritschl, *Deficit Spending in the Nazi Recovery.*

155 Heinz Guderian, *Die panzerwaffe* (Stuttgart, 1937).

156 W. E. Hart, *Hitler's Generals* (London, 1944), 208.

157 It was a point not lost to contemporaries. See "Germany: Wehrwirtschaft," *Time,* May 22, 1939, 3.

158 Cited in James, *The Reichsbank and Public Finance in Germany,* 26.

159 See discussion of his resignation in 1929 in Schacht, *Autobiography,* 257.

160 Tooze acknowledges Schacht's power, but to a lesser extent than other historians of the period. See Barkai, *Das Wirtschaftssystem Des Nationalsozialismus,* chapter 5.

161 Von Epp was a devoted Bavarian who had converted to Nazism and then led an organization familiar with Schacht's thinking, the Colonial Association.

162 German Archives, R 43-I/627, 16–23.

163 Ibid.

164 There is little evidence other than an *ex post* ahistorical reading of post-1937 documents to suggest "important imperialists like Schacht believe that [Hitler] was serious about expansion by promoting a highly visible planning effort [in the colonial sphere]." See Woodruff Smith, *The Ideological Origins of Nazi Imperialism* (New York, 1986), 248.

165 German Archives, NS 26/1294.

166 "Vernünftige Koloniallösung liegt in aller Interesse: Deutschland wünscht keine vollständige Autarkie," *Deutsche Allgemeine Zeitung,* December 16, 1936.

167 Tooze, *Wages of Destruction,* 207.

168 Homze, *Luftwaffe,* 74.

169 For perhaps one of the most famous pictures of World War II aviation, featuring Milch and his men, see German Archives, BA 101I-760–0165N-26.

170 Data in Homze, *Luftwaffe,* 74–75.

171 The company had employed Milch before he became the first director of Lufthansa. Detlef Siegfried, *Der Fliegerblick: Intellektuelle, Radikalismus und Flugzeugproduktion bei Junkers 1914 bis 1934* (Dietz, 2001), especially 287–88; Samuel W. Mitcham Jr., *Eagles of the Third Reich: Men of the Luftwaffe in World War II* (Boston, 2007). For a history of the Luftwaffe's most famous transporter, key to Franco's early war effort in Spain, see Morten Jessen, *The Junkers Ju 52: The Luftwaffe's Workhorse* (London, 2002).

172 Michael Payne, *Messerschmitt Bf 109 in the West* (London, 1998).

5. DAWN OF INTERVENTION

1 See Leonard Mosley, *The Reich Marshal: A Biography of Hermann Göring* (New York, 1974), 212. For the point more generally, see John Keegan, *The Mask of Command* (New York, 1988), 182.

2 Albert Speer, *Inside the Third Reich* (New York, 1971), 153; Hjalmar Schacht, *Account Settled* (London, 1949), 82.

3 For more on the Oberkommando der Wehrmacht (OKW) organization, see *Die berichte des Oberkommandos der Wehrmacht, 1939–1945* (Munich, 1983).

4 Hitler had declared war on the United States, which had originally declared war only on Japan. Ian Kershaw, *Hitler: 1936–1945 Nemesis* (London, 2006), 444.

5 On the "original theory" behind *Führerprinzip,* see Hans Frank, *Das Führerprinzip in der Verwaltung* (Krakau, 1944).

6 Walter Görlitz, "Keitel, Jodl and Warlimont," in *Hitler's Generals,* edited by Correlli Barnett (London, 1989).

7 Adolf Hitler, *Hitlers Tischgespräche im Führerhauptquartier* (Stuttgart, 1976); Adolf Hitler, *Hitler's Table Talk, 1941–1944: His Private Conversations,* edited by Hugh Trevor-Roper, translated by Gerhard Weinberg and Norman Cameron (New York, 1973), 567.

8 See Adolf Hitler, *Mein Kampf* (Munich, 1924), especially chapter 10.

9 Hitler, *Table Talk,* 567n.

10 Ibid.

11 Ibid., 568–69. Picker, the series' first publisher, personally took the notes that night, which quote Keitel directly and Hewel indirectly.

12 Norman Herz, *Operation Alacrity* (Annapolis, Md., 2004), 36–37; Stanley Payne, *Franco and Hitler: Spain, Germany, and World War II* (New Haven, Conn., 2008), especially 271–73.

13 Angel Viñas, *Franco, Hitler y el estallido de la Guerra Civil* (Madrid, 2001), 153–57.

14 Though some sources disagree on whether Canaris was there, reliable accounts put him at the event.

15 Hitler, *Table Talk,* 568. Hitler also claimed Spain would fall back into civil war; hence the reference to a "first one."

16 One of the finest historians of the war arrives at the same conclusion in his Republican trilogy. Angel Viñas, *La soledad de la República* (Barcelona, 2006).

17 Hitler, *Table Talk,* 568. For the finest study of the Falange, see Stanley Payne, *Falange: A History of Spanish Fascism* (Stanford, 1961).

18 Hitler, *Table Talk,* 569.

19 With doctors and mechanics, the number ascends to almost sixteen thousand. See Manfred Merkes, *Die deutsche Politik Gegenüber dem spanischen Bürgerkrieg, 1936–1939* (Bonn, 1961); Hugh Thomas, *The Spanish Civil War* (New York, 2001), appendix 3, 937, who largely takes from Merkes's West German sources.

20 For Francoist figures, see Jesús Salas Larrazábal, *Intervención extranjera en la Guerra de España* (Madrid, 1974). That is Thomas's main source in *Spanish Civil War,* appendix 3, 973. The figures are consistent with Edward Homze, *Arming the Luftwaffe* (Lincoln, Neb., 1976), especially vi.

21 Gerald Howson, *Arms for Spain* (London, 1998), 7–8.

22 For data on production, see Adam Tooze, *The Wages of Destruction* (London, 2006), appendix A4.

23 James Marshall-Cornwall et al., eds., *Documents on German Foreign Policy 1918–1945, from the Archives of the German Foreign Ministry,* Series D, 1937–1945, vol. 3: *Germany and the Spanish Civil War 1936–1939* (Washington, D.C., 1950) (henceforth, *German Documents*), Doc. 2, n2. An internal Nazi Party "recommendation for decorations" from the Auslandorganisation (Foreign Party Office) that outlines the event states, "The first interview with the Führer, on which occasion [Franco's] letter was delivered, took place in Bayreuth in the late evening of the same day [July 25], after the Führer's return from the theatre [*Siegfried*]. Immediately thereafter the Führer summoned Field Marshal Göring, the then War Minister Colonel General von Blomberg, and an admiral who was present in Bayreuth [presumably Canaris]."

24 Viñas's research on this is invaluable. See Angel Viñas and Carlos Collado Seidel, "Franco's Request to the Third Reich for Military Assistance," *Contemporary European History* 11, no. 2 (2002): 191–210.

25 See Viñas, *Franco, Hitler,* 231.

26 Glyn Stone, "Yvon Delbos and Anthony Eden: Anglo-French Cooperation, 1936–38," in *Anglo-French Relations Since the Late Eighteenth Century* (Abington, U.K., 2009).

27 International Military Tribunal, Avalon Project, Yale University, Vol. IX, 281.

28 Whealey claims Hitler gave Göring explicit economic orders, which would fit the time frame of Hitler's thinking. Yet there is no quoted source. See Robert Whealey, *Hitler and Spain: The Nazi Role in the Spanish Civil War, 1936–1939* (Lexington, Ky., 1989), 72–74. Similarly the statement about Göring's "top eco-

nomic" status in the regime is not precise (72). For Göring's initial caution, see Stefan Martens, *Hermann Göring* (Paderborn, 1985), 65–66.

29 For this perspective, see Hans-Henning Abendroth, *Hitler in Der Spanischen Arena* (Nuremberg, 1970), especially 35–36. Abendroth later published a book with interviews featuring Bernhardt, yet we know the latter was prone to embellish his role. For the source, see Hans-Henning Abendroth, *Mittelsmann Zwischen Franco Und Hitler: Johannes Bernhardt Erinnert 1936* (Marktheidenfeld, 1978).

30 *German Documents*, Docs. 9, 10, and 11. For a detailed discussion on von Blomberg, Harold Deutsch, C. *Hitler and His Generals; the Hidden Crisis, January–June 1938* (Minneapolis, 1974), 132–33.

31 *German Documents*, Doc. 11, p. 11.

32 Ibid.

33 Though differently than Göring, Bernhardt also worked on rewriting the past after World War II. This was confirmed in conversation with Angel Viñas in 2010, in correspondence with the author, based on his conversations with Bernhardt.

34 *German Documents*, editor's note, 2, n2, for *Auslandorganisation* document.

35 As with other decisions by Hitler, the historiographic debate is rich with regard to motivation. A key debate is between proponents of the "programmatic" strategy overarching Hitler's decisions or the "polycratic" nature of Nazi power. The former owes much to the work of Hugh Trevor-Roper and Andreas Hillbruger, while the latter view has been popularized by Hans Mommsen, Martin Broszat, and Zygmut Baumann. For the debate, see Eberhard Jaeckel, *Hitler in History* (London, 2000), and, for a Spanish view, Rafael García Pérez, *Franquismo y Tercer Reich* (Madrid, 1994), 56.

36 Paul Preston, *The Coming of the Spanish Civil War* (London, 1994), 134.

37 Though he does not explore the counterfactual, see Thomas, *Spanish Civil War,* 923–28.

38 Michael Alpert, *La guerra civil española en el mar* (Barcelona, 2008), especially 348–51.

39 According to Abendroth, in fact, Milch had been summoned to Bayreuth for planning, along with a maritime expert to coordinate shipments. See also David Irving, *The Rise and Fall of the Luftwaffe: The Life of Luftwaffe Marshall Erhard Milch* (London, 1973), 48.

40 For a reproduction of the original document setting up HISMA, see Viñas, *La Alemania Nazi,* 442.

41 See Archivos del Ministerio de Relaciones Exteriores y Cooperación, Archivo de Guerra de Burgos (henceforth Archivos Españoles), Box (b.) 2187, File 2–3, *Reporte de la Hisma para liquidación,* Madrid, May 28, 1939, signed by Bernhardt. Angel Viñas, *Política Comercial Exterior En España (1931–1975)* (Madrid, 1979), 146.

42 ROWAK would survive until the end of the Nazi regime. S Christian Leitz, *Economic Relations Between Nazi Germany and Franco's Spain: 1936–1945* (New York, 1998), 18–19.

43 *German Documents,* Doc. 101, 113–14, by Hermann Sabath at the Foreign Ministry Economic Office.

44 This is consistent with conclusions from Viñas to Whealey and even García Perez.

45 John Coverdale, *Italian Intervention in the Spanish Civil War* (Princeton, N.J., 1975), 75.

46 *German Documents,* Doc. 33. At the time reports from the Paris Embassy pointed to an average of a hundred men being shipped to Spain per day, along with mili-

tary supplies, which is likely to have influenced early fascist escalation. Italian-German military discussions had been in the ascent since the Ethiopian War.

47 Galeazzo Ciano, *Ciano's Diplomatic Papers* (London, 1948), 60. Next to the Duomo in Milan, Mussolini spoke of an "axis round which all European states which are animated by a desire for collaboration and peace can revolve."

48 Abendroth, *Hitler in der Spanischen arena,* 41.

49 For primary evidence of their duplicitous contacts with the British, see *Dez Anos De Política Externa (1936–1947): A Nação Portuguesa e a Segunda Guerra Mundial* (Lisbon, 1961), vol. 3, Doc. 20 (henceforth *Portuguese Documents*).

50 Payne gets the dates wrong but makes the point that the airlift began with small Spanish aircraft on July 20, when the blockade worked. Stanley Payne, *The Franco Regime: 1936–1975* (Madison, Wisc., 1987), especially 123–24 and n9.

51 Abendroth, *Hitler in der Spanischen arena,* 53; Whealey, *Hitler and Spain,* 7.

52 The issue of control would create many a battle. Burgos Files, Box 812, and underneath, Archivos Españoles.

53 See Burgos Files, Box 2141, Archivos Españoles, for evidence of supply receipts.

54 For detailed analysis on internal finances, see Pablo Martín Aceña and Elena Martínez Ruiz, eds., *La Economía de la Guerra Civil* (Madrid, 2006).

55 Law 15 of August 19, 1936, in *Bandos y órdenes dictadas por el Excmo. Sr. D. Gonzalo Queipo del Llano y Sierra (18.7.36—19.2.37)* (Sevilla, 1937), reproduced in Viñas, *Política comercial exterior,* 144.

56 They did not yet have their own currency. Aceña and Martínez Ruiz, *La Economía de la Guerra Civil.*

57 For the latest data and estimations, see Pablo Martin-Acena, Elena Martinez Ruiz, and Maria A. Pons Brias, "War and Economics: Spanish Civil War Finances Revisited," *University Library of Munich, Germany, MPRA Paper,* no. 22833 (2010).

58 See Viñas, *Política comercial exterior,* 145, for the reproduced junta decrees.

59 For the social uprising in Republican territory in the first few months of the war and its detrimental effect on the Republican economy, see Elena Martínez Ruiz, "Las relaciones económicas internacionales: Guerra, política, negocios," in Aceña and Martínez Ruiz, *La Economía de la Guerra Civil.*

60 For March's role, see Mercedes Cabrera, *Juan March (1880–1962)* (Madrid, 2011), especially 273–75; Ángel Viñas, "La connivencia fascista," in *Los Mitos del 18 De Julio* (Barcelona, 2013).

61 This fits Viñas's conclusions in Viñas, *Política comercial exterior,* 145.

62 For a salient description with particular attention to strategic timing, see Preston, *The Coming of the Spanish Civil War,* especially chapter 12.

63 *El Socialista,* July 25, 1936. See also Cabrera, *Juan March,* 273.

64 This is the main conclusion of the latest documentary revelations on Italian "connivance" in the coup.

65 The "all Popular Front" government in Spain included Communists, who never joined the government in Paris.

66 The request came from the Republican prime minister, and the telegram from Spain confirming the issue with Berlin came on August 1. See *German Documents,* Doc. 21.

67 The reply is included in *German Documents,* Doc. 22.

68 This relationship has been successfully covered by the historiography, in particular through the work of Thomas, Preston, and Radosh. But Viñas's study, *La Soledad de la República* (Barcelona, 2006), stands out for its breadth and quality.

69 See *German Documents,* Doc. 50, 50–52.

70 Von Neurath penned a "strictly confidential memorandum" on August 24, stating, "It seemed to me that it would be well for us to at least make known our desire to cooperate on the neutrality question before this [conscription] announcement." *German Documents*, Doc. 55, 56–57. It was also necessary to agree to the NIC due to the awkward diplomatic incident in which Republicans captured a German plane flown by Franco's men. This worried Dieckhoff; see *German Documents*, Doc. 48.

71 Abendroth, *Hitler in der Spanischen arena*, 52–53.

72 See *German Documents*, Doc. 57, 58–59. A similar complaint was reported on August 29; see *German Documents*, Doc. 62, 61.

73 See *German Documents*, Doc. 58, 59.

74 Glyn Stone, *Spain, Portugal and the Great Powers, 1931–1941* (London, 2005), 132.

75 British "official" perspectives on Franco were positive during the war, which contributed to an all-too-benign view. See Enrique Moradiellos, "The Gentle General: The Official British Perception of General Franco during the Spanish Civil War," in *The Republic Besieged: Civil War in Spain 1936–1939,* edited by Paul Preston and Ann L. Mackenzie (Edinburgh, 1996).

76 The consulted Portuguese files confirm this. See *Portuguese Documents*, vol. 3.

77 The British insights and flow are detailed in Foreign Office, National Archives, Kew (henceforth FO), 371/20584 W15431/9549/41 and FO 371/20588 W18100/9549/41. Stone notes the reports were considered accurate at the Foreign Office. See Glyn Stone, *The Oldest Ally: Britain and the Portuguese Connection, 1936–1941* (London, 1994), 10.

78 Aceña et al. convincingly argue that these initial Republican defeats, in large part due to the effectiveness of Franco's men with Italian and German involvement, handicapped the Republic for the remainder of the conflict. See Aceña et al., *War and Economics*, 1, 25.

79 Though Leitz cites the name as Aurelio Fernández Aguilar from a Du Moulin letter of August 3, 1936, the Messerschmidt piece refers to the name above. He may have used both.

80 This is one of the documentary sources missed by most analyses of the period, including García Perez's exhaustive work, *Franquismo y Tercer Reich.*

81 Soviet Chatos and Moscas would begin changing that balance of aerial power a few weeks later.

82 See *German Documents*, Doc. 80, enclosure, 85–89, 85, n2.

83 *German Documents*, Doc. 80, 3.

84 See *German Documents*, Doc. 83, 91. The War Ministry requested a call-in for the report on September 21, 1936, and classified it as "highly confidential." Yet no history heretofore mentions it.

85 *German Documents*, Doc. 83, 91, n2, emphasis in the original.

86 *German Documents*, Doc. 98, 99, 100, 101, 106–11.

87 See *German Documents*, Doc. 101, 112.

88 Michael Mueller, *Canaris: The Life and Death of Hitler's Spymaster* (London, 2007), 105, 106.

89 The best discussion for this can be found in Garcia Perez, *Franquismo y Tercer Reich,* 61–62; Leitz, *Economic Relations,* 25–26.

90 In the wake of von Blomberg's ungracious Cabinet exit, it would fall on Warlimont to pen the memorandum that created OKW, effectively placing all military decisions under Hitler's purview. For all the organizational parlance, the creation of the Condor Legion and the OKW itself were not that dissimilar. They were

part of the same process of engulfment of traditional military strategies in Hitler's personal sphere of control.

91 See Raúl Arias Ramos, *La Legión Cóndor en la Guerra Civil* (Madrid, 2003); original documents in Karl Ries, *Legion Condor, 1936–1939: Eine illustrierte Dokumentation* (Mainz, 1980).

92 *German Documents,* Doc. 392 and 394 refer to the protocols signed in 1937.

93 *German Documents,* Doc. 101, 114.

94 Ibid.

95 This would be set in stone in the commercial agreements of 1937, a total of four documents. *Colección De Tratados Internacionales Suscritos Por España* (Madrid, 1977), vol. 6, part 1, 251–54.

96 Abendroth, *Hitler in der Spanischen arena,* 61.

97 Finding these must be credited to Charles E. Harvey, "Politics and Pyrites during the Spanish Civil War," *Economic History Review,* n.s., 31, no. 1 (1978): 89–104, see 92–93.

98 CAB 24268 C.P. 80 (37), cited in Harvey, "Politics and Pyrites," 93.

99 FO 371 22634, cited in Harvey, "Politics and Pyrites," 93.

100 García Perez notes the "inability to go beyond hegemonic ambitions," but it is hard to see where the German pressure did not achieve its objectives, particularly focused on the economic sphere after the failed advance to Madrid. See García Perez, *Franquismo y Tercer Reich,* 71. For the best definition of informal empire—rooted of course in the British experience—see John Gallagher and Ronald Robinson, "The Imperialism of Free Trade," *Economic History Review,* n.s., 6, no. 1 (1953): 1–15.

101 For more on the chronology, see Thomas, *Spanish Civil War,* 412.

102 The German Foreign Ministry declined to send an economic legation to Spain when requested by Francisco Agramonte, a former representative of the Republic. Whealey reads this as an issue of legalism from von Neurath's ministry, as does García Perez, yet the outcome did support HISMA-ROWAK. German Foreign Ministry, 629251985–86, U.S. National Archives, cited in Whealey, *Hitler and Spain,* 70, 192, n30.

103 For the best on war tactics, see Gabriel Cardona, *Historia Militar de una Guerra Civil* (Barcelona, 2006). For the foreign role, see the classic Jesús Salas Larrazábal, *Intervención Extranjera en la Guerra De España* (Madrid, 1974).

104 A former military advisor in Argentina and also head of a Freikorps division, Faupel was German representative to the National government, technically in Madrid, but since Franco had failed to conquer it, Salamanca. He was made ambassador in February 1937.

105 *German Documents,* Doc. 132, 142–43.

106 Enge is cited in the document (ibid.).

107 Abendroth, *Hitler in der spanischen Arena,* 124. Leitz has pushed Göring's role in materializing this decision.

108 Whealey makes this point in *Hitler and Spain,* 75.

109 Chief among those investments was of course Rio Tinto, Orconera, and Tharsis. See García Pérez, *Franquismo y Tercer Reich,* 61–62, for a Spanish view of the economic structure.

110 The quantification is in Robert H. Whealey, "Economic Influence of the Great Powers in the Spanish Civil War: From the Popular Front to the Second World War," *International History Review* 5, no. 2 (1983): 229–54, especially 231.

111 For a good overview of the contradictions, see Douglas Little, *Malevolent Neutrality: The United States, Great Britain, and the Origins of the Spanish Civil War* (Ithaca, N.Y., 1985).

112 Harvey, "Politics and Pyrites."

113 Though it does not follow a strict chronological order, there is a good overview of all projects in García Perez, *Franquismo y Tercer Reich,* 71–74.

114 Also known as tungsten, chemical symbol W and atomic number 74. I will keep referring to it as "wolfram."

115 Schacht had many, often violent disagreements with Minister Darré. For more on Darré and his deputy, Herbert Backe, see Adam Tooze, *Wages of Destruction: The Making and Breaking of the Nazi Economy* (London, 2006), especially 166–72.

116 Darré's father had been an active agent of Kaiserreich *Weltpolitik* as an import-export merchant in Buenos Aires, where he was born. For more on his racialist views, see for instance Richard Walther Darré, *Das Bauerntum Als Lebensquell Der Nordischen Rasse* (Munich, 1938).

117 For trade elsewhere, see Christian Leitz, "Nazi Germany and the Luso-Hispanic World," *Contemporary European History* 12, no. 2 (2003): 183–96.

118 *German Documents,* Doc. 163, 179.

119 Ibid.

120 Whealey, *Hitler and Spain,* 76.

6. THE PRECIPICE

1 Hjalmar Horace Greeley Schacht, *Confessions of "the Old Wizard": Autobiography,* translated by Diana Pyke (Boston, 1956), 367.

2 Leonard Mosley, *The Reich Marshal: A Biography of Hermann Göring* (New York, 1974), 212–16.

3 The functionalist view of Hitler as a "weak dictator" can be traced back to Broszat and Mommsen. It is Bracher, however, who speaks of a "chaos state." See Martin Broszat, *The Hitler State* (London, 1981). Tim Mason, meanwhile, has spoken about the "struggle" between Hitler's idealism and the realities of management. Given the evidence cited throughout, my perspective is closer to Kershaw's idea of leaders "working toward the Führer," which necessarily rejects the view of "weak" dictatorship. Yet one must acknowledge a certain "analytical balance" between the two views. See Richard Overy, "Germany, 'Domestic Crisis' and War in 1939," *Past & Present,* no. 116 (August 1, 1987): 138–68; Timothy Mason, "Intention and Explanation: A Current Controversy about the Interpretation of National Socialism," in *The Nazi Holocaust Part 3, The "Final Solution": The Implementation of Mass Murder,* edited by Michael Marrus (Westport, Conn., 1989), 1: 3–20.

4 For the infamous 1932 fundraising efforts, see the standout work by James on Krupp. See Harold James, *Krupp* (Princeton, N.J., 2012), especially 189.

5 Cited in R. J. Overy, *Göring, the "Iron Man"* (London, 1984), 15.

6 Schacht, *Autobiography,* 365.

7 Cited in Overy, *Göring,* 34.

8 I disagree with the causation implied by the otherwise persuasive argument by Athanasios Orphanides, in Athanasios Orphanides, "Is Monetary Policy Overburdened?," Bank of International Settlements, Working Paper 435, December 20, 2013. For a key text of comparative central banking regimes, see Michael D. Bordo and Anna J. Schwartz, *Monetary Policy Regimes and Economic Performance: The Historical Record,* Working Paper, National Bureau of Economic Research, September 1997.

9 Adam Tooze, *Wages of Destruction: The Making and Breaking of the Nazi Economy* (London, 2006), 209, 715, n16. We owe the contemporary account to Norbert Muhlen, *Der Zauberer; Leben Und Anleihen Des Dr. Hjalmar Horace Greeley Schacht* (Zürich, 1938), 166.

10 The British case was more complicated after the 1935 general elections. France introduced a two-year service, preempting Hitler's return to conscription, to be expanded in 1936 as described above. Winston Churchill, *The Gathering Storm* (London, 1948), 117.

11 And yet, according to respected Institut für Demoskopie Allensbach, even in 2014 Germans fear inflation more than cancer. Alexander Jung, "World War I Sowed Seeds of German Hyperinflation in 1923," *Spiegel*, July 2, 2014.

12 Albrecht Ritschl, *Deutschlands Krise und Konjunktur 1924–1934: Binnenkonjunktur, Auslandsverschuldung und Reparationsproblem Zwischen Dawes-Plan und Transfersperre* (Berlin, 2002). For an overview in English, see Albrecht Ritschl, *Deficit Spending in the Nazi Recovery, 1933–1938: A Critical Reassessment* (Zurich, n.d.).

13 International Military Tribunal, Avalon Project, Yale University (henceforth *IMT*), vol. 37, 365ff, for a speech by Schacht on inflation. Also Timothy W. Mason, *Nazism, Fascism and the Working Class* (Cambridge, U.K.?, 1995), 108. For pressures on the Westall and the "imbalance" between agricultural and industrial wages, see Tooze, *Wages*, 265–66. For later inflation, see Willi Boelcke, *Die Kosten Von Hitlers Krieg* (Paderborn, 1985).

14 See Tooze, *Wages*, 266.

15 For a modern view on the holistic concept of "financial repression," see Carmen Reinhart, "The Return of Financial Repression," *Financial Stability Review* 16 (March 2012).

16 See *The League of Nations Treaty Series*, vol. 167. It was technically known as the Franco-Soviet Assistance Treaty, concluded in May 1935.

17 U.K. Cabinet Memoranda, 1935–1937 (or 1937–1939) Cabinet Papers, National Archives, Kew, CAB/24/261. In a report filed in the Cabinet the day after the remilitarization of the Rhineland, Eden was concerned with Hitler's "ways" and his influence under "General Göring and Nazi extremists" (189).

18 CAB/24/261, 190.

19 See the classic Nicholas Rostow, *Anglo-French Relations, 1934–36* (London, 1984), especially 236–38.

20 The July 27, 1936, Commons debate involved not only Lloyd George but also Eden and Chamberlain.

21 Peter Neville, *Mussolini* (London, 2004), 133–34.

22 This translation is Kershaw's. See Ian Kershaw, *Hitler, 1889–1936: Hubris* (New York, 1999), 1.

23 Overy, "Germany, 'Domestic Crisis' and War in 1939," 167.

24 Richard Overy, *The Nazi Economic Recovery, 1932–1938* (New York, 1996), 26.

25 *IMT,* vol. 36, 292; Schacht to Blomberg, cited in Tooze, *Wages,* 209.

26 Rolf Caesar and Karl-Heinrich Hansmeyer, "Kriegswirtschaft und Inflation," in *Währung und Wirtschaft in Deutschland 1876–1975* (Frankfurt, 1976), especially 408–9; Harold James, *The German Slump: Politics and Economics, 1924–1936* (Oxford, 1986), 387.

27 Cited in Hjalmar Schacht, *Account Settled* (London, 1949), 90. The book also references lectures for military audiences in 1935–1936, which von Blomberg later ended. On "his" recovery and the role of monetary expansion, see also Hjalmar Schacht, *The Magic of Money* (London, 1967).

28 For a discussion on this from the microeconomic perspective, see James, *Krupp*.

29 Adam Klug, "The German Buybacks, 1932–1939: A Cure for Overhang?," in *Princeton Studies in International Finance* (Princeton, N.J., 1993), vol. 75, especially 11–15.

30 Caesar and Hansmeyer, "Kriegswirtschaft und Inflation," 382n.

31 See Hjalmar Horace Greeley Schacht, *Abrechnung mit Hitler* (Hamburg, 1948), 16–18. Kershaw, *Hubris,* 9, touches on the issue. Kershaw references a different edition of the German book (corresponding to 61–62).

32 The Westall project offered such attractive wages that it took from other areas of the economy, at times leading the state to compete for labor with itself.

33 At Nuremberg, General Thomas of the Wehrmacht economics office supported the view that Schacht had urged caution on von Blomberg "from 1936 onward." Schacht, *Account Settled,* 90.

34 See Schacht, *Autobiography,* 335; Leon Goldensohn, *The Nuremberg Interviews* (New York, 2004), 218–20.

35 For the escalation of anti-Semitism after the Olympics, see Richard Evans, *Third Reich in Power* (London, 2006), 581–52.

36 For the crucial French perspective (after years of refusing a devaluation), see Kenneth Mouré, "'Une Eventualité Absolument Exclue': French Reluctance to Devalue, 1933–1936," *French Historical Studies* 15, no. 3 (1988): 479–505.

37 Schacht later attempted a second international conference. Patricia Clavin, *The Failure of Economic Diplomacy: Britain, Germany, France and the United States, 1931–36* (Basingstoke, U.K., 1996), especially 187.

38 Kershaw describes Hitler's mood as "effusive" when receiving Ciano in Berchtesgaden that late October. See Ian Kershaw, *Hitler: 1936–1945: Nemesis* (London, 2000), 25. He described Mussolini as the "leading statesman in the world." Galeazzo Ciano, *Ciano's Diplomatic Papers; Being a Record of Nearly 200 Conversations Held During the Years 1936–42 with Hitler, Mussolini, Franco . . . and Many Other World Diplomatic and Political Figures* (London, 1948). For a note on that source, see Chapter 8.

39 Overy is perhaps too kind to say that Göring's economic views "lacked sophistication." See Overy, *Göring,* 52.

40 For a full worldview from his own pen, see Hermann Göring, *Aufbau einer Nation* (Berlin, 1934).

41 David Marsh, *The Bundesbank: The Bank That Rules Europe* (London, 1993), 138. Raising prices was declared "high treason" early in the war (1940).

42 See Fernando M. Martin, "Debt, Inflation and Central Bank Independence." St. Louis Federal Reserve Bank, Working Paper Series, no. 2013–017 (May 2013); Haan de Bevger and S. C. W. Eijffinger, *Central Bank Independence: An Update of Theory and Evidence* (Tilburg, 2000); and Cristina Bodea and Raymond Hicks, "Central Bank Independence, Political Institutions and Economic Growth: New Data and a Global Sample," Princeton University, presented at the 2013 Midwest Political Science Association Conference and 2013 European Political Science Association.

43 Woodruff Smith, *The Ideological Origins of Nazi Imperialism* (New York, 1986), especially 253.

44 Politically driven "geographic" theories then held that the control of central Europe led to the control of Eurasia and the world: "Who rules the World-Island commands the World." The concept originated with Sir Halford Mackinder, but it was likely through Haushofer that it got to the Nazis. See Sir John Halford

Mackinder, *Democratic Ideals and Reality* (New York, 1919), especially 186; Karl Haushofer, *Karl Haushofer: Leben und Werk,* edited by Hans Adolf Jacobsen (Boldt, 1979), vol. 1, for his "geographic" oeuvre.

45 For the "authorized," sycophantic biography, see Gerald Griffin and Erich Gritzbach, *Hermann Göring* (London, 1939), 109.

46 For two examples involving General Fritsch complaining about Göring's interference in the Wehrmacht and the Night of the Long Knives, see Ulrich von Hassell, *The Von Hassell Diaries* (London, 1948), 29; Overy, *Göring,* especially 150–51.

47 Tooze, *Wages,* 210.

48 Overy, *Göring,* 58.

49 Schacht recounts several times in which he complained to Hitler directly about the lack of respect for currency controls from the Party apparatus, both in Germany and abroad. Yet Göring was part of the problem, not the solution. See Frank Bajohr, *Parvenüs und Profiteure: Korruption in Der NS-Zeit* (Frankfurt, 2001).

50 Griffin and Gritzbach, *Hermann Göring,* 107.

51 The dispute seems to have originated when Schacht vetoed a Keppler proposal for steel quotas. Matthias Riedel, *Eisen und Kohle für das Dritte Reich* (Göttingen, 1973), 68–70. Tooze also mentions it in *Wages,* 220.

52 For a well-researched biography focusing on his increasing opposition to Hitler, see Ines Reich, *Carl Friedrich Goerdeler: Ein Oberbürgermeister Gegen Den NS-Staat* (Köln, 1997). Goerdeler would be a leading figure in the 1944 July plot.

53 Overy, *German Recovery,* especially tables in chapter 3.

54 Goerdeler's recommendation would have required a repeat of post-hyperinflationary stabilization. For an account, see Niall Ferguson, *Paper and Iron: Hamburg Business and German Politics in the Era of Inflation, 1897–1927* (Cambridge, 1995), 408–14.

55 See Tooze, *Wages,* 717, n60, for a comprehensive list. Particularly instructive is R2501 6517, on 315–16.

56 Ibid., 219.

57 Kershaw, *Nemesis,* 17–23. Kershaw makes the point that the "four-year" description was not in the memorandum.

58 "Unsigned Memorandum," August 1936, *German Documents,* series C, vol. 5, 853–62; "Aufzeichnung ohne Unterschrift" (1936), in *Akten zur Deutschen Auswärtigen Politik 1918–1945* (Göttingen, 1977), *German Documents,* series C, vol. 5, 2, 490, 793–801.

59 Schacht admitted to this lack of access, though it was surely beneficial to do so at Nuremberg. See *Autobiography,* 351.

60 Ibid.

61 Though known for his theory of "polycratic" power in Nazi Germany, Hans Mommsen acknowledges the centrality of Hitler to Nazi decision making, particularly after 1936. See Hans Mommsen, *From Weimar to Auschwitz* (Princeton, N.J., 1992), especially 163–64. For another example from this historiographic trend, see Lothar Kettenacker and Gerhard Hirschfeld, *Der "Führerstaat," Mythos und Realität* (Stuttgart, 1981).

62 Overy makes the interesting point that given Hitler's distaste for writing, the fact that he wrote this memorandum is telling.

63 "Aufzeichnung ohne Unterschrift," 793, 796.

64 Ibid., 796.

65 Ibid., 801.

66 Hitler was said to be drafting and dictating the memorandum when Göring sent him his commentary on Goerdeler's report earlier in the summer. And Göring traveled to the Berghof when Hitler finished it.

67 Griffin and Gritzbach, *Hermann Göring*, 106.

68 From a historiographical perspective, this lends credence to the Jäckal view on the *Primat der Außenpolitik* in the Hitlerian regime, although Hitler's own words suggest this primacy arises from the effects of "external threat" on German policy, both external and internal. Eberhard Jäckel, *Hitler's World View: A Blueprint for Power* (Cambridge, Mass., 1981).

69 Overy, *Göring*, 51.

70 Despite the many problems with the source, see David Irving, *Göring* (London, 1989), 166.

71 *IMT,* vol. 5, 141.

72 For a fair characterization of Thomas as "ruthless pragmatist," see Tooze, *Wages,* 478.

73 Cited in Kershaw, *Hubris,* 19, originally from *German Documents,* vol. 100, V, 853, N. 1, Doc. 490.

74 Irving, *Göring,* 107.

75 For Schacht's complaints on the economics of the plan, in particular low-quality ores and synthetics, see Schacht, *Account Settled,* 97–105.

76 The hubris here is obvious. Schacht, *Autobiography,* 369–71.

77 Caesar and Hansmeyer, "Kriegswirtschaft und Inflation"; Klaus Hildebrand, *Vom Reich zum Weltreich: Hitler, NSDAP und koloniale Frage, 1919–1945* (Munich, 1969).

78 Overy, *Göring,* especially chapter 3.

79 For more background on this, see the discussion in Diarmuid Jeffreys, *Hell's Cartel* (London, 2008), chapter 4.

80 See also Overy, *Göring,* chapter 3.

81 The all-important discussions with business and the corruption issues are detailed in August Meyer, *Das Syndikat: Reichswerke "Hermann Göring"* (Braunschweig, 1986).

82 Gritzbach and Griffin, *Hermann Göring,* 109.

83 Schacht, *Account Settled,* 100.

84 This is discussed in detail in Chapter 9.

85 *German Documents,* Doc. 196, 219–20. See n2 for the Berlin circulation of the document, which was sent directly to the foreign minister and other officials, according to a Reich Chancellery officer Lammers on January 15, 1937.

86 *German Documents,* Doc. 207, 229.

87 Ibid.

88 Pablo Martin-Acena, Elena Martinez Ruiz, and Maria A. Pons Brias, "War and Economics: Spanish Civil War Finances Revisited," University Library of Munich, Germany, MPRA Paper, no. 22833 (2010), Fig. 8.

89 This is discussed in: Michael Seidman, *The Victorious Counterrevolution: The Nationalist Effort in the Spanish Civil War* (Madison, Wisc., 2011), 110–11.

90 Though limited to British sources, Talbot's research on commercial interests during the war is illuminating with regard to the transfers to Germany. The difference in numbers is given by disagreements over the effective exchange rate (I use FX rates as quoted outside Spain). Ben Talbot, unpublished dissertation, Cambridge University, 2010, especially 35–39. I am grateful to the author and his advisor.

91 A Nationalist takeover of mining facilities—including of course Rio Tinto—in the South and, later in 1937, in the minerals-rich North, had benefited large mining conglomerates.

92 Foreign Office, FO 371/21303, National Archives, Kew, U.K., Rio Tinto to Foreign Office, January 21, 1937.

93 U.K. Cabinet Memoranda, 1935–1937 (or 1937–1939) Cabinet Papers, National Archives, Kew, U.K. (henceforth CAB), 24/268 CP 80 (37), cited in Harvey, "Politics and Pyrites," 99.

94 CAB 23/87, March 3, 1937. For the first sea lord point, see Harvey, "Politics and Pyrites," 99.

95 Harvey, "Politics and Pyrites," 99.

96 German supplies went to Franco, by now the undisputed Nationalist leader. Stanley Payne, Franco and Hitler: Spain, Hitler and World War II (New Haven, Conn., 2008), especially 294–97.

97 The report is signed by Benzler at the Foreign Office. German Documents, Doc. 223, 245–46.

98 Ibid.

99 See Harvey, "Politics and Pyrites," 93–94.

100 Ibid. Despite what Leitz claims, however, this occurred before the "Nazification" of the ministry, which took place only in late 1937, after Göring's formal takeover.

101 On this issue I disagree with Leitz's analysis. See Christian Leitz, Economic Relations Between Nazi Germany and Franco's Spain: 1936–1945 (New York, 1996).

102 The final text of the protocol is reproduced in German Documents, Doc. 234, 256–57.

103 This was Schacht's own terminology in Sofia. See Glasgow Herald, June 16, 1936, 11.

104 For its effects on business, see Overy, Göring, especially 57.

105 For essential background on the birth of Lebensraum ideas, see Vejas G. Liulevicius, War Land on the Eastern Front (Cambridge, U.K.?, 2000).

106 See, for instance, Merkes, Die Deutsche Politik, and Abendroth, Hitler in der Spanischen Arena, for two very dissimilar studies focusing on political motivations. From East Germany the Einhorn thesis focused on German business but not Schacht, even if economic policy was his domain. And of course Leitz focused predominantly on Göring's staff and their role. See Manfred Merkes, Die Deutsche Politik Gegenüber Dem Spanischen Bürgerkrieg, 1936–1939 (Bonn, 1961); Marion Einhorn, Die Ökonomischen Hintergründe Der Faschistischen Deutschen Intervention in Spanien 1936–1939 (East Berlin, 1962); Hans-Henning Abendroth, Hitler in Der Spanischen Arena: Die Deutsch-Spanischen Beziehungen Im Spannungsfeld Der Europäischen Interessenpolitik Vom Ausbruch Des Bürgerkrieges Bis Zum Ausbruch Des Weltkrieges 1936–1939 (Nuremberg, 1970); and, in spite of the issues with Bernhardt's contributions, see Mittelsmann Zwischen Franco Und Hitler: Johannes Bernhardt Erinnert 1936 (Marktheidenfeld, 1978).

107 German Documents, Doc. 256, 287–88.

108 Chamberlain had moved in this direction against Schachtian debt tactics in 1934. See Clavin, Failure of Economic Diplomacy, 184.

109 German Documents, Doc. 257, 288. See reproduction in Wayne Bowen, Spaniards and Nazi Germany (Columbia, Mo., 2000), 33.

110 German Documents, Doc. 257, 289.

111 German Documents, Doc. 231, 253.

112 See Archivos Españoles, Archivo de Barcelona, Archivo de Azaña, b. 136, press clippings. Indeed both Germany and Italy had agreed to limit territorial ambitions in Morocco, but Italy did take over Majorca for a while through a rogue agent.

7. THE SHADOW EMPIRE

1 Hjalmar Schacht, "Germany's Colonial Demands," *Foreign Affairs,* January 1937.
2 Ibid., 226.
3 W. O. Henderson, *The German Colonial Empire, 1884–1919* (London, 1993); Wolfe W. Schmokel, *Dream of Empire: German Colonialism, 1919–1945* (New Haven, Conn., 1964), especially 190 for demands.
4 Schacht, "Germany's Colonial Demands," 226.
5 Ibid., 227. The analysis seems validated by later research. Kenneth Mouré, "'Une Eventualité Absolument Exclue': French Reluctance to Devalue, 1933–1936," *French Historical Studies* 15, no. 3 (1988): 479–505.
6 The language here is almost verbatim that of his 1920s speeches. Schacht, "Germany's Colonial Demands," 224.
7 Holger Herwig, "Geopolitik: Haushofer, Hitler and Lebensraum," *Journal of Strategic Studies* 22, no. 2 (1999): 218–41; Brian Blouet, *Geopolitics and Globalization in the Twentieth Century* (New York, 2004), especially 61–62.
8 Schacht, "Germany's Colonial Demands," 226.
9 Chamberlain came to power on May 28, 1937, replacing the prime minister for whom he had served as Chancellor of the Exchequer. Baldwin had scheduled his retirement after King Edward VIII's "abdication crisis." Robert C. Self, *Neville Chamberlain: A Political Life* (London, 2006), 256–57.
10 Nicholas Rostow, "Conclusions," in *Anglo-French Relations, 1934–36* (London, 1984).
11 Jean Lacouture, *Léon Blum* (New York, 1982), especially 169.
12 For the best accounts of the "gold of Moscow," see Angel Viñas, *El Oro de Moscú: Alfa y Omega de un mito franquista* (Barcelona, 1979); Pablo Martín Aceña, *El Oro de Moscú y El Oro de Berlín* (Madrid, 2001).
13 Archivos Españoles, Archivo de Barcelona, Archivo de Azaña, b. 136, folder 6, Doc. 5, dated April 17, 1937.
14 Similar arguments had been raised in July 1936 and October 1936; in light of internal disagreements within both fascist governments the contingency was real, yet it never translated into policy.
15 Anglo-American outlets continued to refer to him as Nazi Germany's "economic dictator." This would change only at the end of 1937. See, for instance, *Milwaukee Journal,* December 17, 1937, 4.
16 For a contemporary view that resonates with this conclusion, see Arnold Toynbee, *International Survey 1937* (London, 1937).
17 Guadalajara was a painful defeat for the Italian troops in Spain, explained in detail in Chapter 8.
18 Archivos Españoles, Archivo de Barcelona, Archivo de Azaña, b. 136, folder 6, Doc. 5, dated April 17, 1937, 2–3.
19 Ibid., 3.
20 Kershaw outlines the centrality of Hitler's decision making in the foreign sphere in those crucial months, in a way that weakens the "polycratic" reading of the regime at the highest foreign policy echelons. See Ian Kershaw, *Hitler 1936–1945: Nemesis* (London, 2000), 122–28. See Christopher Kopper, *Hjalmar Schacht: Aufstieg*

Und Fall Von Hitlers Mächtigstem Bankier (Munich, 2006) for the "part-time dip-lomat" tendencies, 307–10.

21 Lacouture, *Blum,* 297.

22 Foreign Office, FO 954/8/45, National Archives, Kew, U.K. (henceforth FO), 1–8. The French prime minister briefed Ambassador Clerk himself; Eden then thanked Blum for the courtesy.

23 Ibid., 1.

24 Ibid., 4.

25 Ibid., 2.

26 Lacouture, *Blum,* 297.

27 FO 954/8/36, 1–2. Personal note from Eden to Delbos, September 23, 1936.

28 Ibid.

29 FO 954/8/257, 1. Anthony Eden, October 10, 1936.

30 C. A. MacDonald, "Economic Appeasement and the German 'Moderates' 1937–1939: An Introductory Essay," *Past & Present,* no. 56 (1972): 105.

31 For an example of this view in the historiography, see MacDonald, "Economic Appeasement"; Paul N. Hehn, *A Low, Dishonest Decade: The Great Powers, Eastern Europe and the Economic Origins of World War II* (London, 2005), especially 148–49.

32 Lacouture, *Blum,* 298.

33 Zara Steiner, *The Triumph of the Dark: European International History, 1933–1939* (New York, 2011), i.

34 Lacouture, *Blum,* 298.

35 Archivos Españoles, Archivo de Barcelona, Archivo de Azaña, b. 135, Doc. 9, dated May 14, 1937.

36 Ibid., 2.

37 Granville Roberts, *The Nazi Claims to Colonies: "When a Strong Man Armed . . ."* (London, 1939).

38 Cooper resigned after the Munich Agreement; he would later become a central figure in the Commons' "Norway debate" that sealed the fate of the Chamberlain premiership. John Charmley, *Duff Cooper* (London, 1987).

39 Archivos Españoles, Archivo de Barcelona, Archivo de Azaña, b. 135, Doc. 9, dated May 14, 1937. In 1938 there would be a long diplomatic row about German war supplies in Republican hands through a Greek weapons dealer. This is com-patible with Schacht's views, as relayed to Schlulmeister. See b. 833, folder 4, Docs. 3–22.

40 There is a chance Schacht was referring to the weapons dealing of Veltjens, an in-dependent smuggler who provided war matériel to the Nationalists, particularly General Mola, early in the war. As we shall see, these expenses would later be added to the "German bill" for Spanish authorities.

41 Archivos Españoles, Archivo de Azaña, b. 833, folder 4, Docs. 3–22.

42 This point is best made by Christian Leitz, *Economic Relations Between Nazi Ger-many and Franco's Spain: 1936–1945* (New York, 1998), especially chapter 3.

43 Rafael García Pérez, *Franquismo Y Tercer Reich: Las Relaciones Económicas Hispano-Alemanas Durante La Segunda Guerra Mundial* (Madrid, 1994), especially 89–92.

44 Viñas states that HISMA's auditor was later chased by Bernhardt. He was almost killed and was thrown in prison in 1943, which raises further questions about HISMA management. Angel Viñas, in correspondence with the author, Sep-tember 2011.

45 In his updated biography, Overy accurately reconstructs from the original documents Göring's lack of moral sensitivity. Richard Overy, *Göring: Hitler's Iron Knight* (New York, 2012), 229.

46 Jonathan Petropoulos, *Art as Politics in the Third Reich* (Chapel Hill, N.C., 1996), 196; Frank Bajohr, *Parvenüs und Profiteure: Korruption in der NS-Zeit* (Frankfurt, 2001), 46.

47 Bajohr, *Parvenüs und Profiteure*, x.

48 Gerald Feldman and Wolfgang Seibel, eds., *Networks of Nazi Persecution: Bureaucracy, Business, and the Organization of the Holocaust* (Oxford, 2006), 129.

49 Mark Mazower, *Hitler's Empire* (London, 2012), especially 91–92.

50 Ángel Viñas, in correspondence with the author, September 2011.

51 James Marshall-Cornwall et al., eds., *Documents on German Foreign Policy 1918–1945, from the Archives of the German Foreign Ministry,* Series D, 1937–1945, vol. 3: *Germany and the Spanish Civil War 1936–1939* (Washington, D.C., 1950) (henceforth, *German Documents*), Doc. 263, 293.

52 *German Documents,* Doc. 394, 417–18. It was signed on July 15, 1937.

53 For more on transfers, see Ben Talbot, "British Capital in the Spanish Civil War," University of Cambridge unpublished dissertation, 2010, 38; Angel Viñas, *Franco, Hitler y El Estallido De La Guerra Civil: Antecedentes y Consecuencias* (Madrid, 2001), 223.

54 John Weitz, *Hitler's Banker: Hjalmar Horace Greeley Schacht* (Boston, 1997), 173.

55 Cited in Overy, *Göring,* 59, chart on 58.

56 This features in Kershaw's analysis and is necessarily part of his argument about the centrality of a far from "weak" Hitler, toward whom the apparatus of government worked.

57 Albert Speer, *Inside the Third Reich* (New York, 1971), 152.

58 Ibid. The English translation has Speer mistakenly referring to Schacht—repeatedly—as "Finance Minister." Speer later claims that Hitler "all his life distrusted professionals including, for instance, Schacht" (280).

59 Ibid.

60 Ibid.

61 Hjalmar Horace Greeley Schacht, *Confessions of "the Old Wizard": Autobiography* (Boston, 1956), 375.

62 Overy, *Göring,* especially 72–73.

63 Schacht, *Autobiography,* 372, 373, 377.

64 For Schacht's disappointment with the head of the army, von Blomberg, see ibid., 372.

65 Ibid., 376.

66 Tooze provides enlightening detail in, Adam Tooze, *Wages of Destruction: The Making and Breaking of the Nazi Economy* (London, 2006), 201–12.

67 Norbert Muhlen, *Der Zauberer; Leben Und Anleihen Des Dr. Hjalmar Horace Greeley Schacht* (Zürich, 1938), 182.

68 Kurt von Schleicher had been assassinated in 1934 during the Night of the Long Knives, around the time of Hitler's promotion of Schacht to the ministry. John Wheeler-Bennett, *The Nemesis of Power: The German Army in Politics, 1918–1945* (Basingstoke, U.K., 1967), especially 323–25.

69 International Military Tribunal, via Avalon Project, Yale University, *IMT,* EC-408.

70 Ibid.

71 Overy, *Göring*, 15.
72 Schacht, *Autobiography*, 377.
73 The document itself has generated a wide debate, with historians like Wilburger and Overy claiming it proved expansionist plans in a way with which Kershaw and Mason disagreed. Gerhard L. Weinberg, *The Foreign Policy of Hitler's Germany: Starting World War II, 1937–1939* (Atlantic Highlands, N.J., 1994), especially 39–40.
74 Friedrich Hossbach, "Minutes of a Conference in the Reich Chancellery, Berlin, November 5, 1937, from 4:15 to 8:30 P.M.," Berlin, November 10, 1937. Available at *IMT*, vol. 25, 403–13.
75 Ambassador Magaz was responsible for these complaints. See Archivos Españoles, Archivo de Azaña, box 20, Doc. 12.
76 Ibid., Doc. 12, 2–3.
77 Mogens Pelt, "Germany and the Greek Armaments Industry: Policy Goals and Business Opportunities," in *Working for the New Order: European Business under German Domination, 1939–1945,* edited by Joachim Lund (Copenhagen, 2006), especially 152. See the note on the Powder and Cartridge Company. The transaction further illustrates Republican difficulties in procuring weaponry.
78 Hossbach, "Minutes." This is Göring's only comment at the meeting in the Hossbach copy. According to Müller, however, he participated in questions about the technicalities of further rearmament. See Klaus Jürgen Müller, *Das Heer und Hitler: Armee und Nationalsozialistisches Regime 1933–1940* (Stuttgart, 1969), 240. See also Kershaw, *Nemesis,* 861, n273, for source contrast.
79 Hossbach, "Minutes," 2.
80 This was allegedly his reaction upon seeing a copy of Hossbach's transcript. Klaus Jürgen Müller, *General Ludwig Beck: Studien und Dokumente Zur Politisch-militärischen Vorstellungswelt Und Tätigkeit Des Generalstabschefs Des Deutschen Heeres 1933–1938* (Boppard am Rhein, 1980), 501. See also Kershaw, *Nemesis,* 50.
81 For an accessible overview of the historiographic debate, see Adam Tooze, "Hitler's Gamble," *History Today* 56 no. 11 (2006).
82 Kershaw, *Nemesis,* 50, recounts the episode. The original citation is in Müller, *Heer,* 246.
83 Although he was minister without portfolio, Schacht was no longer receiving documents pertaining to fiscal policy and rearmament, a point corroborated by Nuremberg interrogations. Schacht, *Autobiography,* 451.
84 Ironically Hitler himself had been a witness at the latter's wedding. See Wheeler-Bennett, *The Nemesis of Power.*
85 Omer Bartov, *Hitler's Army: Soldiers, Nazis, and War in the Third Reich* (New York, 1991), especially 3–12. For Warlimont's memoirs, see Walter Warlimont, *Im Hauptquartier Der Deutschen Wehrmacht, 1939–1945: Grundlagen, Formen, Gestalten* (Frankfurt, 1962).
86 See Overy, *Göring,* 79, for the complicated relationship between the two men.
87 Bloch's biography of Ribbentrop is a good study for more on this transition. Michael Bloch, *Ribbentrop* (London, 1983), especially 154.
88 Louis Synder, *Encyclopedia of the Third Reich* (New York, 1976), 295.
89 Cited in Richard Overy, "Germany and the Munich Crisis: A Mutilated Victory?," in *The Munich Crisis, 1938 Prelude to World War II,* edited by Igor Lukes and Erik Goldstein (London, 1999), 200–201.
90 For details, see Leitz, *Economic Relations,* 17.
91 García Perez, *Franquismo y Tercer Reich,* 64.
92 Angel Viñas, *Política Comercial Exterior En España (1931–1975)* (Madrid, 1979), 132.

93 *German Documents,* Doc. 464, 500–502.

94 Ibid., 501.

95 Leitz makes this point well in *Economic Relations,* chapter 2.

96 *German Documents,* Doc. 464, 500–502.

97 Ibid., 501.

98 When Franco reproached British commercial agents, Bernhardt was given the official position of "special German economic representative" in Spain. See Charles E. Harvey, "Politics and Pyrites During the Spanish Civil War," *Economic History Review,* n.s., 31, no. 1 (February 1, 1978): 89–104, especially 103.

99 *German Documents,* Doc. 464, 501. The "economic war" language had clearly permeated into Spain.

100 For a selection of 1938 documents outlining the ongoing debate about the Montaña project, see *German Documents,* Docs. 526, 529, 559, 567, 577, 591, 595. In Spain see Velarda Fuertes, "Un Aspecto del asunto Montana," *De Economía,* no. 21 (March 1968): 131–56.

101 SOFINDUS had been registered in Lisbon and later transferred to Salamanca in November 1938 (curiously in the immediate aftermath of Munich). The original act of foundation is at the Bundesarchiv Koblenz, R 121/838. See García Perez, *Franquismo y Tercer Reich,* 75, as well as its references to Viñas's research, to whom we owe the original find.

102 Archivos Españoles, Archivo de Burgos, b. 833, folder 11, letters dated October 7, October 20, November 10, and verbal note from December 19, 1938.

103 See Archivos Españoles, Archivo de Burgos, b. 827 for letters from Ambassador Magaz mentioning the issue. The military leadership in Berlin had made it clear that a decision had to be reached: either the Legion would be withdrawn or it would be restocked. Hitler opted for the latter.

104 *German Documents,* Doc. 631, 715–17.

105 Ibid.

106 Ibid., 717.

107 For the detailed military view, see Jesús Salas Larrazábal, *Intervención Extranjera en la Guerra de España* (Madrid, 1974).

108 This point is originally made in Paul Preston, "General Franco as Military Leader," *Transactions of the Royal Historical Society* 4, sixth series (1994): 21–41.

109 Christian Leitz, *Nazi Germany and Neutral Europe During the Second World War: Sympathy for the Devil?* (Manchester, U.K., 2001), 116.

110 García Pérez's analysis misses the Magaz reports in the Archivo de Burgos, detailing the strong reaction by German leaders, preferring instead to rely only on reported statements by Hitler. Indeed it seems like the pressure in the economic sphere escalated in the aftermath of Franco's neutrality announcement. García Pérez, *Franquismo y Tercer Reich,* 106. That said, it is true that Beigdeber had tried to reassure Ambassador Stoher. See *German Documents,* series D, vol. 7, Doc. 524.

111 Archivos Españoles, Archivo de Burgos, b. 833, folder 4, letter dated October 18, 1938, 1.

112 Ibid., letters dated November 4 and 8, 1938, 1.

113 Ibid., letter dated November 4, 1938, 1–2.

114 Ibid.

115 Bundesarchiv Lichterfelde (henceforth BAL), R 2501 6521, 291–305. It was a draft memorandum dated October 3, 1938. Cited in Tooze, *Wages,* 285–87.

116 Ibid.

117 Ibid., 286. The translation here is Tooze's.

118 See Tooze, *Wages,* 288. The decision was also cited at the Nuremberg tribunals in the proceedings against Göring.

119 For specific examples, see Kershaw, *Nemesis,* 121–25, as well as Hitler's later regret, 163.

120 *IMT,* Judgment: Schacht, 3.

121 Ibid., 4.

122 *German Documents,* Doc. 703, 808–9.

123 Leitz, *Economic Relations,* especially 120.

124 *German Documents,* Doc. 634, 719. This was reported in a paper by the economic policy director of the Foreign Ministry, who had been in touch personally with Bernhardt.

125 Robert H. Whealey, "Economic Influence of the Great Powers in the Spanish Civil War: From the Popular Front to the Second World War," *International History Review* 5, no. 2 (1983): 229–54.

126 Ibid. A letter dated January 11, 1939, for instance, provides evidence of the "assent from the [Spanish] Ministry of Foreign Affairs to the [Spanish] Ministry of Economics to the payment of 15M *Reichsmarks* to put in the mining societies by Bernhardt."

127 *German Documents,* Doc. 702, 804–5.

8. "HATEFUL TO GOD AND TO HIS ENEMIES"

1 See Galeazzo Ciano, *Diario* (Milan, 1946) and *Diary, 1937–1943* (New York, 2002). The corrected and annotated 2002 version will be quoted throughout, including the Edda Mussolini pages and Carlo Ciucci's additions. See Renzo De Felice, preface to Ciano, *Diary,* v–xvi.

2 On March 11 Ciano had received a report from General Gambara, head of Italian troops in Spain, prophesying that "final action" on Madrid would soon begin. On March 14 the Duke of Aosta, viceroy of Italian East Africa, was optimistic about Ethiopia. Ciano welcomed the news, though he was ambivalent toward the duke: "I do not quite understand whether he was speaking as the Viceroy of Ethiopia or as the son of a French princess." Ciano, *Diary,* 199–200. See also Amedeo, duca D'Aosta, *Studi Africani* (Bologna, 1942).

3 Strictly speaking, the fascistic Hungarian premier Gyula Gömbös was the first to coin the term *axis* in reference to an alliance with Hitler's Germany. Yet Mussolini popularized it. Denis Sinor, *History of Hungary* (New York, 1959), 291.

4 Ciano, *Diary,* March 14, 1939, 200.

5 Jonathan Petropoulos, *Royals and the Reich* (New York, 2006), especially 159.

6 Ciano, *Diary,* March 15, 1939, 201.

7 Italy would be "happy to receive [German] weapons and other equipment." Ciano, *Diary,* March 15, 1939, 201.

8 The invasion materialized a week after the end of the Spanish Civil War, with some of the same units. For a (biased) contemporary take, see Gaspare Ambrosini, *L'Albania nella comunità imperiale di Roma* (Rome, 1940).

9 Ciano, *Diary,* March 15, 1939, 202.

10 *Inferno* 3.63; Ciano, *Diary,* 602.

11 There is general agreement on this issue. See Dante Puzzo, *Spain and the Great Powers* (New York, 1962), 64–66; Hugh Thomas, *The Spanish Civil War* (New York, 2001), 340–53; Javier Tusell, *Franco y Mussolini* (Barcelona, 2006).

12 Thomas, *Spanish Civil War,* 944. For a more detailed account, see John Coverdale, *Italian Intervention in the Spanish Civil War* (Princeton, N.J., 1975), table 7, 393,

with data compiled from the final report from Ciano's ministry, Ufficio Spagna, Ministero degli Affari Esteri, Archivo Storico, Direzione Generale degli Affari Politici, Rome, box 1, 20–22.

13 This estimation does not include Italian exiles fighting for the Republic. As far as we know, the number of Germans in Spain never exceeded fifteen thousand.

14 Puzzo, *Spain and the Great Powers,* 231–45.

15 Roberto Cantalupo, *Fu La Spagna: Ambasciata Presso Franco, Febbraio–Aprile 1937* (Milan, 1948), 10–14.

16 Thomas, *The Spanish Civil War,* 339–45; Paul Preston, *The Coming of the Spanish Civil War* (London, 1994), 121–25; Antony Beevor, *The Spanish Civil War* (London, 1982), especially 199.

17 Rachele Mussolini, *La mia vita con Benito* (Milan, 1948); Thomas, *Spanish Civil War,* 340. Thomas also cites a good example of Mussolini's insistence on the importance of fighting in the making of the "uomo nuovo." Paolo Monelli, *Mussolini, piccolo borghese* (Milan, 1968), 141.

18 Puzzo, *Spain and the Great Powers,* 65.

19 Coverdale, *Italian Intervention in the Spanish Civil War,* 9–12, 401.

20 Regarding two reassessments of the character of Fascism, see Renzo De Felice, *Le interpretazioni del fascismo* (Milan, 1969) and A. James Gregor, *Interpretations of Fascism* (New Brunswick, 1997).

21 Alexander De Grand, *Italian Fascism* (Lincoln, Neb., 2000); Renzo De Felice, *Mussolini* (Turin, 1965). Following Angelo Tasca's 1938 dictum that the best way to define fascism was to write its history, De Grand opened by stating, "Both the man [Mussolini] and the regime he led were a mass of contradictions" (xiii–xvi).

22 De Grand, *Italian Fascism,* 120.

23 Two pages were devoted to comparison. Vincenzo Giura, *Tra Politica ed economia: L'Italia e la Guerra Civile Spagnola* (Naples, 1993), especially 93–4.

24 See De Felice, *Mussolini,* 1: 34–51.

25 Gilles Pécout, *Il lungo Risorgimento. La nascita dell'Italia contemporanea* (Milan, 2011).

26 See R. J. B. Bosworth, *Italy and the Wider World* (New York, 1996), especially 28–29.

27 See De Grand, *Italian Fascism,* 10, for demographic data. For comparison, see Gabriel Tortella, *El desarrollo de la España contemporánea* (Madrid, 1995), 4–22.

28 Aldo Mola, *Giolitti: Lo statista della nuova Italia* (Milan, 2003) and *Giolitti: Fare gli italiani* (Turin, 2005).

29 Giovanna Procacci, "Italy: From Interventionism to Fascism, 1917–1919," *Journal of Contemporary History* 3, no. 4 (1968): 153–76.

30 De Grand, *Italian Fascism,* 30.

31 Paul Thurner et al., "Agricultural Structure and the Rise of the Nazi Party Reconsidered," unpublished manuscript, University of Munich, n.d.

32 De Grand calls it "redemption by club and castor oil," in *Fascism,* 31. According to a 1921 survey, 24 percent of members were land workers, 12 percent landowners, and almost 25 percent were below the voting age. See Juan Linz, "Some Notes toward the Study of Fascism in a Comparative Sociological Historical Perspective," in *Fascism: A Reader's Guide,* edited by Walter Lacqueur (Aldershot, U.K., 1991).

33 Adrian Lyttelton, *The Seizure of Power* (London, 2004), 72–74.

34 For a selection of testimonies, see Carlo Carotti, *Saggi, sguardi e testimonianze sui socialisti a Milano dal 1891 al 2000* (Milan, 2014), 59–60.

35 Lyttelton, *The Seizure of Power,* 76–82.

36 For an original account (with an introduction by il Duce himself) from the late 1920s, see Kurt S. Gutkind, *Mussolini e il suo Fascismo* (Heidelberg, 1927), 23–30.

37 De Stefani later published an overview of his program: Alberto De Stefani, *La restaurazione finanziaria 1922–1925* (Bologna, 1926), especially 16. For the best context, Toniolo's remains the unparalleled economic history of the period: Gianni Toniolo, *L'economia dell'Italia Fascista* (Rome, 1980), especially 46–49.

38 Benito Mussolini, *Opera Omnia* (Firenze, 1951), 19: 21. For an interpretation of the threat to democracy, see Barry Eichengreen, *Golden Fetters: The Gold Standard and the Great Depression, 1919–1939* (New York, 1996), 95.

39 Peter Neville, *Mussolini* (London, 2004), 77.

40 Matteotti had published a critical tome on the early dictatorship: Giacomo Matteotti, *Il Fascismo della prima ora* (Rome, 1924). Most recent accounts agree on Mussolini's personal responsibility for his murder; see Marcello Benegiamo, *A scelta del Duce* (L'Aquila, 2006).

41 Volpi followed De Stefani's writing impulses by publishing a volume with the same title, directed at international audiences: Giuseppe Volpi, *The Financial Reconstruction of Italy* (New York, 1927).

42 Toniolo, *L'economia,* 82–88.

43 De Grand, *Italian Fascism,* 93.

44 Salvatore La Francesca, *La politica economica del fascismo* (Bari, 1972), 19–22.

45 Neville, *Mussolini,* 74.

46 Jonathan Kirshner, *Currency and Coercion* (Princeton, N.J., 1995), 230. Translation and original transcript from Joel Cohen, "The 1927 Revaluation of the Lira," *Economic History Review* 2, no. 25 (1975): 642–54, 649.

47 Although the Quota 90 originated with a discussion with Bank of England governor Montagu Norman and Fed chairman Benjamin Strong in 1926, they both argued the revaluation was too extreme. Charles Maier, *Recasting Bourgeois Europe* (Princeton, N.J., 1975), 541.

48 Ibid., 542.

49 Toniolo, *L'economia,* 121–25; De Grand, *Italian Fascism,* 87.

50 Eichengreen, *Golden Fetters,* 371, includes a useful comparison to France.

51 William G. Welk, *Fascist Economic Policy* (Cambridge, Mass., 1938), 170–72. The Instituto di Riconstrozione Industriale would later become a staple of Italian postwar development. For background on an organization Franco later emulated, see Ajmone Marsan, "Instituto per la Ricostruzione Industriale," in *Public Enterprise: Studies in Organisational Structure,* edited by V. Ramanadham (London, 1986).

52 Welk, *Fascist Economic Policy,* 171.

53 Stanley Payne, *A History of Fascism, 1914–1945* (Madison, Wisc., 1995), 225.

54 Gaetano Salvemini, *Under the Axe of Fascism* (New York, 1936), 10, cited in Christopher Duggan, *The Force of Destiny: A History of Italy since 1796* (London, 2007), 491.

55 For the detrimental effects of these on countries like Italy, see Charles P. Kindleberger, *The World in Depression* (Berkeley, 1986), especially chapter 6; Barry Eichengreen, "The Political Economy of the Smoot-Hawley Tariff," in *International Political Economy,* edited by Jeffry Frieden and David Lake (Boston, 2000).

56 "Preferite il Prodotto Italiano." See Welk, *Fascist Economic Policy,* 175; De Grand, *Italian Fascism,* 85.

57 Toniolo, *L'economia,* 279, n29.

58 Duggan, *Force of Destiny,* 500.

59 For the official story, see Emilio De Bono, *La preparazione e le prime operazioni* (Rome, 1937).

60 For the "official" view, see Alessandro Lessona, *Verso L'impero: Memorie Per La Storia Politica Del Conflitto Italo-etiopico* (Florence, 1939).

61 De Felice argues that Mussolini prioritized the international balance of power and had few to no imperial economic projects. With strong documentary evidence, however, Franco Catalano disagrees. De Felice, *Mussolini,* vol. 1, chapter 6; Franco Catalano, *L'economia italiana di guerra* (Milan, 1969), 6–9.

62 Carlo Manetti, *Etiopia economica, panorama economico agrario dell'Africa Orientale Italiana e dell'Abissinia* (Florence, 1936); Lessona, *Verso L'impero.* The latter was an avid imperial writer in Fascist Italy.

63 Felice Guarneri, *Battaglie economiche tra le due grandi Guerre* (Milan, 1953), especially 473–78.

64 Both Italy and Ethiopia were formal members of the League.

65 Robert W. Whealey, "Mussolini's Ideological Diplomacy: An Unpublished Document," *Journal of Modern History* 39, no. 4. (December 1967), 432–37.

66 Taylor argues that the Hoare-Laval plan "killed the League." A. J. P. Taylor, *The Origins of the Second World War* (New York, 1996), 126. See also Michael Hughes, *British Foreign Secretaries in an Uncertain World* (London, 2006), 136–37. For the interesting counterfactual, see Kenneth Brody, *The Avoidable War* (New Brunswick, N.J., 1999), 300–301.

67 The French documentary evidence suggests Mussolini did get tacit French approval for the invasion from Foreign Minister Pierre Laval: see Bruce G. Strang, "Imperial Dreams: The Mussolini-Laval Accords of January 1935," *Historical Journal* 44, no. 3 (2001): 799–809.

68 Original documents in League of Nations and United Nations Office at Geneva (UNOG) Archives, League of Nations, *Dispute between Ethiopia and Italy* (Geneva, 1936). See also Guarneri, *Battaglie economiche,* 370–76; Franco Catalano, *L'economia Italiana Di Guerra. La Politica Economico-Finanziaria Del Fascismo Dalla Guerra d'Etiopia Alla Caduta Del Regime, 1935–1943* (Milan, 1969), 8.

69 "Il Duce annunzia all'Italia ed al mondo la constituzione dell'Impero fascista," *Il Popolo d'Italia,* March 10, 1936, 1. Mussolini's newspaper, *Il Popolo d'Italia,* alluded to the restoration of peace and reproduced a large picture of Mussolini in military uniform, under which the Latin word *Dux* was printed. Mabel Berezin, *Making the Fascist Self: The Political Culture of Interwar Italy* (Ithaca, N.Y., 1997), 124.

70 R. J. B. Bosworth, *Mussolini* (London, 2002), 310.

71 C. Lowe and F. Marzari, *Italian Foreign Policy, 1870–1940* (London, 1975), 209.

72 Duggan, *Force of Destiny,* 507.

73 C. M. Cresswell, *The Social and Economic System of Italian East Africa* (Rome, 1937).

74 Ibid., 8.

75 Ibid., 31, 42, 45, 49.

76 Alberto Sbacchi, *Ethiopia under Mussolini* (London, 1985); Neville, *Mussolini,* 134.

77 Dennis Mack Smith, *Mussolini* (New York, 1982), 232.

78 A good overview of Italian excesses can be found in: MacGregor Knox, *Mussolini Unleashed, 1939–1941: Politics and Strategy in Fascist Italy's Last War* (Cambridge, U.K., 1982), 3–4.

79 Robert Whealey, "Mussolini's Ideological Diplomacy: An Unpublished Document," *Journal of Modern History* 39, no. 4 (1967): 432–37.

80 Notwithstanding the problems with the source, see Luis Bolín, *España: Los Años Vitales* (Madrid, 1967), 178. Ciano had been stationed in Argentina, where he acquired the accent Bolín noticed. Ray Moseley, *Mussolini's Shadow: The Double Life of Count Galeazzo Ciano* (New Haven, Conn., 1999), 24.

81 See Angel Viñas, "La connivencia Fascista con la sublevación militar otros éxitos de la trama civil," *Los Mitos Del 18 De Julio,* edited by Francisco Sánchez Perez (Barcelona, 2013), 79–182.

82 Coverdale's "demand for immediate payment" is unsubstantiated. There is also debate about how many men the planes airlifted from Morocco; Coverdale advocates ten thousand, Jackson fifteen thousand. See Coverdale, *Italian Intervention,* 74–86; Gabriel Jackson, *The Spanish Republic and the Civil War* (Princeton, N.J., 1965), 248. Their effect on the war is beyond question.

83 Ismael Saz, *Mussolini Contra la Segunda República: Hostilidad, Conspiraciones, Intervención (1931–1936)* (Valencia, 1986), 219–22.

84 Basset claims that Canaris's Abwehr provided weapons to Abyssinian insurgents in spite of Italian ties. See Richard Bassett, *Hitler's Spy Chief: The Wilhelm Canaris Mystery* (London, 2005), 8.

85 "Proposals and Requests Brought by Admiral Canaris on August 28 (1936)," Ministerio degli Affari Esteri, Ufficio Spagna, b. 2 (henceforth *Italian Documents*). We owe the finding to Coverdale, *Italian Intervention,* 103.

86 Minister Hans Frank flew to Rome in late September to invite Mussolini to Germany and reassure him about Spain. Galeazzo Ciano, *L'Europa verso la catastrofe* (Milan, 1948), 42–45.

87 *Italian Documents,* b. 1, cited in Robert Colodny, *The Struggle for Madrid* (New York, 1958), 164–69.

88 This goes beyond the point about war as domestic economic stimulant, which some made at the time. On this issue, see the classic Alan S. Milward, *War, Economy, and Society, 1939–1945* (Berkeley, 1977).

89 "The work you are undertaking is of capital importance for the triumph of Latin and Christian civilization menaced by the international rabble at Moscow's orders," Mussolini allegedly told Rossi. Aldo Santamaria, *Operazione Spagna, 1936–1939* (Rome, 1965), 23.

90 Michael Alpert, *A New International History of the Spanish Civil War* (New York, 2004), 68–69.

91 For an interesting counterfactual arguing Italy could have kept Majorca, see Bruce Strang, *On the Fiery March* (Westport, Conn., 2003), 52.

92 For transcripts, see International Committee for Application of Agreement regarding Non-Intervention in Spain, *The Legislative and Other Measures Taken by the Participating Governments to Give Effects to the Agreement regarding Non-Intervention in Spain* (London, 1936). Ciano's predecessor, Dino Grandi, represented Italy.

93 Antony Beevor, *The Battle for Spain* (London, 1982), 149.

94 Admiral Dönitz discussed the possibility of occupying Spain to take over Gibraltar. International Military Tribunal, Avalon Project, Yale University (henceforth, *IMT*), vol. 13, 348.

95 Ferretti allowed Coverdale to look at his report draft. Coverdale, *Italian Intervention,* 115, n73. I have not been able to corroborate the evidence.

96 "Germany and Italy Recognise Rebel Government," *Guardian,* November 19, 1936, 1.

97 Reproduction in Cantalupo, *Fu la Spagna,* 66–68.

98 Problematically for Mussolini with regard to Abyssinia, Article 16 of the League Covenant stipulated that any aggressive action against a member of the League would be interpreted as an "act of war against all other Members of the League."

99 Views on the treaty differed, but I agree with Toscano that it was "nothing transcendental." Mario Toscano, "L'Asse Roma-Berlino," in *La politica estera Italiana*

dal 1914 al 1943, edited by Augusto Torre (Torino, 1963), 204. For a dissenting view, see Enzo Santarelli, *Storia del movimento e del regime Fascista* (Rome, 1967), 264. See also Coverdale, *Italian Intervention,* 153. Giura largely ignores the debate.

100 For Balkan clearing deals, see Toniolo, *L'Economia,* 279, n29.

101 See Cantalupo, *Fu la Spagna,* 63.

102 Ufficio Spagna. Given these negotiations are not fully detailed in Spanish or German archives, I am relying here on an interview between Coverdale and Count Luca Petromanchi, the head of the Ufficio, from July 7, 1970, cited in Coverdale, *Italian Intervention,* 165.

103 On the eve of their involvement in World War II, Mussolini would famously tell Ciano, "We must keep [Italians] disciplined and in uniform from morning till night. They only understand the stick, the stick, the stick." Though Moseley and other authors translate "the stick" into "Beat them," the original most closely resembles the Miller-Pugliese translation. Ciano, *Diary,* February 7, 1940, 318.

104 Count Luca Petromanchi was in charge. See Ciano, *Diary,* 166.

105 For an original account from the Italian War Ministry, see *Volontari Dell'esercito nella Guerra di Spagna* (Rome, 1939). See also Ernestino Chiappa, *C.T.V., Il Corpo Trppe Volontarie italiane durante la Guerra Civile Spagnola* (Milan, 2003).

106 The Fascist divisions were Dio lo Vuole, Fiamme Nere, and Penne Nere, respectively. For a nostalgic contemporary account from 1941, see Sandro Piazzoni, *Las tropas Flechas Negras en la guerra de España (1937–39)* (Barcelona, 1941).

107 Their average age was between twenty-eight and thirty-two. A group of 2,300 men reported having approximately 7,300 children, rounded to more than three each. See Coverdale, *Italian Intervention,* 186, for data.

108 *Manchester Guardian,* February 17, 1936, cited in Coverdale, *Italian Intervention,* 186.

109 Foreign Office, Private Foreign Office Papers of Sir Anthony Eden, FO/954/13, 1936, National Archives, Kew, U.K. In that lengthy report dated September 18, 1936, Eden states that Grandi told him that any overtures to Italy would be welcomed in Rome, even if many in the regime sought closer Berlin ties. Crucially, however, Grandi did not mention Mussolini.

110 "The Anglo-Italian Agreement," *Bulletin of International News* 15, no. 8 (1938): 11–13.

111 FO/954/13A, 125, 1936.

112 See Robert Whealey, *Hitler and Spain* (Lexington, Ky., 1989), 52.

113 The argument is best made in Glyn Stone, *Spain, Portugal and the Great Powers, 1931–1941* (London, 2005).

114 Zara Steiner, *The Foreign Office and Foreign Policy, 1898–1914* (London, 1986).

115 Robert Alexander, *The Anarchists in the Spanish Civil War* (London, 1999), 158–59.

116 Cited in John F. Coverdale, "The Battle of Guadalajara, 8–22 March 1937," *Journal of Contemporary History* 9, no. 1 (1974): 53–75.

117 See Thomas, *Spanish Civil War,* 501–3.

118 Marshall-Cornwall, ed., *Documents on German Foreign Policy 1918–1945, from the Archives of the German Foreign Ministry,* Series D, 1937–1945, vol. 3: *Germany and the Spanish Civil War 1936–1939* (Washington, D.C., 1950) (henceforth, *German Documents*), Doc. 235, 1, dated March 25, 1937, and based on conversations with French Foreign Minister Delbos. When Blum was replaced by Chautemps in June, Delbos remained foreign minister.

119 Ibid.

120 *Il Popolo d'Italia,* June 17, 1937. This translation is Coverdale's, *Italian Intervention,* 194.

121 In spite of offering no economic analysis, Whealey is indeed right to call Hitler the "principal winner." Whealey, *Hitler and Spain,* 135. He is also correct on the deepening relations between Hitler and Mussolini, as well as the successful use of Spain as a diversion for the prospect of a "Grand Alliance" (137).

122 Guarneri, *Battaglie economiche,* 490–93.

123 Ciano, *Diary,* 7, 12, 28, 30, 40, 54, 93, 112, 238, 253, 320. See also relevant footnote on 615.

124 Ciano, *Diary,* 30, November 27, 1937.

125 Guarneri, *Battaglie economiche,* 593.

126 A direct, econometric comparison of the two closed economies is lacking, though we know the effects of underperformance in the Italian military defeats of World War II.

127 Ciano's diaries suggests Italians in mid-1937 thought the war would be long. Ciano, *Diary,* August 25 and 26, 1937, 2. Guarneri would later complain about Franco's empty promises: "After the battle of Malaga [in 1937], it was thought Franco could take Madrid in 15 days! They were, instead, two years!" Guarneri, *Battaglie economiche,* 682.

128 Catalano, *L'economia italiana di guerra,* especially 3–11.

129 Societá Anonima Fertilizanti Italiani. *Italian Documents, Politica,* b. 32. For a transcript, see Cantalupo, *Fu la Spagna,* 90–97.

130 Coverdale, *Italian Intervention,* 298.

131 Guarneri, *Battaglie economiche,* 682. The free currency was consistently British pounds.

132 Archivos del Ministerio de Relaciones Exteriores y Cooperación, Archivo de Guerra de Burgos (henceforth Archivos Españoles). See b. 13, "Italian proposal for the retirement of merchandise based on the April 29, 1937 Agreement," June 29, 1937. Fagiuoli later worked in the Balkans.

133 *German Documents,* Doc. 207, 229.

134 Archivos Españoles, b. 7628, Doc. 12. Specifically the document cited contains a comparative graph of transfers, in relation to explaining the current deficit due to Nationalist expropriations. See "Rio Tinto LTDA Nota Comparativa" (Comparative Note on Rio Tinto LTDA), June 29, 1937.

135 Coverdale, *Italian Intervention,* 307.

136 Italian Documents, Ufficio Spagna, b. 3, Anfuso telegrammed Ciano on July 4, 7, and 8, 1937. The remaining 75 percent of the amount due for the Italian war supplies was added to the Franco-Fagiuoli credit line, according to the Burgos documents.

137 See Giura, *Tra politica ed economia,* 57–66.

138 Two warships and sixty new planes would fall outside the agreement and would be paid for in cash by Spanish authorities. There is disagreement about the ultimate cost of those war supplies and the loans to cover them. A note by Ciano on August 11 gives 125 million lire as the official number, though Guarneri then says it was closer to 250 million. Italian Documents, Ufficio Spagna, b. 3, telegram of August 11, 1937; Guarneri, *Battaglie economiche,* 534.

139 Bilateral relations deteriorated toward the end of the summer of 1937. Anthony Eden, *Facing the Dictators: The Eden Memoirs* (London, 1962), 506. Coverdale also discusses this trilateral relationship, wondering if Mussolini believed British "passivity and ineffectiveness" to be such that London would not react. Coverdale, *Italian Intervention,* 310–11.

140   Ruggero Zangrandi, *Il Lungo Viaggio: Contributo alla Storia di una Generazione* (Torino, 1948), 147. (Coverdale misquotes the title of the original, citing instead the second edition).

141   Ciano, *Diary,* August 25, 1937.

142   U.K. Cabinet Memoranda, 1935–1937, Cabinet Papers, National Archives, Kew, U.K., CAB/24/273, 2 (1937): "All available evidence regarding stocks of this essential war store tends to refute any suggestion of the immediate likelihood of Italy engaging in a war involving large expenditure of liquid fuel."

143   Coverdale, *Italian Intervention,* 346.

144   Ciano, *Diary,* March 26, 1938, 74.

145   Guarneri, *Battaglie economiche,* 681–82. The translation of this quote is Coverdale's, *Italian Intervention,* 346–47, n89.

146   Archivos Españoles, Box 833, Folder 2528, Doc. 4.

147   At the time the Republic was receiving cutting-edge Soviet aircraft. Walter Boyne, ed., *Air Warfare* (New York, 2002), especially 326–27.

148   Archivos Españoles, b. 833, Folder 2528, telegrams dated July 14 and 17, 1938, from Mosquera, a Spanish envoy, under the title "Informe acerca de las negociaciones en curso para ultimar los suministros de suplementarios de aviación."

149   Archivos Españoles, b. 833, Folder 2528, telegram by Mosquera dated July 17, 1938.

150   Archivos Españoles, b. 833, Folder 2528, telegrams by Mosquera dated July 28 and 31, 1938.

151   Giura, *Tra politica ed economia,* 48–51.

152   Javier Tusell, "La intervención italiana en la Guerra civil española a través de los telegramas de la 'Missione Militare Italiana in Spagna,'" in *Italia y la guerra civil española: Simposio celebrado en la Escuela Española de Historia y Arqueología de Roma* (Madrid, 1986), 238–39.

153   Weary of French intervention, Franco insisted on secrecy. Stanley Payne, *Franco and Hitler* (New Haven, Conn., 2008), 31.

154   Coverdale's otherwise exhaustive analysis is deficient in terms of policy implications. His figures for cost are also understated. Coverdale, *Italian Intervention,* especially 408–9.

155   Italian Documents, Ufficio Spagna, b. 17 and 87, "Appunto S. E. il ministro," Rome, dated November 24, 1939. See Giura, *Tra politica ed economia,* 68. According to Guarneri's data, the full cost up to December 31, 1939, was 8,625 million lire. The actual cost was likely considerably higher.

156   This is based on the Vitali revision of ISTAT data. Via Global Financial Data. See also Mark Harrison, *The Economics of World War II: Six Great Powers in International Comparison* (Cambridge, U.K., 2000), table 5.1 on 179. This was, of course, leaving out other Italian expenditures for restocking and military investments elsewhere.

157   Brown University's Watson Institute for International Studies, "Costs of War" project, March 14, 2013.

158   This is a factor Coverdale, among others, ignores.

159   Archivos Españoles, B. 833, Folder 2528, telegram from Ciano to Beigdeber, dated August 19, 1939.

160   Guarneri, *Battaglie economiche,* 895.

161   See ibid., 908, n44.

162   "Generosísimo." For details on the payments and the opinion, see Angel Viñas, *Política Comercial Exterior En España (1931–1975)* (Madrid, 1979), 1: 232.

163 Instituto de Estudios Fiscales, *Datos básicos para la historia financiera de España* (Madrid, 1976), 257–82; Giura, *Tra politica ed economia,* 87.

164 Ettore Latronico, *Spagna economica, oggi e domani* (Milan, 1938).

165 Mario Roatta, *Otto milioni di baionette: L'Esercito italiano in guerra dal 1940 al 1944* (Milan, 1946), 13.

166 Lowe traces the revival of the Roman term to the 1880s and to poet Gabriele D'Annunzio. See C. J. Lowe, *Italian Foreign Policy, 1870–1940* (London, 1975), 34. Also Neville, *Mussolini,* 209.

167 Gaspare Giudice, *Benito Mussolini* (Turin, 1969), especially 606–8.

168 *German Documents,* vol. 10, Doc. 392, Mussolini to Franco, letter dated August 25, 1940 (XVIII), Rome.

169 For an example of the worries, see the note by Italian Ambassador Henke as early as August 8, 1940, in *German Documents,* vol. 10, Doc. 312, 441–42.

170 Franz Halder, *Kriegstagebuch* (Stuttgart, 1962–1964), 2: 212, cited in Knox, *Mussolini Unleashed,* 1.

9. THE FORMAL EMPIRE

Epigraph: "Göring et la collaboration: Un beau document," *Cahiers d'histoire de la guerre,* May 1950, cited and translated by Alan S. Milward, *The New Order and the French Economy* (Oxford, 1970), 182.

1 For details on the businesses and its activities, see Rafael García Pérez, *Franquismo y Tercer Reich* (Madrid, 1993), 121–24.

2 García Pérez shares this conclusion, even if he questions the efficacy of the whole process in the 1936–1945 timeframe. García Pérez, *Franquismo y Tercer Reich,* 573. See also Christian Leitz, *Economic Relations Between Nazi Germany and Franco's Spain: 1936–1945* (New York, 1996), especially 99–100.

3 Ritschl has a different take on this, yet at the very least some of the effects he sees as of 1938 were due to Germany's war drive. See A. O. Ritschl, "Nazi Economic Imperialism and the Exploitation of the Small: Evidence from Germany's Secret Foreign Exchange Balances, 1938–1940," *Economic History Review,* n.s., 54, no. 2 (2001): 324–45.

4 "El carácter neocolonial de la política exterior alemana con respecto a España." García Pérez, *Franquismo y Tercer Reich,* 575.

5 The Saarland had been reintegrated into Germany in 1935 after a fifteen-year League of Nations mandate. Although the Nazi Josef Bürckel, later a key figure in the Anschluß and occupation, was commissioner for the reintegration *(Reichskommissar für die Rückgliederung des Saarlandes),* the project was not really imperial in the sense that Saarland identity never belonged to any nation-state other than Germany. Its economic resources, particularly coal, were indeed important—and this was rightly recognized even during the referendum campaign.

6 Klaus Jürgen Müller, *Das Heer Und Hitler: Armee Und Nationalsozialistisches Regime 1933–1940* (Stuttgart, 1969), especially 46–47. For a wider discussion, see Weinberg, *The Foreign Policy of Hitler's Germany: Starting World War II, 1937–1939* (Atlantic Heights, N.J., 1994), 303, nn11–12.

7 Ian Kershaw, *Fateful Choices: Ten Decisions That Changed the World* (London, 2007), 63.

8 "A Referendum for Austria," *Economist,* March 12, 1938, 6–7.

9 Mussolini was, as we have seen, a key impediment to a takeover of Austria in 1934. During a visit to Germany in 1937, Göring had pressed the point, and did so

again in 1938. A logistical issue (von Ribbentrop was in the process of moving from London to Berlin to take over the Foreign Ministry) gave Göring considerably more power during the Austrian Crisis. See Richard Overy, *Göring, The Iron Man* (London, 1984), 80.

10 Adolf Hitler, *Mein Kampf* (Munich, 1923), especially 19.

11 Hitler had appointed Nazis to the Austrian Cabinet and obtained pardons for Nazis convicted in Austria. Kershaw provides the best account of the hour-by-hour developments in English in Ian Kershaw, *Hitler: 1936–1945: Nemesis* (London, 2000), 68–69.

12 Miklas had refused to appoint Seyß-Inquart, who himself had reservations about a full annexation of Austria. According to Kershaw and others, "coordination" with an element of compulsion and coercion *(Gleichschsaltung)* had been discussed, though not an outright Anschluß.

13 Müller, *Das Heer,* 56.

14 See Galeazzo Ciano, *Ciano's Diary, 1939–1943* (London, 1947), March 12, 1938, 69.

15 As usual, the message was relayed by Prince Hesse. International Military Tribunal, vol. 31, 369, Doc. 2949-PS, Avalon Project, Yale University. Also in Max Domarus, ed., *Reden Und Proklamationen, 1932–1945* (Wurttemberg, 1962), 813. The translation here is Kershaw's, *Nemesis,* 78.

16 Evan Burr Bukey, *Hitler's Austria: Popular Sentiment in the Nazi Era, 1938–1945* (Chapel Hill, N.C., 2000), especially 43–71.

17 Alfred D. Low, *The Anschluß Movement, 1918–1919: And the Paris Peace Conference* (Philadelphia, 1974); S. W. Gould, "Austrian Attitudes toward Anschluß: October 1918–September 1919," *Journal of Modern History* 22, no. 3 (1950): 220–31.

18 Members of the left, the original hotbed of annexationist dreams during the last years of the Habsburg Empire, supported the outcome, if not the way it was achieved. Social Democrat Karl Renner, later the first postwar president, supported it. Rolf Steininger, "The Road to Anschluß," in *Austria in the Twentieth Century,* edited by Rolf Steininger, Günter Bischof, and Michael Gehler (New Brunswick, N.J., 2008), 85–115.

19 Ralf Banken, "Die Deutsche Goldreserven- Und Devisenpolitik 1933–1939," in *Jahrbuch Für Wirtschaftsgeschichte* (Berlin, 2003), 1, 49–78.

20 "I swear that: I will be faithful, and obedient to the Fuehrer of the German Reich and the German people, Adolf Hitler, and will perform my duties conscientiously and selflessly. (The audience takes the pledge with uplifted hands). You have taken this pledge. A scoundrel he who breaks it. To our Fuehrer a triple 'Sieg Heil.'" For the Reichsbank decree, see *Reichsgesetzblatt,* 1938, I, 254 and *IMT,* EC-297-A, via Avalon Project.

21 As Kirk outlines there was domestic opposition, crushed by the regime. See Timothy Kirk, "Economic Integration and Political Opposition between the Anschluß and the War," in *Nazism and the Working Class in Austria* (Cambridge, U.K., 1996).

22 Austrian taxes had been lower than the Reich's; they were harmonized upward. A "flight tax" was also introduced, which made revenue from mostly Jewish sources at the time. Ernst Hanisch, "Österreichs Wirtschaft und der Anschluß," in *Österreich 1938–1945: Dokumente,* edited by Brigitte Bailer-Galanda et al. (Vienna, 2005).

23 "Germany," *Economist,* April 23, 1938, 12–13.

24 The translation is Overy's, *Göring,* 81.

25 Stefan Zweig, introduction to *Die Welt von Gestern* (Stockholm, 1942).

26 Mazower's masterful account of occupation details this nicely: Mark Mazower, *Hitler's Empire: How the Nazis Ruled Europe* (London, 2009), 49.

27 Though focused strictly on the city, see Gerhard Botz, *Nationalsozialismus in Wien* (Vienna, 2008).

28 An Austrian SS had been active since at least 1934; Seyß-Inquart was one of its local leaders. Wolfgang Rosar, *Deutsche Gemeinschaft. Seyss-Inquart u. d. Anschluß* (Vienna, 1971).

29 Management of the territory was ruled by Führer decrees, reproduced in English in Raphael Lemkin, *Axis Rule in Occupied Europe* (London, 1944), 341.

30 "The Second Republic," in *A History of the Czechoslovak Republic 1918–1948,* edited by Victor Mamatey and Radomír Luža (Princeton, N.J., 1973), especially 153–57.

31 They had already encouraged Slovaks to seek independence earlier.

32 For an accessible overview of the military preparations, see Jochen Böhler, *Auftakt Zum Vernichtungskrieg: Die Wehrmacht in Polen 1939* (Frankfurt, 2006).

33 Wilhelm Frick was minister throughout, only to be replaced in the summer of 1943. Yet the power of the SS in internal administration grew steadily.

34 Stuckart had also been involved in the integration of the Sudetenland a few months before. For an example of his writing from his time in Austria, see Gottfried Neesse and Wilhelm Stuckart, *Partei und Staat* (Vienna, 1938).

35 See Lemkin, *Axis Rule in Occupied Europe,* 342. Mazower details the legal implications of Hitler's decree in *Hitler's Empire,* 60.

36 For an example from 1942, see Lemkin, *Axis Rule in Occupied Europe,* 343.

37 August Meyer, *Das Syndikat: Reichswerke "Hermann Göring"* (Braunschweig, 1986).

38 This is a point well made by Adam Tooze, *The Wages of Destruction: The Making and Breaking of the Nazi Economy* (London, 2006), xxii.

39 It was technically booked as owned by the Bank of the Protectorate before being shipped, in a BIS subaccount. For an analysis of the original documents from the bank, see Arthur Smith, *Hitler's Gold: The Story of the Nazi War Loot* (Berg, 1996), 8.

40 The Czech equivalent dollar amount was $146 million, at the 2.49 official exchange rate. Data from R. L. Bidwell, *Currency Conversion Tables: A Hundred Years of Change* (London, 1970), 22–24.

41 Ritschl considers this the beginning of "Germany's policy of achieving economic growth on the extensive margin through military aggression." See "Nazi Economic Imperialism," 330.

42 *IMT,* EC-369, via Avalon Project.

43 Mazower claims this was a "first in modern European history," involving the "formal imperialism of one European state on another." Yet this overlooks Bonapartist republics in the nineteenth century. Mazower, *Hitler's Empire,* 138.

44 Moses Moskowitz, "Three Years of the Protectorate of Bohemia and Moravia," *Political Science Quarterly* 57, no. 3 (1942): 353–75.

45 Drahomír Jančík, Eduard Kubů, Jiří Novotný, and Jiří Šouša, "Der Mechanismus Der Enteignung Jüdischen Goldes Im 'Protektorat Böhmen Und Mähren' Und Seine Funktionsweise (1939–1945)," *Zeitschrift Für Unternehmensgeschichte/Journal of Business History* 46, no. 1 (2001): 58–76.

46 John Lewis Gaddis, *George F. Kennan: An American Life* (New York, 2011), 121. For the papers, see George Kennan, *From Prague after Munich: Diplomatic Papers, 1938–1940* (Princeton, N.J., 1968).

47 The signing was not public until April, however. In early May Spain withdrew from the League of Nations as promised to Rome and Berlin.

48 James Marshall-Cornwall et al., eds., *Documents on German Foreign Policy 1918–1945, from the Archives of the German Foreign Ministry,* Series D, 1937–1945, vol. 3:

Germany and the Spanish Civil War 1936–1939 (Washington, D.C., 1950) (henceforth, *German Documents*), Doc. 773.

49 Ibid.

50 Viñas covers this topic eruditely. Angel Viñas, *Política Comercial Exterior En España (1931–1975)* (Madrid, 1979), especially 281–85.

51 *German Documents,* Doc. 786.

52 *German Documents,* Doc. 784, dated Berlin, April 6, 1939, see pt. 3 in priorities.

53 Archivo de Burgos, at the Ministerio de Asuntos Exteriores in Madrid. Archivo de Burgos, Folder 1895/6, 2–3

54 Wohlthat had extensive foreign trade negotiation experience from the Baltics to Holland and even the London Whaling Conference, where he represented Germany. He held an MA from Columbia.

55 Hans-Joachim Braun, *German Economy in the Twentieth Century* (1990; London, 2012), especially 101–2. For its later military role, see Cornel I. Scafeş et al., *Third Axis, Fourth Ally: Romanian Armed Forces in the European War, 1941–1945* (London, 1995).

56 Translation is Braun's, *German Economy,* 102.

57 García Perez, *Franquismo y Tercer Reich,* 100.

58 *German Documents,* series D, vol. 3, Doc. 809.

59 "Un dictado económico," *Informe al ministro Suanzes,* June 16, 1939.

60 This would have required the type of clearing agreement that they had sought—and failed to get—in 1937–1938.

61 García Pérez, *Franquismo y Tercer Reich,* 121.

62 Woodruff Smith, *The Ideological Origins of Nazi Imperialism* (New York, 1986), especially 184–87.

63 Signed a week before the invasion, the Molotov-Ribbentrop Pact famously included secret clauses on the division of Poland. Kershaw, *Nemesis,* 162–68.

64 Von Ribbentrop was the most anti-British member of Hitler's entourage. How much this concerned Hitler before the advent of war is contentions. Only when this "bloc" failed decisively did Hitler order preparations for the invasion of the Soviet Union. Geoffrey Roberts, *Stalin's Wars: From World War to Cold War, 1939–1953* (New Haven, Conn., 2006), 56.

65 It is still up for debate whether Hitler foresaw that Britain and France would declare war. For an introduction to the historiographic debate, see Adam Tooze, "Hitler's Gamble," *History Today* 56, no. 11 (2006).

66 For a detailed U.S. army report, see Robert M. Kennedy, *The German Campaign in Poland* (Washington, D.C., 1980).

67 Admittedly a difficult term to translate, technically meaning "special groups" but closer to "task forces." For the rising importance of the SS in the Polish occupation as a precedent to the Final Solution, the sources are extensive, in German, Polish, and English. Christopher Browning, *The Origins of the Final Solution: The Evolution of Nazi Jewish Policy, September 1939–March 1942* (Lincoln, 2007).

68 To manage Poland many fired Nazis were pardoned and returned to work. Müller, *Das Heer,* 47.

69 For Blaskowitz's reports, see Robert Kane, *Disobedience and Conspiracy in the German Army, 1918–1945* (Jefferson, N.C., 2002), especially 167–78.

70 Generals Keitel and Brauchitisch, Blaskowitz's superiors, did not intervene, arguing the role of the SS was Hitler's prerogative. Browning, *The Origins of the Final Solution,* 17.

71 For an excellent and accessible overview, see Timothy Snyder, *Bloodlands: Europe between Hitler and Stalin* (New York, 2010).

72 This is a point well made by Snyder and Mazower among the latest research.

73 Vejas Liulevicius, *War Land on the Eastern Front: Culture, National Identity and German Occupation in World War I* (Cambridge, U.K., 2000), 1–12.

74 Cited in John Connelly, "Nazis and Slavs: From Racial Theory to Racist Practice," *Central European History* 32, no. 1 (1999): 1–33. Also in Mazower, *Hitler's Empire*, 75.

75 For detail on his ruthless rule, see Martyn Housden, *Hans Frank: Lebensraum and the Holocaust* (London, 2003).

76 Ulrich Herbert, *Fremdarbeiter: Politik und Praxis des "Ausländer-Einsatzes" in der Kriegswirtschaft des Dritten Reiches* (Berlin, 1999); Edward Homze, *Foreign Labor in Nazi Germany* (Princeton, N.J., 1967).

77 Ulrich Herbert, "Zwangsarbeiter in der deutschen Kriegswirtschaft 1939–45, ein Überblick," in *De Verplichte tewerkstelling in Duitsland 1942–1945: Acta van het Symposium gehouden te Brussel op 6 en 7 oktober 1992* (Brussels, 1992), 165–80.

78 The Francoist historical perspective asserted for decades that Franco began to distance himself from Hitler as of this point. This was, it turns out, propaganda.

79 Edward Ericson, *Feeding the German Eagle: Soviet Economic Aid to Nazi Germany, 1933–1941* (Westport, Conn., 1999), especially 44–56.

80 Paul Preston, *Franco: A Biography* (London, 1994), 340–41.

81 The Admiralty had long been working on the mechanics of a new blockade in 1939, and it was at least partly implemented—via coordination with the French Ministry—the day after the war declaration. For original documents, see W. N. Medlicott, *The Economic Blockade* (London, 1952).

82 Eric W. Osborne, *Britain's Economic Blockade of Germany, 1914–1919* (London, 2004).

83 See Instituto de Historia y Cultura Aeronáutica, *Historia de la aviación española* (Madrid, 1988), especially 246; José Luis Alcofar Nassaes, *La Aviación Legionaria En La Guerra Española* (Barcelona, 1975).

84 The details of the meetings are available at Documentos Españoles, Archivo de Burgos, Box R. 1895/6. See also Viñas, *Relaciones Comerciales*, 228; García Perez, *Franquismo y Tercer Reich*, 127.

85 The German documents and Spanish reactions show that the Germans were now intent on adding whatever they could to the final bill. Hence the size of the unacknowledged expenses. Viñas has credibly estimated a difference of around 50 million Reichsmarks between what the Spaniards seem to have paid and what the Germans acknowledged they had paid. See Viñas, *Política Comercial*, 260.

86 Robert H. Whealey, *Hitler and Spain: The Nazi Role in the Spanish Civil War, 1936–1939* (Lexington, Ky., 1989), 90–94.

87 García Perez produced the best synthesis from Documentos Españoles, Archivo de Burgos, R. 1895. See García Perez, *Franquismo y Tercer Reich*, 130, for the chart and then 135–39 for a detailed analysis of the "special supply payments" ("suministros especiales") and "other debts" ("otras deudas").

88 García Pérez, *Franquismo y Tercer Reich*, 60.

89 Viñas, *Política Comercial*, 231.

90 Ricardo de la Cierva, *Historia Esencial de La Guerra Civil Española: Todos Los Problemas Resueltos, Sesenta Años Después* (Madrid, 1996), 139.

91 Prime Minister Churchill ordered it on September 3. See *Daily Telegraph*, September 4, 1939, 1.

92 This is a point we owe to Viñas, along with the found documents that detail it (even including one from Wohlthat acknowledging the quality of the new Iberian negotiators). See Viñas, *Política Comercial*, 324–25.

93 García Pérez considers it a "first" for the new state. García Pérez, *Franquismo y Tercer Reich*, 108.

94 This suggests that only commercial attaché Enge returned from the previous team.

95 The team led by Wohlthat tried to triangulate trade via Italy, allegedly creating bilateral commerce between the two nonbelligerents, but Rome was reticent to accept it. It was a system similar to that devised by the ministry to trade with Spain during the Civil War, only it was now reversed.

96 Comisión Interministerial de Tratados.

97 *German Documents*, vol. 8, Doc. 482. In the first appendix, the materials of interest to the Germans are listed, neatly separated into industrial and nonindustrial goods. The main focus remained iron, pyrites, wolfram. For the Spanish copies, see an (edited) version in *Tratados Españoles*, vol. 6, book 1, 495–506. We owe to García Perez the note about the editing of the Iberian documents, which lack the appendixes. García Perez, *Franquismo y Tercer Reich*, 109, n36.

98 It was Article 2 of the treaty, along with the "encouragement" of private exchange in Article 3. Implicitly Article 3 acknowledged that the exchange, as it existed under HISMA-ROWAK, was not "private" but rather state-sponsored.

99 *German Documents*, series D, vol. 8, Doc. 678.

100 García Perez has citations on specific statements, but these are not backed by a clear source.

101 *German Documents*, vol. 8, Doc. 482. García Perez calls this an "abject failure" by the Germans, which unsurprisingly greatly bothered Göring. See García Perez, *Franquismo y Tercer Reich*, 222.

102 Reproduced in *Tratados Españoles*, vol. 6, book 1.

103 Doug Dildy, *Denmark and Norway 1940: Hitler's Boldest Operation* (Oxford, 2007).

104 The force was withdrawn only in June, when the Nazis launched their invasion of France.

105 It was important, from a logistical perspective, to have access to Swedish territory. See Christian Leitz, *Nazi Germany and Neutral Europe During the Second World War* (Manchester, 2000), 54–55.

106 Indeed in the 1943 elections the Nazis received only 2 percent of the vote. Berlin replaced Renthe-Fink that year, seeking tighter control as exploitation escalated.

107 Absolute economic compliance changed only in late 1941. Philip Giltner, *In the Friendliest Manner: German-Danish Economic Cooperation during the Nazi Occupation of 1940–1949* (New York, 1998), 13–52.

108 Milward covers in detail a relationship that went as far back as 1936. See Alan Milward, *The Fascist Economy in Norway* (Oxford, 1972), chapter 1.

109 The puppet regime saw Quisling serve as "minister president" from February 1, 1942, until the end of the war in May 1945. For details on the man and his regime, see Hans Fredrik Dahl, *Quisling: A Study in Treachery* (Cambridge, U.K., 1999).

110 Hans Fredrik Dahl et al., eds., *Norsk Krigsleksikon 1940–45* (Oslo, 1995), "Quisling" and "quisling," 334.

111 The Norwegian camps were not extermination camps, though they imprisoned over fifty thousand people; the camps Grini and Falstadt were the largest. Characteristic of Terboven's brutality was the reaction against the murder of two Gestapo officers in the small seaside village of Tælavåg. Terboven directed the retaliation:

he destroyed the town, sank its ships, imprisoned the women, and deported the men to concentration camps. Terboven married Goebbels's former secretary (and alleged mistress), Ilse Stahl.

112 Hein Klemann and Sergei Kudryashov, *Occupied Economies: An Economic History of Nazi-Occupied Europe, 1939–1945* (London, 2012), 82.

113 Werner Warmbrunn, *The German Occupation of Belgium 1940–1944* (New York, 1993), 68.

114 *German Documents,* series D, vol. 11, 612–19. See also Mazower, *Hitler's Empire,* 106.

115 For his postwar memoirs, see Alexander von Falkenhausen, *Mémoires D'outre-guerre. Extraits: Comment J'ai Gouverné la Belgique de 1940 à 1944* (Brussels, 1974).

116 Klemann and Kudryashov, *Occupied Economies,* 85. The exception, however, was Jewish goods, which continued to be looted. See Avi Beker, *The Plunder of Jewish Property during the Holocaust: Confronting European History* (Basingstoke, U.K., 2001).

117 See John Gillingham, *Belgian Business in the Nazi New Order* (Ghent, 1977), 83–84.

118 Even though the focus is overwhelmingly political, see Dietrich Orlow, *The Nazis in the Balkans: A Case Study of Totalitarian Politics* (Pittsburgh, 1968).

119 Mazower covers this tension well in *Hitler's Empire,* 102–3.

120 "Netherlands: Occupation," *Time,* June 4, 1940.

121 This was the same General Thomas who collaborated closely with Schacht in 1933–1937, later to abandon him during the banker's fall from Nazi grace.

122 The statement appeared in the *Völischer Beobachter,* cited in Klemann and Kudryashov, *Occupied Economies,* 85.

123 The French commander, Gamelin, had suggested an invasion while the Polish campaign was ongoing. See Martin S. Alexander, *The Republic in Danger: General Maurice Gamelin and the Politics of French Defence, 1933–1940* (Cambridge, U.K., 2003), 207–8.

124 Karl-Heinz Frieser, *Blitzkrieg-Legende: Der Westfeldzug 1940* (Munich, 1995), 24.

125 The debate continues as to whether the Germans were necessarily preparing for a "long war." The main proponent of the "Blitzkrieg economy" view is Milward, while Tooze and Overy oppose it. When it comes to the management of the western occupied countries, the failure of Blitzkrieg definitely changed the nature of occupation management.

126 Bloch's contemporary account still stands out: Marc Bloch, *L'étrange Défaite: Témoignage Écrit en 1940* (Paris, 1940). See also Ernest May, *Strange Victory: Hitler's Conquest of France* (New York, 2000).

127 Eberhard Jäckel, *Frankreich in Hitlers Europa: Die Deutsche Frankreichpolitik Im 2. Weltkrieg* (Stuttgart, 1966), 75.

128 Ibid., 77. Bürckel was one of those officials. Forced deportations started in November 1940.

129 The best study of economics in occupied France remains Milward's. See Alan S Milward, *The New Order and the French Economy* (Oxford, 1970), 39.

130 Robert Paxton, *Vichy France: Old Guard and New Order, 1940–1944* (New York, 1972).

131 *Economist,* June 29, 1940, 1.

132 Hitler considered a treaty, but the attack on Mers-el-Kebir in North Africa changed his mind; he then decided to wait until the end of the war with Britain.

133 Klemann and Kudryashov, *Occupied Economies,* 87.

134 Hermann Böhme, *Der Deutschfranzösische Waffenstillstand im Zweiten Weltkrieg* (Stuttgart, 1966), 267.

135 For the use of the system in eastern Europe, see Raphael Lemkin, *Axis Rule in Occupied Europe*, 280.

136 "The Value of the Reichsmark," *Statist*, May 10, 1941, cited in Milward, *New Order*, 55.

137 On July 9 von Ribbentrop himself acknowledged in a letter to Göring that these occupied countries retained their "sovereignty," even if they were to be brought into the "economic area" of the Reich. Milward, *New Order*, 57–63.

138 Tooze, *Wages*, 385.

139 Milward, *New Order*, especially 181–92.

140 Franco wanted "un período de tranquilidad," according to reports from Ambassador Stohrer in 1939. *German Documents*, series D, vol. 3, Doc. 721.

141 Kershaw, *Nemesis*, 327.

142 Ribbentrop and Serrano Suñer did not get along. Michael Bloch, *Ribbentrop* (New York, 1992), 302–10.

143 The *Economist* leader that week was "The French Collapse" (June 29, 1940).

144 Archivos Españoles, Archivo de Burgos, R. 2187, 1–2, letter dated July 5, 1940, cited in García Pérez, *Franquismo y Tercer Reich*, 224.

145 This was the role of the Instituto Español de Moneda Extrajera, under Blas de Huete. Before the Wohlthat agreements in late 1939, they had not been involved in German-Spanish relations. Now they were.

146 This is a common mistake in the historiography that recurs in both García Perez and Leitz.

147 Julian Jackson, *France: The Dark Years, 1940–1944* (Oxford, 2001), especially chapter 4, "The German Problem."

148 See Bloch, *Ribbentrop*, 302–10.

149 Preston has clarified that the train had not been an hour late, but only eight minutes late. Paul Preston, *Franco*, 394–95.

150 Whealey, *Hitler and Franco*, 220–22.

151 This was one of Hitler's negotiating tactics, characteristic of instances when he was exasperated. Kershaw, *Nemesis*, 330.

152 "Mit diesem Kerle ist nichts zu machen." Paul Preston, "Franco and Hitler: The Myth of Hendaye 1940," *Contemporary European History* 1, no. 1 (1992): 1–16.

153 Keeping Spain out of the war was later spun by Francoist propaganda as an act of prudence. Preston, "Franco and Hitler," 1.

154 Nicolaus von Below, *Als Hitlers Adjutant, 1937–45* (Mainz, 1980), 250. See also Kershaw, *Nemesis*, 331. This translation is Kershaw's.

155 On the failure of the "continental option," see, in particular, Andreas Hillgruber, *Hitlers Strategie: Politik und Kriegführung 1940–1941* (Bonn, 1993).

156 Hitler had mentioned Barbarossa before, yet this still seems like a decisive moment for setting on the strategy, particularly given the Italian move against Greece.

157 Ciano, *Diary*, October 10, 1940, 297. See source note in Chapter 8.

158 García Perez found this document in the archive belonging to Handaken Clodius at the Foreign Ministry. See García Perez, *Franquismo y Tercer Reich*, 232, n164.

159 Ibid., 236.

160 The total debt was acknowledged at about 371,800,000 Reichsmarks.

161 Negotiations did resume in 1944 as a last ditch effort to maintain exports of wolfram in spite of the Allied blockade.

162 *Domarus*, 1732.

163 Adam Zamoyski, *Napoleon's Fatal March on Moscow* (New York, 2001).

164 Kershaw, *Nemesis*, 392.

165 Klemann and Kudryashov, *Occupied Economies,* 82.

166 See Giltner, *In the Friendliest Manner,* especially chapter 3. See also Milward, *New Order,* especially chapter 5.

167 Although he is generally on the other side of the debate about the Blitzkrieg economy, Tooze covers this issue in detail in *Wages,* especially chapters 13–15.

168 Tooze makes the point about the "turning point" in December 1941. See *Wages,* 487–88.

169 Klemann and Kudryashov, *Occupied Economies,* 99.

170 See Milward, *New Order,* especially chapter 5.

171 Timothy Mason, *Nazism, Fascism and the Working Class* (Cambridge, U.K., 1995), especially 231–273.

172 Following Mommsen and Broszat, see Jane Caplan, *Government without Administration: State and Civil Service in Weimar and Nazi Germany* (Oxford, 1988). See also her introduction to Mason, *Nazism,* 1–32.

173 The polycratic is characteristic of the so-called functionalist school of Mommsen and Broszat. Kershaw is selectively appreciative of this approach. Ian Kershaw, *The Nazi Dictatorship: Problems and Perspectives of Interpretation* (London, 2000), especially 131–39, and "Working toward the Führer," in *The Third Reich,* edited by Christian Leitz (Oxford, 1999).

174 Cited in Caplan, *Government without Administration,* 309.

175 For the impact on the military, see Müller, *Das Heer,* especially 50–53; John Keegan, *The Second World War* (London, 1989) and *The Mask of Command* (New York, 2004).

176 Pleiger had been a senior manager in Göring's Reichswerke, perhaps the most inefficient venture of the war. In 1942 he was named Reich commissioner for the eastern economy. Matthias Riedel, *Eisen und Kohle für das Dritte Reich: Paul Pleigers Stellung in der NS-Wirtschaft* (Göttingen, 1973).

177 Frank Bajohr, *Parvenüs und Profiteure: Korruption in Der NS-Zeit* (Frankfurt, 2001).

178 This is a point well made in Tooze, *Wages,* xi–xxvii. See also Mazower, *Hitler's Empire,* 261–65; Milward, *New Order,* 271.

179 Data from table 60 in Milward, *New Order,* 273.

180 This is a central point in Snyder, *Bloodlands,* especially 155–87.

181 Mazower and Kershaw make this point clearly.

182 Among the many sources, see Browning, *Origins of the Final Solution.*

183 Bernhardt received it as a local representative of ROWAK. García Pérez deserves credit for finding these files. For the detailed schedule of payments, as confirmed by Bernhardt to Franco on February 23, 1942, see García Pérez, *Franquismo y Tercer Reich,* 271, n89.

184 Preston confirms this from another perspective in *Franco,* 540–60.

185 For an interesting treatment, see Wayne H. Bowen, *Spaniards and Nazi Germany: Collaboration in the New Order* (Missouri, 2000), 103–56.

186 García Pérez, *Franquismo y Tercer Reich,* 275.

187 Hartmut Heine, "El envío de trabajadores españoles a la Alemania nazi, 1941–1945," *Migraciones y Exilios,* July 2006, 9–26.

188 *Acuerdo Hispano-Aleman para el Empleo de Trabajadores Españoles en Alemania,* signed in Madrid on August 21, 1941. Non-Spanish sources seem to understate the number of workers; the latest Iberian sources put the number of workers around fifteen thousand to twenty thousand.

189 Whealey, *Franco and Spain,* 217–19.

190 It most likely referred to the second Battle of El Alamein and subsequent battles in Tunis. See Erwin Rommel, *The Rommel Papers,* edited by Basil Liddel-Hart (New York, 1953), especially 318–21.

191 The letter was also published in the Department of State *Bulletin*. William Franklin et al., eds., *Foreign Relations of the United States, Diplomatic Papers* (Washington, D.C., 1966) (henceforth *FRUS*), series 1942, vol. 3, Europe, Spain, 306.

192 Preston chronicles this in detail in *Franco: A Biography* (London, 1994), especially 480–82.

193 This policy was not exclusive to Spain, for a similar embargo was being negotiated with Salazar's Portugal. Douglas Wheeler, "The Price of Neutrality: Portugal, the Wolfram Question, and World War II," *Luso-Brazilian Review* 23, no. 1 (1986), 107–27.

194 See Tooze, *Wages,* chapter 18, for a discussion of weapons development in the (in)famous Mittelbau factories, focusing on the V2 and the Me 210.

195 *FRUS,* series 1944, vol. 4, 297.

196 Ibid., 298–306.

197 Ibid., 320–30. Hayes, a history professor at Columbia University before taking on the Madrid Embassy, wrote a book about his mission upon his return to the United States. Carlton J. H. Hayes, *Wartime Mission in Spain: 1942–1945* (New York, 1946).

198 *FRUS,* series 1945, vol. 5, 668–69, letter dated March 24, 1945.

199 Partly drafted by exiled Republicans, the resolution prevented nations aided by any country that had fought against UN forces from obtaining membership.

200 *FRUS,* series 1945, Potsdam Conference, vol. 2, 1071–75.

201 Preston, *Franco,* 528.

202 Although Share focuses on the 1975 transition, the discussion of the succession "dilemma" is important to understand the internal changes within the long-lived Francoist dictatorship. Donald Share, "The Franquist Regime and the Dilemma of Succession," *Review of Politics* 48, no. 4 (1986): 549–75.

203 *FRUS,* series 1946, vol. 6, 1071.

204 Rafael García Perez, "El envío de trabajadores españoles a Alemania en la Segunda Guerra Mundial," *Hispania* 170 (1988), 1031–65. See also Leitz, *Nazi Germany and Neutral Europe,* 136.

205 Preston, *Franco,* 553.

206 *FRUS,* series 1946, vol. 5, 1033–34.

207 Julio Aróstegui and Jorge Marco, *El último frente: la resistencia armada antifranquista en España, 1939–1952* (Madrid, 2008) and Secundino Serrano, *Maquis: historia de la guerrilla antifranquista* (Madrid, 2001).

208 *FRUS* 1045, n1. The declaration was made public while President Truman was meeting with Churchill. A day later the latter would deliver his famous "Iron Curtain Speech."

209 During the last days of the war, Franco still believed Hitler would use "miraculous" rockets to win. I have written about Francoist isolation and its end elsewhere. See Pierpaolo Barbieri, "From UN Outcast to U.S. Partner: Steering Francoist Spain toward the Economic Miracle," *Hemispheres: The Tufts Journal of International Affairs,* no. 30 (March 2009): 89–128.

CONCLUSION

1 Walther Funk, *The Economic Future of Europe* (Berlin, 1940). See also Walther Funk, *Wirtschaft im Neuen Europa* (Lübeck, 1941); Maurice Pernot, *German Trade Policy, Dr. Funk's System* (Paris, 1938).

2 Göring was "acting" minister of economics—just like Schacht before him—between Schacht's dismissal and Funk's appointment. Thereafter he maintained informal power over the ministry. Funk's economic ideas were largely indistinguishable from

Schacht's, save perhaps for his closer contacts to the Nazi Party and Göring. Henry Ashby Turner, *German Big Business and the Rise of Hitler* (New York, 1985), 149, 185.

3 Funk, *Economic Future of Europe*, 12.

4 Ibid., 12.

5 Ibid., 8.

6 Paolo Fonzi, "Nazionalsocialismo e Nuovo Ordine Europeo: La Discussione Sulla 'Großraumwirtschaft,'" *Studi Storici* 45, no. 2 (2004): 313–65.

7 Hein Klemann and Sergei Kudryashov, *Occupied Economies: An Economic History of Nazi-Occupied Europe, 1939–1945* (New York, 2012), 85–90.

8 Funk, *Economic Future of Europe*, 7, 9–10. Funk added, "The European economic system will have to be directed toward this goal. The development will take place in stages; today it is weighted down by uncertainties, for we must not forget—we are still in a state of war! This united Europe will allow no influence from outside Europe" (10–11). *Grossraum*, written in German even in the English version, translates into "a large territory," most often with imperial connotations. See Nazi theorist and jurist Carl Schmitt's classic use in *Völkerrechtliche Grossraumordnung, mit Interventionsverbot für Raumfremde Mächte* (Berlin, 1939). See also Vejas Gabriel Liulevicius, "The Languages of Occupation: Vocabularies of German Rule in Eastern Europe in the World Wars," in *Germans, Poland, and Colonial Expansion to the East: 1850 through the Present,* edited by Robert L. Nelson (New York, 2009).

9 Mazower adds that Hitler rebuked Funk in Mark, *Hitler's Empire* (London, 2009), 122–24.

10 Speer tells the story of planning for a monument to be forty-six feet higher than the 151-feet high Statue of Liberty. See Albert Speer, *Inside the Third Reich* (New York, 1971), 108.

11 Klaus Fischer, *Hitler and America* (Philadelphia, 2011), especially 9–45.

12 Geoffrey Pridham and Jeremy Noakes, *Documents on Nazism, 1919–1945* (New York, 1975), 900. See also Mazower, *Hitler's Empire,* 120.

13 Robert Skidelsky, *John Maynard Keynes: A Biography* (London, 2000), 3: 196. Skidelsky makes the point that the clippings were incomplete and that Keynes got a better idea of the plans from a paper he had edited for the *Economic Journal* from Guillebaud (195). I am grateful for Lord Skidelsky's help in researching this issue.

14 Elizabeth Johnson and D. E. Moggridge, eds., *The Collected Writings of John Maynard Keynes* (London, 1971), 25: 1.

15 John Maynard Keynes, *A Tract on Monetary Reform* (New York, 1924).

16 Skidelsky, *Keynes,* 2: 103.

17 Melchior was Max Warburg's right-hand man and had arranged many of the German contacts, most likely including Schacht. Niall Ferguson, *The Pity of War* (London, 1999), 400.

18 Skidelsky, *Keynes,* 2: 129.

19 Keynes had picked the topic himself to build from a recent *Times* article. It was written before the dismal news from the conference but made public only after the "reflationary package" failed.

20 Skidelsky, *Keynes,* 2: 476.

21 Johnson and Moggridge, *The Collected Writings,* 25: 3–4.

22 Ibid.

23 The United Nations Monetary and Financial Congress yielded what we now know as the "Bretton Woods system" of organized exchange rates under the aegis of the U.S. dollar, along with the World Bank Group and the International Mon-

etary Fund. Harry Dexter White from the U.S. Treasury and Keynes were its central architects. See Filippo Cesarano, *Monetary Theory and Bretton Woods: The Construction of an International Monetary Order,* Historical Perspectives on Modern Economics (New York, 2006); Michael Bordo and Barry Eichengreen, eds., *A Retrospective on the Bretton Woods System: Lessons for International Monetary Reform* (Chicago, 1993).

24 Johnson and Moggridge, *The Collected Writings,* 25: 7.

25 See Alan S. Milward, *The New Order and the French Economy* (Oxford, 1970), 270–72; Avraham Barkai, *Das Wirtschaftssystem Des Nationalsozialismus: Ideologie, Theorie, Politik, 1933–1945* (Frankfurt, 1988), 226.

26 See Niall Ferguson, *The War of the World* (London, 2007), especially 466–504.

27 John Gallagher and Ronald Robinson, "The Imperialism of Free Trade," *Economic History Review,* n.s., 6, no. 1 (1953): 1–15.

28 Hugh Thomas, *The Spanish Civil War [New Edition]* (New York, 2001), 902.

29 This is a point well made by Christian Leitz, *Economic Relations Between Nazi Germany and Franco's Spain: 1936–1945* (Oxford, 1996).

30 Vejas G. Liulevicius, *War Land on the Eastern Front: Culture, National Identity and German Occupation in World War I* (Cambridge, U.K., 2000), 258.

31 Ian Kershaw, *Nemesis,* especially xxxvii–xxxix; Woodruff D. Smith, *The Ideological Origins of Nazi Imperialism* (New York, 1986), 251–55.

32 Bernd Wenger, "Hitler, der Zweite Weltkrieg und die Choreographie des Untergangs," *Geschichte und Gesellschaft* 26 (2000): 493–518.

33 Schacht, *Autobiography,* 345.

34 U.S. Treasury Secretary Morgenthau appears to have summarily dismissed the possibility. Harold James, "Schacht's Attempted Defection from Hitler's Germany," *Historical Journal* 30, no. 3 (1987): 729–33.

35 Hjalmar Horace Greeley Schacht, *Confessions of "the Old Wizard": Autobiography* (Boston, 1956), 345.

36 Hugh Trevor-Roper, ed., *Hitler's Table Talk, 1941–1944: His Private Conversations* (New York, 2008), 342.

37 Schacht, *Autobiography,* 278.

38 Robert Gellately and Leon Goldensohn, *The Nuremberg Interviews* (New York, 2004); Florence Miale, *The Nuremberg Mind: The Psychology of the Nazi Leaders* (New York, 1975).

39 "Rearmament in itself is not a crime . . . the case against Schacht depends on the inference that Schacht did in fact know of the Nazi aggressive plans . . . the Tribunal . . . comes to the conclusion that this necessary inference has not been established beyond a reasonable doubt. The Tribunal finds that Schacht is not guilty on this indictment," read Francis Biddle at Nuremberg on October 1, 1946. See *IMT,* Judgment: Schacht. http://avalon.law.yale.edu/imt/judschac.asp.

40 His bank was the *Deutsche Außenhandelsbank Schacht & Co.* For the criticism and his self-defense, see Hjalmar Horace Greeley Schacht, *The Magic of Money* (London, 1967), 209.

ACKNOWLEDGMENTS

In writing what follows, I have accumulated more debts than pages.

Spending five years at Harvard is a rare honor; to single out anyone amid such a faculty is no easy task. And yet, this project could not have been possible without the dedication and guidance of Charles Maier, Emma Rothschild, and Patrice Higonnet. When Borges imagined "Paradise as a kind of library," he surely envisioned Charlie's, an endless spring of both literature and inspiration.

I am most grateful to Niall Ferguson. His teaching and work ethic set a standard that has inspired me ever since our concurrent first semester at Harvard. Over a decade I have found in him the best mentor one could hope for, always generous with the rarest of commodities: time. It was Niall who believed in this author and this book since before either could be called such; and it is in no small measure thanks to him that they are.

The research herein could not have been possible without the generous support of the Minda de Gunzburg Center for European Studies—a second home at Harvard—the Krupp Foundation, the Real Colegio Complutense, and the Weatherhead Center for International Affairs.

I am grateful to the master and fellows of Trinity College, Cambridge, and Cambridge University's History faculty, in particular Natalia Mora-Sitja, Martin Daunton, John Adamson, and Paul Kennedy. I fondly recall rehearsing arguments at the Centre of History and Economics, a bridge between the two Cambridges. I am obliged to the Harvard-Cambridge Scholarship Committee for trusting me with the Lt. Charles Henry Fiske III and the Gates Cambridge Scholarships for their vote of confidence. I owe to Rob Shapiro as much or likely more than the whole Harvard-Cambridge community does, and to Marty Peretz the first opportunity to write for a wide audience. It is a joy to call them friends as well as teachers.

I am also grateful to the Harvard Kennedy School and its Belfer Center for Science and International Affairs. Having studied under the late Ernest May, I was especially honored to be Ernest May Fellow. My gratitude goes to Graham Allison, Paul Tucker, and Susan Lynch.

It was one afternoon at Cambridge that I met Rob Johnson, who invited me to join the Institute of New Economic Thinking at inception; he has welcomed and inspired me ever since. I hope that these pages are worthy of the Institute's goal to make crucial economic debates accessible to wider audiences.

I am thankful to the Berggruen Council for the Future of Europe, especially Nicolas, Dawn Nakagawa, Juan Luis Cebrián, and Nathan Gardels, not only for their stimulating work on European integration but also for inviting me to be a part of it.

To discuss the past and future of Europe with men of the stature of George Soros and Mario Monti has been an immense privilege; it has only deepened my belief in what an integrated Europe can achieve. I hope the dystopia between these covers can help place debates about federalization in a fuller historical context, underscoring the need for strong democratic pillars in the worthy edifice of ever closer union.

To my colleagues at Greenmantle I owe the ideal work environment. I learn from them daily and thank them for graciously understanding my absences to work on this project. I am especially grateful to Dimitris Valatsas, whose erudition has been nothing short of invaluable. Equally invaluable has been Dan Loeb's earliest and enduring support.

Because distance does not diminish debts, I must thank Cristina Rins for instilling a love for history and Francis Cahn for opening doors to Harvard.

I am fortunate to have the best agent in the world, Andrew Wylie, who took a chance on a young, first-time author writing about a distant war long ago. I am also grateful to Kristina Moore and all those who make up the Wylie Agency in New York and London. For their support at a critical time in this project, Emma and John Makinson deserve my most sincere gratitude.

This is a Harvard University Press book on both sides of the Atlantic. It has been an honor and a pleasure to work with Kathleen McDermott, my tireless editor, as well as Andrew Kinney and the Press's wonderful staff. Their unflagging support has not gone unnoticed.

Historians rely on archives and archives depend on their oft-neglected staff. I must thank everyone at the Bundesarchiv Koblenz and Berlin-Lichterfelde, the Ministerio de Asuntos Exteriores y Cooperación in Madrid, Ministero degli Affari Esteri, Servizio Storico, in Rome, the British National Archives in Kew, as well as the Library of Congress, the New York Public Library, and the incomparable Widener Library.

Friends and colleagues—beyond the above—have read this manuscript in full or in part. I am particularly indebted to Lev Menand, Jason Rockett, and Sarah Wallington for their research help. I am also grateful to the eminences in the field that have provided comments and criticism at different stages, including John Coverdale, Barry Eichengreen, Stanley Fisher, Peter Hayes, Harold James, Richard Overy, Paul Preston, Gianni Toniolo, Adam Tooze, and Ángel Viñas. I am motivated by the work of the late Alan Milward and grateful to Frances Lynch.

Thanks also go to Ayaan Hirsi Ali, Marshall Auerback, Tony Barber, Nicolás Belgorosky, Ramsen Betfarhad, Lewis Bollard, Piotr Brzezinski, Lucy Caldwell, Jason Cummins, Patrick Daniel, Santiago Dañino-Beck, Rowan Dorin, Agustino Fontevecchia, Chloe Frank, Federico Fubini, Janan Ganesh, Cecilia Garibotti, Adam Goldenberg, Charlotte Grogan, David Haber, Omar Halabi, Roxanne Krystalli, Audrey Kim, Ian Klaus, Jacob Kline, Joshua Lachter, Charlie Laderman, Sahil Mahtani, Lawrence Minicone, Ryan Orley, Nan Ransohoff, Felipe Razquin Goñi, Andreas Schaab, Christopher Sealey, Jason Shure, Jamie Sterne, Federico Taiano, Juliet Wagner, Jonathan Weigel, Eric Weiner, and Christopher Wiegand.

Any mistakes are my responsibility. What remains is for my parents, Adriana and Franco, to whom my debt knows no bounds—and for Davina, without whose inspiration I would have never finished this book.

INDEX